Lecture Notes
in Business Information Processing

305

Series Editors

Wil M.P. van der Aalst
Eindhoven Technical University, Eindhoven, The Netherlands
John Mylopoulos
University of Trento, Trento, Italy
Michael Rosemann
Queensland University of Technology, Brisbane, QLD, Australia
Michael J. Shaw
University of Illinois, Urbana-Champaign, IL, USA
Clemens Szyperski
Microsoft Research, Redmond, WA, USA

More information about this series at http://www.springer.com/series/7911

Geert Poels · Frederik Gailly
Estefania Serral Asensio · Monique Snoeck (Eds.)

The Practice of Enterprise Modeling

10th IFIP WG 8.1. Working Conference, PoEM 2017
Leuven, Belgium, November 22–24, 2017
Proceedings

Springer

Editors
Geert Poels ⓘ
Ghent University
Ghent
Belgium

Frederik Gailly ⓘ
Ghent University
Gent
Belgium

Estefania Serral Asensio ⓘ
KU Leuven
Leuven
Belgium

Monique Snoeck ⓘ
KU Leuven
Leuven
Belgium

ISSN 1865-1348   ISSN 1865-1356 (electronic)
Lecture Notes in Business Information Processing
ISBN 978-3-319-70240-7   ISBN 978-3-319-70241-4 (eBook)
https://doi.org/10.1007/978-3-319-70241-4

Library of Congress Control Number: 2017957841

Printed on acid-free paper

This Springer imprint is published by Springer Nature
The registered company is Springer International Publishing AG
The registered company address is: Gewerbestrasse 11, 6330 Cham, Switzerland

Preface

Enterprise modelling has established itself as the research discipline that aims at producing knowledge and solutions to effectively integrate information and communication technologies into business operations and the management of enterprises. Through the design of novel concepts, models, methods, and techniques, enterprise modelling offers the frameworks and instruments required to analyze the application of innovative IT solutions and to engineer them into the business. Empirical studies on the use of enterprise modelling provide insights into the effectiveness of these artefacts and their relationship to the context of application, including the human factor. Over the years, considerable progress has been made regarding knowledge creation and solution design. Many of those actively involved in enterprise modelling research and application meet at the annual Practice of Enterprise Modelling (PoEM) conference, which was created by the International Federation for Information Processing (IFIP) Working Group 8.1 to offer a forum for knowledge transfer and experience-sharing between the academic and practitioner communities.

We are proud to present the proceedings of the 10th IFIP WG 8.1 Working Conference on the Practice of Enterprise Modelling (PoEM 2017), held in Leuven (Belgium) during November 22–24, 2017, and jointly organized by two of Flanders' most outstanding universities: KU Leuven and Ghent University. Both universities have research teams actively involved in enterprise modelling research and we were very honoured by the invitation of PoEM's Steering Committee to host the 10th anniversary conference. A decennium of PoEM conferences indicates that enterprise modelling is not only a lasting phenomenon but also a field that has matured and continues to attract the interest of researchers and practitioners. We believe that this anniversary could not be celebrated better than in Leuven, which is –with its almost 800 year's old university and over 40,000 students– not only a place of wisdom and scholarship, but also of joy, pleasure, and good living. An ideal place for people to meet, exchange ideas, discuss, explore new avenues, strengthen existing collaborations, and establish new ones.

We were happy to receive for this anniversary edition of PoEM 70 submissions for the main conference, including research papers, practitioner/experience papers, and work-in-progress papers. Submissions were received from all corners of the globe. There were submissions from newcomers to the field as well as from established scholars in enterprise modelling. Each paper was sent to three anonymous reviewers who scrutinized them using strict criteria of scientific quality to uphold the standard we are used to for PoEM. Over 60 Program Committee members were involved in the review process. Their hard work resulted in the acceptance of 20 full papers and four short papers, i.e., an acceptance rate of 28% (or 34% including the short papers).

These 24 accepted papers were organized into eight sessions covering diverse topics related to enterprise modelling and its application in practice. Other conference events included a PhD consortium, an industry track, and the PrOse workshop for enterprise modelling in the OMiLAB scientific experimentation phase. We further invited two keynote speakers. On Thursday, November, 23, Steven Alter, Professor Emeritus of the University of San Francisco, gave a keynote entitled "A Work System Perspective for Enterprise Modelling." Steve is the originator of the work system theory (WST) that grew out of the work system method, which is a systems analysis method intended for use by business professionals without the help of IT professionals or consultants. The WST has been applied in many fields including information systems, service and service systems, business process management, work-arounds and noncompliance, adoption and diffusion of technology, enterprise engineering, and agile development. Steve's keynote showed how WST can be used as a basis for enterprise modelling, identified some of its limitations for that purpose, and illustrated how it can be used as a point of comparison for deciding what to include in an enterprise modelling effort.

A second keynote speech was given on Friday, November 24, by Mia Vanstraelen, now HR director at IBM, who has a long-standing experience in enterprise modelling, in particular with the foundation of IBM's Insurance Application Architecture (IAA) Framework. She shed light on a somewhat underexposed topic in enterprise engineering: how changing an enterprise model impacts workforce. She discussed challenges in how to deal with the impact of enterprise re-engineering on human resources and proposed a research agenda.

September 2017   Geert Poels
                                                     Frederik Gailly
                                                    Monique Snoeck
                                                    Estefania Serral

Organization

Steering Committee

Anne Persson — University of Skövde, Sweden
Janis Stirna — Stockholm University, Sweden
Kurt Sandkuhl — University of Rostock, Germany

General Chair

Monique Snoeck — KU Leuven, Belgium

Program Chairs

Geert Poels — Ghent University, Belgium
Frederik Gailly — Ghent University, Belgium

Organizing Chair

Estefanía Serral Asensio — KU Leuven, Belgium

Doctoral Consortium Chairs

Jolita Ralyte — University of Geneva, Switzerland
Ben Roelens — Ghent University, Belgium

Industrial Chair

Serge Demeyer — University of Antwerp and Inno.com Institute, Belgium

Program Committee

Hans Akkermans — Vrije Universiteit Amsterdam, The Netherlands
Pouya Aleatrati Khosroshahi — Technische Universität München, Germany
Raian Ali — Bournemouth University, UK
Joao Paulo Almeida — Federal University of Espirito Santo, Brazil
Judith Barrios Albornoz — University of Los Andes, Colombia
Giuseppe Berio — Université de Bretagne Sud and IRISA UMR, France
Dominik Bork — University of Vienna, Austria
Xavier Boucher — Ecole Nationale Supérieure des Mines de Saint Etienne, France
Robert Andrei Buchmann — Babeş-Bolyai University of Cluj Napoca, Romania

Rimantas Butleris   Kaunas University of Technology, Lithuania
Albertas Caplinskas   Vilnius University, Lithuania
Tony Clark   Sheffield Hallam University, UK
Rolland Colette   Université Paris 1 Panthéon Sorbonne, France
Sergio De Cesare   The University of Westminster, UK
Wolfgang Deiters   Fraunhofer ISST, Germany
Serge Demeyer   Universiteit Antwerpen, Belgium
Dulce Domingos   Universidade de Lisboa, Portugal
Michael Fellmann   University of Rostock, Germany
Hans-Georg Fill   University of Bamberg, Germany
Guido Geerts   University of Delaware, USA
Marcela Genero   University of Castilla-La Mancha, Spain
Giovanni Giachetti   Universidad Tecnológica de Chile, Chile
Jaap Gordijn   Vrije Universiteit Amsterdam, The Netherlands
Jānis Grabis   Riga Technical University, Latvia
Giancarlo Guizzardi   Federal University of Espirito Santo (UFES), Brazil
Yoshinori Hara   Kyoto University, Japan
Stijn Hoppenbrouwers   HAN University of Applied Sciences, The Netherlands
Jennifer Horkoff   Chalmers University of Gothenburg, Sweden
Manfred Jeusfeld   University of Skövde, Sweden
Paul Johannesson   Royal Institute of Technology, Sweden
Ivan Jureta   University of Namur, Belgium
Håvard Jørgensen   Commitment AS, Norway
Monika Kaczmarek   University of Duisburg Essen, Germany
Dimitris Karagiannis   University of Vienna, Austria
Lutz Kirchner   Scape Consulting GmbH, Germany
Marite Kirikova   Riga Technical University, Latvia
John Krogstie   IDI, NTNU, Norway
Robert Lagerström   Royal Institute of Technology, Sweden
Birger Lantow   University of Rostock, Germany
Wim Laurier   Facultés Universitaires Saint-Louis, Belgium
Ulrike Lechner   Universität der Bundeswehr München, Germany
Moonkun Lee   Chonbuk National University, South Korea
Florian Matthes   Technische Universität München, Germany
Raimundas Matulevicius   University of Tartu, Estonia
Heinrich C. Mayr   Alpen-Adria-Universität Klagenfurt, Austria
Graham Mcleod   Inspired.org, South Africa
Haralambos Mouratidis   University of Brighton, UK
Christer Nellborn   Nellborn Management Consulting AB, Sweden
Selmin Nurcan   Université Paris 1 Panthéon Sorbonne, France
Andreas L Opdahl   University of Bergen, Norway
Oscar Pastor Lopez   Universitat Politecnica de Valencia, Spain
Anne Persson   University of Skövde, Sweden
Michael Petit   University of Namur, Belgium
Ilias Petrounias   The University of Manchester, UK
Andrea Polini   ISTI – CNR, Italy

Simon Polovina   Sheffield Hallam University, UK
Henderik Proper   Public Research Centre Henri Tudor, Luxembourg
Jolita Ralyte   University of Geneva, Switzerland
Ben Roelens   Ghent University, Belgium
Kurt Sandkuhl   The University of Rostock, Germany
Ulf Seigerroth   Jönköping University, Sweden
Estefania Serral Assensio   KU Leuven, Belgium
Khurram Shahzad   University of the Punjab, Pakistan
Nikolay Shilov   SPIIRAS, Russian Federation
Keng Siau   Missouri University of Science and Technology, USA
Pnina Soffer   University of Haifa, Israel
Janis Stirna   Stockholm University, Sweden
Darijus Strasunskas   POSC Caesar Association, Norway
Eva Söderström   University of Skövde, Sweden
Victoria Torres   Universidad Politécnica de Valencia, Spain
Irene Vanderfeesten   Technische Universiteit Eindhoven, The Netherlands
Jan Vanthienen   KU Leuven, Belgium
Olegas Vasilecas   Vilnius Gediminas Technical University, Lithuania
Hans Weigand   Tilburg University, The Netherlands
Eric Yu   University of Toronto, Canada
Jelena Zdravkovic   Stockholm University, Sweden

Contents

Regular Papers

Domain Modelling in Bloom: Deciphering How We Teach It

Daria Bogdanova[✉] and Monique Snoeck

Research Center for Management Informatics, KU Leuven, Naamsestraat 69,
3000 Leuven, Belgium
{daria.bogdanova,monique.snoeck}@kuleuven.be

Abstract. Domain modelling is a crucial part of Enterprise Modelling and considered as a challenge in enterprise engineering education. Pedagogy for this subject is not systematized and teachers or book authors develop the curriculum based on their own experience and understanding of the subject. This leads to a wide diversity of pedagogical methods, learning paths and even drastic differences in the applied terminology. In this paper, we identified and classified learning outcomes from several educational resources on domain modelling according to the revised Bloom's taxonomy of educational objectives. We identified the similarities and gaps among the resources, such as lack of evaluation-related tasks, as well as the insufficient presence of procedural knowledge related tasks. The examples of most popular tasks are given, along with the directions to the future development of a systematic educational framework and guidelines for domain modelling pedagogy.

Keywords: Conceptual modelling · Domain modelling · Education · Revised Bloom's taxonomy · Scaffolding · Cognitive process

1 Introduction

Enterprise modelling consists of different perspectives such as goal modelling, business process modelling, value modelling, etc. Amongst those perspectives, the 'what' or data perspective, addressed through domain modelling, is considered one of the crucial aspects of Enterprise Modelling [1]. However, any educator that starts teaching domain modelling faces several challenges. First, domain modelling often means formalizing an ill-structured domain or problem description formulated in natural language. This applies to any field where domain modelling or conceptual data modelling is used: engineering design, software development or enterprise engineering. Ill-structured problems are domain- and context-dependent, so in addition to the knowledge of modelling techniques *per se*, novice modellers should grasp the context and the specifics of the domain in which they have to work [2].

Second, there is no existing generally accepted framework for modelling pedagogy – educators have to come up with the entire course design, tasks and learning paths on their own, based on their professional experience and views on learning process.

© IFIP International Federation for Information Processing 2017
Published by Springer International Publishing AG 2017. All Rights Reserved
G. Poels et al. (Eds.): PoEM 2017, LNBIP 305, pp. 3–17, 2017.
https://doi.org/10.1007/978-3-319-70241-4_1

Third, not only the approaches to teaching, but even the terminology significantly varies, bringing the entire field of domain modelling close to a "Babylonian" state, where everyone names the same notion in a different way. Though some modelling methods are similar or even identical across communities (object-oriented modelling community, database modelling community, and others), the fact that they may implement completely different terminology and notation hampers the exchange of knowledge. As an example, in [3], the term "domain object" or "object" for short, is used to address a wide variety of concepts, such as entities, associations, agents and events, all of which are considered subtypes of "Object". Consequently, the terms "object model" (as in [3, 4]) and "object diagram" have completely different meanings: according to the current version of the UML standard, "object diagram" refers to the concrete instances that exist in the system in a given moment, while in [3] and in many other resources "object model" refers to the equivalent of a UML class diagram describing the model in general. To avoid confusion, in this paper we will stick to the standard terminology of UML [5].

Last, but not least, though there are many insights available on what makes a good model (a large review on that matter was made as early as in 1994 [6]), the portrait of a good modeller is still somewhat blurry. The skill set that he/she is expected to possess is not formalized, and, subsequently, the identification of learning outcomes is complicated, so as the development of assessment criteria.

In this work, we aim to make an initial step towards the systematic educational framework for enterprise modelling. As a first step, we limit our research to the data modelling aspect only, not concerning the aspects such as business processes, goals, or business object behaviour, which will be subjects of future studies. We investigate the current state of practice by identifying and classifying learning outcomes pursued in samples of educational literature [3, 4, 7, 8], massive open online courses [9–11] and university level courses exams from KU Leuven, Université catholique de Louvain and University of Namur [12–16]. Inspired by learning outcomes categorization works conducted in different fields of studies, such as biology [17], social sciences [18], computer science [19], and others, we use the revised Bloom's taxonomy of educational objectives [20] as a classification tool.

The following research questions are to be answered in this work:

RQ1: What learning outcomes can be identified in current domain modelling education?
RQ2: What is the positioning of the identified learning outcomes in the revised Bloom's taxonomy of educational objectives?
    RQ2a: How are the learning outcomes distributed among various knowledge levels?
    RQ2b: What are the most frequently appearing types of tasks?
RQ3: What is the range of domain modelling concepts addressed by the educators?

Apart from providing information on the state of practice, developing the methodology for the analysis of the current practice allowed for additional contributions to the field of teaching domain modelling. The analysis required a field-specific revision of the Bloom's taxonomy (Sect. 3), an analysis of how the learning of domain modelling concepts is scaffolded, and the categorization of the learning goals provides a set of typical tasks that can be used as inspirational templates by teachers.

The remainder of this paper is structured as follows. Section 2 presents related research. Section 3 presents the methodology, amongst which a revised Bloom's taxonomy for domain modelling (Sect. 3.1), and a scaffolding of domain modelling concepts (Sect. 3.2). Section 4 then presents the results of classifying 291 exercises and tasks from 12 different sources. A discussion follows in Sect. 5 and Sect. 6 presents the conclusions and topics for further research.

2 Related Research

2.1 Pedagogical Resources on Domain Modelling

As already mentioned in the introduction, there is no general agreement on how to teach domain modelling. Existing standards, such as MSIS 2006 [21] or IEEE SE 2014 curriculum guidelines for software engineering education [22], only give a general perspective on the large educational field, such as software engineering, and only briefly mention the aspect of domain modelling. As for domain modelling as a discipline, though there are plenty of approaches to how to model, there is no comprehensive literature or published guidelines on how to teach modelling.

Several attempts were made to determine the criteria of competence of novice modellers and propose the learning paths for their professional growth. [23] describes teaching practices aimed at building a bridge between a novice conceptual data modeller and an expert. Such practices include a high-level four-step strategic plan for training modellers comprising familiarization with data modelling constructs, adopting an expert's strategies, gaining exposure to different application domains and reviewing the developed data models. Another attempt of improving the understanding of conceptual modelling by novice modellers was made in [24], based on observations of novice versus expert modellers going through all steps of developing a conceptual modelling project, including data collection and domain modelling. The observations show that the patterns applied by novice modellers differ drastically from those applied by the experts. Thus, the identified experts' patterns could be used to improve procedural knowledge of novice modellers. In [25], the authors propose to assess students' understanding of the concept of inheritance based on a five-level scale: from understanding the difference between abstract and concrete classes to understanding of complex models with more than one inheritance hierarchy.

The examples of works above demonstrate that the available sources on modelling education propose very high-level approaches that never go into the details, such as the topics learned on each stage or the type of tasks given to the students. Though the available textbooks propose various learning paths, no study was found that analyses the effectiveness of proposed scaffolding methods.

2.2 Implementations of Bloom's Taxonomy

Bloom's taxonomy [26] and the revised Bloom's taxonomy [20] continue to attract the attention of educators in a wider and wider variety of fields. Since the 1960s, when the first handbook proposing the taxonomy was published, the educational community conducted tens of classification works.

In 2008, Bloom's taxonomy was applied in the University of Washington for developing the Blooming Biology Tool – an assessment tool to assist the biology educators to align the assessments they use with the teaching activities and help develop classroom materials and exams based on a unified evaluation kit [27]. Later the same year, Science published the report on the application of Bloom's taxonomy to the major biology-related exams [17], based on the exam questions ratings from [27]. The findings were rather surprising for the biology education community, as the analysis of MCAT (Medical College Admission Tests) showed that its tasks, perceived as heavily based on content knowledge (lower-order thinking), contain a large proportion of tasks requiring higher-order thinking, such as problem-solving ability and critical thinking. Later on, the "Blooming" tools expanded to more narrow fields of biology: consequently, the Blooming Anatomy Tool [28] and the Bloom's Taxonomy Histology Tool [29] were successfully applied in the corresponding fields. In [30], the revised Bloom's taxonomy was applied to classify a large collection of biology-related assessment packages into a two-dimensional taxonomy; the study showed the lack of procedural and metacognitive knowledge-related questions.

Biology is not the only field where Bloom's taxonomy was applied: [31] presents a successfully implemented self-assessment tool based on Bloom's taxonomy for students of programming classes; in [32], the authors developed a set of core learning objectives for accounting ethics using Bloom's taxonomy; it was applied for assessing the software engineering curriculum and the IEEE software engineering body of knowledge [19]. However, to this moment none of the existing studies attempted to apply Bloom's taxonomy to domain modelling or enterprise modelling education.

3   Methodology

3.1   Revised Bloom's Taxonomy for Domain Modelling

As the revised Bloom's taxonomy itself was developed as a general one and applicable to a wide variety of fields, the criteria for classification given in the description of the taxonomy should be narrowed and tailored to be implemented in domain modelling education. The revised Bloom's taxonomy of educational objectives [20] is a matrix identifying 6 cognitive process levels and 4 different knowledge levels. As the result of the tailoring to domain modelling, the following criteria of categorization (with examples) were applied in this work.

Cognitive Process Levels
Remembering tasks imply recalling and reproduction of previously learned material. This includes giving definition to terms, recognition of notation and copying/duplicating existing learning material. In case of domain modelling, such tasks may include giving a definition to a given modelling concept (e.g. inheritance, aggregation, association class), or naming a given modelling notation element.

Understanding tasks refer to the previously learned material, possibly by interpreting it (explaining, translating from one form to another), or by comparison. Typical understanding level tasks would include interpreting a given model and providing its textual description or giving an example (instance) of a given class or association.

Applying tasks imply using the previously learned information in new ways and/or implementing a learned technique. Applying domain modelling knowledge may include modification of a model using an available example or the application of a given technique to create an association between two classes.

Analysis tasks imply deconstructing the material to understand its inner structure and the general principles of relationships between different elements. Examples are the comparison of two models for a domain or generalizing a given model.

Evaluation tasks aim at assessing the ability of students to make judgements based on given criteria, standards or guidelines. Examples in domain modelling education are finding mistakes in a given domain model by comparing it to the given description or choosing the model that describes the given domain best and motivating one's decision.

Creating tasks imply the use of the learned material to create a new structure or to enhance an existing one. This is the highest cognitive level of the taxonomy. Examples in conceptual modelling education are building a model according to a given description and completing an incomplete model.

Knowledge Levels

Factual knowledge includes the basics of the studied disciplines, such as basic terminology. In domain modelling, factual knowledge refers to the knowledge of modelling notation and definitions of various terms and concepts.

Conceptual knowledge implies understanding of the connections and interrelationships between the elements learned on factual level. For domain modelling, conceptual knowledge is related to the understanding of relationships between modelling concepts and between various elements of a given model or model fragment.

Procedural knowledge refers to the subject-specific methods, procedures and rules. Procedural knowledge means knowledge of modelling techniques and criteria for their implementation; it may include the step-by-step approaches to modelling and knowledge of guidelines and procedures specific to the discipline of domain modelling.

Metacognitive knowledge implies strategic knowledge and the student's awareness of his/her own knowledge. Metacognitive knowledge in domain modelling is related to knowledge about the (typical) mistakes a student (or a group) tends to make, the most successful strategies for learning, and the knowledge of cognitive processes that would be involved in a given task.

3.2　Scaffolding Levels

At first, we attempted to classify the assessment tasks directly into the Bloom's taxonomy. We however soon faced the problem that certain tasks require prerequisite knowledge. This scaffolding of knowledge is not adequately captured by either the cognitive process levels or the knowledge levels. Therefore, based on the existing learning paths for domain modelling education, we created the following scaffolding tree (Fig. 1), according to which the modelling levels addressed by learning outcomes were additionally classified.

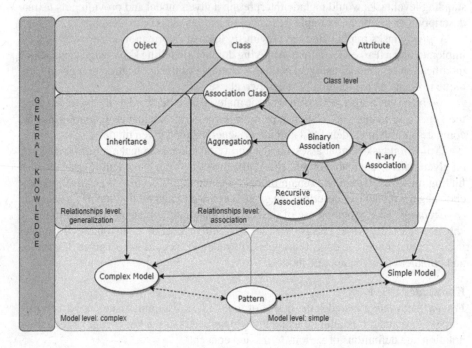

Fig. 1. Scaffolding tree for domain modelling education

This scaffolding tree comprises four major levels:

- Class level, which includes the concepts of object, class and attribute;
- Relationships level subdivided into generalization and association sections. The generalization section includes the concept of inheritance, while the association section includes binary, n-ary and recursive associations, aggregation and partly the concept of association class, which was included in both class and relationships levels;
- Model level subdivided into simple and complex model sections. These two sections are introduced to emphasize the pedagogical difference between models that utilize only a limited amount of modelling concepts and those that use a wide variety of concepts: "simple" model and "complex" model. A simple model implies the use of the whole class level and binary associations, while a complex model may include the whole set of relationships level concepts;
- General knowledge level includes knowledge of modelling notation languages, general conventions and guidelines for modelling, and other necessary information, which is out of the scope of the above three levels.

The arrows should be read "A is a prerequisite for B", if the arrow starts in A and points at B.

3.3 Materials

For the assessment of current practice, different sources could be used. As explained in the introduction, general curricula designs identify learning goals at a too high level to be useful for everyday educational practice. Better sources would therefore be the individual courses and how they address domain modelling. Here too, different starting points can be used. The learning goals formulated for a course, often found in online course descriptions, could be a potential source. However, such descriptions are still quite high level. Moreover, they only specify what is planned to be addressed, rather than what is effectively addressed by the course. Better sources are therefore the actual assessment questions used to assess the students' knowledge of domain modelling. This is also in line with previous research on educational frameworks based on Bloom's taxonomy, which used the applied assessment items to build evaluation tools and frameworks for their subjects.

Other issues are that domain modelling appears as a sub discipline in different fields (object-oriented modelling, conceptual modelling and database design) and that courses have different formats. In order to achieve a sample as representative as possible, the choice of materials was made such as to cover different forms (books, online courses (MOOCs), and face-to-face courses) and different communities. This resulted in the following sources:

- Four books were chosen from different modelling communities: object-oriented modelling, conceptual data modelling and database design [3, 4, 7, 8]. For each of the books we chose a seminal work having more than 100 references on ResearchGate and, at the same time, containing exercises. Though some books had higher citation rating than those that were picked, the majority of those books did not contain a set of exercises based on which learning outcomes could be derived.
- All openly available higher-education level MOOCs. Each from a different platform: edX, Open University and Stanford Lagunita [9–11].
- Face-to-face courses from three universities in Belgium: KU Leuven, Université Catholique de Louvain and University of Namur [12–16].

For the books and the MOOCs, all relevant exercises and assessment tasks were classified. Hence, both intermediate and final assessment tasks were represented. For the face-to-face courses, exam questions (final assessment) were collected directly from the teachers. In this case, material from exercise sessions were not collected, to minimize the burden for the teachers willing to share their material with us. In total, 291 assessment tasks from 12 resources were analysed.

3.4 Classification Process

The classification was conducted by the two authors of the paper. The assessment packages were assessed separately, with a high level of interrater agreement (less than 10% of the learning outcomes had to be discussed due to the disagreement in classification). In case of a disagreement, a thorough discussion and study of materials of the particular educational resource was conducted to determine the exact meaning and logic of the task and when necessary, the domain specific interpretation of the Bloom's taxonomy was further clarified.

4 Results

4.1 Illustration

As an illustration, we are giving an example of how the classification of learning outcomes (LOs) was done for one task from [8].

LO4.9: Discuss the conventions for creating a class diagram.
For this task, the following levels were determined:

- Cognitive process level – *understanding*. Discussion tasks, by definition, are aimed at understanding a given concept or a set of rules/conventions. The border between brainstorming (creating a new set of conventions) and discussing (trying to understand the meaning and logic of the existing conventions) is crucial in such types of tasks.
- Knowledge level – *procedural*. Conventions can be considered a subject-specific procedural knowledge: the knowledge of how the model is designed and why it is designed this way and not any other in order to comply with community standards and be readable by other modellers.
- Scaffolding level – *general*. General level includes the general knowledge about modelling; rules and conventions, as well as modelling notation languages, are considered part of this general knowledge.

A similar way of reflection was conducted for every learning outcome analysed in this work. The full list of identified learning outcomes translated into UML terminology is available online [33].

4.2 Bloom's Taxonomy for Domain Modelling

Table 1 demonstrates the normalized results of the classification. The results are normalized to avoid overrepresentation of data from resources that contain more assessment items than others do (e.g., the average amount of exercises in books exceeds the amount of exercises in MOOCs). The table should be read as follows: the columns represent the assessment packages classified in this study ("B" stands for "Books", "M" for "MOOCs", "U" for "University exams"). The rows represent the dimensions of the revised Bloom's taxonomy: in bold the cognitive dimension, as sublevels the knowledge dimension. If a certain knowledge dimension of the four (factual, conceptual, procedural, metacognitive) does not appear in the table, it means that none of the assessment items fit into the category.

As can be seen from the last column (Grand Total) of Table 1, in the cognitive dimension (boldface), the most frequent tasks are related to the "Understand" level, then, the second place is almost equally distributed between "Analyse" and "Create", while the third is given to "Apply". The most underrepresented levels are "Remember" and

Table 1. Summary of the results per assessment package – normalized

Sum of 1 Row Labels	Column B1	B2	B3	B4	M1	M2	M3	U1	U2	U3	U4	U5	Grand Total
⊟Remember	0,0%	0,0%	0,0%	13,1%	1,9%	0,0%	0,0%	0,0%	0,0%	0,0%	25,0%	0,0%	4,1%
Factual	0,0%	0,0%	0,0%	13,1%	1,9%	0,0%	0,0%	0,0%	0,0%	0,0%	0,0%	0,0%	3,1%
Conceptual	0,0%	0,0%	0,0%	0,0%	0,0%	0,0%	0,0%	0,0%	0,0%	0,0%	25,0%	0,0%	1,0%
⊟Understand	29,2%	17,5%	48,5%	41,0%	37,0%	47,2%	22,2%	0,0%	0,0%	0,0%	0,0%	0,0%	32,4%
Factual	16,7%	0,0%	0,0%	9,8%	1,9%	0,0%	0,0%	0,0%	0,0%	0,0%	0,0%	0,0%	3,8%
Conceptual	8,3%	15,0%	48,5%	11,5%	33,3%	41,7%	22,2%	0,0%	0,0%	0,0%	0,0%	0,0%	22,8%
Procedural	4,2%	2,5%	0,0%	19,7%	1,9%	5,6%	0,0%	0,0%	0,0%	0,0%	0,0%	0,0%	5,9%
⊟Apply	16,7%	2,5%	9,1%	13,1%	7,4%	5,6%	33,3%	69,2%	0,0%	0,0%	41,7%	0,0%	13,4%
Conceptual	4,2%	0,0%	3,0%	3,3%	0,0%	2,8%	0,0%	69,2%	0,0%	0,0%	41,7%	0,0%	6,6%
Procedural	12,5%	2,5%	6,1%	9,8%	7,4%	2,8%	33,3%	0,0%	0,0%	0,0%	0,0%	0,0%	6,9%
⊟Analyse	8,3%	15,0%	6,1%	13,1%	50,0%	30,6%	44,4%	15,4%	25,0%	33,3%	16,7%	0,0%	22,8%
Conceptual	8,3%	12,5%	3,0%	11,5%	50,0%	27,8%	44,4%	15,4%	25,0%	33,3%	8,3%	0,0%	21,0%
Procedural	0,0%	2,5%	3,0%	1,6%	0,0%	2,8%	0,0%	0,0%	0,0%	0,0%	8,3%	0,0%	1,7%
⊟Evaluate	0,0%	10,0%	3,0%	3,3%	3,7%	8,3%	0,0%	7,7%	25,0%	0,0%	0,0%	0,0%	4,8%
Conceptual	0,0%	7,5%	0,0%	3,3%	3,7%	8,3%	0,0%	7,7%	25,0%	0,0%	0,0%	0,0%	4,1%
Procedural	0,0%	2,5%	3,0%	0,0%	0,0%	0,0%	0,0%	0,0%	0,0%	0,0%	0,0%	0,0%	0,7%
⊟Create	45,8%	55,0%	33,3%	16,4%	0,0%	8,3%	0,0%	7,7%	50,0%	66,7%	16,7%	100,0%	22,4%
Conceptual	41,7%	40,0%	27,3%	9,8%	0,0%	0,0%	0,0%	7,7%	50,0%	66,7%	16,7%	100,0%	16,9%
Procedural	4,2%	15,0%	6,1%	6,6%	0,0%	8,3%	0,0%	0,0%	0,0%	0,0%	0,0%	0,0%	5,5%
Grand Total	100,0%	100,0%	100,0%	100,0%	100,0%	100,0%	100,0%	100,0%	100,0%	100,0%	100,0%	100,0%	100,0%

"Evaluate". In the knowledge dimension, the metacognitive knowledge level is not represented in any of the assessment packages. The most represented level is Conceptual, with much lower amount of Procedural level questions and almost none Factual.

In Fig. 2, a plot for the summary of results per category is presented. As can be seen, the books give the most evenly distributed tasks among the cognitive levels, while Exams and MOOCs tend to concentrate more on a few cognitive levels. The large majority of exam questions we analysed focus on applying conceptual knowledge and on creating and contained no assessment items related to the understanding level.

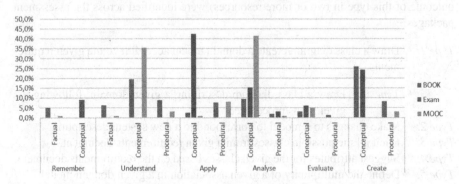

Fig. 2. Summary of results per category

At the same time, MOOCs are more focused on understanding and analyzing. Unlike the books and the exams, MOOCs provide hardly any creative questions.

4.3 Scaffolding Levels

Figure 3 shows the normalized summary of results related to the scaffolding levels addressed by the assessment tasks. It can be seen from the plot that the majority of questions address model and relationships levels (with particular concentration on complex model sublevel and associations sublevel). Books and exams put most focus on complex models, while MOOCs are rather aimed at assessing knowledge related to associations and simple models.

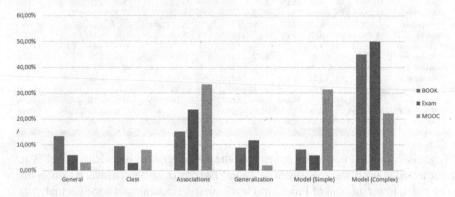

Fig. 3. Scaffolding levels per category – normalized

4.4 Frequent Tasks

The following frequent learning outcomes (more than two appearances of a learning outcome of this type in two or more resources) were identified across the assessment packages[1]:

Type 1:   Draw a class diagram/create a domain model according to the given require-
           ments.

           Type 1a: Draw a class diagram describing a given domain, following the
                       given steps/procedure.

Type 2:   Make changes to a model to correspond to a new system description.

Type 3:   Elicit all the possible classes from a given requirements document.

Type 4:   Suggest attributes for the given classes based on the requirements document.

Type 5:   Define the multiplicity of a given association in a given domain model.

Type 6:   Analyze the lifecycle of a given object.

Type 7:   Find structural issues/ways to improve the given domain model.

Type 8:   Refine a given model by using a given modelling technique.

Type 9:   Develop an alternative design for a model.

Type 10: Draw an object diagram of a given model.

---

[1] The learning outcomes were formulated as tasks similar to how the authors formulated them;
"draw a class diagram" corresponds to "The student should be able to draw a class diagram".

Type 11: Propose the improvements for a given modelling notation.
Type 12: Write a complete narrative description of a given class diagram/explain a given class diagram.

Table 2 shows the frequent learning outcomes positioned in the revised Bloom's taxonomy. When grouping learning outcomes into types, we observed slight variations in the formulation of similar learning outcomes, which resulted in slight differences in classifications. In this table, only the derived learning outcome types are classified.

Table 2. Distribution of the most frequent task types in the revised Bloom's taxonomy

Cognitive process dimension						
Knowledge	Dimension					
	Remember	Understand	Apply	Analyse	Evaluate	Create
Factual						
Conceptual		Type 5 Type 10 Type 12		Type 3 Type 4 Type 6	Type 7	Type 1 Type 2 Type 9
Procedural			Type8			Type 1a Type 11
Metacognitive						

5 Discussion

When looking at the above results, the following limitations of the study should be taken into consideration: The amount of studied literature sources cannot be considered fully representative for the entire field of domain modelling. In order to reach a deeper and more accurate understanding of the current state of the field and the learning outcomes pursued by the educators, more assessment packages from different sources should be analysed. Nevertheless, because materials were sourced from different communities and formats, the results can to a large extent be considered as sufficiently representative for obtaining a first indicative image of the field. Also, the classification process may be improved by introducing a more formal rating system and inviting more raters to evaluate the positioning of each learning outcome in the revised Bloom's taxonomy. Nevertheless, the fact that the current two raters obtained agreement on almost all items without discussion, is an indication of reasonable confidence in the correct classification. All in all, while the list of material could be extended and the classification could be further strengthened by adding more raters, the overall validity of the results is estimated as fair given the spread of the material sources and the high interrater agreement.

Looking at Fig. 2, one can see that the results show a difference between different educational sources in terms of the addressed cognitive and knowledge dimensions. MOOCs have the least amount of creative learning outcomes compared to exams and textbooks. This may be explained by the nature of traditional MOOC questions: to enable the automated assessment of students' knowledge, the MOOCs apply multiple-choice questions. Though multiple-choice questions can possibly be designed in a way that they would address higher cognitive levels of Bloom's taxonomy [17], the development of such questions is time-consuming. The "easier to create" multiple choice questions typically address the lower levels of the cognitive dimension. Nevertheless, all three MOOCs still have a relatively high rating of their learning outcomes, with more than a half of the questions addressing higher levels such as "Apply", "Analyse", "Evaluate" and "Create".

Exams on the other hand show a strong focus on the outcomes related to the higher cognitive dimensions applying, analysing and creating, while outcomes focusing on understanding were not present at all. This could possibly be explained by the fact that only (summative) assessment items of the final exams were collected. Teachers may possibly use other types of (ungraded) formative assessments in the course of a semester, but we did not request this material from them to limit the burden of their participation. Books provided the most equally distributed learning outcomes among the three learning material types. This can be explained by the fact that exercises included in books are designed for gradual scaffolding rather than for summative assessment, as in the exams.

All three types have "Remember" and "Evaluate" levels underrepresented, with only a few tasks related to "Remember" and slightly more related to "Evaluate". The first may be explained by the nature of the discipline itself: unlike some disciplines (e.g. biology with a very high rating of "Remember" [30]), domain modelling is perceived as a skill acquired exclusively through practice rather than through remembering terms and definitions. The lack of evaluation-related tasks is evident not only in the field of domain modelling: a categorization of the main unified exams questions for biology also found that evaluation level was not addressed in any of the five types of assessment packages [17]. Nevertheless, it would make sense to have more "Evaluate" types of assessments as this is the intermediate scaffolding step between "Analyse" and "Create". The absence of this type of assessments indicates a gap in the scaffolding.

In the knowledge dimension, the most represented level is the conceptual level, while none of the analyzed sources addressed the metacognitive level. The second least represented level is the factual level (which correlates with the underrepresented "Remember" level), and the third least represented is the procedural level. The lack of the procedural level outcomes may be a reflection of the state of the field as such: this could be an indication of an absence of unified (or agreed upon) guidelines, standards and procedures for domain modelling.

Regarding scaffolding levels, the majority of outcomes are related to model- and relationships levels, with books and exams mostly focused on complex models and MOOCs – on simple models. General and class levels are the least represented in the assessment packages. This again could indicate a lack of proper scaffolding: assessments seem to jump immediately to higher levels without proper testing of the lower ones. These gaps are also reflected in the identified frequent tasks: they have a high amount of "create"-related learning outcomes among them, with "understand" and "analyse" in the second place.

Obviously, these results are specific to the discipline of domain modelling and cannot be generalized to a different domain. Even generalisation to other sources from the discipline of domain modelling (books, exams, etc.) should be done with much care: as one can see from Table 1 there are substantial differences between sources, even between sources of the same type.

6   Conclusion and Further Research

In this work, we made the first attempt to classify the domain modelling-related assessment packages into the revised Bloom's taxonomy and find the positioning of the learning outcomes according to the scaffolding levels indicated in Fig. 1. This first classification exercise leads to the conclusion that, generally speaking, assessment packages of a single source (a book, a face-to-face course, a MOOC) show considerable gaps in scaffolding and overall evaluation of student's knowledge. Several levels both in terms of cognitive and knowledge dimensions seem to be missing. The most underrepresented is the metacognitive knowledge level, associated with strategies of learning and awareness of student's own cognition. Factual knowledge level, along with the "Remember" cognitive process are the next least represented in all of the assessment packages, with Procedural knowledge level insufficiently addressed by every source. "Evaluation" cognitive process, which can be considered one of the most important high-level cognitive processes on the way to creation of a model, is also addressed insufficiently in all the analysed materials. Exams and textbooks focus mostly on "Create" cognitive process, while in MOOCs this level is heavily underrepresented.

Similar inequalities are observed in the scaffolding levels addressed by the assessment material: it is highly focused on model and relationships levels, while knowledge about classes and the general knowledge on domain modelling is rarely tested.

Summing the above glimpse into the current state of the domain modelling education, we can conclude that the examined assessment materials are considerably unbalanced, which may cause difficulties both in the teaching and the learning processes. A thorough revision of the existing learning materials and assessment packages and their scaffolding can be suggested to the domain modelling educators.

For the future, we plan to develop a systematic educational framework for domain modelling, based on the revised Blooms taxonomy. This framework will include sample classroom tasks, learning paths and scaffolding approaches, as well as a validated assessment tool for domain modelling. Domain modelling educators could benefit from the identified learning outcomes and use the revised Bloom's taxonomy as an inspiration for creating their own classroom material and assessment packages. The analysis of learning outcomes could be expanded to other levels of modelling, such as object behaviour and process modelling. In addition, the best scaffolding approach should be identified among those proposed in the educational literature and in the university curricula.

Acknowledgement. The authors wish to thank the teachers of the analysed university courses for their willingness to share exam questions.

References

1. Bernaert, M., Poels, G., Snoeck, M., De Backer, M.: CHOOSE: towards a metamodel for enterprise architecture in small and medium-sized enterprises. Inf. Syst. Front. **18**, 781–818 (2016)
2. Jonassen, D.H.: Instructional design models for well-structured and III-structured problem-solving learning outcomes. Educ. Technol. Res. Dev. **45**, 65–94 (1997)
3. van Lamsweerde, A.: Requirements Engineering: From System Goals to UML Models to Software Specifications. Wiley, Hoboken (2009)
4. Blaha, M., Premerlani, W.: Object-Oriented Modeling and Design for Database Applications. Prentice Hall, Englewood Cliffs (1998)
5. Booch, G., Jacobson, I., Rumbaugh, J.: OMG unified modeling language specification. Object Management Group 1034 (2001)
6. Lindland, O.I., Sindre, G., Solvberg, A.: Understanding quality in conceptual modeling. IEEE Softw. **11**, 42–49 (1994)
7. Olivé, A.: Conceptual Modeling of Information Systems. Springer, Heidelberg (2007)
8. Elmasri, R., Navathe, S.: Fundamentals of Database Systems. Addison-Wesley, Boston (2011)
9. Snoeck, M.: UML class diagrams for software engineering. edX. https://www.edx.org/course/uml-class-diagrams-software-engineering-kuleuvenx-umlx
10. The Open University: Modelling object-oriented software – an introduction. http://www.open.edu/openlearn/science-maths-technology/computing-and-ict/modelling-object-oriented-software-introduction/content-section-0
11. Widom, J.: DB9 unified modelling language. Stanford Lagunita. https://lagunita.stanford.edu/courses/DB/UML/SelfPaced/info
12. Snoeck, M.: Architecture and modelling of management information systems - KU Leuven. https://onderwijsaanbod.kuleuven.be/syllabi/e/D0I71AE.htm
13. Poelmans, S.: Design of a business information system - KU Leuven. https://onderwijsaanbod.kuleuven.be/syllabi/v/e/HMH28EE.htm#activetab=doelstellingen_idp1415488
14. Kolp, M., Pirotte, A.: UCL/IAG/ISYS - Unité de Systèmes d'Information (ISYS) – UCL. http://www.isys.ucl.ac.be/etudes/cours/geti2101/
15. Heymans, P.: Analyse et modélisation des systèmes d'information - Université de Namur. https://directory.unamur.be/teaching/courses/IHDCB335/2015
16. Faulkner, S.: Bases de données - Université de Namur. https://directory.unamur.be/teaching/courses/EIMIB212/2016
17. Zheng, A.Y., Lawhorn, J.K., Lumley, T., Freeman, S.: Application of bloom's taxonomy debunks the "MCAT Myth". Science **319**, 414 (2008)
18. Gezer, M., Sunkur, M.O., Sah, F.: An evaluation of the exam questions of social studies course according to revized bloom's taxonomy. Educ. Sci. Psychol. **28**(2), 3–17 (2014)
19. Dolog, P., Thomsen, L.L., Thomsen, B.: Assessing problem-based learning in a software engineering curriculum using bloom's taxonomy and the ieee software engineering body of knowledge. ACM Trans. Comput. Educ. **16**, 1–41 (2016)
20. Krathwohl, D.R.: A Revision of Bloom's taxonomy. Theory Pract. **41**, 212–218 (2002)
21. Gorgone, J.T., Gray, P., Stohr, E.A., Valacich, J.S., Wigand, R.T.: MSIS 2006. ACM SIGCSE Bull. **38**, 121 (2006)
22. Ardis, M., Budgen, D., Hislop, G., Offutt, J., Sebern, M., Visser, W.: Curriculum guidelines for undergraduate degree programs in software engineering. Computer **48**, 106–109 (2014)

23. Venable, J.R.: Teaching novice conceptual data modellers to become experts. In: Proceedings 1996 International Conference Software Engineering: Education and Practice, pp. 50–56. IEEE Computer Society Press (1996)
24. Wang, W., Brooks, R.J.: Improving the understanding of conceptual modelling. J. Simul. **1**, 153–158 (2007)
25. Sedrakyan, G., Snoeck, M.: Effects of simulation on novices' understanding of the concept of inheritance in conceptual modeling. In: Jeusfeld, M.A., Karlapalem, K. (eds.) ER 2015. LNCS, vol. 9382, pp. 327–336. Springer, Cham (2015). doi:10.1007/978-3-319-25747-1_32
26. Bloom, B.S.: Handbook on Formative and Summative Evaluation of Student Learning (1971). https://eric.ed.gov/?id=ED049304
27. Crowe, A., Dirks, C., Wenderoth, M.P.: Biology in bloom: implementing Bloom's Taxonomy to enhance student learning in biology. CBE Life Sci. Educ. **7**, 368–381 (2008)
28. Thompson, A.R., O'Loughlin, V.D.: The Blooming Anatomy Tool (BAT): a discipline-specific rubric for utilizing Bloom's taxonomy in the design and evaluation of assessments in the anatomical sciences. Anat. Sci. Educ. **8**, 493–501 (2015)
29. Zaidi, N.B., Hwang, C., Scott, S., Stallard, S., Purkiss, J., Hortsch, M.: Climbing Bloom's taxonomy pyramid: lessons from a graduate histology course. Anat. Sci. Educ. (2017)
30. Lo, S., Larsen, V., Yee, A.: A two-dimensional and non-hierarchical framework of Bloom's taxonomy for biology. FASEB J. **30**, 662 (2016)
31. Alaoutinen, S., Smolander, K.: Student self-assessment in a programming course using bloom's revised taxonomy. In: Proceedings of the Fifteenth Annual Conference on Innovation and Technology in Computer Science Education – ITiCSE 2010, p. 155. ACM Press, New York (2010)
32. Kidwell, L.A., Fisher, D.G., Braun, R.L., Swanson, D.L.: Developing learning objectives for accounting ethics using bloom's taxonomy. Account. Educ. **22**, 44–65 (2013)
33. Bogdanova, D., Snoeck, M.: Learning outcomes in domain modelling education, Mendeley Data (2017). http://dx.doi.org/10.17632/285d6jhdg9.1

Information Security Risk Management

Salimeh Dashti[✉], Paolo Giorgini, and Elda Paja

DISI, University of Trento, Via Sommarive, 14, 38123 Trento, Italy
salimeh.dashti@studenti.unitn.it, {paolo.giorgini,elda.paja}@unitn.it

Abstract. Security breaches on the socio-technical systems organizations depend on cost the latter billions of dollars of losses each year. Although information security is a growing concern, most organizations deploy technical security measures to prevent security attacks, overlooking social and organizational threats and the risks faced because of them. In this paper, we propose a method to information security risk analysis inspired by the ISO27k standard series and based on two state-of-art methods, namely the socio-technical security requirements method STS and the risk analysis method CORAS. The method captures social interactions among stakeholders, while capturing both the risks that threaten their assets as well as those arising while interacting with others. Then, the method suggests how assets are to be protected based on the information classification and potential losses incurred by security breaches. An example from the healthcare domain is used throughout the paper to illustrate the method.

Keywords: Information security · Security risk analysis · Security requirements engineering

1 Introduction

Organizations are increasingly investing on information security to protect informational assets and avoid huge monetary losses [22]. Yet the number of security incidents continues to increase [20]. Evidence suggests that most organizations deploy only technical information security countermeasures, such as encryption of data in transit and intrusion detection systems [10,23]. But organizational systems operate in a socio-technical context where they interact with other systems, humans and organizations by exchanging data, sharing information or outsourcing tasks [18]. As such, they may wreck confidentiality by disclosing information in an unauthorized way, crash the integrity of private data, affect availability by relying on untrusted third parties, etc. Therefore, the design of a secure organizational system cannot be handled with traditional security methods (e.g., [4,6,15,26]) but should rather begin with a thorough analysis of its socio-technical context, thereby considering not only technical attacks, but also social and organizational ones [5,12,18].

Moreover, regulations such as Basel II, the Turnbull report and the Sarbanes-Oxley Act, stress on the need for conducting information security and risk analysis conjointly, since the lack of adequate mechanisms for controlling the flow

G. Poels et al. (Eds.): PoEM 2017, LNBIP 305, pp. 18–33, 2017.
https://doi.org/10.1007/978-3-319-70241-4_2

of information through the organization would incur massive financial costs. Information security is therefore an inseparable and important factor in analyzing risk [2]. Despite many Information Security Risk Management (ISRM) approaches [9,14,29,30] have been proposed, they are mainly for certification purposes and related to specific standards, and do not offer any clear and systematic method.

According to the 2015 PWC report [21], the two main reasons for organizations to fail in risk analysis are: (i) *incomplete risk plans*, and (ii) *ineffective risk prioritization*, that is, focusing on a single-criteria such as financial impact rather than a combination of quantitative and qualitative criteria.

In this paper, we propose an integrated and tool-supported method to information security and risk analysis. We combine and extend two state-of-art methods, namely the socio-technical security requirements method STS [3] and the risk analysis method CORAS [13]. STS is a security requirements engineering method expressly thought for socio-technical systems, it considers information a first-class citizen and deals with security issues arising from social and organizational factors (in particular during interaction). STS allows understanding the impact of threats over stakeholders' assets, but it is not meant thorough risk analysis. Hence, we follow the CORAS method [13], which offers a clear step-by-step method to conduct risk analysis. Following CORAS steps, we address the *incomplete risk plan* problem, by guiding user from identifying risk till treating them, and also we deal with the risk prioritization problem, by analyzing not only the financial impacts of risk but also brand, reputation, and other potential impact factors specific to companies and their industries. However, CORAS does not deal with the risk organizations face over social interactions between stakeholders and clients. By integrating with STS we overcome this limitation. On the other hand, although STS captures security over information, it treats all informational assets equally important from a security point of view. According to the ISO27K security standard series [7,8], information classification is a key concept in the structuring and development of an effective information security method. Thus, we follow the ISO27k principles to specify the classification of a particular informational asset in order to determine how it is to be protected. This helps introducing a balance between protection and costs.

Particularly, our integrated method makes the following contribution: (i) it combines information security and risk analysis providing a systematic method; (ii) it evaluates and classifies assets based on the ISO27k standard series; (iii) it introduces security requirements based on asset classification, and last but not least (iv) it provides a balance between cost and protection.

The rest of the paper is organized as follows. Section 2 introduces the baseline and the running example. Section 3 illustrates step by step the modeling phase of our method and how the CORAS steps are placed in our method. Section 4 describes the reasoning techniques and a brief description of the support tool. Section 5 discusses related work. Finally, Sect. 6 describes lessons learned in using the method in the healthcare case study and concludes the paper.

2   Baseline and Running Example

This section introduces the two states-of-art we employed to build our method, and our running example taken from healthcare domain.

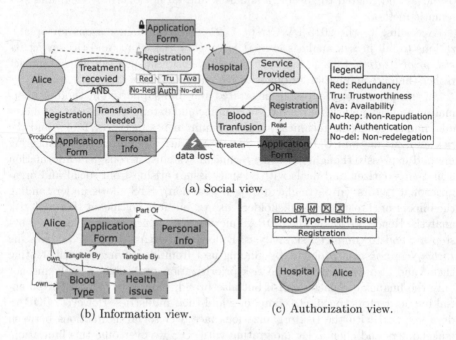

(a) Social view.

(b) Information view.   (c) Authorization view.

Fig. 1. The three views of the STS.

STS [3] is a model-based and tool-supported security requirements engineering method for designing socio-technical systems. Models are created based on the Socio-Technical Security modeling language (STS-ml), with STS-Tool[1], which allows constructing models by iteratively building three views (*social*, *information*, and *authorization*), each focused on different aspects of the socio-technical system. The *social view* (Fig. 1a), represents actors as intentional and social entities. STS-ml supports two types of actors: agent–concrete participants (e.g., Alice), and role–abstract actors (e.g., Hospital), used when the actual participant is unknown. Actors may possess documents, which are represented by rectangles (e.g., Application form). Possession indicates that actor has the document and can performing operations and transferring them. The operations are *read*, *modify*, or *produce* documents while achieving their goals, represented by ovals (e.g., Registration). As shown in Fig. 1a, Alice's main goal is to obtain Treatment received which is and-decomposed into two subgoals: Transfusion needed and Registration; to obtain the latter, she *produce* the document Application form.

Threats are represented in terms of *event* in STS. For instance, event data lost has threatened Application form. Security requirements are specified over interactions, namely goal delegations and document transmissions. The locks placed in top-left side of the goal/document indicate that security requirement has been set. Double-clicking on the closed lock opens it and shows the set security requirement which are expressed by small rectangle under asset/goal (e.g., No-Rep, No-del, etc.).

Informational content of the documents manipulated in the social view, are captured in information view (Fig. 1b). The view allows for specifying information ownership (*owns*) which indicates that an actor is the legitimate owner of the asset and can make use of it. For instance, Fig. 1b shows that the agent Alice owns the information Blood type and Health issue, represented by dashed-boarder rectangle. The view also gives a structured representation of information and documents, through *Part-of*, and how they are inter-connected, through *Tangible-by* relation. Figure 1b illustrates that the document Personal info is *part of* the document Application form; the latter represents two pieces of information, namely Blood type and Health issue, via *Tangible-by* relation.

The *authorization view* shows the authorizations that actors grant to others over information, specifying which operations they are allowed (prohibited) to do, for which goals (scope). Plus, specifying whether authorization can be further transferred or not. Figure 1c shows that Alice authorizes Hospital to *read* and *modify* (R and M shown with check sign), but prohibits *transmission* and *producing* (T and P shown with cross sign) information Blood type and Health issue in the scope of the goal Registration. The authorization is transferable since the arrow is solid, while nontransferable authorization is captured by dotted arrow.

CORAS [13] is a model-driven risk analysis method that consists of 8 steps. The first 5 are concerned with the definition of assets and the scope of their analysis. Then, it follows a discussion with stakeholders to order assets accordingly to their relevance. Threats are identified and modeled by using *threat diagram*, as shown in Fig. 2. The CORAS supports three types of threats: *non-human threat* (e.g., System failure), *human-deliberate threat* (e.g., Hacker), and *human-accidental threat* (e.g., Physician). The diagram identifies the vulnerabilities (weaknesses) that opens for, or may be exploited by a threat, to initiate a chain or series of events (threat scenarios) that leads to unwanted incident(s) which harms or reduces the value of an asset(s). As can be seen in Fig. 2, due to the vulnerability Ineffective protection, human-deliberate threat Hacker initiates the threat scenario Breaks in. The scenario leads to the unwanted incident Record theft which impact asset Application form. The frequency of threat scenarios and unwanted incident will be estimated and assigned as *likelihood scale*. Moreover, the impact of incident over asset will be estimated and assigned as *consequence scale*. For instance, the Hacker *certainly* (likelihood scale) exploit the weakness and breaks into system, which has a *Major* (consequence scale) impact on the asset. *Risk evaluation matrix* is used to evaluate risks based on the scales and risk evaluation criteria, which aids the analyst by highlighting risks with green,

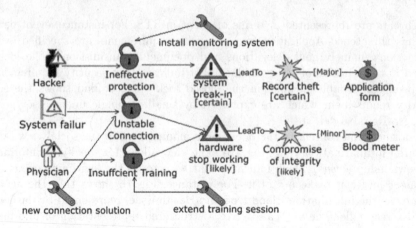

Fig. 2. The CORAS threat diagram. (Color figure online)

orange and red colors; the threats that fall in the range of cells highlighted in red cells will be treated. In the example shown in Fig. 2 all the captured threats are treated. For example, the suggested treatment to avoid harm by Physicion is to conduct training sessions.

Running Example. A healthcare system is a socio-technical system in which hospitals and healthcare centers allow physicians or general practitioners to perform medical tests and give advice to patients who have registered for medical services. Such a scenario sees as main participants not only the hospitals, patients, and physicians, but also laboratories for specialized tests as well as research centers that conduct data analysis to make forecasts on the need for blood banks. This is complex socio-technical system in which involved participants (actors) need to rely on each other to fulfill their objectives, by interacting and exchanging information. Information in such system is sensitive, for instance personal information, health status, etc., which should be protected from possible attacks. A threat is not necessarily an outsider, like a hacker, it also can be a careless employee or a connection failure. This example integrates two scenarios from the healthcare used to apply CORAS and STS, the methods that serve as a baseline for our work. As such, the illustration of the integrated method can show of the added values of the latter compared to the underlying methods.

3 Information Security Risk Modeling

Our method consists of two main macro phases: *modeling* and *automated analysis*. In this section, we focus on the modeling phase, while automated analysis and also the reasoning techniques and the supporting tool will be described in the next section.

The modeling phase consists in the creation of four different models, each focused on a specific aspect of socio-technical system. We start with the *social model* and continue with describing *asset* and *authorization modeling*. Then, we conclude with *threat modeling*.

1. Social Modeling. This model represents the organization of the overall socio-technical system. Figure 3a represents part of the *Social Model* of our example. We have extended the concept of asset in STS by adding three different types of assets: (1) *hardware*, which is represented by round-corner rectangle (e.g., Blood meter); (2) *software*, which is represented by pentagon (e.g., Registration software), and (3) *system*, which is represented by hexagon (e.g., Hospital service). Actors *use* these assets while achieving their goals. Figure 3a shows that Physician *uses* hardware Blood meter to achieve two subgoals: Blood type performed and Transfusion via specialist.

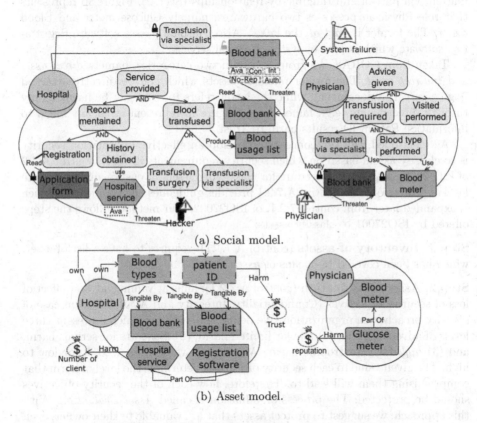

(a) Social model.

(b) Asset model.

Fig. 3. Part of the models of the running example.

STS supports clause A.6.2.3 of ISO27002 and control A.6.2.1 of ISO27001 which require covering security requirements on agreements with third parties. We have gone further by acknowledging the importance of protecting assets *within organizations*, with respect to control A.6.1 of ISO27001 and Clause 6.1 of ISO27002. For instance, role Hospital wants to ensure the availability of the service Hospital service to achieve subgoal History obtained. Thus, security requirements availability (Ava) has been set.

Another extensions to this model is to identify threats in a technical way by specifying the type of threats, that is, to employ proper and better treatment. Consider that careless employee is the threat, as they remained the most cited source of compromise [20], the first treatment could be training him instead of implementing other expensive security countermeasures. Thus, the STS event concept has been refined to the three types of threats (refer to Sect. 2), from CORAS. Figure 3a shows, threat System failure threaten document Blood bank.

2. Asset Modeling. As mentioned, we have added three more information assets which their structures also need to be modeled, as document and information, via part-of and tangible-by relationships (Sect. 2). Figure 3b represents that role Physician possesses two hardwares, namely Glucose meter and Blood meter. The former is *part of* the latter. Also, Hospital posses software Registration software which is part of system Hospital service.

Taken from CORAS, we group assets in two categories, namely *direct asset* and *indirect asset*. The former refers to assets which can be directly attacked (e.g., a server, a document), while the latter refers to what can be harmed only through direct assets (e.g., fame, trust). Figure 3b represents that any harm to information Patient ID results harm to Trust.

As mentioned, the key concept to develop an effective information security is to classify assets based on which security requirements are set. Control A.7.2 of ISO 27001 requires a procedure for classifying assets to ensure an appropriate level of protection, and control A.7.2.1 provides guidelines on classification which is expanded later from control 7.2.1. of ISO27002. Our method follows the steps offered by ISO27001 to classify assets:

Step 1. Inventory of assets (control A.7.1.1): requires to have a list of asset, which has been covered by means of *asset model*.

Step 2. Asset classification (control A.7.2.1): aims at valuing adverse effect of loss of security objectives (Confidentiality, Integrity and Availability) in case of security breaches on organization. We define three classes which represent three levels of adverse effects: (1) *low* for limited harm; (2) *moderate* for serious harm, and (3) *high* for catastrophic harm. We assign a value from 1 to 3, for low to high. The given value to each security objectives determine the level of harm that compromising them will lead to. Therefore, how each of the security objectives should be protected. The process of valuation is called *Asset Evaluation*. With this approach, we suggest to protect assets that are valuable to their owner, even if there is no captured threat against them; that is because the ways that are impossible to attack system yesterday may get possible tomorrow as technology is growing dramatically.

Asset evaluation has to be done over meetings with stakeholders. Understanding the impact of indirect assets on organization, is a starting point to evaluate direct assets. Thus, the process begins with valuing indirect assets, from 1 (low) to 3 (high). As shown in Fig. 4, role Hospital has evaluated the adverse effect of

Name	Blood usage list	Value	C	I	A	Type	Document	
			2	2	2			

Number of user	1			Number of copy	1		

Direct Asset							Indirect asset	
Name	Num. of user	Num. of copy	type	C	I	A	Name	Value
Blood type	4	1	Info	2	2	2		
Patient ID	1	2	Info	1	2	2	Trust	2

Fig. 4. Asset valuation table

Trust, *moderate* as valued 2. After valuing indirect assets, we need to value direct assets, for which asset structure is so helpful, since value of an asset is defined by value of what it is composed of. Subsequently, we start from asset constituent by answering questions such as: *"how much harm will the unauthorized disclosure of this asset cause to the organization?"* to evaluate confidentiality. Same sort of question to evaluate all security objectives. Once evaluation of all constituents is done, the highest given value to security objectives among constituents of an asset, will be automatically assigned to corresponding security objectives of that asset.

Values are set, using Asset Valuation Table, shown in Fig. 4. The figure depicts that document Blood usage list represents information Blood type and Patient ID, which are valued 2, 2, 2 and 1, 2, 2 for CIA, respectively. Thus, the automatic assigned value to confidentiality is 2, since it is the highest among 1 and 2; same for integrity and availability.

By considering indirect assets while valuing the loss of organization in case of harm to their direct asset, we offer a multi-criteria evaluation which addresses the mentioned "single-criteria" problem from [21].

Step 3. Asset handling (control A.7.2.2): We follow STS's principle [3] in classifying security requirements. Due to space limitation, in the following we describe only the added security requirements type to STS, for the rest please refer to [3]:

– *Confidentiality:* where we introduce:(i) Number of copies (ISO27002 clause 6.2.3): to restrict the number of instances that can exist from information to avoid disclosing information; (ii) Number of users (ISO27002): to control number of permitted users to access information asset; (iii) Duration of authorization (ISO27002 clause 6.2.3), and (iv) Act on termination (ISO27001 control A.8.3.1 and A.8.3.2). The last two requirements allow capturing access control when giving authorization to another party which are introduced during *Authorization Modeling.* While, requirements *Number of copy* and *Number of user* are set in this model by Asset Valuation Table (Fig. 4).
The figure shows that, *Number of user* and *Number of copy* are 4 and 1 for information Blood type and 1 and 2 for information Patient ID, respectively.

Unlike value of CIA, the lowest given value to these security requirements among constituents will be automatically assigned to corresponding security requirements of their main asset. The reason is that, if it is required to have one instance from a piece of information, surly there should be only one document which contain it. Otherwise, the security requirement for that piece of information is violated. The same goes for *number of user*. Accordingly, the requirements for document Blood usage list are 1 and 1.

– **Accountability** refined as: (i) *Non-repudiation of transmission*: expressed by receiver who requires sender not to repudiate the transmission of asset; (ii) *Non-repudiation of acceptance*: expressed by sender who requires receiver not to repudiate receiving transmitted asset. Figure 3a shows the requirements over transmission of document Blood bank. (iii) *Separation of information* (based on effect of aggregation concept by ISO27002): aggregation of information may cause a large quantity of non-sensitive information to become sensitive. This security requirement can be set among information which their aggregation makes them sensitive. For instance, information health issue might not be sensitive as long as it is anonymous. Once it appears with the patient name, then confidentiality of it may become important.

As said, the classification given to a particular information asset determines how it is to be protected. We introduce three different levels of security requirements for each level of value: (1) non-negotiable: refers to the security objective valued 3. Such requirement has to be implemented otherwise the company face a severe harm. (ii) negotiable: refers to the security objective valued 2. These requirements may or may not be implemented. Stakeholders and the risk analyst can discuss over it and decide based on the likelihood of captured threat. (iii) No protection: refers to the security objective valued 1 that will pose any harm to organization. If confidentiality of an asset is 3, while integrity and availability are 2, the method requires *non-negotiable* security requirements for confidentiality and *negotiable* for the other two security objectives, so that, we invest more where needed to make a balance between protection and cost. Note that, the requirements are automatically assigned as user enter the values. Graphically, non-negotiable security requirement is expressed by dashed-line border and negotiable ones by dotted-line border. As shown in Fig. 4, document Blood usage list has been valued 2, 2, 2. Therefore, *negotiable* security requirements should be assigned, as shown in Fig. 3a.

3. Authorization Modeling. STS authorization model has been extended to support two security requirements: (1) *duration of authorization*: to specify how long the given authorization is valid; and (2) *act on termination*: to determine the proper action once the authorization is over that could be either to *return* or to *destroy* the asset.

By now, the first fifth steps of CORAS are taken by identifying target of analysis (goals and assets) and threats using *social* and *asset* model. Next, we cover step six (risk estimation) and seven (risk evaluation). To do so, we need to model captured threats.

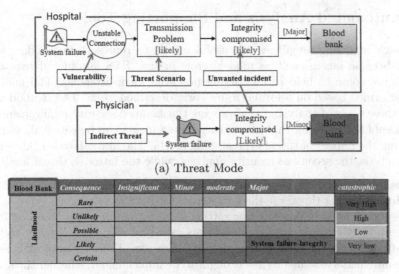

(a) Threat Mode

Blood Bank	Consequence	Insignificant	Minor	moderate	Major	catastrophic
Likelihood	Rare					Very High
	Unlikely					High
	Possible					Low
	Likely				System failure-Integrity	Very low
	Certain					

(b) Risk Evaluation Matrix of Blood bank.

Fig. 5. Threat modeling.

4. Threat Modeling.

To model threat, we use the CORAS concept but fault tree analysis [27] notations which are widely adopted for risk analysis. Figure 5a illustrates that, due to Unstable Connection (vulnerability), it is *likely* (likelihood scale) that the document Blood bank faces Transmission problem (threat scenario); the problem can have a *major* (the consequence scale) impact on the document Integrity (unwanted incident).

Threats can propagate via interactions, namely goal delegation and asset transmission. As shown in Fig. 6a, a non-human threat System failure attacks document Blood bank which has been transmitted to the role Physician to be modified while achieving subgoal Transfusion via specialist. Thus, the compromised document can have side effect not only on functionality of Hospital, but also on the Physician. These types of threats are called *indirect threats*. As Fig. 5a shows, the indirect threat System failure (illustrated in gray) has *minor* impact on Physician, while it has *major* impact on the Hospital. Note that, modeling *indirect threat* only requires *unwanted incident*, since the vulnerability existed where the threat has raised and carried out the events.

To evaluate threats, we use *Asset Evaluation Matrix* (Fig. 5b), from CORAS. The matrix will be automatically filled for each victim asset, based on assigned *likelihood* and *consequence* scales. The threats that fall in the range of the cells highlighted in red need to be treated. The matrix cell can be modified to adjust for each asset based on the risk tolerance of stakeholder (please refer to [13]). Figure 5b illustrates that the threat *System failure* against document Blood bank is unacceptable.

4   Automated Analysis and Supporting Tool

Although modeling languages are useful means to represent knowledge, they might become inconsistent as models grow in size. STS automated reasoning techniques come to help in identifying potential inconsistencies. The analysis are performed based on a formal framework, described in [3]. The method supports three types of analysis: (1) approving the assigned security requirements as treatments (2) verifying that all security requirements can be satisfied, and (3) verifying the impact of threats threatening assets. The first analysis is known as risk analysis, the second as security analysis, while the latter as threat analysis.

(I) Risk Analysis. Risk estimation and evaluation has been covered by *threat modeling*. Treating threats is the last step of CORAS to take.

Assets are already protected by setting security requirements based on their values and any extra security requirements asked by stakeholders (refer to [3]). Yet, after evaluating threats, it needs further checks. The *Non-negotiable* security requirements assigned to assets ought to be implemented, whether the assets are attacked or not. Whereas, *negotiable* security requirements can be further discussed to be or not to be implemented based on frequency of threats. As the result of risk analysis, the tool highlights in red the assets which are under unacceptable attack with negotiable security requirements, so that, stakeholders can decide whether to keep the protection as they are or improve them to non-negotiable type. As shown in Fig. 5b, the threat against the document Blood bank, is unacceptable and we also have shown in Fig. 3a that its security requirements are negotiable. The decision is to protect document Blood bank, strictly. So that, its security requirement has been improved. Graphically, Fig. 6a shows that the security requirements of the document became dotted-border.

(II) Security Analysis. STS supports: (i) identifying possible conflicts among security requirements, and (ii) identifying conflicts between actors own business policies and the security requirements imposed on them. Figure 6c depicts part of this analysis. We extended STS analysis to check the following conflicts over assets as well: (1) fulfillment of security requirement *number of copy*. For instance, the requirements for information Blood type is 1 (Fig. 4). While, as shown in Fig. 6b, the information is represented in two documents, namely Blood usage list and Blood bank. Thus, the requirement is violated, so that, the tool is highlighted them. (2) fulfillment of security requirement *number of user*. This requirements for hardware Blood meter is set one. Figure 6a shows that, the hardware need to be accessed for achieving two subgoals, namely blood type performed and transfusion via specialist, which may lead to conflict if they be achieved by two different user. To avoid such conflicts, we use security requirement *Goal-based combination of duties* between two goals. This requirement implies the fact that the user who fulfills the former, ought to be the same as the one who fulfills the latter. Graphically, this is represented as an arrow between two entities annotated with the "equal" (=) symbol. In our example, as the result of security analysis, *Goal-based combination of duties* between the two mentioned subgoals is suggested, to ensure that the same Physician will achieve both goals.

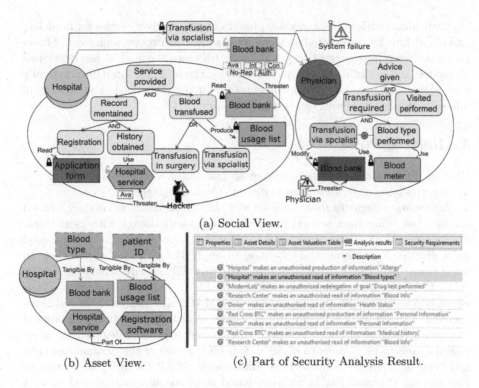

(a) Social View.

(b) Asset View.   (c) Part of Security Analysis Result.

Fig. 6. Automated analysis result. (Color figure online)

(III) Threat Analysis. This analysis identifies the followings: (1) the threat propagation through the model. Figure 6a, illustrate the result of threat System failure propagation. Earlier we described how we take care of the indirect threat. (2) Specifying critical and non-critical actors. There are two groups of actors in a socio-technical systems: (i) actors who hold assets (even one) with *negotiable* type of protection, called *non-critical actors*; (ii) actors who *only* hold asset with non-negotiable security requirements, called *critical actors*. The entire socio-technical systems can be attacked through one single entry. Thus, the latter group may be more concerned about the level of protection of actors they interact with. Distinguish between these two groups, help stakeholders to either emphasizing strictly on security while interacting with uncritical ones or possibly avoid interactions with them. In our example the role Physician is a critical actor who receives document from a non-critical role. Graphically, the role is highlighted in red, as shown in Fig. 6a.

The Supporting Tool. Our method is fully supported by a prototype CASE tool. It has been developed as an eclipse plug-in of the STS-Tool, which is a modeling tool for STS-ml. It is a standalone application written in Java, and its core is based on Eclipse RCP Engine. AS STS-Tool, our tool is compatible for multiple platforms (Windows 32 and 64 bits, Mac OS X, Linux). The tool supports all activities of our method providing graphically facilities for modeling and algorithms for automated analysis over models. Moreover, a number of functionalities for report generation is implemented. Once the analyst has developed all models and performed the required analysis, the tool generated automatically a set of documents as support documentation for the work done. The tool is still under implementation and can be found soon in[2].

5   Related Work

We can differentiate two areas related to our work: *information security risk management* and *information security management systems.*

Information Security Risk Management (ISRM) methods are mainly focused on risks but suffer from several issues: lack of a methodology with clear steps, overlooking information security risks, expensive documentation, and the need for a deep understanding and expertise to apply the proposed approaches. In some cases, like *Dutch A&K analysis, Austrian IT security handbook, MARION, ISAMM,* the information is only available in the local language. These issues have been tackled by some works: The MAGERIT risk analysis and management method identifies and groups assets according to their organizational hierarchy. Then, it analyzes potential threats and required safeguards to meet security objectives. It aims to make stakeholders aware of the existence of risks and keep them under control. In a similar way, SREP (Security Requirement Engineering Process) [16] is an asset-based iterative and incremental process that uses misuse case diagrams to model threats and MAGERIT tables to assess them. Despite their systematic nature, both methods overlook vulnerabilities derived from interactions, whether from the system and its environment or from social interactions among stakeholders. IRAM [31] is a workshop-based and tool-supported model, focused on the organization's information systems and information threats. The approach helps determine the criticality and prominence of information systems. Unfortunately, the actual risk calculation formula is not openly available. Mehari [17] provides a complex process, including cyclic risk management and a knowledge base to support semi-automated risk analysis based on a set of input factors. While the method supports quantitative, scenario-based analysis of risk, it lacks the identification of organizational assets, valuing them, and capturing threats against them. Finally, The Facilitated Risk Assessment Process (FRAP) [19] aims to sketch how a "facilitator-led" qualitative risk analysis and assessment can be applied in order to enable stakeholders to produce findings which are understandable by non-experts. However, FRAP strongly relies on the role of the Facilitator to guide the stakeholder, it does not valuate the asset and presents the same drawbacks as MAGERIT and SREP regarding interactions.

Information Security Management Systems (ISMS) is focused on standards for IT Governance which lead to information security, such as PRINCE2, OPM3, MMI, P-CMM, PMMM, ISO27K series, BS7799, PCIDSS, COSO, SOA, ITIL

---

[2] http://www.sts-tool.eu/downloads/.

and COBIT. In the following, we discuss the five most prominent ISMS standards. *BS7799* [28] contains several parts, the first part containing best practices for ISMS, whereas the second part focuses on how to implement ISMS referring to BS 7799-2, which later became ISO 27001 [7]. The Control Objectives for Information and related Technology (*COBIT*) [11] is a certification which is globally accepted to ensure that IT operations are aligned with business goals and objectives. However, [24] reveals that there is relatively little academic literature making use of COBIT, and [25] claims that a big effort is required to understand and apply it. The Information Technology Infrastructure Library (ITIL) [1] is an approach to service management based on "do what works". It unites all areas of IT service provision into a single goal based on two main concepts of a service: (i) delivering value and (ii) not caring how a service is implemented. However, its monolithic analysis does not capture which actors in the organization generate the values that are later delivered to the customers. Finally The Payment Card Industry Data Security Standard (PCIDSS) [32] is a worldwide information security standard defined to help industry organizations processes card payments.

6   Conclusion

In this paper, we have presented an integrated method for information security and risk analysis built on top of the STS security methods and the CORAS risk analysis method. We adopted principles from the ISO27k series and provided a method to evaluate information-related assets based on their potential impacts in case of security breaches, to classify them and ensure an adequate level of security according to their value. We also find weak actors of the system to warn the analyst to limit interaction with them.

The running example used throughout the paper is part of a larger case study we developed[3]. The main findings while developing the running example are summarized as follows: (1) although the asset classification has provided a number of advantages, grouping them in three categories was in many cases too restrictive. As future work, we will support a customizable classification, so that, based on the socio-technical system under analysis, a different classification will be adopted; (2) the method performs in a high level of abstraction, which provides a rationale on how the business analyst should decide upon security requirements. This makes the estimation of costs difficult. For a more accurate evaluation, we plan to extend our method by estimating the costs of asset acquisition and security requirements implementation; (3) although our method enriched STS by modeling and analyzing information-related assets, the language was not expressive enough to represent how assets are manipulated to achieve goals.

Acknowledgments. This project has received funding from the SESAR Joint Undertaking under grant agreement No. 699306 under European Union's Horizon 2020 research and innovation program.

---

[3] http://disi.unitn.it/~pgiorgio/IRM-HealthCareCase.pdf.

References

1. Abid, M.: Information technology infrastructure library (ITIL). JIT **1**(1) (2012)
2. Continuity Central: Information risk co-existance. https://www.continuitycentral. com/feature0189.htm
3. Dalpiaz, F., Paja, E., Giorgini, P.: Security Requirements Engineering: Designing Secure Socio-Technical Systems. MIT Press, Cambridge (2016)
4. Firesmith, D.: Security use cases. J. Object Technol. **2**(3), 53–64 (2003)
5. Giorgini, P., Massacci, F., Mylopoulos, J.: Requirement engineering meets security: a case study on modelling secure electronic transactions by VISA and Mastercard. In: Song, I.-Y., Liddle, S.W., Ling, T.-W., Scheuermann, P. (eds.) ER 2003. LNCS, vol. 2813, pp. 263–276. Springer, Heidelberg (2003). doi:10.1007/ 978-3-540-39648-2_22
6. Haley, C., Laney, R., Moffett, J., Nuseibeh, B.: Security requirements engineering: a framework for representation and analysis. IEEE Trans. Softw. Eng. **34**(1), 133–153 (2008)
7. ISO/IEC: ISO/IEC 27001 information security standard (2013)
8. ISO/IEC: ISO/IEC 27002 information security standard (2013)
9. ISO/IEC 15408: ISO/IEC 15408–1:2009 information technology standard (2009)
10. Kessel, P.: Into the cloud, out of the fog: EY 2011 global information security survey (2011)
11. Lainhart IV, J.W.: A method for controlling information and information technology risks and vulnerabilities. JIS **14**(s-1), 21–25 (2000)
12. Liu, L., Yu, E., Mylopoulos, J.: Security and privacy requirements analysis within a social setting. In: Proceedings of RE Conference, pp. 151–161. IEEE (2003)
13. Lund, M., Solhaug, B., Stølen, K.: Model-Driven Risk Analysis: The CORAS Approach. Springer Science & Business Media, Heidelberg (2010)
14. McEvoy, N., Whitcombe, A.: Structured risk analysis. In: Davida, G., Frankel, Y., Rees, O. (eds.) InfraSec 2002. LNCS, vol. 2437, pp. 88–103. Springer, Heidelberg (2002). doi:10.1007/3-540-45831-X_7
15. Mead, N., Stehney, T.: Security Quality Requirements Engineering (SQUARE) Methodology, vol. 30. ACM, New York (2005)
16. Mellado, D., Fernández-Medina, E., Piattini, M.: Applying a security requirements engineering process. In: Gollmann, D., Meier, J., Sabelfeld, A. (eds.) ESORICS 2006. LNCS, vol. 4189, pp. 192–206. Springer, Heidelberg (2006). doi:10.1007/ 11863908_13
17. Mihailescu, V.: Mehari. JABIS **3**(4), 143 (2012)
18. Paja, E., Dalpiaz, F., Giorgini, P.: Modelling and reasoning about security requirements in socio-technical systems. Data Knowl. Eng. **98**, 123–143 (2015)
19. Peltier, T.: Facilitated risk analysis process (FRAP). Auerbach Publication, CRC Press LLC, Boca Raton (2000)
20. PWC: Turnaround and transformation in cybersecurity. https://www.pwc.com/ sg/en/publications/assets/pwc-global-state-of-information-security-survay-2016. pdf
21. PWC: Why risk assessments fail. https://www.pwc.com/us/en/risk-assurance/ publications/assets/preventing-erm-risk-assessment-failure.pdf
22. PWC: 2015 information security breaches survey (2015). https://www.pwc.co.uk/ assets/pdf/2015-isbs-technical-report-blue-digital.pdf
23. Richardson, R.: CSI computer crime and security survey, 2011 (2010)

24. Ridley, G., Young, J., Carroll, P.: COBIT and its utilization: a framework from the literature. In: Proceedings of the 37th HICSS. IEEE (2004)
25. Simonsson, M., Johnson, P., Wijkström, H.: Model-based it governance maturity assessments with COBIT. In: ECIS, pp. 1276–1287 (2007)
26. Sindre, G., Opdahl, A.L.: Eliciting security requirements with misuse cases. Requirements Eng. **10**(1), 34–44 (2005)
27. Stamatelatos, M., Vesely, W., Dugan, J., Fragola, J., Minarick, J., Railsback, J.: Fault Tree Handbook (2002)
28. British Standard: Code of practice for ISM British Standards Institution (1995)
29. British Standard: Standard 100-2: It-grundschutz-vorgehensweise. BSI (2008)
30. Stoneburner, G., Goguen, A.Y., Feringa, A.: SP 800-30. Risk management guide for information technology systems (2002)
31. Sun, L., Srivastava, R., Mock, T.: An information systems security risk assessment model under the Dempster-Shafer theory of belief functions. JMIS **22**(4), 109–142 (2006)
32. Virtue, T.: Payment Card Industry Data Security Standard Handbook. Wiley, Hoboken (2009)

Using Grounded Theory for Domain Specific Modelling Language Design
Lessons Learned from the Smart Grid Domain

Sybren de Kinderen[✉]

University of Duisburg-Essen, Essen, Germany
sybren.dekinderen@uni-due.de

Abstract. This paper shows how Grounded Theory (GT), a method for domain understanding predominantly used in the social sciences, can be useful for the design of a Domain Specific Modelling Language (DSML). Using a pilot study from the smart grid domain, we discuss how GT can be used to systematically derive the abstract syntax of a DSML from domain data. From this, we derive lessons learned from the application of GT, the most relevant being that (1) with GT, one systematically derives an abstract syntax of a DSML, reflecting domain commonalities and variation points, (2) in line with its explorative character, with GT one gains a grounded domain understanding, and the domain goals that a DSML should satisfy, (3) GT does imply a notable time investment, which one needs to weigh against its prospective benefits. Finally we present a concluding outlook in terms of implications for DSML design mechanisms.

Keywords: Grounded Theory · Domain Specific Modelling · Language design · Smart grid

1 Introduction

Domain Specific Modelling Languages (DSMLs) reconstruct the concepts of a specific domain (e.g., electricity, healthcare), thereby increasing their expressiveness of the particulars of that domain [8,16]. DSMLs steadily gain in proliferation [13,15] in part due to: fostering communication with domain experts, by staying close to domain-specific terminology [8]; increasing modeling productivity, by not having to reconstruct domain specific knowledge from scratch [9,16], and; acting as a thinking tool [25, p. 41], since DSMLs abstract from unnecessary details.

Being reconstructions of domain concepts, the design of DSMLs should naturally reflect the commonalities and variations of a domain. As an example, consider the "browsing" domain captured in [16]. It has the common features "get", "post", and "index" (which are features necessary for browsing), but has a variable set of plug-ins, such as the feature "flash" (specific plug-ins being

G. Poels et al. (Eds.): PoEM 2017, LNBIP 305, pp. 34–48, 2017.
https://doi.org/10.1007/978-3-319-70241-4_3

features that differ across the different domain solutions, reflected in different specifications).

To ensure that DSML design is close to a domain, existing DSML design literature aims at purposeful, "top-down", DSML design, and eliciting user feedback. It ranges from comprehensive approaches such as [8, 16, 24], to language design guidelines [13], to supporting diagram types [25, p. 521]. As a precursor to language design [8] [24, p. 152] suggest use scenarios. These ensure purposeful language design, and foster feedback from prospective users [24, p. 152]. Similarly, for feedback purposes, [8] suggests the use of mockup diagrams. Further, [13] provides language design guidelines such as "Reflect only the necessary domain concepts" [13], which points towards purposeful language design. Also, [25, p. 521] [16] propose feature diagrams to capture the commonalities and variation points of domain features.

However, comparatively little attention is paid to systematically reconstruct a DSML inductively, "bottom-up", from existing representations of a domain [7, 26], such as technical specifications, source code, or requirements documents. Consequently, one risks that a rich domain variety is not fully accounted for in a DSML. Also, by forgoing a systematic grounding in domain data, current DSML design approaches make little effort to systematically reconcile the externalized knowledge of different domain experts (e.g., in the form of interview transcripts, or meeting minutes). As such, one does not systematically compare the results of elicitation efforts across different prospective language users, in terms of differences and commonalities in their points of view.

One method that is promising for uncovering domain variation is Grounded Theory (GT) [6]. GT is a method for domain understanding that is used predominantly in the social sciences. Two key features of GT make it also of interest for DSML engineering: (1) GT aims at studying *variations and commonalities* between different qualitative sources, deriving its concepts inductively from a qualitative data set. As a result, GT synthesizes commonalities and variation points of domain data, and can be used to systematically compare different points of view of different stakeholders. (2) In GT concepts are key to theory development [3]. Starting from the qualitative data sources one has, one reconstructs the key domain concepts, their perceived meaning and interrelations. Thus, in developing a domain understanding, it complements the way of thinking used in DSML design.

The goal of this paper is to show how GT can be used for DSML design. Using a case study from the smart grid industry, we show how GT can be used to systematically create (1) an object oriented diagram, representing the abstract syntax of a DSML, and (2) a domain goal diagram. In line with the explorative spirit of GT, this goal model complements the abstract syntax with a grounded understanding of the domain goals behind it.

Note here that we focus on developing the abstract syntax of a DSML, plus the understanding of the domain goals behind it. The concrete syntax (i.e., the visualization) is out of scope.

This paper is structured as follows. In Sect. 2, we introduce the key ideas of GT in the light of DSML design. In Sect. 3, we introduce our case study from the smart grid domain. Subsequently, Sect. 4 shows how GT can be useful for DSML design, using the case study as a running example. It also discusses lessons learned. Section 5 presents related work. Finally, Sect. 6 provides a concluding outlook, setting out implications for DSML design.

2 Theoretical Foundations: Grounded Theory

GT is a *qualitative* research method that produces a *domain* conceptualization in a largely *inductive* manner. As a *qualitative* research method, the research questions driving GT are exploratory [6, p. 25]. As such, in line with qualitative research generally, GT is aimed at increasing understanding of a phenomenon about which relatively little is known. Key to a qualitative research project carried out with GT, is that it concerns itself with systematic *domain conceptualization* from a qualitative data set [3,6]. Here, "domain conceptualization" refers to characterizing a domain in terms of concepts and their properties, as well relationships between concepts [3]. In deriving the conceptualization from a qualitative data set – hence a theory "grounded" in a data set – GT is largely (though not exclusively [23]) *inductive*. In line with its explorative character, its point of departure for theory building is less a well established body of knowledge, more a pool of qualitative data in the form interview transcripts, technical documentation, or otherwise.

The systematic domain conceptualization by means of induction is what makes GT an especially appealing method for supporting DSML design, in that (1) for both DSML design and GT, concepts are in focus. This helps in combining their respective insights. (2) The systematic domain conceptualization by means of induction helps to structurally "ground" a DSML in domain data, as well as, as we shall see, to systematically establish a solid understanding of a relatively unexplored domain.

Finally, of note is that GT is concerned with helping to analyse "...the actual production of meanings and concepts used by social actors in real settings" [23], quoting [10]. As such, it is aimed at understanding commonalities and differences in how different actors *interpret* a certain phenomenon. It is not aimed at defining one true and final positivist account of a domain. However, due to the predominantly technical nature of the pilot study (the conceptualization of IT infrastructure for the smart grid), this particular side of GT will be considered as out of scope for the remainder of this paper.

Next, we explain the case study used for our GT-driven DSML design effort.

3 A Smart Grid IT Infrastructure DSML

Study Setup. This case study is part of a larger research project with the objective of providing model-driven support for doing a technical as well as a cost-benefit analysis of smart grid initiatives. Smart grid initiatives refer to initiatives in the electricity domain that are enabled by developments in ICT [2, p. 14], such as smart meters. Once a smart grid initiative is shown to be technically feasible, the next step is to actually realize it as an economically viable business [18]. For example, one needs to assess who will be involved, we well as the involved costs and benefits, both purely quantitatively (e.g., investments in equipment) and qualitatively (e.g., societal benefits such as CO_2 reduction).

In this paper, we focus on developing a language for expressing a technical IT infrastructure of a smart grid initiative. The technical details of such a smart grid IT infrastructure have an influence on the corresponding economic side [20], hence they need to be considered together with the economic analysis.

For DSML design with GT the advantages of this focus are as follows:

- It is a relatively unexplored domain, in terms of conceptual modelling languages that detail technical IT infrastructure for the smart grid. The closest that we have is the Smart Grid Architecture Model (SGAM [2]). However, due to its high level of abstraction SGAM is mainly suitable as an abstract reference model (e.g., to state that we consider "components" but not "communication", or "data", at the levels of "customer premises" and "distribution"). It is less suited for modelling specific IT infrastructure components and their relations.
- Technical specifications are appropriate for a pilot study: they are diverse enough to capture variation of domain concepts, yet concrete enough to minimize the risk of "getting lost".

For scoping reasons, we focus on conceptualizing one specific part of the IT infrastructure: a substation PC. Electricity substations transform electricity from the high-voltage grid into low-to-medium voltage for the end-users (such as households). Substation automation, then, can help with monitoring this electricity transformation, e.g., in noticing an electricity overload or outage before customers place a call.

Materials. Our qualitative data set consists of technical specifications of substation automation solutions: hardware, software, and the pricing of both.

The specifications consist of two parts: purely technical specifications (e.g., permanent storage having a "RAID1" capability), and advertising text (e.g., "maximize data availability" [21] for "RAID1" capabilities). We analysed both parts, to find both purely technical features (which would be interesting for specifying the technical hardware capabilities), and to gather input for domain understanding. Concerning the latter: one needs of course be careful with advertising texts, but the used wording does hint at what is important for the domain, thus - especially over multiple documents - helping us to gather core goals that the technical specifications should comply with.

We coded the specifications in MAXQDA[1], a software tool that supports qualitative research. Apart from supporting qualitative research activities (such

---

[1] http://www.maxqda.com/products/maxqda-standard.

as, as explained in Sect. 4.1: code reuse over multiple documents, having a memoing function, the ability to build coding trees), we find that the main advantage
of using a software tool for qualitative research is that we have a direct trace
between codes and parts of the document they belong to. Thus, one can always
revisit assumptions made on the basis of existing codes, or complement already
generated codes if approached from a different angle.

In total we coded eleven documents: two for pricing, five for hardware, two
for software, two all-in-one solutions. We continued coding specifications until
no new insights would be gained by coding additional specifications.

In addition, we had an informal feedback session with an academic expert
from the smart grid domain to discuss our developed models. This session acted
mainly as a sanity check for the features emphasized in the advertising texts.

4   Grounded Theory for DSML Design

We now explain how GT is used for DSML design. Our GT-driven design process
consists of two steps. In Step 1, we use GT to develop a domain conceptualization
in terms of GT coding trees derived from domain data. In Step 2, we use the
GT coding trees to develop diagrams for DSML design.

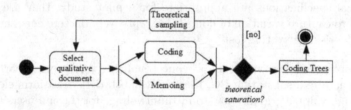

Fig. 1. The key GT activities for qualitative data analysis

4.1   Step 1: Using Grounded Theory to Develop Coding Trees

Figure 1 shows the key activities of GT to derive a domain conceptualization
from qualitative data: for each additional data source, we do coding and memoing
for qualitative analysis. Then, using theoretical sampling, the next document is
selected. Subsequently it is analyzed using, again, coding and memoing. This
process continues until theoretical saturation is reached [3].

In what follows, we discuss the activities of coding, memoing, theoretical
sampling, and theoretical saturation, and guidelines for each. These guidelines
follow a Straussian interpretation of GT (cf. [6]). We follow Straussian GT since
it provides more guidance in carrying out GT activities compared to Glaserian
GT, the key alternative interpretation of GT. See [5] for a detailed comparison
of Glaserian and Straussian GT. In our discussion, we highlight points that play
an important role in language design. Note here that, since GT is a qualitative
research method from the social sciences, we speak here of "guidance" rather
than a specific algorithm to follow.

Coding. With coding, the researcher assigns meaning to qualitative data [17]. While there is no "wrong way" of coding in GT, it is important to keep in mind that coding is a central analysis activity, requiring one to work actively with the qualitative data at hand. It is not mere labeling of text [23].

In GT coding happens in parallel to data collection [6, p. 57]. This means that one starts coding with the first qualitative document, and progressively modifies the code system while coding additional documents. To avoid drowning in the dataset, in Straussian GT, the qualitative analysis is guided by a research question which should be specific enough to focus of the coding effort [6, p. 24].

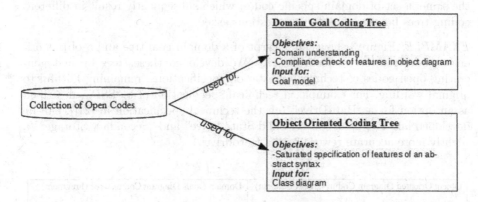

Fig. 2. Grounded Theory for creating a domain goal coding tree and an object oriented coding tree

Straussian GT distinguishes three types of coding: open, axial, and selective/focused (cf. [6]). With *open coding* one breaks qualitative data apart by labeling blocks of raw data with concepts. Note that for open coding there is no fixed unit of analysis: it can happen on a word, sentence or paragraph level [3]. With *axial coding* one relates concepts to each other. Finally, with *selective/focused coding* one defines the concepts that are important to explain the phenomenon at hand [3]. In GT, such concepts are referred to as *categories*. Categories are created either by the open codes directly, or - often the case - by aggregating multiple codes under a more abstract category. To aid in the definition of categories, Straussian GT provides several hints such as asking journalistic questions: "why", "who", "when", "with what consequences" [6, p. 199].

It is important to note that these coding activities are not necessarily orthogonal to each other. For one, [6, p. 118] point out that open and axial coding often take place in parallel. This is because, by delineating codes from each other, naturally ideas emerge on possible relations between them.

The result of a coding effort is a coding tree, which summarizes how detailed (often open) codes are gradually aggregated into more abstract categories. Such a coding effort then also acts as a key input for DSML design. As depicted in Fig. 2, for DSML design we develop two such coding trees: an object oriented coding tree, and a domain goal coding tree. We do so because for DSML design we desire to create two diagrams: (1) a domain goal diagram, providing an understanding of a domain, and identifying requirements that the domain imposes on a DSML, and (2) an object oriented diagram, in terms of the abstract syntax of the DSML. The creation of a separate domain goal diagram is also in line with DS(M)L design literature such as [25], who propose to use feature diagrams as a precursor for DS(M)L development.

As per Fig. 2 notice that a set of codes is reused amongst the two coding trees. This was done because, although the domain goal diagram and object oriented diagram evolve in different directions, their starting point is essentially the same: a set of domain specific codes, which subsequently result in different coding trees because of different questions asked.

EXAMPLE: Figure 3 shows an excerpt of a domain goal tree and a object oriented code tree for a substation PC. We developed these trees by first generating open codes of technical substation specifications, remaining faithful to original wording. For example, a technical specification of a "SSD", described as an option for a "HardDrive" (cf. the technical specification in [21]), can be developed into two open codes: "Solid State Drive" and "Secondary Storage" (a slightly more accurate rewording of "Harddrive").

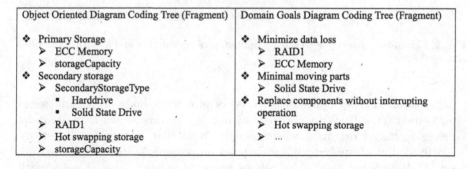

Fig. 3. Creating two different coding trees while reusing a set of open codes

However, developing categories can sometimes require textual interpretation. While the category development of the object oriented code tree can largely follow the natural hierarchy of technical specifications (e.g. we group the code "Solid State Drive" under the category "Secondary Storage"), for the domain goal code tree one needs predominantly interpretive coding.

For example, for the domain goal tree we found the following qualitative data to indirectly refer to the code "Solid State Drive": "...eliminating all moving parts, including rotating hard drives" [21]. Thus, we developed a category "minimize moving components" and grouped the code "Solid State Drive" under this. Then, in coding a different - later - technical specification, this category and the link to "Solid State Drive" was consolidated by interpreting the snippet "No rotating parts (except for hard disk drive option)" [22].

Finally, note that by means of such coding we created two coding trees while reusing open codes of the technical specification (this reuse was especially well supported by the software tool that we used for our coding effort). For example, the open code "Solid State Drive" is present in both an object oriented diagram and a domain goal diagram. It is just that, when developing the coding trees, the categorization of respective trees differs: in an object oriented tree, "Solid State Drive" is part of a category "Storage Type", whereas for the domain goal tree it is part of the category "minimize moving parts".

Memoing. While coding, GT recommends to write down analytic notes called memos [3]. This forces one to (1) make explicit speculations that emerge while thinking about the qualitative source one is coding, and (2) to keep track of how ideas evolve over time [6, p. 118]. With memoing, one records ideas that emerge during coding of the initial data set, which inspire the coding of additional data. In turn, this helps one to mature the conceptualizations in the coding trees.

EXAMPLE: Memoing has mainly aided us in structuring our understanding while creating the domain goal coding tree. For example, while coding the first qualitative documents, we created the following memo for hot swapping of storage devices: "Exchange component without interrupting the system at hand. It seems to increase serviceability/system maintenance operations". The latter part of this (admittedly rough) memo speculates at maintenance being a theme, prior to maintenance actually becoming a category in its own right.

Later the category becomes important while coding that a front panel provides "easy access to hardware", thus leading to "easier maintenance" (according to the advertising text). Looking back at the notes, one sees common themes emerge, leading one to (1) define maintenance as a category in its own right, and (2) to aggregate under the category "maintenance" the categories "easy access to hardware" and "exchange component without interrupting operations".

Theoretical sampling. This sampling method means that one decides what additional data to analyze next based on the conceptualization of qualitative data already gathered [6, p. 143]. As such, theoretical sampling is exemplary for GTs idea of staying close to a data set, rather than following an existing theory.

EXAMPLE: In our data selection, the newly developed categories did not lead us away from coding substation PC specifications as originally intended.

Theoretical saturation. One continues coding until theoretical saturation, i.e. until no new insights emerge while coding further qualitative data. This means that variation and commonality between the categories in qualitative data is accounted for, and importantly: that a consistent explanatory story can be told on the basis of the developed conceptualization [6, p. 197].

EXAMPLE: we analysed substation specifications until no new insights were gained from coding further specifications. This meant that elements of both the object-oriented coding tree and domain goal coding tree were stable.

For the domain goal coding tree, additionally a stopping criterion is that it can be used to "tell a consistent explanatory story" (cf. [6, p. 197]) about the hardware of a substation PC, especially in terms of what sets this apart from "regular" PC hardware. In this case, a substation PC was found to have domain goals such as continuity of operations, and minimal maintenance.

4.2 Step 2: Develop DSML with Coding Trees

In this step, we develop our diagrams for DSML design from the coding trees that result from the GT effort.

Mirroring the two coding trees developed in Sect. 4.1, we develop two diagrams for language design: (1) an object-oriented model, developed in terms of a UML class diagram [19], depicting an abstract syntax, and (2) a goal model, created in the Goal Requirements Language (GRL, [1]). As stated in Sect. 4.1, the goal model complements the abstract syntax by providing a domain understanding, and explicating the key goals behind the abstract syntax.

For the domain goal diagram, we turn leaf-level codes of the domain goal code tree into resources, and use more abstract categories to develop a goal structure. Furthermore, we ask what actors actually state the domain goals.

For the object oriented diagram we have to decide, for each element of the tree, whether to turn it into a an element of a class diagram (class, attribute, constraint, generalization, etc.). Actually, part of the hard work has already been done during the coding effort. Nevertheless, to support this decision we offer the following commonsense guidelines: (1) categories form classes and enumerations. Here, enumerations refer to datatypes with a fixed set of values [19, p. 173]. Once defined, the enumeration allows one to restrict the values one can select for the datatype. E.g., to restrict the values of the datatype "SecondaryStorageType" to "SSD" or "HDD", (2) codes at the leafs of the coding tree form attributes and enumeration elements. Furthermore one of course decides on the attribute type, (3) one category subsuming another forms a generalisation/specialisation relation, (4) redundant leaf codes in categories that are subsumed by other categories form attributes of the subsuming category. Finally, we identify (5) constraints by reviewing what codes would constrain an object-oriented model, rather than specifying it further. The idea is that we develop constraints in part from domain goals captured in the domain goal model. We can do this due to the close relation between the domain goal model, and the object oriented model (recall Fig. 2).

EXAMPLE: Figures 4 and 5 depict, respectively, the domain goal and object oriented models of a substation PC. For reference, compare these to the excerpt coding trees developed in Fig. 3.

For the domain goal model, we see how the leaf level codes of the domain goal coding trees have been used to develop resources, such as "Hotswapping power supply", and "Solid State Drive". Furthermore, mirroring the coding tree we see how these resources contribute to achieving domain goals: "Replace components without interrupting operations" for the resource "Hotswapping power supply",

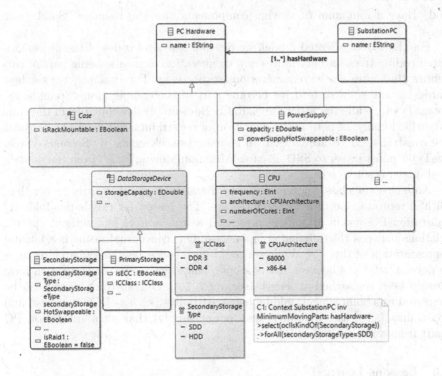

Fig. 4. Excerpt of the substation PC Object Oriented Diagram, cf. UML [19]

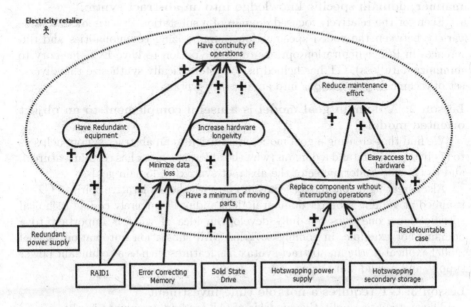

Fig. 5. Excerpt of the substation PC Domain Goal Diagram, cf. GRL [1]

and "Have a minimum of moving components" for the resource "Solid State Drive".

For the object oriented model, we develop leaf level codes of the object oriented coding trees into attributes and enumeration elements, being part of categories that form classes/enumerations respectively. For example, we see how harddrive and solid state drive become part of the enumeration "SecondaryStorageType", while the attribute "isRaid1:Boolean" is developed from the code "Raid1". Finally, of note is the definition of constraints. For example, consider the constraint C1. It states that all enumeration elements of "SecondaryStorageType" must be set to SSD, in case "MinimumMovingParts" from the domain goal model is set to true.

Note that the class diagram depicts a hierarchical set of features rather than faithful reproduction of a PC architecture. The reason for this is two-fold: (1) substation PC specifications are presented as taxonomies (so: without specific relations between the different components). Our conceptualization is a faithful representation of this. (2) While we could have coded regular PC architectures to develop relations between the concepts, languages for PC configuration have already been researched at length (see, e.g., [12]). Our abstract syntax can be perceived as a complement, adding extra attributes (such as ECC memory) and constraints (such as redundancy of a power supply) that set a substation PC apart from a regular PC.

4.3   Lessons Learned

Lesson 1: GT is a suitable instrument for synthesizing, in a structured manner, domain specific knowledge into an abstract syntax

Even for the relatively focused domain of a substation PC, we found a large variety between the coded specifications, emphasizing commonalities and differences in PC configuration options (e.g., the option to have ECC memory to minimize data loss). GT has helped us to systematically synthesize this diverse set of technical specifications into an abstract syntax.

Lesson 2: A domain goal model is a useful complement to an object oriented model

We find that creating a goal model in addition to an abstract syntax helps us to (1) better understand a domain (why the abstract syntax has certain features), and to (2) test conformance of the abstract syntax to domain goals.

Also, creating a goal model seems in line with the explorative spirit of GT: it is aimed at gaining a better domain understanding. By merely coding technical specifications, one does not fully develop an idea of what is important to a domain. For example, in coming to grips with substation automation, a goal model explicates *why* an abstract syntax has features such as a redundant power supply, and a solid state drive.

Lesson 3: GT requires a notable time investment

The systematic qualitative analysis of GT (coding, memoing) implies a considerable time investment. Thus, prior to using GT for DSML design, the implied time investment needs to be weighed against its prospective benefits.

To reduce time investment, we additionally foresee combinations with scenario-driven approaches, whereby scenario analysis ad interim the qualitative analysis can help to focus the qualitative analysis effort.

5   Related Work

Similar to goal models, for DS(M)L design feature diagrams can describe commonalities and variabilities of a domain [16] [25, p. 521]. In feature diagrams, one specifies an abstract feature (for example "browsing") into more detailed ones (for example "get" or "post" features for "browsing") using logical operators such as (X)OR, AND. The resulting "configuration tree" of features can be used to reason about valid sets of features, that can be subsequently translated into valid combinations of model elements [25, p. 523].

Importantly however, the capture of domain features has largely been supported by top-down scenarios. For example, [24, p. 93] suggest user stories to elicit features. A systematic grounding of feature models in qualitative domain data is lacking.

In [7] GT is proposed for the design of conceptual modelling languages. However, this is an (early stage) position paper; while it discusses the idea of using GT as a means to develop an empirically grounded conceptual modelling language, it provides no specifics on how this should be actually done. For example, in terms of choosing between Glaserian and Straussian GT, while this has a significant influence on how one proceeds. Similarly [14] suggests the use of GT for grounding a formal ontology in a qualitative dataset. However, as also admitted by [14] only partial end results of the GT are provided: a set of open codes with, for each, the number of occurrences in the studied dataset.

The closest to our work comes [26], who has applied GT to develop a class diagram of blade servers with the help of Grounded Theory. Particularly [26] uses GT to synthesize technical specifications, such as different types of harddisks, or different types of RAM memory. However, by focusing on aggregating technical specifications, no deeper domain understanding is gained of what is actually a Blade Server. Thus, while [26] succeed in systematically deriving detailed technical specifications with GT, arguably they forego one of the key tenets of doing explorative research: to better *understand* the phenomenon at hand. The same holds true for [11], who has used GT for requirements analysis. While [11] succeeds in developing a class diagram summarizing the most important concepts of the system to be developed, a deeper understanding of the reasoning behind them (in line with the explorative nature of GT) remains implicit.

6   Concluding Outlook

In this paper, we showed how Grounded Theory (GT) can be used for DSML design. Using a case study from the smart grid domain, we discussed how GT is useful for grounding two DSML design diagrams in qualitative domain data: (1) an object oriented diagram, providing the abstract syntax of the DSML as synthesized inductively from qualitative domain data, and (2) a domain goal diagram which, in line with the explorative spirit of GT, provides a grounded understanding of the domain goals behind the abstract syntax.

For further work, we first of all work towards what we term *metamodel provenance*. This means that we further establish an explicit trace between features in an abstract syntax, the domain goals behind it, and the coded fragments of the qualitative sources on which the domain goals are based.

For instance, such metamodel provenance allows us to selectively "switch on and off" elements of the abstract syntax or goals in the domain goal model, and see how this influences the domain goal model respectively object oriented model. Here, an interesting starting point is work on feature models, and how these relate to actual language design considerations. Also we aim to further capitalize on GRL, whose supporting software tool JUCMNav[2] actually supports automated reasoning on goal satisfaction. Given relations between goals, and their respective importance, the impact of satisfying/denying leaf level goals can be propagated towards calculating satisfaction/denial of top-level goals. This can contribute to establishing automated reasoning about satisfaction of goals desired by domain actors, and the impact this has on features of an abstract syntax.

Second, we aim at further developing domain goal models by making explicit the context variables under which a certain domain understanding is relevant (in terms of geography, timeframe or otherwise). At the very least such context is relevant for our ongoing case study in the smart grid, where many concerns that one wants to express depend on context (e.g., regional differences in regulation). In this light constructivist grounded theory is a particularly promising research strand. It makes explicit such context variables by means of a conditional/consequential matrix [6, p. 95], and situation maps [4]. Third, we wish to explore how conceptual modelling can be useful for GT. In this paper we focused GT as a complement to DSML design, however we suspect that the relation can be mutually beneficial. For example, while remaining faithful to GT one can use a domain goal diagram during coding tree development, to help structure codes into categories rather than developing the domain goal model ex-post.

Finally we intend to gain experiences with using GT for creating DSMLs in domains wherein the *social* aspect plays an important role, for example by interviewing domain experts and thus gaining insights into how a particular phenomenon is interpreted. In the Smart Grid domain, this concerns for instance regulatory or valuation aspects. We aim at this because, while the used case study was sufficiently non-trivial to act as a first experiment, in the end it boiled down to the analysis of technical specifications (with the exception of a final informal feedback round with a domain expert). As such GT's claimed ability to uncover how domain stakeholders interpret a particular phenomenon remains under explored.

---

[2] http://jucmnav.softwareengineering.ca/ucm/bin/view/ProjetSEG/WebHome.

Acknowledgements. The author would like to thank Qin Ma and Monika Kaczmarek-Heß for their valuable feedback.

References

1. Amyot, D., Ghanavati, S., Horkoff, J., Mussbacher, G., Peyton, L., Yu, E.: Evaluating goal models within the goal-oriented requirement language. Int. J. Intell. Syst. **25**(8), 841–877 (2010)
2. Bruinenberg, J., Colton, L., Darmois, E., Dorn, J., Doyle, J., Elloumi, O., Englert, H., Forbes, R., Heiles, J., Hermans, P., et al.: Cen-cenelec-etsi smart grid coordination group smart grid reference architecture. Technical report (2012)
3. Charmaz, K.: Grounded theory as an emergent method. In: The Sage Handbook of Qualitative Research, pp. 155–172. The Guilford Press (2008)
4. Clarke, A.: Situational Analysis: Grounded Theory After the Postmodern Turn. Sage, Thousand Oaks (2005)
5. Cooney, A.: Choosing between glaser and strauss: an example. Nurse Researcher **17**(4), 18–28 (2010)
6. Corbin, J., Strauss, A.: Basics of Qualitative Research, 3rd edn. Sage, London (2008)
7. Feller, J., Finnegan, P., Nilsson, O.: Applying theory-building techniques to the design of modelling languages. In: European Confernce on Information Systems (ECIS). AISNet (2009)
8. Frank, U.: Domain-specific modeling languages: requirements analysis and design guidelines. In: Reinhartz-Berger, I., Sturm, A., Clark, T., Cohen, S., Bettin, J. (eds.) Domain Engineering, pp. 133–157. Springer, Heidelberg (2013). 10.1007/978-3-642-36654-3_6
9. Frank, U.: Multi-perspective enterprise modeling: foundational concepts, prospects and future research challenges. Softw. Syst. Model. **13**(3), 941–962 (2014)
10. Gephart, R.P.: Qualitative research and the academy of management journal. Acad. Manag. J. **47**(4), 454–462 (2004)
11. Halaweh, M.: Using grounded theory as a method for system requirements analysis. JISTEM **9**(1), 23–38 (2012)
12. Heise, D.: Unternehmensmodell-basiertes IT-Kostenmanagement als Bestandteil eines integrativen IT-Controllings. Logos, Berlin (2013)
13. Karsai, G., Krahn, H., Pinkernell, C., Rumpe, B., Schindler, M., Volkel, S.: Design guidelines for domain specific languages. arXiv preprint arXiv:1409.2378 (2014)
14. Lamp, J., Milton, S.K.: Grounded theory as foundations for methods in applied ontology. In: QualIT 2007: Qualitative Research: from the Margins to the Mainstream Abstracts and Papers, pp. 1–13. Victoria University of Wellington (2007)
15. Malavolta, I., Lago, P., Muccini, H., Pelliccione, P., Tang, A.: What industry needs from architectural languages: a survey. IEEE Trans. Software Eng. **39**(6), 869–891 (2013)
16. Mernik, M., Heering, J., Sloane, A.M.: When and how to develop domain-specific languages. Software Engineering [SEN] E 0309 (2003)
17. Miles, M.B., Huberman, A.M.: Qualitative Data Analysis: An Expanded Sourcebook. Sage, Thousand Oaks (1994)
18. Niesten, E., Alkemade, F.: How is value created and captured in smart grids? a review of the literature and an analysis of pilot projects. Renew. Sustain. Energy Rev. **53**, 629–638 (2016)

19. Object Management Group: The OMG Unified Modeling Language (OMG UML), version 2.5. Technical report (2015)
20. Razavian, M., Gordijn, J.: Consonance between economic and IT services: finding the balance between conflicting requirements. In: Fricker, S.A., Schneider, K. (eds.) REFSQ 2015. LNCS, vol. 9013, pp. 148–163. Springer, Cham (2015). 10.1007/978-3-319-16101-3_10
21. Selinc: SEL-3355 Computer. Technical report. Last accessed 20 April 2017
22. Siemens: SICAM - Substation Automation and RTUs. Technical report. Last accessed 20 April 2017
23. Suddaby, R.: From the editors: what grounded theory is not. Acad. Manag. J. **49**(4), 633–642 (2006)
24. Villanueva Del Pozo, M.J.: An agile model-driven method for involving end-users in DSL development. Ph.D. thesis, Universidad Politecnica de Valencia (2016)
25. Voelter, M., Benz, S., Dietrich, C., Engelmann, B., Helander, M., Kats, L.C., Visser, E., Wachsmuth, G.: DSL engineering: Designing, implementing and using domain-specific languages (2013). dslbook.org
26. Zwanziger, A.: Reconstructing the blade technology domain with grounded theory. In: Salinesi, C., Pastor, O. (eds.) CAiSE 2011. LNBIP, vol. 83, pp. 187–196. Springer, Heidelberg (2011). 10.1007/978-3-642-22056-2_20

Towards Meta Model Provenance:
A Goal-Driven Approach to Document
the Provenance of Meta Models

Sybren de Kinderen[1]([✉]), Monika Kaczmarek-Heß[1], Qin Ma[2],
and Iván S. Razo-Zapata[3]

[1] University of Duisburg-Essen, Essen, Germany
{sybren.dekinderen,monika.kaczmarek}@uni-due.de
[2] University of Luxembourg, Esch-sur-Alzette, Luxembourg
qin.ma@uni.lu
[3] Luxembourg Institute of Science and Technology, Esch-sur-Alzette, Luxembourg
ivan.razo-zapata@list.lu

Abstract. This paper introduces the notion of meta model provenance.
Meta model provenance helps to understand the origins of meta model
elements, such as language concepts, attributes, or constraints. Thus, it
should answer questions such as: where did this language concept come
from? under which assumptions was it introduced? Among others, meta
model provenance is intended to support the controlled evolution of languages and informed language (re-)design. In this paper, we focus on a
goal-driven meta model provenance approach. This is one specific operationalization of the meta model provenance concept, which shows how
goal models help to understand the origins of the elements of a conceptual
modeling language. To illustrate our goal-driven provenance approach,
we use a scenario from the electricity domain.

Keywords: Meta model provenance · Modeling language design · Goal-
driven meta model provenance

1 Introduction

With the proliferation of modeling languages and sharing of created models
[1,2], questions regarding origins of a language specification emerge, e.g., where
did this language concept come from? for what purpose it was specified, under
what particular assumptions, and for what use scenarios? Existing approaches
to design modeling methods postulate an informed language design process,
within which, among others, use scenarios or requirements [3] are defined that
subsequently drive the definition of the language. However the dissemination of
modeling languages typically boils down to its abstract syntax, usually in the
form of a meta model (i.e., a set of concepts, their attributes, relations and
constraints), concrete syntax and semantics [4]. Thus, information regarding the

G. Poels et al. (Eds.): PoEM 2017, LNBIP 305, pp. 49–64, 2017.
https://doi.org/10.1007/978-3-319-70241-4_4

language's intension and domain constraints/requirements are either lost, or are captured in separate documentation that is not always available to an interested audience.

Such a language specification with lacking documentation can result in an ad hoc language (re-)design, expressing itself most prominently in an uncontrolled evolution of modeling languages. Consider the Enterprise Architecture modeling language ArchiMate [5]. For the core ArchiMate language, a set of requirements and assumptions were defined [6], such as conceptual parsimony (meaning, to keep the amount of concepts in the language to a minimum). However, these language requirements were never part of the core language specification. Largely as a result of this, later extensions to ArchiMate have been defined that ignore these language requirements. The resulting extensions are therefore not fully in line with the ideas behind the original language. In the case of the ArchiMate's motivation extension, this has resulted in concepts that can confuse language users and/or concepts that are obsolete [7]. For example, the motivation extension has both the concepts of a driver and a goal, whereas according to the principle of conceptual parsimony having the concept of a goal would arguably suffice.

In this paper, we focus on information regarding the origins of elements of language specification. We term this information as "provenance". The term provenance refers to the origin, history or pedigree of some artifact [8]. In the Information Systems (IS) domain, the concept of data provenance is widely used to denote origin or history of data [8–11]. Similarly, while not under the banner of provenance, the conceptual modeling community, particularly Thalheim [12], emphasizes analysis of conceptual models and modeling languages using a set of questions based on the classical rhetorical frame introduced by Hermagoras of Temnos[1]. Various modeling language design methods, such as [3,13–15], concretize a subset of these questions, focusing for example on stakeholder (who) and scenario (why) analyses. Yet, in the light of provenance as we find it in the IS discipline, both such questions and the language design approaches fall short. Particularly, in terms of how this information concretely relates to a language specification, in which form this information can be captured, and (related) what particular value this information as a language's provenance has.

Therefore, motivated by the shortcomings of the current state of documenting the information on origins of language specification, we propose a concept of a *meta model provenance* recording the intention standing behind the configuration of a language specification. To capture the origins of a modeling language, there is a need to define (1) the provenance concept that would account for peculiarities of language design as well as (2) corresponding methods that would help trace that provenance. Thus, we define the concept of meta model provenance considering the following aspects: (1) its scope, i.e., what it describes, (2) the way it should be represented and the representation's formality level, and finally, (3) the way it should be visualized and disseminated. We argue that capturing explicitly meta model provenance contributes to the *understandability* of the

---

[1] Who, what, when, where, why, in what way, by what means?

meta model and its current configuration. Thus, it supports *controlled language evolution.* Furthermore provenance contributes to *informed language (re-)design*, i.e., (re-)designing a language based on domain "rules", use scenarios, (prospective) language users, and purposes of language users.

In this paper we first sketch the core idea of the meta model provenance concept and show its overall design. Thereafter, we focus on goal-driven meta model provenance, whereby we use goal models to capture the intension of the elements of an abstract syntax. We use a case scenario from the electricity domain to illustrate the goal-driven approach.

This paper is structured as follows. First, we introduce different aspects covered by Domain-Specific Modeling Language (DSML) design methods, and subsequently discuss how these are reflected in different DSMLs. Next, we introduce the concept of meta model provenance and motivate its role in the design and application of DSMLs. Then, we introduce a goal-driven meta model provenance approach. Subsequently, the proposed approach is illustrated with a scenario from the electricity domain. The paper concludes with final remarks.

2   The Design of Domain-Specific Modeling Languages

Typically DSML design methods take domain characteristics as a point of departure, particularly in the form of the purposes of a DSML, prospective use scenarios, and domain constraints, cf., [3, 13–15]. Further, they propose to document the design decisions along the way. This all leads to what we term"informed language design", meaning that the elements of a DSML are systematically reconstructed from the domain that they represent.

As a synthesis of different DSML design methods we observe that the following selected aspects inform the DSML design (note that, due to space considerations we cannot discuss each aspect in detail): (1) *Use scenarios*, either in terms of (a succession of) tasks to be supported by a DSML [3], or in the form of user stories [14]. (2) *Purposes*, which are similar to scenarios, but without the specific temporal ordering. Purposes are reflected in selected DSML design guidelines from [15], and in the requirements engineering approach from [16]. (3) Having a *feedback loop* between initial versions of a DSML and its prospective users, in terms of both agile process [13,14], and the use of mock up diagrams to elicit end user feedback [3]. (4) *Capturing domain features*, prominently in terms of feature diagrams [14,17]. Here "features" capture the variability of a domain, in terms of features common to the domain (e.g., for the "browsing" domain of [17], "get" and "post"), and features that differ across the domain (e.g., for "browsing": each browser can have a different set of plug-ins).

However, even if the above mentioned aspects are important for the design of a DSML, the resulting DSMLs usually lack a concrete relation to them. Either the aspects are (1) documented, but the documentation exists separate from the DSML specification, it is not publicly available, or the documentation is written in a natural language that is different from the DSML specification, or (2) the documentation is not at all provided. Indeed, we have observed such a lack of traceability not only in state-of-the-art enterprise modeling approaches such as ArchiMate [5] or in some DSMLs being part of Multi-perspective Enterprise Modeling (MEMO) [4], but also in de facto standards such as Unified Modeling Language (UML) [18].

During the design of ArchiMate requirements for modeling, analysis and visualization have been identified [6], and have helped to shape the core ArchiMate language specification. However, these requirements are not explicitly traceable to the final language specification. This, consequently, increases the risk of developing extensions to ArchiMate that do not meet the initially defined requirements anymore (as with the motivation extension, discussed in the introduction).

Furthermore, recent languages being part of MEMO have been designed following the DSML design method by Frank [3]. As a result the relevant use scenarios, general and specific requirements, as well as justification of designed decisions have been documented, e.g., [19]. However, this information is not always available to a wider audience as (1) it might be unclear where this information is stored, (2) it is disseminated only in German, as in [19].

UML presents similar issues in the sense that its initial general requirements do not say much about how the final language specification was decided upon [18]. As a result, there are concepts in UML whose rationale is not clear, which leads to different (mis)interpretations (e.g., purely in terms of semantics an aggregation relationship can be substituted by an association relationship with corresponding cardinalities [18]).

To sum up: during language design there exists initial documentation about the language purposes, their requirements and the intended use of a language. However, that information is not linked to the resulting language specifications, neither is it always available to audiences interested in extending those languages. This introduces the danger of *uncontrolled evolution*, which can already be observed in standard languages such as ArchiMate. Therefore, we argue that whenever the designed domain-specific modeling approach is to be used beyond the specific group of people involved in its creation, it is imperative that one captures the provenance of the language specification in terms of its origins: the purposes standing behind a language, its use scenarios, and domain constraints. Thereby, one fosters controlled language evolution, and the informed (re-)design of conceptual modeling languages.

3   Meta Model Provenance

In this section, we first characterize meta model provenance based upon a synthesis of language design literature and literature on data (visualization) provenance (in Sect. 3.1). Following this, we focus on our exemplary provenance approach: goal-driven meta model provenance (in Sect. 3.2).

3.1 Characterizing Meta Model Provenance

For our research purposes, the provenance of a language specification is of importance. As most languages are defined by using a meta model, we further denote it as **meta model provenance** and focus on provenance of meta model elements such as concepts, their attributes, relations, and constraints.

As per the introduction, the term "provenance" is used in a wide array of domains [20,21]. Two of these are relevant to us: data provenance and data visualization provenance. Data (visualization) provenance approaches focus on a static world view when defining the cornerstones of provenance. This is in contrast to capturing the provenance of dynamics, as prominently happening within workflow provenance [22]. Hence, in their way of thinking, data (visualization) provenance approaches are close to what we intend to capture. Thus, in characterizing meta model provenance, we turn to key questions as defined in data (visualization) provenance cf. [20,21]: (1) what is the scope of the meta model provenance, in terms of the type of information that can be captured? (2) how it is represented and what level of formality is used? and (3) how can provenance be visualized?

Accordingly, we structure our discussion on the proposed idea of meta model provenance in line with these three aspects.

The scope of meta model provenance. Different research initiatives have been undertaken with the aim to standardize the scope of data (visualization) provenance. One important effort is the so called W7 model [23,24]. The W7 model represents different components of provenance, namely *what, when, where, how, who, which* and *why*, and their relationships to each other. In the W7 model, data provenance is conceptualized as consisting of various events that happen during the lifetime of the data from its creation to destruction, cf., [23]. Each of the 7 Ws has its subtypes, for instance, *what* has among others subtypes including creation, modification and publication, and ownership, whereas *how* can be classified into single and complex actions [10].

Likewise, but without using the term provenance per se, in the conceptual modeling domain Thalheim [12] uses W-questions as a baseline for developing a "Theory" of modeling. Thereby, he first characterizes modeling by four core characteristics: wherefore (purpose), whereof (origin), wherewith (language), and worthiness (value). Subsequently, he details each of the core characteristics by means of further Ws. For example, in the case of wherefore (purpose): how, why, whereto, when, for which reason [12].

Although the proposed dimensions from both data provenance as well as the theory of conceptual modeling by [12] constitute a comprehensive framework regarding different types of provenance information, it is unclear how – concretely – this information complements conceptual modeling languages, and what purpose the capturing of this information should particularly serve. Also, the respective W frameworks provide few hints regarding the way in which the information should be stored, retrieved, and visualized.

Turning now to the aspects informing the DSML design methods from Sect. 2, we observe that each of them provides an answer to a subset of W-questions.

For instance, scenario- and goal-driven methods answer questions like *for whom?* and *for which purpose(s)?*, whereas methods that capture domain features help to partly answer *what?* questions. However, while providing a valuable input, the aspects mentioned by the DSML design methods as such are insufficient for our purposes since they have not be designed with the idea of provenance in mind. Thus, as discussed in Sect. 2, the provenance information resulting from these design methods is insufficiently documented and/or insufficiently related to a language specification.

Representation and the used level of formality. Provenance can be represented at different levels of formality, depending on the analysis task to be supported [20,22]. Here the formality ranges from plain text annotations, up to formalisms that can be automatically processed, such as the query inversion described in [20] to retrieve data lineage in a database. The manner in which provenance is represented has implications for the costs of recording it, the set of analysis tasks it supports, and for its ease of use [20,22]. For one, due to their unrestrictive nature *plain text annotations* offer rich expressiveness, but at the same time introduce the challenge of storing and retrieving the relevant data [20]. In contrast, purely formal provenance approaches offer rich possibilities for automated analyses, but often are difficult to come to grips with for average end users [22]. As a semi-formal approach, conceptual modeling combines the respective strengths of a purely plain text approach, and a purely formalized approach. Like plain text annotation approaches it offers possibilities for rich expressiveness, yet at the same time, it offers a subset of computer-supported analysis capabilities from purely formal provenance approaches.

Provenance visualization. Depending on its audience and intended use, provenance information can be visualized in different ways. In line with [20,22] this can be an informal way, e.g., by means of plain text notes, by means of query results represented in the syntax of a query language, or by means of visual graphs. Each visualization of provenance information comes with some advantages and some drawbacks. Like the level of formality, a plain text description can be relatively easily prepared and requires no prior knowledge (only the knowledge of the natural language it was expressed in is required). On the other hand, using formal techniques, such as query languages, automated reasoning, requires prior training and/or an engineering background.

3.2   A Goal-Driven Approach to Document Meta Model Provenance

In what follows, we show how meta model provenance can be operationalized by focusing on the intention standing behind the current language specification. Thus, we focus on the following subset of W-questions: (1) **for what reasons?** This question concerns the goals and/or information needs of involved stakeholders that are going to be fulfilled; and (2) **what?** This question concerns elements of the (meta) model that are affected by the purposes of a language, or have been defined because of it.

In line with [16], we consider the goals of both direct users of a language (such as language designers, or information analysts), and those that receive results out of the use of a language (such as CxOs being interested in certain analysis results). The goal-driven approach to document meta model provenance should be able to: express why different concepts have been included in the language specification and which application scenarios the different meta model elements are to support. Also, by relying on goal models one can check to what extent models that are instantiated from the meta model comply with domain goals.

Requirements. To provide transparency with respect to assumptions and desired features for our provenance approach (thus in a sense providing rudimentary provenance of our approach), we first explicate the requirements for our goal-driven meta model provenance approach. Thereafter, we discuss the provenance approach itself.

R1: *Having a semi-formal provenance approach.* With our goal-driven provenance approach we are, on the one hand, interested in expressing domain goals, the stakeholders behind these goals, and relations between goals. Thus, we are interested in having an approach with a rich expressiveness. On the other hand, we are interested in performing computational analyses with our approach, prominently to check to what extent a model generated with the meta model is in line with the domain goals. This implies computational reasoning capabilities for the approach. Thus, all in all we are interested in a semi-formal provenance approach: sufficiently rich in expressiveness to capture various facets of intentionality, yet sufficiently computational to support reasoning.

R2: *The visualization should fit the users of this information, and the desired use scenario.* Thus, a minimal learning effort should be accounted for. As a result, one should also decide on the way this information should be visualized for the involved stakeholders so that the desired use cases can be supported. Here our assumption is that goal models are at least accessible to the primary stakeholder of a language: a language designer. Thereby, based on the existing modeling expertise we assume that a language designer has familiarity with goal modeling or, if not, that the effort to learn goal modeling is low.

R3: *Having a close relation between language provenance and language specification.* As already discussed in Sect. 2, keeping the documentation separate from the language specification makes the specification less accessible to an interested audience. In addition, post hoc tracking of provenance introduces difficulties such as forgetting the provenance over time, or by introducing an additional "rationalization" bias by making up provenance reasons in retrospect. Therefore, capturing the provenance should ideally be done at the same time as, and together with, the definition of the language specification.

R4: *Supporting different levels of granularity.* We should capture information regarding both the intentional elements, and the origin of elements of the language specification at different levels of granularity. If we desire to keep the language specification close to the corresponding provenance information, it follows that we should cover comprehensively relations between different elements of the language specification and elements of the language provenance. Concretely, this implies that provenance should be tracked both at (i) a fine-grained level, i.e., on the level of attributes, roles, relations and cardinalities, and at (ii) the level of meta types, constraints, or even clusters of those.

R5: *Having software tool support.* As stated, we are interested in a semi-formal approach, in part because this provides us with computational reasoning support. In particular, we are interested in compliance checking of language specification elements with provenance elements, as well as compliance of the models instantiated from the meta model with the domain goals. To support us in this task, a software tool is required that provides reasoning capabilities.

The GRL4DSML Approach for Goal-Driven Meta Model Provenance. Guided by the above requirements we now introduce the GRL4DSML approach for capturing the provenance of the language specification using goal models. GRL4DSML consists of two parts: (1) a meta model, for conceptually expressing elements of an abstract syntax, intentional elements, and a relationship between abstract syntax elements and intentional elements; and (2) a process, for using the GRL4DSML meta model to capture language provenance in a goal-driven manner.

The GRL4DSML meta model is shown in Fig. 1. It integrates concepts from both GORE (Goal-Oriented Requirement Engineering) and DSML design, and defines connections among these concepts. On the GORE side, we use a core subset of the Goal-oriented Requirements Language (GRL) [25] meta model. GRL offers the following main concepts. Goals are objectives that a stakeholder (modeled as an actor) would like to achieve. To achieve goals, actors may employ resources (physical or informational entities) and perform tasks. We take GRL as the baseline because it is standardized by the Telecommunication Standardization Sector (ITU-T) and has a mature tool support in terms of jUCMNav[2].

On the DSML design side, a core set of meta modeling concepts is extracted and included. Meta modeling is a means to specify DSMLs, where the abstract syntax of a DSML includes the following elements: (1) a meta model that defines the constructs of the DSML, and (2) a set of well-formedness constraints. In the example we use the MEMO Meta Modeling Language (MML [26]). It offers meta types, their attributes and relations, as well as possibility to define OCL constraints. MML, when compared to 'traditional' meta modeling languages (e.g., the Meta Object Facility of UML), provides additional language constructs such as intrinsic attributes and relations. Such intrinsicness means that the attribute/relation is instantiated only at the instance level and not at the type level, and is visualized with a white letter "i" on a black background.

We enumerate the following main constructs in the GRL4DSML meta model: "meta types", "attributes", and "relations". Recall that the purpose of GRL4DSML is to guide the DSML design with goals of DSML stakeholders and to document such a provenance. To this end, we require the traceability from

---

[2] http://jucmnav.softwareengineering.ca/ucm/bin/view/ProjetSEG/WebHome.

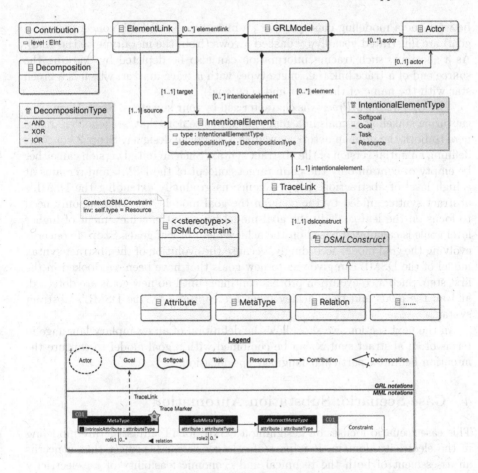

Fig. 1. GRL4DSML design meta model

DSML constructs to goals of stakeholders to indicate that the latter motivates the existence of the former.

Well-formedness constraints associated with a DSML further restrict the shape of instances the DSML can express for the purpose of goal achievement: all instances of the DSML must make these constraints true, and the validity of the constraints guarantees (to an extent) the fulfillment of goals. As a consequence, constraints resemble a special type of informational resources offered by the DSML to contribute to the fulfillment of goals. To capture this in the GRL4DSML meta model, we extend the Resource concept from GRL with a stereotype «DSLConstraint».

The legend at the bottom of Fig. 1 summarizes the visual notation that we use to illustrate the application of GRL4DSML in the case scenario (Sect. 4). For GRL concepts, we reuse GRL's concrete syntax. For meta modeling concepts, we reuse MML's concrete syntax, which is similar to class diagrams. The trace links between meta modeling concepts (e.g., a meta type) and GRL concepts (e.g., a goal) are illustrated visually by dashed arrows (from the meta type to the goal). As a shortcut, such tracing information can also be depicted by marking the source end of a trace link (i.e., meta type) with a trace marker, which is a green star with the name of the target end (i.e., goal).

The GRL4DSML Process is characterized by four key steps. **Step 1** concerns capturing stakeholder goals in a goal model. Please note that "stakeholder" refers here to both the domain actors as well as a language designer. **Step 2** concerns defining an initial version of the abstract syntax. Such an initial version can either be empty or contain only the main target concept of the DSML and remains at a high level of abstraction. **Step 3** concerns gradually extending the DSML's abstract syntax guided by the goals in the goal model. Note that we only need to focus on the leaf goals in the goal model because the achievement of higher level goals is calculated based on the achievement of leaf goals. **Step 4** concerns evolving the goal model accordingly, because the evolution of the abstract syntax model of the DSML can give rise to new goals that have been overlooked in the first step. Such a co-evolution process continues until no new goals are detected, and all the goals and their achievement are captured by the DSML's abstract syntax.

In the next section, we show how the definition of an exemplary language in terms of an abstract syntax can be combined with a goal model to capture the intention behind a particular language specification.

4   Case Scenario: Substation Automation

This case scenario focuses on designing a DSML for IT infrastructure modeling in the electricity domain. It is part of a larger research project that concerns an assessment of both the technical and economic feasibility of an electricity domain initiative. The idea is that while more and more initiatives in the electricity domain are enabled by IT (IT being, e.g., smart meters), the realization

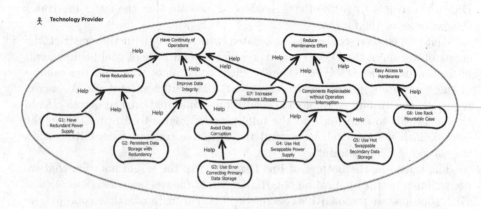

Fig. 2. Goal model capturing the intentions of the technology provider

of such initiatives in the marketplace requires an economic assessment next to the technical one, prominently in terms of the actors involved and what they exchange of value with one another [27]. Since characteristics of an IT infrastructure influence the economical side and vice versa [28], we thus have a need to model IT infrastructure as part of this project.

For scoping reasons, we focus our example on the modeling of substation PCs. In the electricity grid, substations transform high-level voltage, as usually generated by large power plants, to medium to low level voltage suitable for end users (households or small businesses). Substation PCs, then, act as a single point of contact for monitoring the activities in a substation. This concerns both regular activity, such as transmitting metering data, and signaling abnormalities, such as power spikes or disruptions in the electricity flow.

We start with a goal model (Fig. 2) that captures the intentions of the technology provider (**Step 1**). Then, the *DSML Initialization* (**Step 2**) takes place. As shown in Fig. 3a the DSML initially has a single meta type "SubstationPC" to designate the substation PCs being modeled. Each substation PC possesses a unique serial number, modeled by an attribute "SN" of type string.

DSML Extension to Support G2. We elaborate in the following how the DSML is extended to enable the discussion of the fulfillment of the leaf goals in the goal model (**Step 3**). This is done by including the necessary elements in the DSML. For example, consider "G2: Persistent Data Storage with Redundancy". The description of G2 uncovers two concepts: "persistent data storage" and "redundancy". As a response, for capturing the concept of "persistent data storage" the language designer introduces a new meta type "SecondaryStorage" into the abstract syntax. In addition, to characterize a data storage device, a brand name, a model number, and its capacity are also included in the abstract syntax by means of three new attributes for "SecondaryStorage": "dataStorageBrand" and "dataStorageModel" of type string, and "capacity" of type double. Moreover, a new (containment) relation is also introduced, from the "SubstationPC" meta type to the meta type "SecondaryStorage", to indicate that data

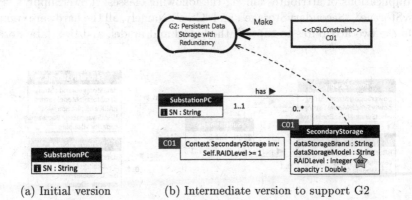

(a) Initial version   (b) Intermediate version to support G2

Fig. 3. Evolution of Substation PC DSML design

storage devices are components of a substation PC. No restriction is imposed on the cardinalities of the association. Thus, they are set to the most general one, namely "0..*".

For capturing the concept of "redundancy", the language designer adds a property to express redundancy to data storage devices. This is done by referring to the RAID (Redundant Array of Independent Disks) technology, which is a data storage virtualization technology for the purpose of data redundancy. More specifically, yet another new attribute "RAIDLevel" of type integer is introduced to class "SecondaryStorage", to indicate at which level the RAID technology is implemented in a given data storage device.

Figure 3b now shows the modified version of the abstract syntax, including the elements for expressing secondary storage characteristics. The motivation of the current version of the DSML design is documented by tracing the new language constructs in the abstract syntax of the DSML to the corresponding goal in the goal model, in this case goal G2.

Note that the new constructs introduced in the DSML make it possible to express instances (i.e., substation PCs), with which one can discuss about the achievement of G2. However, the actual level of fulfillment of G2 is still to be decided by the value of the "RAIDLevel" attribute in the instances. More specifically, no redundancy is provided if the RAID level is 0. We add a new constraint C01 in the abstract syntax of the DSML to reflect the checking of this value. This constraint is captured in the goal model as a resource offered by the DSML which contributes to the full achievement of G2 (marked by label "make").

DSML Extension to Support G1–G6. By applying **Step 3** to the other leaf goals (except for G7, which is considered only later) in a similar manner, the abstract syntax of the substation PC DSML further evolves to the version captured in Fig. 4. We mark the motivation of each construct directly by the name of the corresponding goal in the abstract syntax, to avoid repeating the goal model diagram.

Goal Model Extension. At this stage, the language designer notices that there are duplications of attributes among the following classes: "PowerSupply", "PrimaryStorage", "SecondaryStorage", and "Case". Namely, all the hardware components use two attributes to capture the brand and model, and two data storage

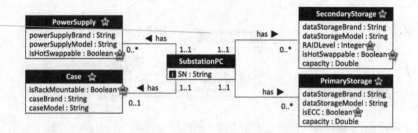

Fig. 4. Substation PC DSML intermediate version to support leaf goals G1–G6

classes share the capacity attribute. Instead of duplicating these attributes from one to another, a better way to implement this would be to introduce generalization/specialization. Such an intention of the language designer is captured by a new goal "G8: Reuse" (**Step 4**), which acts as the motivation of the new abstract meta types "HardwareElement" and "StorageDevice", and the corresponding inheritance relations (**Step 3**).

DSML Extension to Support G7. Finally, the DSML is extended to support also G7 (**Step 3**). This is done by introducing yet another attribute "averagelifespan" of type integer to class "HardwareElement".

Figure 5 presents the final version of the substation PC DSML (at the bottom) and the updated goal model with new goals and constraints (at the top). Note that by enforcing all the constraints in the DSML, the corresponding leaf goals are achieved fully for any substation PC instantiated from it. Please also note that with our approach, the constraints can be switched on and off,

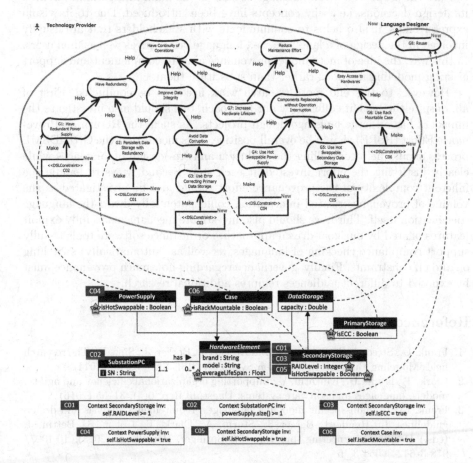

Fig. 5. Updated Goal Model (top) and DSML (bottom), and traceability

depending on the needs of the language user. For example, if at a later stage the technology provider notices that there is also a market for substation PCs without hot swappable power supply, the corresponding constraint C04 can be switched off. The resulting DSML would then also allow the specification of substation PCs without this feature.

5   Conclusions and Outlook

In this paper we have introduced the overall idea of meta model provenance and presented a goal-driven approach to achieve it. We argued that meta model provenance must be able to record the intension behind the elements of a given abstract syntax, to support the controlled evolution and the informed (re-)design of languages.

The goal-driven approach offers a semi-formal representation that helps to capture the scope of a given language as well as the main motivation(s) behind its design decisions, i.e., why concepts have been introduced. Due to its visual expressiveness, it also helps to communicate with stakeholders that are usually involved in the design of a language, i.e., language designers as well as final users. In this way, the idea of meta model provenance aims to complement and support existing modeling methods rather than substitute them.

However, to this end more research work needs to be conducted. First of all, despite the benefits offered by our approach, one should also investigate the impact it has on large language design projects. As such, the Return on Provenance Effort (RoPE) should be overall positive. This means that the GRL4DSML process should help controlling the evolution and (re-)design of languages while clearly justifying the effort invested at each step. Second, ways to handle the inherent complexity of the provenance effort should also be investigated as the volume of provenance-related information could potentially dwarf the language specification itself. Third, we should also investigate mechanisms to fully exploit features offered by our goal-driven approach. For instance software tools to fully support compliance checking of languages, as well as (automatically) switching on and off constraints. Finally, governance regarding how much provenance must be exposed to different audiences requires additional research.

References

1. Frank, U., Strecker, S., Fettke, P., vom Brocke, J., Becker, J., Sinz, E.: The research field 'Modeling Business Information Systems'. BISE **6**(1), 39–43 (2014)
2. Clark, T., Frank, U., Kulkarni, V.: Supporting organizational efficiency and agility: models, languages and software systems. Dagstuhl Rep. **6**(5), 31–55 (2016)
3. Frank, U.: Domain-specific modeling languages: requirements analysis and design guidelines. In: Reinhartz-Berger, I., Sturm, A., Clark, T., Cohen, S., Bettin, J. (eds.) Domain Engineering, pp. 133–157. Springer, Heidelberg (2013). 10.1007/978-3-642-36654-3_6
4. Frank, U.: Multi-perspective enterprise modeling: foundational concepts, prospects and future research challenges. SoSyM **13**(3), 941–962 (2014)

5. The Open Group: ArchiMate 2.1 Specification: Open Group Standard. The Open Group Series. Van Haren, Zaltbommel (2013)
6. Lankhorst, M.M., Proper, H.A., Jonkers, H.: The anatomy of the ArchiMate language. Int. J. Inf. Syst. Model. Des. (IJISMD) 1(1), 1–32 (2010)
7. Engelsman, W., Wieringa, R.: Understandability of goal-oriented requirements engineering concepts for enterprise architects. In: Jarke, M., Mylopoulos, J., Quix, C., Rolland, C., Manolopoulos, Y., Mouratidis, H., Horkoff, J. (eds.) CAiSE 2014. LNCS, vol. 8484, pp. 105–119. Springer, Cham (2014). 10.1007/978-3-319-07881-6_8
8. Tan, W.C.: Research problems in data provenance. IEEE Data Eng. Bull. 27, 45–52 (2004)
9. Gupta, A.: Data provenance. In: Liu, L., Özsu, M.T. (eds.) Encyclopedia of Database Systems, pp. 608–608. Springer US, Boston (2009)
10. Ram, S., Liu, J.: A semantic foundation for provenance management. J. Data Semant. 1(1), 11–17 (2012)
11. Kramer, F., Thalheim, B.: Metadata as support for data provenance. In: Jaakkola, H., Thalheim, B., Kiyoki, Y., Yoshida, N. (eds.) 26th International Conference on Information Modelling and Knowledge Bases XXVIII (EJC 2016). FAIA, vol. 292, pp. 195–214. IOS Press (2016)
12. Thalheim, B.: The science and art of conceptual modelling. Trans. Large-Scale Data- Knowl.-Center. Syst. 6, 76–105 (2012)
13. Karagiannis, D.: Agile modeling method engineering. In: Proceedings of the 19th Panhellenic Conference on Informatics, PCI 2015, pp. 5–10. ACM, New York (2015)
14. Villanueva Del Pozo, M.J.: An agile model-driven method for involving end-users in DSL development. Ph.D. thesis, Universidad Politecnica de Valencia (2016)
15. Karsai, G., Krahn, H., Pinkernell, C., Rumpe, B., Schindler, M., Völkel, S.: Design guidelines for domain specific languages. arXiv preprint arXiv:1409.2378 (2014)
16. De Kinderen, S., Ma, Q.: Requirements engineering for the design of conceptual modeling languages. Appl. Ontol. 10(1), 7–24 (2015)
17. Mernik, M., Heering, J., Sloane, A.M.: When and how to develop domain-specific languages. ACM Comput. Surv. (CSUR) 37(4), 316–344 (2005)
18. OMG: The OMG Unified Modeling Language, v. 2.5. Technical report (2015)
19. Heise, D.: Unternehmensmodell-basiertes IT-Kostenmanagement als Bestandteil eines integrativen IT-Controllings. Logos, Berlin (2013)
20. Simmhan, Y.L., Plale, B., Gannon, D.: A survey of data provenance in e-science. SIGMOD Rec. 34(3), 31–36 (2005)
21. Ragan, E.D., Endert, A., Sanyal, J., Chen, J.: Characterizing provenance in visualization and data analysis: an organizational framework of provenance types and purposes. IEEE Trans. Vis. Comput. Graphics 22(1), 31–40 (2016)
22. Herschel, M., Hlawatsch, M.: Provenance: on and behind the screens. In: Proceedings of the 2016 International Conference on Management of Data, pp. 2213–2217. ACM (2016)
23. Ram, S., Liu, J.: Understanding the semantics of data provenance to support active conceptual modeling. In: Chen, P.P., Wong, L.Y. (eds.) ACM-L 2006. LNCS, vol. 4512, pp. 17–29. Springer, Heidelberg (2007). 10.1007/978-3-540-77503-4_3
24. Liu, J., Ram, S.: Improving the domain independence of data provenance ontologies: a demonstration using conceptual graphs and the W7 model. JDM 1(28), 43–62 (2017)
25. ITU-T: User requirements notation (URN)-language definition (November 2008) Recommendation Z.151 (11/08). http://www.itu.int/rec/T-REC-Z.151/en. Last accessed 28 July 2017

26. Frank, U.: The MEMO Meta Modelling Language (MML) and Language Architecture, 2nd edn. ICB-Research Report 43, University of Duisburg-Essen (2011)
27. Niesten, E., Alkemade, F.: How is value created and captured in smart grids? a review of the literature and an analysis of pilot projects. Renew. Sustain. Energy Rev. **53**, 629–638 (2016)
28. Razavian, M., Gordijn, J.: Consonance between economic and IT services: finding the balance between conflicting requirements. In: Fricker, S.A., Schneider, K. (eds.) REFSQ 2015. LNCS, vol. 9013, pp. 148–163. Springer, Cham (2015). 10.1007/978-3-319-16101-3_10

Light Touch Identification of Cost/Risk in Complex Socio-Technical Systems

Iliada Eleftheriou[✉], Suzanne M. Embury, and Andrew Brass

School of Computer Science, University of Manchester,
Oxford Road, Manchester M13 9PL, UK
iliada.eleftheriou@manchester.ac.uk

Abstract. Information sharing within complex organisations is often source of considerable cost and risk. In previous work, we showed that points of highest IT cost/risk within an organisation are often located at the points where data moves from one context of use to another. We proposed a lightweight method of modelling the journeys data make within an organisation, and showed how to identify risky or costly boundaries. In this paper, we build on this previous work by evaluating the stability and completeness of the three core boundaries of our proposed method with staff from different clinical genomics hospital departments in the UK. Assessing our boundaries in the four new studies we found that although our core boundaries are stable in the new area of Clinical Genomics, domain-specific requirements of organisations can drive the need for additional boundaries. Finally, we discuss the feasibility of a general, low-cost process for identifying further boundaries of interest when applying the method to a new domain.

Keywords: Data movement boundaries · Data journeys · Information sharing · Risk identification · Cost identification

1 Introduction

Information systems in complex organisations are often sources of considerable cost and risk to their owners, as well as delivering business value. When resources must be stretched to deliver as much value as possible, we need to discover the places in the organisation where costs are higher than necessary and where value opportunities are being missed. However, by the same token, organisations can't afford to divert resources into expensive new developments or re-engineering activities. Any efforts to optimise current processes, or to create new processes, must be cheap and effective to carry out.

In previous work, we set out to design a lightweight method for identifying points of high cost and risk in organisations, in respect of the creation, management and use of data, that can be used for early stage decision making. That is, the method should not require a detailed model of the organisation or its

© IFIP International Federation for Information Processing 2017
Published by Springer International Publishing AG 2017. All Rights Reserved
G. Poels et al. (Eds.): PoEM 2017, LNBIP 305, pp. 65–80, 2017.
https://doi.org/10.1007/978-3-319-70241-4_5

processes to be produced before it can make predictions. Using 18 case studies of software failure and success in the UK National Health Service (NHS), we developed a method called *data journey modelling*, in which the broad movement of data within and between organisations can be mapped [5]. Onto this model, we overlay information about key "boundaries": places in the journey where data moves to another context causing the use and interpretation of data to alter in a way that can endanger the portability of data and introduce high costs/risks to the organisation. For example, when data is moved out of the context of the department that created it, and is used by others, the perceived data quality often drops dramatically, since much of the metadata that allows it to be interpreted correctly is not gathered or transferred explicitly with the data.

We identified three core boundaries from the information in the case studies: boundaries between organisational sub-units; boundaries between human participants on different salary scales; and boundaries where the medium of representation for data changes (e.g., from digital to paper). We confirmed their usefulness in a retrospective evaluation of a cost-saving effort in an NHS radiography department [6]. All three boundaries proved quick and easy to apply, and were able to indicate the points which the human experts had selected for change in the cost-saving exercise, as well as a number of additional points where, the experts agreed, cost could have been saved. Having assessed the usefulness and accuracy of the boundaries, a number of questions arose. Would these boundaries be similarly effective in other domains? And are they a complete set, or are other boundaries needed to capture the major costs and risks?

In this paper, we describe our efforts to answer these questions, by working with staff from several different Clinical Genetics departments in the NHS. Clinical genomics involves a more complex patient pathway than we had observed in our previous work, and raises different data management challenges. We describe 3 new case studies in which our standard boundary set was able to predict points of cost/risk (Sect. 4). We also describe a further case study, in which we examine the completeness of our boundary set. We found types of cost that our core boundaries did not predict, and propose two new boundaries to cover the gap in this new domain (Sect. 5). Finally, we present a tentative method for the low-cost up-front identification of new boundaries, to ensure that any data journey modelling effort within new domains is equipped with the boundaries it needs to perform effective cost/risk identification (Sect. 6).

2   Related Work

Despite decades of research on risk management and cost estimation, still no lightweight decision making approach has been proposed for the early-stages of the development cycle. Existing techniques focus principally on creating detailed predictions based on substantial models of the planned development [2,7,8,12, 13]. They support project managers throughout the development process itself, rather than giving a low-cost indicator for use in *early-stage* decision making.

Other modelling methods, like UML models, capture fine-grained flows, between low-level processing units within a system, making it hard to focus on higher-level aspects of the enterprise that can bring cost and risks, i.e. social factors [3,11]. Other high-level approaches (e.g., Data Flow Modelling, Business Process Modelling, and data provenance) can implicitly model data movements between a network of systems, they typically contain much more detail than is needed for our purposes [1]. They provide no abstraction as to which parts of the system should be captured for early-stage cost/risk identification and which can be safely ignored. Others, identifying and combining both technical and social aspects, require detailed organisational knowledge which is often hard, and time consuming to acquire [10,14,15]. Although they are powerful mechanisms to understand actors of an organisational infrastructure, they do not give us any specific means to identify likely costs.

In summary, we found no predictive approach that is sufficiently lightweight to be used as a decision-making aid in the very early stages of a development.

3 Background: Boundaries in Data Journey Modelling

To give the context for the work reported in this paper, we first give a brief overview of the data journey modelling approach. A data journey model is an abstract representation of the broad movements of data within and across collaborating organisations [5]. It is a socio-technical model in that it combines information about the movement of data between networks of people, as well as software systems of often different organisations. Since data journey models are intended for early-stage decision making (ideally before any implementation is initiated), they must be cheap to produce. This is achieved by keeping the focus on the broad information flows, rather than modelling the detailed processes of how data is captured, managed and used. Data journey models are intended to quickly show the major points of stress in organisational and cross-organisational data movement: the points where the meaning of data may inadvertently (and invisibly) change, where changes of media or governance requirements block the movement of data and where data may be lost in translation.

Figure 1 gives an example of a simple data journey model from a hypothetical NHS setting in which a general practitioner (GP) requests a blood test from a local pathology lab. As can be seen from the example, the data journey model shows the major containers (both electronic and physical) where data "rests" in between legs of its journey, from point of creation to point of use. Electronic containers are shown as cylinders and physical data containers as cuboids. Actors in various roles are also shown, indicating people or systems who interact with containers to create or consume information. The solid arrows indicate the legs of the journey where data moves between containers, while the dashed arrows indicate data creation and use by actors. Journey legs are labelled with the information type that moves along them.

The first step in the data journey modelling process is to create the data journey model. Our experience in working with a variety of NHS practitioners is that journey models can typically be created in 1–2 h, and that clinical staff can create them as easily as those with an IT function. Although modelling the

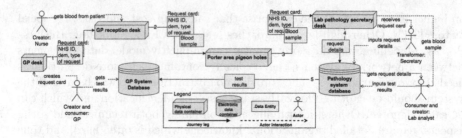

Fig. 1. Data journey model for a primary care blood test scenario

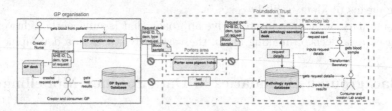

Fig. 2. Organisational boundary overlaid on the Pathology lab data journey model.

data journeys is only the first step in our technique, we found that it had value in itself, in helping health care practitioners (HCPs) to quickly gain an overview of how their organisation uses and shares data, when in their daily work they see only the detail of the parts of the journey they are directly involved with.

The second step is to add layers on top of the data journey model describing the key cost and risk factors likely to affect the successful movement of data. These layers group containers and actors that share similar characteristics relevant to the handling of data. The idea is that data movement within these groupings is likely to be low cost and low risk. However, when a journey leg takes data across a boundary between groups, then the risk of error, data loss, and additional data management costs increases. By overlaying several groupings/boundaries on a data journey model, a heat map of likely cost/risk points can be created. From our earlier work with 18 case studies of software failure and success, written by NHS staff, we extracted the following three boundaries:

- The 'Organisational' boundary, which groups containers and actors that are part of the same organisational unit (e.g. same department). Figure 2 shows the organisational boundaries overlaid on the pathology lab journey model.
- The 'Media' boundary, which groups containers that use the same media for information transfer and storage (e.g. paper files, x-rays, digital images).
- The 'Actors pay-scale' boundary, which groups actors who are at the same or similar salary level (e.g. clinician, secretary). This boundary is a low-cost proxy identifying groups of people of similar vocabularies and expertise, to identify points of information loss when data is shared across them.

The final stage of the model is to extract predictions of the places where operational costs might be high, or where the risk of significant costs occurring is high. This involves simply identifying the places where journey legs cross boundaries in the heat map, with legs that cross more boundaries being considered at greater risk than legs which cross fewer. Stakeholders are then asked to consider the identified legs, and to identify whether a genuine cost (or risk of cost) is present. Since our method is intended for early stage decision making, no attempt is made to quantify the costs or risks predicted. The information needed for that is typically not available at this stage, and could be costly to acquire. Our aim is to quickly provide a broad brush picture of the likely costs and risks.

A previous study in an NHS radiology department demonstrated the ability of this method to correctly identify points of high cost within a real setting [6]. Despite the simplicity of our method, almost all the predicted optimisation points were found to be valid by hospital staff, with only 2 false negative results. However, this single study could not completely validate the data journey modelling technique, and a number of open questions remained:

- How 'stable' are the boundaries across different organisations and domains? Are these three boundaries capable of identifying points of cost/risk in other settings, or does each new setting require us to identify a new set of boundaries? If data journey modelling is to be truly low cost to apply, then we need to have a stable set of boundaries that can be used across many domains. We can't afford to have a lengthy boundary discovery process bolted onto our lightweight method.
- How 'complete' is this set of boundaries? Even if the three boundaries we have identified in our previous work are stable across domains, that leaves open the possibility that some important costs and risks are not being identified by our method, because they cross boundaries that we are not modelling.
- How expensive is it to determine possible important boundaries for new settings, before full data journey modelling has taken place? Even if we identify a set of boundaries that is stable and (largely) complete across domains, there is still the possibility that some particular area might have highly specific requirements that should be taken into account in the identification of costs and risks. Can we find a low-cost, up-front way to determine whether a setting has specific boundary requirements not covered by our standard boundary set?

We set out to obtain answers to these questions by working with groups of health care professionals in the Clinical Genomics area, a different domain than the one we had previously worked with. The processes we followed, and the results we obtained, are described in the following sections.

4   Stability of the Core Boundaries

In this section, we assess the stability of our method's three core boundaries in identifying places of high costs and risks in a new domains. To do so, we worked with health care professionals (HCPs) in the area of Clinical Genomics. Clinical genomics is a branch of medicine in which the genome of the patient is sequenced, and interpreted by a multi-skilled team of experts, in order to assist with diagnosis of hereditary conditions, inform treatment decisions, and to determine the likelihood of conditions or symptoms appearing in the future [9]. The Clinical Genomics patient pathway is more complex than those we have worked with before, as it requires sharing of a rich variety of information between numerous actors, with very different skill sets, from different organisational units.

4.1 Study Design

During the period covered by this paper, we were lucky enough to have access to three separate groups of HCPs, working in different hospital foundation trusts across the UK, and having quite different roles in the clinical genomics patient pathway (varying from managerial positions to specialist technicians). In working with each group, our research question was: are the core boundaries stable for this group? That is, if used alone, can our core boundaries identify some costs/risks deemed significant by the domain experts in domains different from the ones from which they were originally identified? We did not require that the core boundaries find all cost/risk points, only that significant ones could be identified.

We followed a method inspired by action research, but adapted to fit the circumstances of the opportunities we had to work with domain experts (some of which arose at short notice). In each case, we began by defining a procedure to follow, and took care only to document domain expert responses, and not to lead them to answers we might have wished they had given.

4.2 Clinical Genomics Study A: Phenotype Pathway

In the most extensive study of the three, we worked with staff in a Genomic Medicine department of a Foundation Trust hospital in Greater Manchester which had recently undertook a re-engineering phase to improve the efficiency of their processes. To evaluate the stability of our method's boundaries in this domain, we carried out a retrospective analysis of the data journeys needed to capture the patient's phenotype (the set of observable characteristics of the patient's genotype). We modelled the journeys of data before and after the information infrastructure redesign to assess the predictive power of our method's boundaries, using the following approach:

1. We conducted semi-structured interviews with a Bioinformatician in the Genomics department of the trust, to gather the necessary domain knowledge.
2. We modelled the old data journeys before any improvements were made by hospital staff and overlaid our core boundaries to identify the journey legs with likely high costs and risks.

3. Then, we modelled the data journeys of the *new* system after the hospital re-engineering team improvement efforts.
4. Finally, we compared the predicted costly journey legs of the old model with the staff's improvements to assess the stability of our method's boundaries in predicting places of high costs and risks. These improvements were at a sufficiently advanced stage to give some confidence that they were indeed cost-saving, though we had no way to confirm that in the scope of the study.

The journey models we produced from this exercise are shown in Fig. 3. In the pathway we modelled, the phenotype of the patient is gathered by a specialist clinician from retinal images. The clinician examines these images and writes a report documenting the observed phenotype of the patient as hand written notes. Clerical staff then type up the reports. Before the re-engineering, several technical and social challenges caused considerate costs to the department. Diagnostic data was stored on a very old computer not connected to the network. To retrieve data, staff had to physically go to the room where the devices are stored and retrieve data using a USB drive, or sometimes even a floppy disk. Moreover, patient phenotype information was often needed by bioinformaticians and other actors working in the pathway, but no official sharing protocol existed, obstructing the dissemination of vital information. Another expensive issue was that phenotype data was not always coded (converted into standard medical codes) on input to the local computer system, making machine processing challenging.

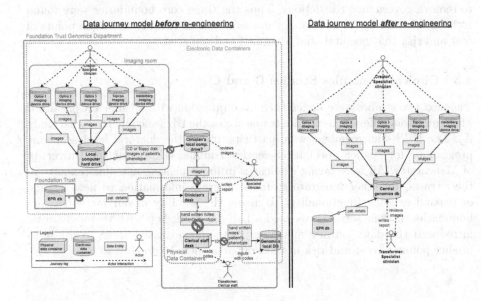

Fig. 3. Data journey model *before* and *after* the re-engineering process. (Color figure online)

With the help of the bioinformatician, we created the data journey model of the old system prior to the re-engineering phase, as shown in the left part of Fig. 3[1]. Once the bioinformatician approved the model, we overlaid the three core boundaries. In Fig. 3, organisational boundaries are denoted with a green colour solid line, the change of media boundaries with a red dotted line, and the change in pay-scale boundary with a large red warning sign. The journey legs that cross the boundaries are legs 6, 7, 8, 9, and 10, indicated in the figure with a small red warning sign. The place of highest cost/risk as predicted by our method is journey leg no 8, since it crossed two of the three boundaries (organisational and media boundaries).

Next, we worked with the bioinformatician to model the current (improved) data journeys, as illustrated in the right part of Fig. 3. The new system replaced the old report-based process with a new computer system for storing patient phenotype electronically. Now the phenotype is stored in a central database for access by all members of the genomics team. Data captured by the retinal imaging devices are also uploaded to the central database.

Comparing the two models, we found that all but one of the predicted costly journey legs in the old model were removed in the current model. The one that remains (journey leg #8) in fact crosses two boundaries, and one of these (the media boundary) was removed by the re-engineering effort. The bioinformatician felt that cost savings were possible by removing the organisational boundary at this point, but that it would be challenging because this part of the journey was under the control of the wider Foundation Trust and therefore subject to hard-to-remove governance restrictions. Thus the three core boundaries were found to be stable and useful in this new domain, able to identify the same points of cost and risk that hospital staff identified and replaced.

4.3   Clinical Genomics Studies B and C

The next two studies were undertaken in conjunction with 4 Clinical Consultant Managers from different Genomics teams across the UK (unconnected with study A). The NHS staff members were participating in the doctoral level academic programme for Higher Specialist Scientist Training (HSST) at the University of Manchester. All were facing challenges in implementing new functionality in their trusts, to either integrate systems, migrate information to new servers, or expand existing functionality. To assess the stability of our method's core boundaries in their settings, we held a half-day workshop with them where we introduced the data journey modelling method, and asked them to use it to predict points of cost and risk in their departments. To do this, we:

---

[1] As with many governmental institutions, aspects of this case study are confidential. Although the results presented were produced from the actual models, the illustrative models given in the paper are generalised, to show the typical journeys expected in a clinical genomics setting.

1. Introduced data journey models as a tool to map the information infrastructure of an organisation and the data journeys happening within (without yet mentioning the predictive part of our method's boundaries).
2. Asked the clinical consultant managers to create models of the key data journeys happening in their departments.
3. Before mentioning the boundaries, we asked them to note on their models the journey legs they think are the most expensive (in terms of time, effort and resources) based on their experience.
4. Introduced the use of boundaries to predict places of high costs/risks, and asked them to apply the core boundaries to their data journey models.
5. Compared the places that clinical consultants assessed as most costly with the places our boundaries identified to assess their predictive power.

Working in pairs, the clinical consultants created data journey models corresponding to areas of concern in their respective departments. Each model was thus an amalgam of behaviours in two different Clinical Genomics departments in the UK. Each team focused (at their own choice) on slightly different parts of the patient pathway. Study B focused on the data journeys needed to collect information from several actors across the pathway for the bioinformatician to process. Study C focused on the data journeys needed to collect variant information from several external resources (e.g., Decipher and ClinVar).

Interestingly, all participants agreed that even this first step (of creating the data journey model) was valuable. Prior to the experience, they had a bioinformatics-centric picture of the work in their departments, since that was the focus of their everyday activities. The data journey model helped them to gain a different perspective on the processes and interactions taking place within their teams. In particular, the study B pair was surprised by the number of journey legs needed to collect required information for one key task in their pathway (exome assembly). The Study C pair focused on the external data sources that bioinformaticians rely on to feed their computational analysis pipeline. Before they started modelling, they planned to model the journeys data make from the external data sources to the bioinformatician's machine. However, while modelling these journey legs, they realised that the legs depend on a larger set of journey legs. Having created the data journey model, they recognised the value of other actors in the pipeline in getting accurate information to work with. The journey model brought home to all of them the complexity of the interactions between people and systems involved.

Having completed the data journey models, and before the boundaries had been added, we asked both pairs to identify the journey legs where most effort (cost) was expended, and where they were most concerned to see an efficiency gain. Having done this, we introduced the three core boundaries of our method and showed the participants how to layer the boundaries over the model and draw predictions from them. In both cases, the points of cost/risk identified by the boundaries differed from the problematic legs already identified by the teams. But upon consideration, both teams agreed that the predicted legs *were* sources of highest cost; they just hadn't been aware of them beforehand.

The case study B pair initially identified the bioinformatician's part of the model as the most costly, where the heavy data processing happens. The boundaries, however, identified a single point of failure in their current infrastructure — the majority of the journeys started and ended at a single system, maintained by one particular staff member. They had not realised the dependence of their processes on this one person before this exercise. Having identified it, they can look at re-engineering their processes and remove the single point of failure.

In case study C, the pair initially identified the legs moving data from the external sources to the bioinformatician's workplace as most costly, because of the need to pay data access fees. While the boundaries did predict these points of cost, they predicted a different leg as being of highest cost/risk: the point of information handover from the bioinformatician to the genetic counsellor, which crossed all three boundaries. On consideration, both HCPs agreed that the point predicted by the boundaries was probably more costly, since it happens on a daily basis (the cost is accumulated daily), whereas the area they had been concentrating on happened more rarely.

Thus, in both cases (and in less than 2 h, including training in data journey modelling) our 3 core boundaries were able to identify points of cost that the domain experts agreed with. In fact, in both cases, the predictions differed from the participants prior perceptions of the risks, giving them an insight into the needs of their departments that they did not have before. Taken together, studies A, B and C indicate that even this simple set of boundaries can have significant predictive power, at very low cost, in the Clinical Genomics domain.

5   Completeness of the Boundaries (Study D)

Case studies A, B and C allowed us to test the stability of our core boundaries in the Genomics domain. However, the nature of the case studies, and the small number of stakeholders involved, did not allow us to draw any conclusions about the completeness of this set of boundaries. This was the focus of our next case study, in which we set out to answer whether the core boundaries were able to identify most of the key points of cost and risk, or whether there are significant aspects of cost and risk that they cannot identify.

In this case study, we investigated the entire Clinical Genomics patient pathway, looking for significant costs/risks not captured by our 3 core boundaries. For this, we worked with the group of HSST staff from studies B and C, but also with another group of NHS staff attending the Clinical Bioinformatics Genomics Masters course at the University of Manchester. They came from various NHS Foundation Trusts in the Greater Manchester and Liverpool area, and worked in a range of positions within the Genomics patient pathway, such as Genetic Counsellor, Genome Technician, and Clinical Geneticist. To assess the completeness of the core 3 boundaries in identifying significant costs/risks, we:

1. Worked with clinical genomics staff to create a data journey model for the full patient pathway.

2. Observed the clinical bioinformatics module to collect socio-technical challenges across the entire patient pathway that NHS staff report facing in their everyday work and that cause significant costs for their departments.
3. Assessed each challenge to see if they were predicted by our core boundaries over-layed onto the patient pathway data journey model.

To look for costs/risks in the pathway, we asked the participants to discuss challenges they face in their everyday work. We collected not just technical challenges stemming from the data and technologies used, but also social and organisational challenges that all introduced some type of cost/effort to their everyday processes. The challenges identified from this process are summarised in Table 1. We examined each challenge to determine whether costly/risky points relating to it would be picked up on a data journey model using our 3 core boundaries. To do so, prior to this study, we had developed a comprehensive data journey model for the full clinical genomics pathway, with the help of the clinical genomics team at a nearby hospital. We looked at the points on this model where these challenges might materialise, to see if they coincided with the legs predicted to be cost/risk hot spots by our three standard boundaries. We present the boundary indicative of the cost described by each challenge to the second column of the table. Costly points not captured by any of the boundaries are noted with a question mark symbol.

From the table, we see that more than half the challenges (62%) can be identified by our core boundaries. The people-oriented challenges were all identified by our actor boundary, since it identifies points where data moves between members of staff with different kinds and degrees of specialist expertise. In our Clinical Genomics data journey model, this happens principally at the point of data handover from the clinical geneticists to the bioinformaticians, and *vice versa*. These groups of people have very different specialisms, and do not always share the same understanding of the data.

The organisational boundary was able to indicate all the obstacles of sharing information with external sources. No change-of-media challenges were in evidence in the set of challenges we elicited from the domain experts in this case. However, some challenges were not identified by our standard boundaries. Specifically, those involving data volume and governance procedures were not captured by any of the standard boundaries. Both these factors limit the portability of data, and introduce additional costs to the patient pathway.

The data volume is a major obstacle to the movement of data between key actors in the pathway. Sequencing a patient's genome can produce millions of data files, resulting in large volumes of data (typically 10–100 GB per patient). Given the complex nature of the pathway, with different actors typically working in different locations, and using their own dedicated software systems, large data volumes can be a real barrier to effective sharing and collaboration.

To validate the newly found obstacle of the volume of the data, we referred back to the case studies B and C. Examples of volume-related challenges were experienced by participants in both studies. One of the participants reported the need to establish a new journey to move information from an old data reposi-

Table 1. Challenges identified in the Clinical Genomics domain.

Challenges and potential costs/risks	Boundary
Data can be misunderstood by consumers when it is produced by teams with different backgrounds and expertise from the consumers	Actor
Data that is used by one group of people but collected by another are often found to be inaccurate/incomplete. The consumer of the data in this case often experiences a decreased quality of the data	Actor
Lack of communication between stakeholders and the development team	Actor
Staff can be reluctant to share variants with other pipelines because of the governance frameworks in place	?
Heterogeneity issues between external data sources. E.g. use of different IDs. Some sources may have older versions of the same data entity. Also, different sources represent the same data in different ways.	Org.
There are governance issues whenever data is transferred between networks of different organisations (university and hospital networks)	Org.
Information governance caused issues when integrating different parts of different pipelines (research and clinical)	?
Some data are 30–40 years old. Corrections to data over time cause duplicate versions of information (which are not explicitly marked at the source)	?
The sequencing machines produce very large volumes of data, causing storage and sharing problems	?
Different bioinformaticians use different workflows to process the data, leading to potentially different results	Actor
Needed information might not exist (i.e. never-seen-before variants). It can be hard to distinguish between non-existent data and data that is only absent from the source	?
Information available in the literature is not always as accurate as claimed	Org.
Clinical geneticists have only 10 min to comprehend findings produced by the bioinformaticians before making a potentially life-threatening decision	Actor

tory to a newly created one. However, no connection has been yet established to migrate information between the two repositories (there are no governance barriers, since the movement is within the same hospital). Apart from communication problems between the stakeholders and the development team, the major problem is the volume of data that needs to be shared. Since there is no direct network connection they currently have to copy each day's work (some 10 GB of data) to the new repository, through external hard disks, every night. Another participant reported the need for exome data to move between two geographically distant sites (two UK cities). However, exome data sets are typically around

5 GB, and attempts to transfer them cause the archive system which is used for transferring data to crash. Moreover, in another data movement example in a university hospital, data needs to be transferred from the external university network to the internal NHS network. Both machines are in the same room, but are on different networks. The volume of data to be transferred is large, and the network is slow. The participant reported that sometimes they have to plug the machine physically into the other network to transfer data.

The other new boundary retrieved from the challenges relates to information governance. In domains where information is highly private and confidential such as clinical genomics, information sharing must be tightly regulated and controlled. Governance protocols must be established to ensure that patient data is kept securely, and only used for agreed purposes. To complicate matters, governance protocols do not coincide with organisational boundaries. For example, within clinical genomics, there are two main protocols in use: a research oriented pipeline of processes and a clinical oriented pipeline. Each pipeline must follow the respective governance framework and guidelines. Audit information is captured along the pipeline based on the specific governance framework that applies. If governance protocols conflict, or are not fit for purpose, serious delays and additional costs can affect data sharing efforts.

Thus, this study identified two additional boundaries needed to root out the key obstacles to data sharing in a clinical genomics setting: data volume and information governance. Although these boundaries arose out of highly domain specific situations, they are applicable across a broad range of domains. In the era of big data, clinical geneticists are not unique in having to work with much larger data sets than their IT infrastructure are designed for. Nor are information governance protocols limited to the handling of genetic data.

Since, it seems reasonable to assume that these boundaries will have wider applicability than just this one domain, the next step is to convert these high level concepts into actual "boundaries" that can be added to a data journey model. To be a useful boundary in our context, the information needed to decide which containers/actors are on which side of the boundary must be quick and cheap to acquire. To apply the volume boundary on the model, we group together containers storing data sets of similar size. A simple and quick way to categorise the volume of the data entities is by using the agile approach of 'tee shirt sizing', in which size is described by broad categories (small, medium, large) [4]. Then, boundaries show where data moves from containers handling large volume of data into containers set up to handle small volume, and vice versa. Similarly, to identify costs arising from the governance boundary, we group together containers and actors set to follow the research-oriented pipeline, and the clinical-oriented pipeline. Since containers and actors can work on both governance protocols, costs will arise when a journey leg moves data to a target container of a different protocol than those followed by the source.

Finally, identifying the new boundaries of data volume and information governance, suggests that domain-specific requirements of organisations might drive the need for additional boundaries during data journey modelling. The next section presents a new method to identify potential boundaries in other domains.

6   Identifying Boundaries in New Domains

Our work with the clinical genomics teams indicated that certain areas might have domain-specific costs and risks that may not be identified using our core set of boundaries. It seems likely that many new domains may share this characteristic: the generic boundaries can be applicable, but some domain-specific boundaries may also be needed. In this section, we discuss a method to identify additional boundaries to use when modelling data journeys in a new domain. It is an up-front approach that takes place before any data journey modelling is initiated, and low-cost, so as not to jeopardise the lightweight nature of the combined boundary-discover/data journey modelling technique. The process we propose for this is as follows:

1. "Grumble Analysis": hold a brainstorming session with stakeholders and domain experts to capture socio-technical challenges stemming from technical, organisational, regulations, guidelines, and social aspects, that they face in their everyday work.
2. "Good/Bad Analysis": for every challenge identified, check whether an already established boundary matches it. If not, a new boundary may be waiting to be discovered. Ask the experts to suggest characteristics that differentiate participant organisational elements causing the problems described by the challenge, from those which do not. Primarily, we look for binary properties of the participants ("good" or "bad" characteristics) that are simple and cheap-to-acquire. For example, if data shared from external sources is often incomplete, we might distinguish sources based on their data admin response times. "Good" suppliers respond within 2 days, "bad" suppliers respond less promptly.
3. For each such characteristic, we look for cheap-to-acquire surrogates that can be used to form boundaries on the data journey model. An easy and quick way to do this is the tee-shirt agile approach mentioned above; categorise properties into simple broad classes, such as large, medium, small. Having categorised the properties of the participant organisational elements, we can group together those with similar size to form boundaries. Whenever data crosses a boundary, data moves from a source with a good property to a target of a different property that would impose costs to the journey.

Having identified a pool of potential boundaries, we then apply them on the data journey models we create within the new domain to check their usefulness in identifying costs and risks in the new domain. So, over time, we can build up a core set of boundaries to be used within that particular domain.

7   Conclusion

In this paper, we tested the three boundaries we had identified in previous work for stability across different settings, and for completeness. We applied the boundaries in three new case studies, in a different clinical domain than used in our previous work, and with staff in different roles in the patient pathway. We found that the boundaries performed consistently well across all three case studies; they were able to identify points of cost/risk that the staff agreed with, and (perhaps most importantly) were able to identify points of cost/risk that the staff themselves were not aware of before the modelling exercise. We also undertook a study of the entire clinical genomics patient pathway, looking for costs and risks that were not identifiable by our standard boundaries. We found that although many of the challenges were picked up by the standard boundaries, some were not suggesting that domain-specific organisational requirements can drive the need for additional boundaries. From this, we provide two new boundaries (data volume and data governance) to fill in the gap. We also present a low-cost technique for identifying new candidate boundaries in other domains, so that unique characteristics of the domain will not be missed during data journey modelling. In future work, we will check the applicability and power of our new boundaries, as well as testing that our proposed method for discovering boundaries is indeed quick and effective to apply in other domains and other contexts.

References

1. Aguilar-Saven, R.S.: Business process modelling: review and framework. Int. J. Prod. Econ. **90**(2), 129–149 (2004)
2. Boehm, B., Abts, C., Chulani, S.: Software development cost estimation approaches - a survey. Ann. Softw. Eng. **10**(1–4), 177–205 (2000)
3. Li, Q., Chen, Y.L.: Data flow diagram. In: Li, Q., Chen, Y.-L. (eds.) Modeling and Analysis of Enterprise and Information Systems, pp. 85–97. Springer, Heidelberg (2009). doi:10.1007/978-3-540-89556-5_4
4. Cobb, C.G.: The Project Manager's Guide to Mastering Agile: Principles and Practices for an Adaptive Approach. Wiley, New York (2015)
5. Eleftheriou, I., Embury, S.M., Brass, A.: Data journey modelling: predicting risk for IT developments. In: Horkoff, J., Jeusfeld, M.A., Persson, A. (eds.) PoEM 2016. LNBIP, vol. 267, pp. 72–86. Springer, Cham (2016). doi:10.1007/978-3-319-48393-1_6
6. Eleftheriou, I., Embury, S., Moden, R., Dobinson, P., Brass, A.: Data journeys: identifying social and technical barriers to data movement in large, complex organisations. Technical report, School of Computer Science, UoM (2016). www.datajourney.org/publications/tech_rep_data_journey.pdf
7. Jørgensen, M., Grimstad, S.: Software development effort estimation - demystifying and improving expert estimation. In: Tveito, A., Bruaset, A., Lysne, O. (eds.) Simula Research Laboratory, pp. 381–403. Springer, Heidelberg (2010). doi:10.1007/978-3-642-01156-6_26
8. Mendes, E.: Effort and risk prediction for healthcare software projects delivered on the web. In: Mendes, E. (ed.) Practitioner's Knowledge Representation, pp. 107–122. Springer, Heidelberg (2014). doi:10.1007/978-3-642-54157-5_1
9. Mount, D.W.: Bioinformatics: sequence and genome analysis. J. Bioinform. **28** (2001)
10. Pardo, T., Cresswell, A.M., Dawes, S.S., et al.: Modeling the social and technical processes of interorganizational information integration. In: Proceedings of the 37th Annual Hawaii International Conference on System Sciences, p. 8. IEEE (2004)

11. Simmhan, Y.L., Plale, B., Gannon, D.: A survey of data provenance in e-science. ACM SIGMOD Rec. **34**(3), 31–36 (2005)

12. Trendowicz, A.: Software Cost Estimation, Benchmarking, Risk Assessment: The Software Decision-Makers' Guide to Predictable Software Development. Springer, Heidelberg (2013). doi:10.1007/978-3-642-30764-5

13. Trendowicz, A., Jeffery, R.: Principles of effort and cost estimation. In: Trendowicz, A., Jeffery, R. (eds.) Software Project Effort Estimation, pp. 11–45. Springer, Cham (2014). doi:10.1007/978-3-319-03629-8_2

14. Yu, E.S.: Social modeling and *i**. In: Borgida, A.T., Chaudhri, V.K., Giorgini, P., Yu, E.S. (eds.) Conceptual Modeling: Foundations and Applications. LNCS, vol. 5600, pp. 99–121. Springer, Heidelberg (2009). doi:10.1007/978-3-642-02463-4_7

15. Yusof, M.M., Kuljis, J., Papazafeiropoulou, A., Stergioulas, L.K.: An evaluation framework for health Information Systems: human, organization and technology-fit factors (HOT-fit). Int. J. Med. Inform. **77**(6), 386–398 (2008)

The OntoREA© Accounting and Finance Model: A Retroactive DSRM Demonstration Evaluation

Christian Fischer-Pauzenberger📵 and Walter S.A. Schwaiger(✉) 📵

Institute of Management Science, Technische Universität Wien, Theresianumgasse 27,
1040 Vienna, Austria
{christian.fischer-pauzenberger,walter.schwaiger}@tuwien.ac.at

Abstract. Derivative instruments have special characteristics that make them difficult to understand and to handle in financial instrument accounting. In the OntoREA© Accounting and Finance Model [1] such instruments are conceptualized and integrated into the REAC Business Ontology [2] as well as the OntoREA Accounting Model [3]. But the OntoREA© model is developed at a very abstract level so that no real cases are used for demonstration and evaluation. This shortcoming is addressed in this article by demonstrating and evaluating the *Collective* conceptualization of derivative instruments in OntoREA© from a retroactive design science methodological (DSRM) [4] perspective within the model driven software development (MDD) context. Along the model transformations in this context the OntoREA© model serves as platform independent (PIM) model. For demonstration purposes its direct translation into a platform specific (PSM) as well as an implementation specific (ISM) model are demonstrated for a real derivative instrument. The evaluation shows that the requirements of derivative instruments are met adequately.

Keywords: OntoREA© accounting and finance model · OntoUML · Model driven development · Design science research methodology

1 Introduction

A derivative is a financial instrument:

- *Whose value changes in response to the change in an underlying variable such as an interest rate, commodity or security price, or index;*
- *That requires no initial investment, or one that is smaller than would be required for a contract with similar response to changes in market factors; and*
- *That is settled at a future date* [5].

This is the definition of derivative instruments in the International Financial Reporting Standards (IFRS). The three characteristics of derivative instruments say that their value is derived from an underlying variable (that's where their name comes from), the zero or low investment comes from the fact that these instruments are only contracted commitments that are fulfilled in the future where the underlying and the contracted

© IFIP International Federation for Information Processing 2017
Published by Springer International Publishing AG 2017. All Rights Reserved
G. Poels et al. (Eds.): PoEM 2017, LNBIP 305, pp. 81–95, 2017.
https://doi.org/10.1007/978-3-319-70241-4_6

prices are exchanged between the contracting agents. The zero investment means that a derivative instrument can have a value of zero. A good example for such a contract is a forward which is defined as follows: *Contracts to purchase or sell a specific quantity of a financial instrument, a commodity, or a foreign currency at a specified price determined at the outset, with delivery or settlement at a specified future date. Settlement is at maturity by actual delivery of the item specified in the contract, or by a net cash settlement* [6].

At the *contracting date* the buyer and the seller of the forward contract agree to exchange at the future *expiration date* the underlying good. In e.g. a *stock forward* the *underlying* of the contract is an explicitly defined *stock* (e.g. the XY stock). In the easiest case the forward *contract size* is one stock. In this instance the buyer of the forward receives in the future the stock from the seller. In reciprocity for this receipt the buyer pays the seller the *forward price*. Normally the forward price is set at the contracting date so that the initial value of the forward is equal to zero. This valueless property of the forward causes a problem in accounting as such contracts cannot be considered neither as assets nor as liabilities.

In Fig. 1 the stock forward is conceptualized with an UML-activity diagram. The contracting between the two agents, i.e. the buyer and the seller, is the activity that initiates the forward contract. There are no exchanges at the contracting date. In the contract only the future related commitments are specified. This can be seen in the figure where the buyer has a debit commitment to the stock which is a credit commitment for the seller who has to deliver the stock. On the other hand the reciprocity requires that at the expiration date the buyer has to pay in cash the forward price to the seller.

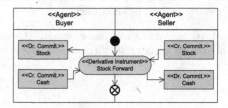

Fig. 1. Derivative instrument – UML-activity diagram

The OntoREA© accounting and finance model [1] integrates the REAC Business Ontology [2] with the OntoREA Accounting Model [3]. Its name suggests that it is specified in the OntoUML language [7]. Derivative instruments are included according to the *no-arbitrage pricing theory* form the Nobel laureates Black/Scholes [8] and Merton [9]. Specifically the derivative instruments are conceptualized according to their corresponding *hedge portfolio* [10] – which underlies the no-arbitrage pricing theory – as *Collective* with a *MemberOf* relationship to two *Economic Resources*.

This abstract conceptualization of derivative instruments is hard to grasp. In the following this understanding problem is solved by demonstrating the precise meaning of the *Collective* conceptualization with a *stock forward* running example. Furthermore the usage of the OntoREA© model will be demonstrated in the model driven (software) development (MDD) context [11]. The UML activity diagram in Fig. 1 corresponds to the computational independent *CIM model*, the OntoREA© model constitutes the platform independent *PIM model*. According to the *forward engineering* approach in MDD the PIM model is transformed into a platform specific *PSM model* and finally into an implementation specific *ISM model*. More precisely, the MySQL [12] database model (PSM) and RStudio dataframe model (ISM) [13, 14] are derived in two transformation steps. For demonstrating the MDD process up to the software application a prototypical ISM application will be developed in RStudio Shiny.

A design science research methodology applied in accounting information systems [4] consists of six activities, i.e. problem identification and motivation, definition of the objectives of a solution, design and development, demonstration, evaluation and communication. In this light the OntoREAC Accounting and Finance model [1] addresses the first three activities quite well. This can be seen by the developed accounting and finance model which integrates the special temporal modal and identity-related peculiarities of financial instruments into the REA-based Asset-Liability-Equity (ALE) accounting model. Due to its publication the model also accomplishes the DSRM communication activity. With respect to the demonstration and evaluation activities there are shortcomings: there is no demonstration of the models' usage in e.g. an MDD context and its adequacy concerning the representation of the derivative instruments is not evaluated.

The primary research objective is twofold: Firstly, fostering the meaning of OntoREA©'s *Collective* conceptualization of financial instruments. Secondly, the DSRM validation of this conceptualization in two steps

- by demonstrating its usage in the two model transformations within the MDD context, i.e. from the PIM to the PSM model as well as from the PSM to the ISM model, and
- by evaluating the adequate coverage of the financial instruments' special peculiarities.

The paper is organized as follows. In the subsequent section the OntoREA© accounting and finance model is presented. In the MDD context this model constitutes the abstract PIM model that is successively transformed into more specific models. In the next section the two transformations are demonstrated. Firstly, the MySQL database model (PSM) is derived. Of special importance is the specification of exclusivity constraint, which underlies the OntoUML *Collectives* constraints, for the MySQL database in the object constraint language (OCL). Secondly, the derived PSM model is transformed into an RStudio data model (ISM). In this transformation step the exclusivity constraint is via the switch function already expressed in the R programming language. This specification has the advantage that it can be directly used in the prototypical ISM application in RStudio Shiny. The prototypical application is shown in the next section. In the final section the paper is concluded.

2   The OntoREA© Accounting and Finance Model: PIM Model

The OntoREA© accounting and finance model is based upon the *REAC Business Ontology* [2] as well as the *OntoREA Accounting Model* [3]. Both models can be seen in Fig. 2. The REAC business ontology extends the original *REA Accounting Model* [15] by including among others a forward looking perspectives in form of commitments. The REA©-based ALE accounting model eliminates deficiencies in the REAC business ontology in order to make it appropriate for Asset/Liability/Equity (ALE) accounting purposes.

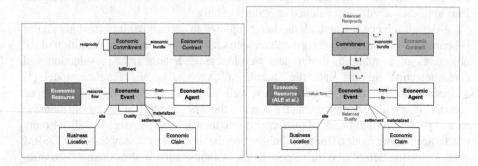

Fig. 2. REAC Model (left) and REA©-based ALE accounting model (right)

In Fig. 3 the REA©-based ALE accounting model is slightly modified in order to enhance its expressiveness with respect to the OntoREA© accounting and finance model. The modification consists of the reification of the *Balanced Duality* relationship and the *Balanced Reciprocity* relationship. Now it is explicitly expressed that each business transaction is based upon a contract, i.e. a spot contract in a spot market and a future contract in a future market.

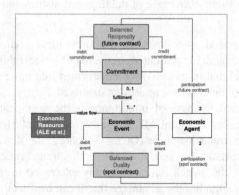

Fig. 3. REA©-based ALE accounting model – modified version

For understanding the meta-physical semantics of the OntoUML languages a short primer is given: "In conceptual modeling entity types and relationship types are the most fundamental constructs" [16]. Taken from [3] the following entity types (subsequently marked in bolded letters), which are derived from the UFO typification tree (marked in italic letters) are of importance for the OntoREA accounting model:

- **Kinds** are *rigid substance sortals* and they provide their own identity principle (rather than just carrying it). *Kinds* are also considered as an OntoUML model's backbone [17] and they are used to model resources, events and agents as endurants.
- **SubKinds** are *rigid sortals* and do not provide their own identity principle, they are merely inheriting the principle from another *Substance Sortal*.
- **Roles** are *anti-rigid sortals* and therefore can change their instantiation in a modal sense according to an extrinsic generalization condition. Furthermore, Roles are relational-dependent, they have to rely on at least one other universal. Roles get their identity principle through the generalization relation from the instance of its parent universal.
- **Phases** are *anti-rigid sortals* as well with a significant distinction to Roles. Phases are relational (i.e. external) independent. Due to the predetermined disjoint and complete generalization sets, instances of Phases, in contrast to instances of Roles, can change according to their intrinsic (and not extrinsic) generalization condition. As Roles, Phases also get their identity principle through the generalization relation.

Next to the above mentioned entity types the following relationship types will be important for the OntoREA accounting model to be developed:

- **Relator Universals**, are *moment universals* which represent the objectification of a relational property. Relator Universals are existentially dependent on a multitude of individuals, thus, mediating them. Relators are the foundation of the so-called **Material Relations** [18] and act as truthmakers of the relation.
- **Formal Relations** hold directly between entities without requiring any intervening individual. [1].

Next to that, two additional *meronymic* meta-properties are used in the OntoREA© accounting and finance model in order to address the peculiar *parthood relationship* associated with derivative instruments:

- **Collectives** are – like Kinds – *rigid substance sortals* and that provide their own identity principle. The difference to *Kinds* lies in the scope of the universals. The *Kind* universal specifies individual universals whereas the *Collective* universal goes beyond individual universals by specifying collections.
- **MemberOf Parthood-Relationships** are relationships where both the *Collective* and its constituting *Kinds* have their corresponding identity principles. The *Beatles* are an example for such a collection. Seen as an instantiation of a *Collective* universal the Beatles as a group has its own identity. The members of the Beatles as persons are instantiations of a *Kind* universal and consequently have their personal identity.

The remaining entity types and relationship types of UFO are not needed for the OntoREA© accounting and finance model. The current and complete version of UFO is specified in the UFO reference [19].

Equipped with the vocabulary and syntax given in the OntoUML primer the OntoREA© accounting and finance model [1] can be presented. Figure 4 shows the model. The OntoUML meta-physical properties are marked with ≪Guillemet≫ parentheses. In contrast to the original version of the model one minor modification is included in order to avoid mis-understandings within the MDD contextual model transformations:

The *Null* naming of the third derivative instrument phase is replaced by the word *Off Balance* due to the special importance of the *Not Null* restriction used in platform specific database PSM models.

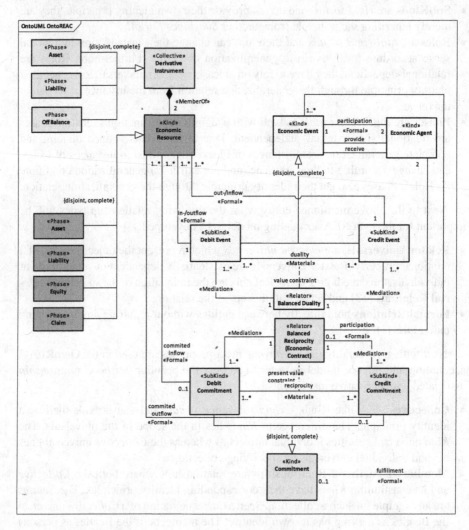

Fig. 4. OntoREA© accounting and finance model – conceptual model (PIM)

For the exploration of the OntoREA© accounting and finance model in Fig. 4 it's advisable to start with the *Balanced Duality* and the *Balanced Reciprocity* classes. As is indicated in the REA©-based ALE accounting model in Fig. 3, both classes are *Relator* classes that reify the monetary balancing between the associated debit and credit entries. As such they possess a truthmaker that mediates between the debit and credit entries. In both cases the truthmaker is a contract, i.e. a *spot market contract* in the balanced duality case and a *future market contract* in the balanced reciprocity case. For simplicity this connection to the truthmaker is referenced explicitly only in the balanced reciprocity case by setting the *Economic Contract* in parentheses.

A derivative instrument, which is the primary focus in this article, is an *Economic Contract* that obeys the *Balanced Reciprocity relationship* between its debit and credit commitments. Furthermore there is a 0..1 cardinality from the *Economic Resource* class to the *Debit Commitment* class as well as to the *Credit Commitment* classes. If there are economic resources linked to the debit and credit commitments then these are the resources in the hedge portfolio of the derivative instrument. As such the derivative instruments are economic contracts that are linked to their corresponding hedge portfolio. In the top-left corner of Fig. 4 the *Collective* class Derivative Instrument is shown. "This class has a *MemberOf* relationship to the *Kind* class Economic Resource. The cardinality says that derivative instruments have two economic resource members, i.e. one asset and one liability. Furthermore the *Collective* class Derivative Instrument is typified via a *Phase* partition that consists of the *Phase* classes Asset, Liability and Off Balance. According to this the derivate instruments can change the phases over time without losing its identity by switching from the *Phase* Off Balance, i.e. an off-balance position, into an on-balance position either to the *Phase* Asset or the *Phase* Liability and so on." [1].

The *Collective* conceptualization of derivative instruments in the OntoREA© is quite different to the ALE phases of economic resources. The asset, liability, equity and claim phase partition of economic resources relate to individual resources of a *Kind* class whereas the asset, liability and off balance phase partition of derivative instruments relate of a *Collective* class that consists of the 2 economic resources in its hedge portfolio. Accordingly the two phase partitions will be treated differently in the transformation from the PIM model into the PSM model.

3   The OntoREA© Model in the MDD-Context: Transformations from PIM via PSM into ISM

Let's start with a concrete derivative instrument example, i.e. a long position in a stock forward contract. At the beginning of the year (*contracting date*) we are buying a stock forward where we receive one XY stock (*contract size*) at the end of the year (*expiration date*) and for which we have to pay the forward price. Currently the one-year interest rate, which corresponds to the contract's *initial time to maturity* of 12 months, amounts to 4% (4% = 0.04). By taking the interest rate as the substitute for the cost of carry, the forward price is equal to 104, which is the current stock price of 100 plus the 4% interest rate. For this forward price the fair value of the stock forward is equal to zero. This means, the stock forward is a valueless position taken at the contracting date. Considering such a position from the accounting recognition perspective shows the problem that according to the valueless property in the initial measurement it cannot be assigned neither as asset nor as liability.

Over time the fair value of the contract, i.e. the stock forward value, depends on the actual stock prices and the remaining times to maturity. In the mid-year pricing, where the stock price is assumed to be 100, the forward value amounts to −1.98. In this case the forward contract appears due to its negative value as a liability position in the balance sheet. For the final measurement at the expiration date it is assumed that the stock price is 120. In this case the forward contract has a positive value of 16 so that it appears as an asset in the balance sheet.

Considering the evolution of forward value over its life cycle, i.e. from the contracting date up to the expiration date, shows the temporal modal nature of the balance sheet recognitions. Starting from an off balance position the stock forward changes to a liability and ends up as an asset position. This recognition structure mainly depends on the assumed development of the stock prices which is taken for illustrative purposes. In general there are different stock price developments possible so that the stock forward recognitions are different as well. As stock prices are stochastic over time, the stock forward's balance sheet assignments also have a *stochastic temporal modal nature*. This specific nature of forward contracts can be seen in Table 1 in the boldfaced rows.

Table 1. Stock forward (running example) – contract specification and pricing

```
Contracting date:        01.01.2020
Expiration date:         31.12.2020
Initial stock price:     100
Initial interest rate:   4%
Stock Asset:             100
Loan Liability:          100
Forward value: = A - L   0 (Off B.)
Pricing date #1:         30.06.2020
Actual stock price:      100
Actual time to maturity: 6 months
Stock Asset:             100
Loan Liability:          101,98
Forward value: = A - L   -1,98 (L)
Pricing date #2:         31.12.2020
Actual stock price:      120
Actual time to maturity: 0 months
Stock Asset:             120
Loan Liability:          104
Forward value: = A - L   16 (A)
```

Furthermore, Table 1 shows the *hedge portfolio* at each pricing date in form of the *stock asset* and the *loan liability*. The net value of this portfolio gives the forward value. In parentheses the balance sheet assignments are given which depend on the sign of the net values, i.e. a zero value gives an off balance position, a positive value gives an asset position and a negative value gives a liability position.

The hedge portfolio forms the conceptual basis of the no-arbitrage pricing theory. In the case of forward contracts a *static hedge portfolio* is sufficient to exactly replicate (duplicate) the forward values over time. The static portfolio consists of buying one stock (asset), financing the purchase price with a loan (liability) and holding this asset/ liability hedge portfolio until the forwards expiration date. In the absence of transaction costs the static buy-and-hold portfolio gives the same forward value development as the long position in the forward contract.

Equipped with this profound understanding of the initial and subsequent pricing of the stock forward contract the transformation of the OntoREA© PIM model into PSM models can be addressed. According to the chosen platform there are different possible

PSM models. In this article the popular MySQL database platform [12] is taken which specifies the *MySQL database model* as *MySQL PSM model*.

As in this article the focus lies on the transformation of the *Collective* conceptualization of derivative instruments, the *Collective* transformation from the OntoREA© PIM model into the MySQL PSM model is addressed now. The result of this transformation can be seen in Fig. 5. At the center is the *Derivative_Instrument* table. The relationships to its phases are the links to left side located tables for *Asset*, *Liability* and *Off_Balance*. To each table there is a 0..1 cardinality so that the derivative instrument can but must not be in each phase, and each table has the *Derivative_ID* as its primary and foreign key (pfK). The three phases of the derivative instruments are transformed into separate tables due to the phases' anti-rigidity. All three phase tables have the Boolean *Mark_to_Model* attribute specified as TINYINT data type in the MySQL PSM model. This attribute allows the switching between the representation of derivative instruments either in form of their hedge portfolio, i.e. the mark-to-model attribute is true, or in form of the portfolio's net value if the mark-to-model attribute is false. Furthermore the *Off_Balance* table does not contain the *Fair_Value* attribute like the *Asset* and *Liability* tables as its valueless property is automatically given whenever the net value of the hedge portfolio is neither positive nor negative.

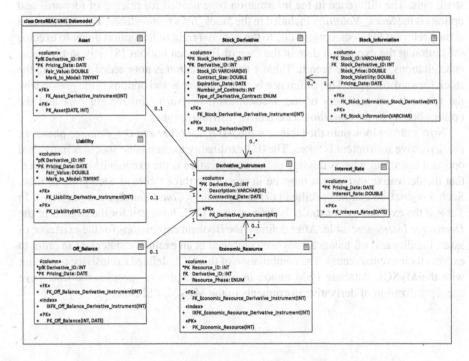

Fig. 5. Relational database model – MySQL database model (PSM)

Next to the relationships to the balance sheet phases of the *Derivative_Instrument* class, Fig. 5 also contains the relationship to the hedge portfolio. This relationship is set by the 0..1 cardinality to the *Economic_Resource* table so that one economic resource can but must not be associated with a derivative instrument. Furthermore this option is indicated by the missing * (NOT NULL CONSTRAINT) in the *Derivative_ID* foreign key (FK) attribute of the *Economic_Resource* table so that the relationship can be *Null*. On the other side of the relationship there are two economic resources assigned to the derivative instrument via the cardinality of 1..*. The two related economic resources are an asset as well as a liability position. To be precise, in the IFRS reporting standards not the hedge portfolio constituents but only the portfolio's net value is recognized in the balance sheet. Due to the rigid relationship of the hedge portfolio's constituting resources to their balance sheet phases, these resource phases are modeled via an enumeration with respect to asset, liability, equity and claim.

The final important point to mention in Fig. 5 relates to the specification of the derivative instrument. The concrete specification of stock derivatives can be seen by the relationship of the *Derivative_Instrument* table to the *Stock_Derivative* table. The cardinality of 0..1 says that derivate instruments can but must not be a stock derivative. On the other side each stock derivative is a derivative instrument. The stock derivative's main defining attributes are the *Contract_Size*, the *Expiration_Date* and the *Type_of_Derivative_Contract*. The inclusion of the contract type information allows the differentiation between stock forwards and stock options, e.g. in form of stock calls and stock puts. The difference in the information base needed for pricing of forwards and options is the *Stock_Volatility* included in the *Stock_Information* table. This information is only relevant for stock options due to the optional right of the option buyer to execute the option at the expiration date in the case of European options [8] only in favorable constellations. As can be seen in Table 1 this information is not needed for pricing the stock forward contract. This difference between forwards and options is the reason why the forwards are members of the *unconditional derivative instrument type* and the options belong to the *conditional derivative instrument type*.

Now a closer look onto the tables for the *Asset*, *Liability* and *Off_Balance* phases of the derivative instrument is taken. The 0..1 cardinality to each table specifies individual optional links. But what is missing in this specification is the exclusivity constraint, i.e. that the derivative instrument must be in one of the three tables at each point in time. Such a restriction can be specified [17] in the *Object Constraint Language* (OCL). In Table 2 the exclusivity constraint is defined as an OCL *invariant* for the *context* of the *Derivative Instrument* table. After defining the Boolean expressions for the existence of asset, liability and off balance, they are combined in an exclusive statement in order to express their exclusiveness. The combination of this OCL defined exclusivity constraint with the MySQL database PSM model in Fig. 5 completely specifies the *Collective* conceptualization of derivative instruments in the MySQL PSM model.

Table 2. OCL exclusivity constraint – MySQL database model (PSM)

```
Algorithm. OCL invariant for the exclusivity of derivative instrument phases in PSM

context d: Derivative_Instrument inv exclusivePhaseReferences :
def : assetExists : Boolean =
      Asset.allInstances()->exist (a|a.Derivative_ID = d.Derivative_ID)
def : liabilityExists : Boolean =
      Liability.allInstances()->exist (l|l.Derivative_ID _d = d.Derivative_ID)
def : offbalanceExists : Boolean =
      Off_Balance.allInstances()->exist (o|o.Derivative_ID _d = d.Derivative_ID)
(assetExists xor liabilityExists) xor offbalanceExists
```

After the OntoREA© PIM model is transformed into the MySQL PSM database model, the second transformation can be performed, i.e. the transformation from the MySQL PSM model into the RStudio Shiny dataframe ISM model. The dataframes in the ISM model are a composite data type in the R programming language that can contain several variables with different individual data types. Accordingly all tables in the MySQL PSM model can be represented as dataframes in the RStudio Shiny ISM model.

Figure 6 contains the RStudio Shiny dataframe ISM model which is visualized with the R package *datamodelr*. This model consists of 8 dataframes that have the same naming like the 8 tables in the MySQL PSM model. The dataframes of the three derivative instrument phases, i.e. *Asset*, *Liability* and *Off_Balance* have the foreign key (annotated by the tilde ~) as their primary key (annotated by its underlining). This corresponds to the primary foreign key (pfK) specification in the MySQL PSM model.

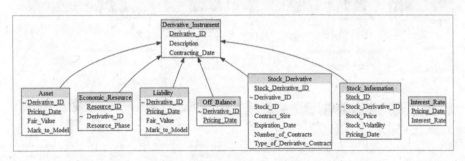

Fig. 6. Data.frame model – RStudio shiny data model (ISM)

The exclusivity constraint with respect to the three derivative instrument phases derived from the corresponding OCL constraint is specified as *switch function*. The switch exclusivity constraint is given in Table 3. The exclusive assignment to one phase at each point in time is given by the hedge portfolio's net value dependent specification of all phases as cases (case 1: positive net value -> asset; case 2: negative net value -> liability; case 3: else -> off balance) and the exclusiveness of the assignment within the switch function.

Table 3. Switch exclusivity constraint – RStudio shiny data model (ISM)

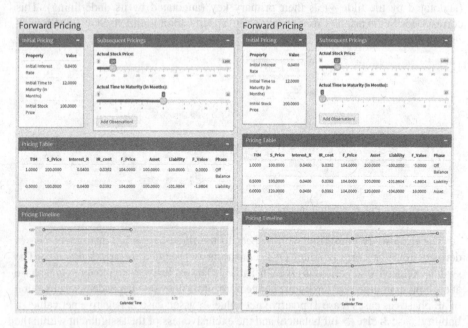

```
z <- function(n) {
  switch(n,
         '0' = "Liability",
         '1' = "Asset",
         '2' = "Off Balance")
}

F_Value <- c(0, -1.98,16)
F_Value_Categories <-
+ sapply(F_Value, function(y) if(y<0) '0'
+ else if (y>0) '1' else '2')
F_Phase <- sapply(F_Value_Categories,
+ function(y) z(y))
```

Switch Expression
F_Value

case= F_Value < 0 — Liability

case= F_Value > 0 — Asset

default — Off Balance

4   The OntoREA© Model: RStudio Shiny ISM-Based Application

The RStudio Shiny ISM dataframe model can easily be translated into an RStudio Shiny application (ISM-based application) as all dataframes in the RStudio Shiny ISM dataframe model (Fig. 6) and the switch exclusivity constraint for the three derivative instrument phases (Table 3) are already specified in the R programming language.

Fig. 7. Prototypical ISM-based application (Subsequent Pricings)

Figure 7 shows in the top left corner the user interface for the initial pricing of the *prototypical RStudio Shiny application* which is based upon the RStudio Shiny ISM dataframe model and which implements the switch exclusivity constraint. In the upper left panel the parameters for the initial pricing are specified, i.e. the initial interest rate of 4%, the initial time to maturity of 12 months and the initial stock price of 100. The resulting no-arbitrage forward price of 104 is shown in the middle of the lower panel. Furthermore this panel also shows the stock asset value of 100, the loan liability value of −100 and the resulting net value of the hedge portfolio amounting to zero. According to the switch function this corresponds to an off balance phase assignment of the stock forward at its contracting date.

Figure 7 shows the user interface for the subsequent pricing of the stock forward for two different dates. In both dates it is assumed that the initial interest rate did not change compared to its original level of 4%. So only the stock price and the time to maturity are changing over time. Their actual values are set with the sliders that are available in the subsequent pricing activity.

- The left hand side contains the input parameters and the results for the mid-term pricing at the end of June: The actual stock price is still 100 and the time to maturity reduced to 6 months. In this constellation the stock asset value is 100, the loan liability value is −101.98 and the resulting net value of the hedge portfolio amounts to −1.98. The negative portfolio value evaluated in the switch function gives a liability phase assignment of the stock forward.
- The right hand side contains the input parameters and the results for the final pricing at the end of December: The actual stock price rose to 120 and the time to maturity reduced to zero. In this constellation the stock asset value is 120, the loan liability value is −104 and the resulting net value of the hedge portfolio amounts to +16. The positive portfolio value evaluated in the switch function gives an asset phase assignment of the stock forward.

This prototypical ISM-based application illustrates the *stochastic modal temporal behavior* of forward contract which is captured in OntoREA© via the *Collective* OntoUML meta-property of derivative instruments.

Although only a stock forward contract is used in the running example, it has to be mentioned that the *Collective* conceptualization also holds for derivative instruments in form of options. Options are defined as follows: *Contracts that give the purchaser the right, but not the obligation, to buy (call option) or sell (put option) a specified quantity of a particular financial instrument, commodity, or foreign currency, at a specified price (strike price), during or at a specified period of time. These can be individually written or exchange-traded. The purchaser of the option pays the seller (writer) of the option a fee (premium) to compensate the seller for the risk of payments under the option* [5].

The no-arbitrage pricing theory also holds for options. For options a *dynamic hedge portfolio* exactly replicates (duplicates) the option value over time. In the dynamic hedging fractions of the stock are bought and they are partially financed by a loan liability. Over time the investment and financing has to be continuously adjusted according to the revealing stock prices. At the expiration date the hedge portfolio gives the same result as the initial buying an option contract.

5   Conclusions

The title of this article indicates a design science research methodological (DSRM) demonstration and evaluation [4] associated with the OntoREA© accounting and finance model. This investigation necessitates due to the missing real case usage and the missing adequacy evaluation in the original [1] OntoREA© artifact. By using a stock forward contract as running example the hedge portfolio meaning of the derivative instrument's *Collective* conceptualization with a *MemberOf* relationship to two *Economic Resources* was enlightened and illustrated with a real derivative instrument.

The *Collective* conceptualization served as starting point in the MDD's PIM model which was successively transformed in two steps into a MySQL PSM database model and an RStudio Shiny ISM dataframe model. The exclusivity constraint of the derivative instrument's asset, liability and off balance phases were specified in the OCL language for the MySQL PSM model and the switch function in the R programming language for the RStudio Shiny ISM model. The setup of the ISM model in the R programming language finally allowed a direct coding that resulted in a prototypical RStudio Shiny application.

Overall, the consistent usage of the *Collective* conceptualization in the MDD context and the real case demonstration of its appearance in the different model transformations demonstrate the conceptualization's usage required in the corresponding DSRM activity. The DSRM evaluation activity is performed by showing with the stock forward example that the derivative instruments are adequately represented with respect to their identity-related peculiarity, their temporal modal peculiarities in the asset liability and off-balance phases as well as the exclusivity constraint defined thereupon.

Summing up. The two research objectives are met as follows: By using a rolling example the OntoREA©'s *Collective* conceptualization of derivative instruments is presented in a numerical and easy-to-grasp manner. With the demonstrated usage and adequacy evaluation of the *Collective* conceptualization the second research objective is met. By fulfilling this objective the DSRM required real case usage demonstration and adequacy evaluation are provided which are missing in the most innovative part of the original OntoREA© artifact. Having provided this kind of DSRM validity evidence the next step should be a formal validation of the OntoREA© model for detecting possible misspecifications by performing e.g. a model simulation in the logic-based Alloy language.

References

1. Fischer-Pauzenberger, C., Schwaiger, W.S.A.: The OntoREA© Accounting and Finance Model: Ontological Conceptualization of the Accounting and Finance Domain. In: Proceedings of 36th International Conference on Conceptual Modeling, ER 2017, Valencia, Spain, 6–9 November 2017. LNCS. Springer, Heidelberg (2017, to appear)
2. Geerts, G.L., McCarthy, W.E.: Policy level specifications in REA enterprise information systems. J. Inf. Syst. **20**, 37–63 (2006)

3. Fischer-Pauzenberger, C., Schwaiger, W.S.: The OntoREA accounting model: ontology-based modeling of the accounting domain. Complex Syst. Inform. Model. Q. (11), 20–37 (2017)
4. Geerts, G.L.: A design science research methodology and its application to accounting information systems research. Int. J. Account. Inf. Syst. **12**, 142–151 (2011)
5. IFRS: international accounting standard 39 financial instruments: recognition and measurement. http://ec.europa.eu/internal_market/accounting/docs/consolidated/ias39_en.pdf
6. IAS 39—financial instruments: recognition and measurement. https://www.iasplus.com/en/standards/ias/ias39
7. Guizzardi, G.: Ontological Foundations for Structural Conceptual Model (2005). http://doc.utwente.nl/50826
8. Black, F., Scholes, M.: The pricing of options and corporate liabilities. J. Polit. Econ. **81**, 637 (1973)
9. Merton, R.C.: Theory of rational theory option pricing. Bell J. Econ. **4**, 141–183 (1973)
10. Cox, J.C., Ross, S.A., Rubinstein, M.: Option pricing: a simplified approach. J. Financ. Econ. **7**, 229–263 (1979)
11. Pastor, O., España, S., Panach, J.I., Aquino, N.: Model-driven development. Informatik-Spektrum **31**, 394–407 (2008)
12. Sparks, G.: Database modelling in UML. www.sparxsystems.com/downloads/whitepapers/Database_Modeling_In_UML.pdf
13. An introduction to R. https://cran.r-project.org/doc/manuals/r-release/R-intro.pdf
14. Hillebrand, J., Nierhoff, M.H.: Mastering RStudio–Develop, Communicate, and Collaborate with R. Packt Publishing Ltd., Birmingham (2015)
15. McCarthy, W.E.: The REA Accounting Model - A Generalized Framework for Accounting Systems in a Shared Data Environment (1982)
16. Guizzardi, G., Wagner, G., Almeida, J.P.A., Guizzardi, R.S.S.: Towards ontological foundations for conceptual modeling: the unified foundational ontology (UFO) story. Appl. Ontol. **10**, 259–271 (2015)
17. Rybola, Z., Pergl, R.: Towards OntoUML for software engineering: transformation of anti-rigid sortal types into relational databases. In: Bellatreche, L., Pastor, Ó., Almendros Jiménez, J.M., Aït-Ameur, Y. (eds.) MEDI 2016. LNCS, vol. 9893, pp. 1–15. Springer, Cham (2016). doi:10.1007/978-3-319-45547-1_1
18. Sales, T., Barcelos, P., Guizzardi, G.: Identification of semantic anti-patterns in ontology-driven conceptual modeling via visual simulation. In: 4th International Workshop on Ontology Information System (ODISE 2012), Graz, Austria (2012)
19. Ontology Project: UFO-A specification. http://ontology.com.br/ufo-a/spec/

Goals, Workflow, and Value: Case Study Experiences with Three Modeling Frameworks

Jennifer Horkoff[1,2]($\boxtimes$), Imed Hammouda[1,2,3], Juho Lindman[1],
Jamel Debbiche[1], Martina Freiholtz[1], Patrik Liao[1], Stephen Mensah[1],
and Aksel Strömberg[1]

[1] University of Gothenburg, Gothenburg, Sweden
imed.hammouda@cse.gu.se, juho.lindman@ait.gu.se
[2] Chalmers Institute of Technology, Gothenburg, Sweden
jenho@chalmers.se
[3] Mediterranean Institute of Technology,
South Mediterranean University, Tunis, Tunisia

Abstract. It is beneficial to understand the benefits and drawbacks of enterprise modeling approaches in certain contexts. We report experiences applying different combinations of three modeling approaches to industrial cases. Specifically, we report on experiences from four companies using a combination of goal modeling, e^3 value modeling, and workflow modeling. Our findings help to guide enterprise modeling approach selection in similar contexts, and can be used to make recommendations to improve future applications of the selected modeling approaches.

1 Introduction

A wide variety of modeling methods have been introduced in order to capture, visualize, and analyze various aspects of an enterprise. Although enterprise modeling can provide clear benefits, every modeling approach has its advantages and disadvantages. It is beneficial for the enterprise modeling community to better understand the factors which make a particular modeling approach more or less appropriate in a particular context. Such experiences can be gathered through application of one or modeling methods to case studies.

In this work we report experiences applying three modeling approaches to industrial cases conducted in the context of Bachelor/Master thesis work. From these experiences in this context, we report benefit and drawbacks of individual methods in practice, as well as comparative experiences between some methods. More specifically, we report on modeling results for four cases (companies) using three modeling notations: two cases conducted using goal modeling (iStar) [5], one case conducted using goal and e^3 value modeling [10], and one case conducted by a further group using goal and workflow modeling [7].

The case studies were conducted as part of a Chalmers Software Center project investigating strategic API design for software-intensive businesses.

Published by Springer International Publishing AG 2017. All Rights Reserved
G. Poels et al. (Eds.): PoEM 2017, LNBIP 305, pp. 96–111, 2017.
https://doi.org/10.1007/978-3-319-70241-4_7

We focus on practical experiences with the three modeling frameworks, reporting qualitative experiences in order to address the following research questions:

Q1. What are the benefits and drawbacks of applying each modeling approach in our industrial context?

Q2. How do experiences with goal modeling and workflow modeling compare?

Q3. How do experiences with goal modeling and value modeling compare?

This work makes several contributions: (1) Our results allow potential modelers conducting projects in similar contexts to weigh the benefits and drawbacks of enterprise modeling approaches, facilitating informed selection. (2) Our findings outline improvements for the evaluated modeling languages, giving method developers feedback for future work.

This paper is structured as follows. Section 2 gives background on the modeling approaches and the cases. Section 3 outlines the methodology followed by the groups, while Sect. 4 contains the main observations of our studies. We discuss results and validity threats in Sect. 5, related work in Sect. 6, and provide conclusions and outline future work in Sect. 7.

2   Background

2.1   Modeling Methods

We give a brief introduction to the modeling techniques applied in our cases.

Goal Modeling. The cases used the iStar goal modeling framework, based on the recent iStar 2.0 Standard [5] consolidating versions of i* originating from [22]. Although we use iStar, we believe our observations would apply to qualitative versions of similar goal modeling languages (e.g., GRL or Tropos).

In iStar, goals are defined as objectives which the system should achieve through different tasks and dependencies on other actors [5]. Goal models include qualities, goals which are achieved or denied via positive or negative contribution links (e.g., helps, hurts). The model shows a hierarchy of goals assigned to actors, tracking the high-level goals of the system to low-level tasks, resources, or to dependencies on other actors. See Fig. 1 for example resulting goal models.

Workflow Modeling. Workflow refers to actions, a sequence of activities, or tasks set in a certain order enabling a system to serve its purpose [7]. The workflow focuses on the use of entities (e.g. actors and activities) to explain the sequence of operation or work procedures. In this study UML activity diagrams (with swimlanes for actors) are used to model the workflows of interest.

Value Modeling. The e^3 value model has been developed to identify the exchange of value objects between different actors in a business network [10]. Value objects can represent a service, right or a quality attribute. Value models include actors, value objects which belong to at least one actor, value ports with value interfaces which are used by actors to exchange values, and value activities, which are the activities the actor must do in order to deliver the value object. In the case we used e^3 models as per [10].

2.2   Research Context: Project and Company

The purpose of the ongoing project is to explore techniques for strategic API design, viewing APIs as a means to protect and expose business aspects. The Chalmers Software Center project works in six-month sprints, and has completed its second sprint focusing on API analysis and design [1]. This paper reports results from the most recent sprint, applying three enterprise modeling techniques to the elicitation and analysis of API designs for four companies. We leave reporting of API insights to future work, focusing on modeling observations. Although all companies were dealing with high-level API design challenges, each company was interested in particular analysis questions, leading us to choose differing modeling methods for each case (see API Challenges and Modeling Approaches in Table 1). All companies were interested in mapping their API ecosystem(s); given the existing work using goal models for ecosystem mapping (e.g., [20]), we applied goal models in each case. Company C3 was particularly interested in Workflow modeling, while C4 wanted to explore API value.

We summarize each company and their interests in Table 1, keeping identities anonymous. Each of the four companies are large (minimum 2000+ employees), with headquarters in Scandinavia and operations worldwide. The companies develop products and systems that include software, hardware, and mechanical components. For some companies, we modelled API systems which were in place or in development, in other cases the API framework was in the planning stages.

Table 1. Summary of cases for each company

Company	Sector	Country	API maturity	API challenges	Modeling approaches	Group
C1	Communications	Sweden	Partial	Mapping API ecosystems	iStar	G1 [6]
C2	Packaging	Sweden	Planning	Planning incremental API development	iStar	G1 [6]
C3	Manufacturing	Denmark	Partial	Workflow bottlenecks, evaluating API design plans	Workflow modeling, iStar	G2 [4]
C4	Telecommunications	Sweden	Complete	Understanding API value, motivations	Value modeling, iStar	G3 [18]

In terms of modeling background, company participants had a technical background and were generally familiar with modeling, including workflow modeling, but were not familiar with goal or value modeling. The students involved were senior students in a Software Engineering Bachelor or Masters (3rd or 5th years students) who had been introduced to UML modeling as part of their education, but also did not have explicit experience with goal or value modeling. G1 and G2 consisted of 3 Bachelor students, while G3 had two Masters students.

3 Methodology

We summarize the elicitation and modeling methodology of each of the three groups. More information (can be found in the full theses [4,6,18].

Elicitation Modeling. Each of the three research groups conducted a series of group and individual workshops and interviews in order to collect qualitative data to facilitate modeling. G1 and G2 conducted workshops with each company at the company location, as well as follow-up online interviews. The general elicitation process can be summarized as follows:

1. **Introductory Group Interview:** Necessary to understand the API ecosystem of the companies.
2. **Off-site Modeling:** Using available context knowledge and the scenario of focus (user story) to create initial model versions.
3. **Interactive Workshop:** Starting with the initial models, expand and correct the models interactively using group input.
4. **Follow-up Online Interview(s):** Finalize data collection and fill gaps discovered while modeling. Discussed experiences with modeling approaches.
5. **Dissemination Workshop:** Summarizing modeling and analysis results in a workshop with all company representatives present.

Workshops had 3–6 company participants including roles such as developer engineers, development managers, software engineers, product managers, and expert engineers. Online interviews were conducted with individual representatives from each company, who had been present in the workshops. Workshops lasted about three hours, while individual interviews were typically one hour.

G3 also conducted an introductory group interview and off-site modeling with C4, but gathered further data with individual semi-structured interviews and a survey, selecting participants involved in the API Framework (FW). Ten interviews and two surveys were conducted with the same questions, interviews lasting 45 min. G3 also had access to archival data concerning the FW.

Information gathered from workshops and interviews, including a selection of technical documentation, was used to create models. It was agreed with the companies that the first round of modeling should focus on a particular scenario or user story, to keep the scope of the models in check. Each group attempted to classify their resulting goal models in terms of a layered API architecture developed as part of the ongoing project (containing the Business Asset, API, SW App, and Domain Layers). The modeling process was iterative, with the students receiving iterative feedback from someone knowledgeable in the modeling approaches (the first author) and the company contacts.

G1 used goal model element colors as a means to indicate which elements were problematic, or which solved problems. In contrast, G2 had time to make explicit use of systematic qualitative goal model analysis to find issues in the current or planned design captured in the model [16]. In this analysis, each goal and softgoal in the model is given a label showing its satisfaction level, which is dependant on how the tasks in the model contribute to each goal.

Tooling. G1 and G3 used Microsoft Visio with appropriate stencils to make the iStar and Value models. G2 used Visual Paradigm to draw the workflow models. G2 drew iStar models in Creative Leaf [15], a free online iStar modelling tool, and OpenOME [17], an Eclipse-based open-source i* tool.

Model Validation. For G1 and G2 model creation was iterative and continuous, with workshops and interviews presenting and receiving feedback on the models. G3 explicitly used member checking to improve the accuracy, credibility and validity of the collected data [13]. Four new interviews were scheduled with previous participants, each lasting around an hour, during which G3 described and went through the models step by step, receiving feedback.

Feedback and general impressions on the process and modeling approaches were collected mainly by the students, via recorded interviews. Interviews were transcribed and feedback was coded to provide input to the theses.

4   Modeling in Practice: Observations and Comparisons

In this section we report the qualitative observations encountered by the three groups when using the modeling techniques in practice. As we used goal modeling in all four companies, but workflow and value modeling in only one company, we have more data to report on goal modeling. Figure 1 shows simplified goal models resulting from G1 for C2, showing the transition from the current to distant future and the use of colors to highlight issues (red) and solutions (blue). Here we can see the goal model divided into the API layers. The actual resulting goal models had 50+ elements, the workflow models had 10+ activities, while the value model had 20+ value exchanges. Further example models, including workflow and value models, can be found in the theses [4,6,18].

We report observations mainly from the viewpoint of the student groups conducting the modeling (G1, G2, and G3), but also observations and impressions from the company representatives, and occasionally the group supervisors.

4.1   Goal Modeling

General Impressions. G2 observed that goal models captured the dependencies between actors in the API ecosystem and this provided valuable information to the company. G3 noted that while the goal models were initially perceived as difficult to read by the company representative, the details in these models got a positive response in later member checking validation. While the main purpose of the validation was to validate the data itself, the model was perceived as easy to understand quickly and displayed the relevant information clearly.

G1 noted advantages of capturing an API ecosystem in goal models rather than text, with a C2 representative noting *"It is a big advantage that this is an image and not text... I see a lot of advantages with this"*. A participant from C1 noted the benefits of having a high-level graphical overview. *"benefits and strength (of goal modeling) is definitely giving the overview understanding... it is good that it combines all the elements so you can see the connection in the*

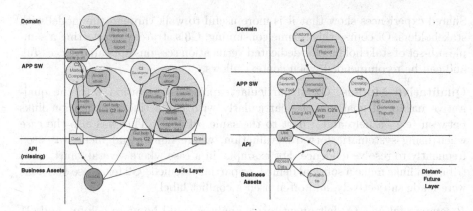

Fig. 1. Simplified version of current and distant future for C2 (Color figure online)

big picture". The same participant confirmed the benefits of graphics over text *"Once you get the goal modeling syntax, you understand all of this, otherwise you will have to use and write a lot of text to explain the same thing"*.

One could argue that this observation – the benefits of graphics over text – is common to all models. Still, it is useful to confirm this result, particularly for goal modeling, showing that the model size and complexity does not cancel out the benefits of graphical visualization.

Recommendations. Goal models can initially be overwhelming, but with time and knowledge of the syntax, can provide a rich way to capture strategic data. Their selection should depend on the level and depth of modeling in a particular case: they are likely not appropriate for "light" or quick modeling, but more appropriate for cases where more extensive modeling can take place.

Validation. G1 and G2 went through a process of iterative validation, where models and associated questions (gaps) were sent via email to company representations, and feedback was received during online meetings. These groups noted difficulties in getting company time in order to validate the model, due to the time and resource constraints of the companies. G1 further noted that the syntax of the models had to be re-introduced with every discussion. Nevertheless, these groups did receive feedback which results in changes to the models; however, most of the feedback was not framed in model terms, leaving the groups to interpret them in terms of the model.

G3 had a more specific validation stage, selecting a subset of C4 representatives for model member checking, walking the participant through the model. In this case, participants generally agreed with the goal model. Participants were engaged enough to make a few corrections, adding a few goals, softgoals, and tasks, changing the responsibility for some tasks, and adding two new actors.

Recommendations. We observe that although model validation is generally possible, letting stakeholders look through the model on their own is likely not fruitful.

Shared experiences show that it is more useful to walk through the model with stakeholders. Of course this is time consuming, G3's strategy of selecting a sample sub-set of stakeholders for dedicated verification sessions appeared successful, and can be recommended when context allows.

Qualitative Models. G2 in particular expressed frustration with the qualitative nature of goal models, particularly with conflicting contribution links between (e.g., a help and a hurt to the same softgoal). This was also the case when using systematic forward evaluation, where human judgment was used frequently to resolve evidence. For example, in a case where several "hurt" contribution links make a softgoal denied, or partially denied? G2 felt these decisions were made subjectively, and often used a conflict label.

Recommendations. G2 felt quantitative analysis could be more helpful, and G1 made a similar recommendation. Goal modeling should support quantitative data and analysis whenever possible.

Layers Views. The groups reported experiences dividing the goal model into API layers. Overall, G1 and G2 found that using the layered API framework with the goal model increased the readability of the models. G2 noted that structuring the actors into clearly defined layers made them easier to locate, both while communicating about the models and during the modeling. G1 agreed, the C2 contact also provided positive feedback on the layers, with a C1 representative adding *"It is much more useful to make it layered... otherwise it just gets, it's just a big spiderweb that you look at and think that it is too much."*.

However, G2 noted that layers limit the placement of dependency- and contribution links, particularly when there are many links between the top and bottom layers. G1 noted a further limitation in that the reader must understand the purpose of each layer, requiring additional training or explanation.

G2 found that it was not always obvious where in the layered API framework a specific actor belongs, this often depended on perspective. In fact, G1 created different layer configurations for different perspectives. G1 had some initial negative experiences mapping actors to layers in the initial stages, when their understanding of the domains was incomplete.

In addition to using layers, G1 dealt with the complexity of their models using views, sub-sets of the models captured in separate files, receiving positive feedback from the company contacts. However, G1 noted that the larger context of the entire API ecosystem must be considered – the views cannot replace this model. The C1 representative noted *"I think that whatever comes up in those discussions needs to go in there. Because some of them will prove that you have some connections that might show up to be problematic."*.

Recommendations. Layers and views are helpful for managing and highlighting key points on large and complex goal models. However, each layer must have a clear semantic meaning, communicated to participants; layers should be added in later stages, when domain knowledge is more complete; and, modelers should be aware that placement of an actor in a layer may change depending on perspective. Views cannot replace the full complexity of the model.

Complexity and Completeness. When it comes to the complexity of the goal models, C1 and C2 provided similar feedback, stating that it is both a strength and a weakness. One participant stated *"... it becomes messy and complex and I don't know in terms of complexity what the upper limit is"*. Participants also noted that knowledge was cumulative, based on past sessions, *"... for those who haven't been in discussion of the layers, it would be hard to discuss the business assets and APP SW as separate layers"*.

G1 noted that modeling with the companies helped trigger discussions revealing information that was not available in the documents received. However, G1 also noted that it was difficult to determine when the model should be considered complete. As the companies cooperate in the modeling process, new gaps were identified and the modeling continued iteratively. A C3 participant stated *"There is all the information here, but it is a little bit messy"*.

As they iterated over the models, G2 found that they had to make decisions based on a trade-off between completeness and simplicity. The models should be complete enough to be useful for analysis. As the group added more actors and elements to the model, the models became more difficult to understand, which had a negative impact on the effectiveness of the model.

The groups noted the presence of a goal model learning curve, a C2 participant explained *"it is hard to understand for people who don't know goal modeling"*. G1 noted that they had to continuously share a document reminding the stakeholders of the syntax of goal modeling and explanation of the different layers used. The participants for G2's case made the point that differing levels of understanding were needed depending on the level of involvement in modeling. However, a C3 participant stated *"I wouldn't say I feel that is any harder than some other modeling languages."*.

Recommendations. Some complexity is unavoidable. One recommendation is to create an initial large model which covers much of the domain, then remove actors not involved in the analysis. The learning curve can be mitigated with training, and the level of training can vary depending on participation.

Scope. G2 noted that they limited the scope of the goal models by excluding actors which are judged to be unrelated to the changes implemented in the to-be model. Both G1 and G2 focused their early modeling efforts on a particular use case or scenario provided by the companies, while G3 focused only on modeling the existing FW. This early material was necessary to help the groups focus and start modeling, but the later modeling diverged from this initial scope. In the case of C1, the scenario description was quite brief, and the resulting model was relatively small, resulting in a significant expansion of the model in the interactive workshop. In the case of C2, the initial user stories were long and detailed, resulting in relatively large starting models, much of which was removed or changed as a result of in later scoping discussions.

Recommendations. Setting an initial scope for modeling is essential, starting the scoped modeling process from an existing use case or scenario, ideally documented, is also a good practice. However, it may be better to limit the size of this starting point, to avoid modeling effort which is deemed out of scope, and to make it easier for participants to understand and contribute to the model.

Methodology. G1 commenting on the lack of explicit methodology for iStar. Although some methods exist (e.g., [16]), there is no one established method purported by the iStar 2.0 standard. G1 recommends the method in Sect. 3 as a starting point for those working with goal models in an industrial project.

Recommendations. Experiences in this study indicate that a general goal modeling method is needed.

Highlighting and Analysis. G1 used element coloring to show problematic and "fixed" model elements. This helped to show the improvements and transitions through planned API deployment in the C2 case. In the C1 case, where time transition was not emphasized, the colors were less helpful. The goal modeling expert/supervisor noted that the colors did not always reflect the semantics of the model. For example, an element would be marked by the group as red, when the incoming contribution links were all positive (help). G2 used systematic goal model analysis (i.e., [16] with some success. They were able to use the analysis to find unfulfilled softgoals, which helped them to ask relevant questions and enabled them start thinking about ways to resolve unfulfilled elements.

Recommendations. We avoided introducing systematic evaluation for G1 mainly to avoid overwhelming them with detail (they were covering an additional case compared to the other groups). In retrospect, it seems this analysis was generally usable by the G2, and in fact G1 came up with their own, less systematic and less semantically consistent method to make similar points using the models. Given these experiences, we can recommend the user of systematic analysis for student modelers conducting case studies.

Interactive Modeling. G1 conducted explicit interactive modeling sessions with two companies (G3 did offline modeling, while G2 used their second workshop to iterate over their current models with one company representative). G1 noted that every participant adds their own insight and perspective, and the goal model can quickly drift away from the original scope. This was apparent during the C1 workshop where questions like "is this relevant to the API ecosystem?" or "is this considered inside the scope of the API ecosystem?" were frequently asked. However, company participant expressed support of the interactive workshop *"... it is good if there is some kind of workshop and brainstorm and everyone knows the syntax and then build them together."*.

Recommendations. Interactive workshops build model content, stakeholder investment and familiarity with the model. However, participants should be given initial training, and care should be taken to direct and focus the discussion.

Tooling. When selecting a goal modeling tool, G1 and G3 used Microsoft Visio, in part because it is a stable commercial tool, but also because it allows flexibility in terms of syntax and notation, e.g., element colors and splitting the model into layers. G2 had trouble acquiring an academic license for Visio. They started with the Create Leaf online tool, but eventually moved to the desktop Eclipse-based OpenOME tool. They did so because they felt their increasingly larger models were more visually pleasing in OpenOME.

Recommendations. iStar-specific tools should allow more flexibility in terms of what can be drawn. Care should be taken for the visual appearance of models.

4.2   Workflow Modeling

General Impressions. G2 felt that the workflow models were important tools for the researchers to understand and get an overview of the current and planned workflow. The models effectively communicated how different actors in the API ecosystem interact. However, they were not frequently used in the analysis of the ecosystem once the workflow was understood by the researchers. The aspects captured by the models did not provide new insight for the case company, i.e., they only modelled what was already known.

Recommendations. Workflow models are useful in early project stages to understand actor interaction, particularly for analysts to confirm their domain understanding.

Layering. G2 attempted to apply the API layers to the workflow models as well as the goal models, but had difficulties. They considered using swimlane notation for layers, but this would conflict with their use of swimlanes for actors.

Recommendations. Instead of graphical layers, one could try other visual indicators, like colors, for adding layers to workflow models. Else it seems the structure of workflows are less amenable to classification and layering of elements.

Analysis. G2 did not perform any sort of systematic analysis on their workflow models, e.g., model checking [7]. This was mainly due to: (1) the learning curve and tool support barriers for bachelor students to understand and apply this type of analysis, and (2) difficulty to get the specific historical or constraint information needed for such analysis from C3.

G2 did note a desire to capture action duration (the time it takes to complete an action) in their workflow models, in order to support an analysis of potential bottlenecks. They believe that the ability to tell at a glance where the time is spent would assist in the development of an improved workflow. Generally, approaches to address duration or time in workflow BPMN models do exist (e.g., [9]), but again, these approaches are difficult to apply without great effort in the context of an industrial bachelor thesis.

Recommendations. Formal or quantitative workflow analysis should be more accessible, particularly via tools. An easy way to capture task duration is needed.

Workflow vs. Goal Modeling Generally, the use of workflow and goal models together provided analysis value, representing two different ways to look at the same thing (the ecosystem in terms of goal fulfillment and the ecosystem in terms of activities). The use of workflow models in addition to the goal models made it possible to gain an initial understanding of the underlying process of profile (/API) development of the company.

As mentioned in Sect. 3, G2 was able to exploit the links between workflow and goal models. Although this link can be exploited in either direction G3 chose to start with workflow models and use them to help create goal models, inspired by existing work [21]. Specifically, tasks in the goal models correspond to the actions in the process models, and the actors in the goal models are represented as swimlanes in the process models. They also used these links to help maintain consistency between the models. G2 notes that in order to exploit these links, the vocabulary between the models must remain consistent.

G2 notes that more focus was put into the workflow models at the start of the elicitation. These models worked largely as an initial one-way communication tool between the company representative and the researchers: G3 verified their understanding of the workflow by asking for feedback. During the latter half of the study, most of the attention of the group of researchers and the company went to the goal models. The natural tendency within the study was to use the two types of models sequentially rather than together. According to G2, once the goal models had been finalized, the process models did not offer much valuable information for the analysis of the company's API ecosystem.

Although iStar is not designed to be temporal, G2 noted that it was easier to represent time constraints in goal models using softgoals such as "fast documentation" and "fast approval". Furthermore, G2 noted that goal models were able to imply a temporal ordering, even though this is not explicitly part of the language. For example, the necessary sequence of actions can be implied with dependencies, if A depends on B, B must be done before A.

Recommendations. Tooling should exploit the links between the two types of models, helping modelers to keep the vocabulary and models consistent, and partially auto-generating one model from the other. Our experiences showed that workflow models were more useful at the beginning of the elicitation and analysis process, as the researchers were trying to get a handle on basic domain flows, while goal modeling was more useful later in the process, when domain understanding had increased. Inferring temporal information from goal models as is may be problematic, as this information may be interpreted differently by different modelers. However, if this implicit ordering can be clarified, standardized, and made consistent with workflow models, particularly with tool support, this can further enhance the use of goal and workflow models together.

4.3 Value Modeling

General Impressions. G3 did not explicitly ask for feedback about the models from C4 company representatives; nevertheless, while member checking the model, they received some feedback. Generally, the feedback during the member checking process was positive. While the main purpose of the validation was to validate the data itself, the models were perceived as easy to understand quickly and displayed the relevant information clearly.

Value vs. Goal Modeling. G3 reports that their industrial supervisors initially liked the value model more than the goal model. However, this model was presented in a shorter status update meetings, where they did not go through the goal model in a step-by-step manner. As the value model is more straight forward and smaller, G3 found that they needed less time presenting it to make someone grasp the model, compared to a goal model.

G3 used the goal model as a means to compliment the value model: the goal model visualized the identified challenges and values and maps them to the relevant actors. Tasks or lack of tasks can show why these challenges and values exist. G3 made an explicit link between the actors in the goal and value models, but did not explicitly link values to any iStar elements. Overall, G3 found that applying e[3] value modeling did not find new information compared to analysis of the goal model, it only presented the values gained in a more direct and abstract manner. The value model can serve as a quick visualization of which stakeholders gain what value, but it does not explain why or how they gain value.

Recommendations. Value and goal modeling can be seen to be complementary, with value models showing a simpler, more understandable view of actors and value exchanges. However, goal models were more effective at assigning values to actors, and to capturing the "why" for values, although this comes with a complexity price. As with workflow models, tooling could better support the link between goal and value models, linking actors to actors, and mapping values to one or more iStar elements.

5   Discussion

We can summarize our results to answer **Q1–3**. In terms of benefits and drawbacks of industrial application (**Q1**) goal models were found difficult to understand at the beginning of a project, with a significant learning curve. However, the longer-term results and impressions were more positive. Goal model validation is possible, but time consuming. The models are complicated and capture much information, this is both a drawback, and a strength, as capturing the same magnitude of information with text would be daunting. The groups saw the qualitative nature of goal models as a drawback, even though it is unclear how easy it would have been to gather quantitative data in the cases. The groups complained about the lack of explicit method for goal modeling. Our results show that systematic evaluation for goal models is an advantage, but that goal model tooling can still be improved. Interactive group modeling is possible, but only with attention to focus and participant training.

Workflow models were helpful at the start of the project to clarify actors and flows, but the group found they were missing specific duration information, and could not easily apply any analysis to find or show bottlenecks. Value modeling was initially quite easy to understand, and helpful as a summary view.

Comparing goal to workflow modeling (**Q2**), our evidence supports the idea that these models are complementary. Workflow models clearly show process, which is only informally implied in the goal models. However, workflow models were not as helpful in analysis, and proved more useful later in the project. Similar results were found for value models (**Q3**), they were initially helpful as they were easily understood, and were seen as a helpful summary view as compared to the goal models; however, the goal models were seen as more helpful for analysis, with the value models not providing any new insights.

Our experiences lead to a number recommendations. Goal modeling is useful for projects with sufficient modeler and stakeholder time, for a deeper analysis of motivations. For shorter projects where motivation or dependencies are understood, this type of modeling is less applicable, while value and workflow models could be appropriate. Workflow analysis would be improved by the ability to easily capture task duration and by more accessible analysis techniques. When there is sufficient time or need, the combination of these types of models is beneficial in practice. Available tools, which are accessible to students and case-study-ready, should better support links between these types of models, supporting consistency checks and partial derivations.

Threats to Validity. In terms of *Construct Validity*, it is possible that the student modelers and the company representatives misunderstood the syntax or semantics of goal, workflow, or value models. We mitigated this threat by giving an overview of the modeling language or the models themselves at multiple points in the study. In particular, we note that G3 did not use the calculations available with e^3 value modeling (e.g., [10]); however, collecting cost measures for an internal API framework would have been challenging.

Considering *Internal Validity*, all groups used some form of triangulation, collecting data from workshops, documents, archival data, and interviews. For C1, C2 and C3, validation rounds after the interactive workshop only involved one person per company. However, we mitigate this effect by collecting impressions from more than four people from four different companies in different areas.

Examining *External Validity*, all case companies are located in Scandinavia; however, these companies are large and international. Applying the same modeling process to different companies with different challenges, different workshop participants, and different validation stakeholders may produce differing observations. However, we mitigate this possibility by involving a number of people from four different companies. The focus on strategic API modeling may bias results; however, we feel it was useful to focus on a concrete challenge and problem within each case. In a different case with more complicated or varied workflows, workflow modeling may have been perceived as more useful.

Finally, considering *Reliability*, our study had the participation of a goal model expert, a co-author of the recent iStar 2.0 guide. For demonstration purposes she made one of the first versions of the model for one of the user stories provided by C2. The other user story and all other models in the studies were created by the students. The students received feedback on goal model syntax and semantic issues, but most changes were on the small-scale, e.g., wrong link direction, wrong element choice, etc. The majority of the detailed impressions of the models and modeling experience were elicited by the students from the company directly, with little participation of the supervisors. The students and company representatives report both benefits and drawbacks of goal modeling, and most of the data reported in this work is from their perspective.

6   Related Work

Goal Models. Existing work has reported experiences with goal models in practice, for example the iStar Showcase [2] contains summaries of a number of case studies using goal modeling, a number of which mention scalability, complexity, and learning curve as iStar issues. Our experiences confirm these findings; however, we are able to give further recommendations for improvements based on our experiences, without significantly extending and complicating the language.

Earlier work from Estrada et al. [8], applying iStar in industry, find that it is expressive and applicable to the domain, but does not well support modularity, scalability, or complexity management. We find the same issues, but work towards modularity solutions with our practical experiences in layers and views.

Goal and Workflow Models. Work exists evaluating workflow models, although it seems much of this work focuses on controlled experiments (e.g., [19]), or on evaluating a specific aspect (e.g., configurability [12]).

Much work has looked at goal models and some form of workflow model (process, BPMN) together, typically with a focus on methods which map or transform elements from one model to the other (see [14] for a recent survey on goal model mappings/transformations). Few papers report practical experiences with basic workflow models, [14] reports that 92% of the papers found were (technical) solution papers, with evaluation focusing on new solutions.

G2 were particularly inspired by de la Vara et al. [21], who provide guidelines on deriving goal models from process models. This derivation method has been used to achieve consistency between the goal and workflow models in our study.

Goal and Value Models. Horkoff et al. find six papers using goal models with value models [14]. Most of these papers introduce rules, mapping, and methods to explicitly link goal and value models (e.g., [3]). G3 did not explicitly use any of these approaches, mainly as an evaluation of these methods was not the focus of their thesis. Work by Gordijn et al. links goals and e^3 value model, making deeper use of their connections for iterative modeling than G3 did in their case [11]. This is due in part on G3's focus, on analyzing benefits and drawbacks of the C4 FW, and not explicitly on evaluating the models.

7   Conclusions and Future Work

We have presented experiences applying three different modeling languages to analyze strategic API development for four case companies. Our experiences can help enterprise modelers to choose between the modeling languages, depending on their analysis needs, expertise, the depth of the required study, and the time available. We also provide feedback for improving the language, methods, and tools associated with these approaches, with an emphasis on goal modeling. Future work should implement and evaluate our recommendations.

Overall, feedback from the case companies given at the final cross-company workshop was positive, with the modeling providing sufficient insights on strategic API ecosystem development. Although positive feedback was collected for the goal and workflow models, the companies are particularly interested in ensuring API value and having high-level summary models. Thus the next sprint will focus on modeling and measuring value.

Acknowledgments. Thanks to company contacts and the Chalmers Software Center for support.

References

1. Chalmers Software Center. https://www.software-center.se/
2. iStar Showcase'11: Exploring the goals of your systems and businesses, practical experiences with i* modeling. http://www.cs.toronto.edu/km/istar/iStarShowcase_Proceedings.pdf
3. Andersson, B., Johannesson, P., Zdravkovic, J.: Aligning goals and services through goal and business modelling. Inf. Syst. e-Business Manag. **7**(2), 143–169 (2009)
4. Bedru, F., Freiholtz, M., Mensah, S.: An empirical investigation of the use of goal and process modelling to analyze API ecosystem design and usage workflow. Bachelor thesis (2017). http://hdl.handle.net/2077/52648
5. Dalpiaz, F., Franch, X., Horkoff, J.: iStar 2.0 language guide. arXiv preprint arXiv:1605.07767 (2016)
6. Debbiche, J.: Str Applying goal modeling to API ecosystems: a cross-company case study. Bachelor thesis (2017)
7. Eshuis, R., Wieringa, R.: A formal semantics for UML activity diagrams-formalising workflow models (2001)
8. Estrada, H., Rebollar, A.M., Pastor, O., Mylopoulos, J.: An empirical evaluation of the i* framework in a model-based software generation environment. In: Dubois, E., Pohl, K. (eds.) CAiSE 2006. LNCS, vol. 4001, pp. 513–527. Springer, Heidelberg (2006). doi:10.1007/11767138_34
9. Friedenstab, J.P., Janiesch, C., Matzner, M., Muller, O.: Extending BPMN for business activity monitoring. In: HICSS, pp. 4158–4167. IEEE (2012)
10. Gordijn, J., Akkermans, H., Van Vliet, J.: Designing and evaluating e-Business models. IEEE Intell. Syst. **16**(4), 11–17 (2001)
11. Gordijn, J., Petit, M., Wieringa, R.: Understanding business strategies of networked value constellations using goal-and value modeling. In: 14th IEEE International Conference on Requirements Engineering, pp. 129–138. IEEE (2006)
12. Gottschalk, F., Wagemakers, T.A.C., Jansen-Vullers, M.H., Aalst, W.M.P., Rosa, M.: Configurable process models: experiences from a municipality case study. In: Eck, P., Gordijn, J., Wieringa, R. (eds.) CAiSE 2009. LNCS, vol. 5565, pp. 486–500. Springer, Heidelberg (2009). doi:10.1007/978-3-642-02144-2_38
13. Harper, M., Cole, P.: Member checking: can benefits be gained similar to group therapy? Qual. Rep. **17**(2), 510–517 (2012)
14. Horkoff, J., Li, T., Li, F.L., Salnitri, M., Cardoso, E., Giorgini, P., Mylopoulos, J.: Using goal models downstream: a systematic roadmap and literature review. IJISMD **6**(2), 1–42 (2015)

15. Horkoff, J., Maiden, N.A.: Creative leaf: a creative iStar modeling tool. In: iStar, pp. 25–30 (2016)
16. Horkoff, J., Yu, E.: Evaluating goal achievement in enterprise modeling – an interactive procedure and experiences. In: Persson, A., Stirna, J. (eds.) PoEM 2009. LNBIP, vol. 39, pp. 145–160. Springer, Heidelberg (2009). doi:10.1007/978-3-642-05352-8_12
17. Horkoff, J., Yu, Y., Eric, S.: OpenOME: an open-source goal and agent-oriented model drawing and analysis tool. iStar **766**, 154–156 (2011)
18. Hussein, M., Lundén, A.: An industrial assessment of software framework design: a case study of a rule-based framework. Master's thesis (2017). https://tinyurl.com/y9td34v6
19. Moody, D.L., Sindre, G., Brasethvik, T., Sølvberg, A.: Evaluating the quality of process models: empirical testing of a quality framework. In: Spaccapietra, S., March, S.T., Kambayashi, Y. (eds.) ER 2002. LNCS, vol. 2503, pp. 380–396. Springer, Heidelberg (2002). doi:10.1007/3-540-45816-6_36
20. Sadi, M.H., Yu, E.: Modeling and analyzing openness trade-offs in software platforms: a goal-oriented approach. In: Grünbacher, P., Perini, A. (eds.) REFSQ 2017. LNCS, vol. 10153, pp. 33–49. Springer, Cham (2017). doi:10.1007/978-3-319-54045-0_3
21. de la Vara, J.L., Sánchez, J., Pastor, O.: On the use of goal models and business process models for elicitation of system requirements. In: Nurcan, S., Proper, H.A., Soffer, P., Krogstie, J., Schmidt, R., Halpin, T., Bider, I. (eds.) BPMDS/EMMSAD-2013. LNBIP, vol. 147, pp. 168–183. Springer, Heidelberg (2013). doi:10.1007/978-3-642-38484-4_13
22. Yu, E.S.: Towards modelling and reasoning support for early-phase requirements engineering. In: RE, pp. 226–235. IEEE (1997)

An Evaluation Framework for Design-Time Context-Adaptation of Process Modelling Languages

Jing Hu, Ghazaleh Aghakhani, Faruk Hasić[(⊠)],
and Estefanía Serral[(⊠)]

Leuven Institute for Research on Information Systems (LIRIS),
KU Leuven, Leuven, Belgium
{jing.hu,ghazaleh.aghakhani}@student.kuleuven.be,
{faruk.hasic,estefania.serralasensio}@kuleuven.be

Abstract. To enhance the performance and efficiency of business processes, it is essential to take the dynamics of their execution context into account during process modelling. This paper first proposes an evaluation framework that identifies the main requirements for supporting the modelling of context-adaptive processes. Using this framework, we analyse four popular business process modelling languages: Coloured Petri Nets (CPN), Business Process Modelling and Notation 2.0 (BPMN), Yet Another Workflow Language (YAWL), and Unified Modelling Language Activity Diagrams (UML AD). The analysis is carried out by evaluating how the respective language notations fulfil the identified requirements in several real-life scenarios. Lastly, a comparative analysis of the languages focussed on their support for modelling context-adaptive business processes is provided.

Keywords: Context adaptation · Business process modelling · Process notation

1 Introduction

The central focus of business processes is on the way the activities are performed within an organization. The modelling of business processes has the goal of mapping the current process of the organization ("as-is") to the future process ("to-be"). Successful modelling eventually leads to favourable results in Business Process Management (BPM), which incorporates the improvements. Therefore, business process modelling is the most critical step in the BPM lifecycle [1, 2].

Essentially, a business process is designed to achieve certain objectives and goals. Nevertheless, it may fail to do so due to the divergence caused by the dynamic changes and unexpected events during the lifetime of the business process [3]. Being unable to adapt accordingly to the ever-changing business environment results in a high failure rate of BPM projects [4]. To tackle this problem, [5] suggests that one of the critical principles for success is the principle of context adaptation, which means the practitioners must understand and identify relevant context factors when designing a business

G. Poels et al. (Eds.): PoEM 2017, LNBIP 305, pp. 112–125, 2017.
https://doi.org/10.1007/978-3-319-70241-4_8

process, hence enabling flexibility to deal with internal and external contingencies. Therefore, it is of paramount importance to employ a process language that supports context-adaptation. Such language must provide high expressiveness in terms of control flow, as well as in capturing the significant execution contexts.

Considerable number of approaches have been proposed to support the above principle in terms of both modelling perspectives and business languages. Yet, neither of these approaches provide a solid universal way to construct a Context-Adaptive Business Process (CABP), nor are the proposed different modelling languages compared in this aspect. Hence, this paper aims to compare the most popular business process languages (CPN, BPMN, YAWL and UML AD) to answer the following research question: *"How do business process modelling languages support CABPs?"*

Based on the standing point of CABP modelling, a framework for comparing modelling notations in terms of supporting context adaptation is proposed. This framework is constructed by a comprehensive list of requirements towards the modelling of CABP. This list of requirements is the result of both repetitive review of relevant literature and eleven CABP scenarios from empirical studies. By applying this framework, the selected business languages are examined and their modelling support towards context adaptation is compared against these requirements.

The rest of the paper is structured as follow. Section 2 handles the related work. Section 3 details the proposed framework. Evaluation of business notations regarding their fulfilment of the framework in terms of used scenarios is elaborated upon in Sect. 4. Finally, Sect. 5 delivers the conclusions and discusses future work.

2   Background and Related Work

A business process cannot adapt to the changing situations without being aware of the situational context in which it is executed. Many studies, such as [6–11], make contributions to define context in order to formulate a more precise definition of CABP. Despite all these efforts, there is no uniquely adopted definition so far. This is because each of these definitions is formulated from different perspectives or based on different process design approaches. In this paper, we refer to the definition provided by [3, 12–14]. The context towards context-aware business process is therefore defined as: *"Context is any information that is relevant to and might affect the execution of a business process. This information includes aspects of the process itself, the business environment in which it is embedded as well as any other entities that interact with the process."*

A context-adaptive business process, on the other hand, is defined as: *"A business process with the ability to recognize relevant contexts, integrate the relevant knowledge and information into the execution."*

In terms of constructing context-aware business processes, [3] examines the role-based modelling approach where assignment of relationships between roles and functions can be changed according to the dynamic context, given that roles and functions are more static. [15] proposes an extended CPN tool with ontology-based context models to support context adaptation. [16] explains how Worklet, an extended tool of YAWL, supports dynamic workflow and exception handling. In terms of extended tools of BPMN, [17] introduces uBPMN to support ubiquitous processes while [18] proposes to integrate BPMN with Internet of Things (IoT) devices and its native software components to support IoT dynamism.

Some analyses provide a comparative analysis between the most commonly used traditional modelling notations, such as [10, 19–25]. Yet, none of them concern context-adaptive BPs. They aim at normal control flow capability or specific applications like Web of Things (WoT) [1, 26]. Though the targets and perspectives of these comparative analyses are different from the purpose of this paper, their research sheds light on the methodology in terms of properties and requirements for comparison criteria.

3 Framework

To obtain the essential requirements that will compose the framework, a literature survey is performed where roughly 50 relevant papers have been analysed. Firstly, these papers are categorized based on their relevant aspects, including definition of context/context-awareness/context adaptation, context-aware or context-adaptive scenarios, CABP modelling, and CABP modelling with extended languages and tools. The second step is to identify scenarios related to CABP and extract all potential requirements. This step iterates until the most fitting scenarios are found, and a comprehensive list of CABP requirements is identified.

3.1 Relevant Scenarios

From the literature survey, eleven relevant scenarios are extracted based on their representativeness. These scenarios are listed and briefly described below; for a full description of the scenarios, source papers are presented.

- **Scenario 1 - Ambient Assisted Living (AAL) system** [27]: The AAL system consists of three parts: the Set Top Box (STB), the remote computer, and the smart phone. Each enclose an individual process and interact with the other in terms of exchanging data and information, yet executed independently by different actors. The STB process makes use of the sensors on the patients to detect their location. It interacts with the smart bio-medical devices on patient to collect the patients' health measurement data when the patient is at home. When it is detected "not at home", STB requests the smartphone to take-over and perform the monitoring and reporting of the health data. All the health data is eventually sent to the remote computer process in the hospital for analysis. In case of abnormal data, (e.g. high or low blood pressure), on-site doctors are notified and the corresponding actions take place.
- **Scenario 2 - E-business shop process** [19]: The entire online shopping process is executed by two resources, customer and the shop, all interacting. Depending on the customer's action, activities from the shop are triggered and executed. This requires flexible sequence order among the activities of the shop process.
- **Scenario 3 - Dynamic pricing process in supermarket** [18]: Price of orchid is automatically reduced if the temperature rises as it affects the quality. The process

includes a temperature sensor which estimates the quality of orchid and Electronic Shelf Label (ESL) which indicates the price.

- **Scenario 4 - Online banking system for international transfer** [28]: The online banking for international transfer process is performed via an internet banking application. It starts with a user logging into the online banking system; the user location is automatically detected by the device-installed GPS sensor at the same time. A feasibility check-up is then activated based on the detected location. If the check-up returns true, the user must manually input the destination country, which again is checked for validity by the system. In the case of an invalid country, an exception arises, and the process flow is channelled to display error message. Otherwise, the system will determine the corresponding transaction fee and exchange rate based on the predefined business rules and situational information, respectively.

- **Scenario 5 - Vehicle repair process** [19]: Vehicle repair process is triggered by the reception of a vehicle, and completed after handing over the vehicle back to the customer. Within this process, the vehicle does not receive any repair until a diagnosis is confirmed. Furthermore, the repair types are determined according to the diagnosis.

- **Scenario 6 - Post-production phase of film** [16]: The post production process can be broken into three major stages, pre-edit, edit and post-edit. The following tasks are identified across the three stages: prepare film/tape for edit, video effect production (VFX), offline task, edit sound and music, online task, film finishing task, finishing tape/disk task, and release printing. In addition, in the pre-edit stage, post-edit stage, and the high-resolution editing, more than one task is involved. Execution of involved tasks is required to be flexible according to the context or to be skipped.

- **Scenario 7 - Product promotion process in department store** [8]: The product promotion process normally starts with sales assistant being notified with the promotion event by the manager, and ends with closing a sales deal. To increase the chances of successful sales and be more efficient, it is essential to identify potential buyers rather than to approach every customer. The potential buyers' identification is context sensitive, and involves large number of deterministic context information and facts, which are necessarily integrated into the process.

- **Scenario 8 - Health checking process** [19]: The health checking process starts with the admission of the patient, and ends by discharging the patient. Within this process, preconditions are held for the execution of some examination activities, such as MRT test, puncture, etc. This gives rise to different variants of the process, which require adaptation of the initial process.

- **Scenario 9 - Process of handling incoming call in insurance company** [10]: The process of handling incoming calls for insurance claims is impacted by the environmental elements. Different approaches are required depending on the weather factors to ensure smooth workflow, for example, hiring external staff during storm season.

- **Scenario 10 - Air ticket reservation and check-in process** [10]: The process specifies the foreseen exceptions and the corresponding strategies during ticket reservation and check-in process in an airline company. For example, weather

condition or holiday season may lead to more traditional check-ins and special arrangement is required.
- **Scenario 11 - Environmental monitoring system** [29]: Numerous sensors are installed for measuring various environmental index. Once there is a deviation, alert will be sent to the central system to trigger adaptation of the overall process.

3.2 Identified Requirements

From the literature and the scenarios, we have extracted a set of requirements that are classified into three main categories: support for context modelling, support for flexibility, and support for scalability. The reason for such classification is that each category plays an indispensable role in supporting the construction of CABP as is next detailed. Table 1 lists the three categories of the identified requirements along with their sub-requirements. Among the sub-requirements, support for creating sub-processes and support for decision logic can be classified into both scalability and flexibility as they apply in both cases. All three categories and the sub-requirements are explained in detail in what follows. Furthermore, among the eleven scenarios, scenario 1, 4, 6 and 7 are selected to evaluate the support of the languages towards the requirements for CABP. The selection is based on the fact that these scenarios demand together all the specified requirement. This is also demonstrated in Table 1.

Table 1. CABP requirement framework & Selected scenarios with involved respective requirements

Requirements	Scenarios			
	1	4	6	7
Support for context modelling				
Support for interoperability [11]	X			X
Support for use of external context [30, 31]		X		
Support for context fusion [31, 32]	X	X		
Support for time constraint [33]	X			
Support for flexibility				
Support for sub-processes [8, 10, 34]	X	X	X	X
Support for flexible activity execution [33]		X		
Support for decision logic [8]		X	X	X
Support for routing logic [10, 19]	X	X	X	
Support for exception handling [16]	X	X		
Support for scalability				
Support for sub-processes [29]	X	X	X	X
Support for separation of concerns [35]		X	X	X

3.2.1 Support for Context Modelling

The ability to represent and manage the context data is crucial for dynamic processes. A dynamic environment generates massive context data at any point in time that needs to be expressed in the model. These context data may affect the execution of relevant activities in a process and its overall outcome. The following four sub-requirements are identified to support context modelling.

Support for interoperability. Interoperability means heterogeneous systems involved in one business process can interact with each other in real-time mode [11]. More precisely, when activities or processes within a system or among different systems can make use of data flow between different applications or users, this process or system is interoperable.

Support for use of external context. In the domain of IoT, hardware sensors and virtual sensors are usually used to capture the external contexts by which process activities are triggered. Nevertheless, regardless of the domain, there are other sources that can provide usable contextual information [30]. Irrespective of the ways the external context is acquired, a modelling language is expected to support real-time data retrieval from the physical world to enable dynamic business processes.

Support for context fusion. Context fusion refers to the aggregation of data being collected from multiple sources prior to being propagated for use. Especially in cases where data from single sources may not carry sufficient information to understand the full situation [32]. Therefore, it is necessary to fuse data from multiple sources to achieve more accurate information [31]. However, data may be acquired in different forms, such as data captured by sensors and contextual data like business rules and relevant regulations. Depending on the data forms, different fusion methods apply.

Support for time constraint. Within a workflow, the result or execution of one activity may influence others. Such influence may closely be linked with time-related aspects like activity duration, time constraints between activities (such as deadline, interval, temporality [33]), and their feasibility (i.e. time constraints do not contradict each other). Time constraints play a crucial role in designing and managing processes. It ensures the consistent state of workflow instances. If it is violated, an exception error must arise during the execution. In addition, in case of redesigning an existing business process, the information provided by time constraints about the actual time consumption of activity execution is indispensable to ensure business process improvement [36].

3.2.2 Support for Flexibility

Process flexibility is essential to deal with variations caused by a changing environment, and occurring during run time A flexible business process has the ability to alter itself, or the parts affected by the context, at runtime, to support execution alternatives that deal with foreseen and unforeseen changes [10, 37]. The following five sub-requirements are identified to support flexibility.

Support for creating sub-processes. A business process usually aims at achieving one ultimate hard-goal. Use of sub-processes allows to decompose a process into several soft adjustable sub-goals, represented by their respective sub-processes. In this way, a better understanding of the relevant contexts is ensured by linking them to each sub-goal, and corresponding context variables are modelled into the sub-processes. Eventually, the chance of failing to achieve the ultimate hard-goal is reduced by mitigating the risk of being affected by context changes via sub-processes. Moreover, sub-processes enable the modelling of situations without detailing the relevant context information in the master process. Whenever a situation arises, the relevant sub-process is activated to adapt to the context changes, while the master process remains unaffected [34].

Support for flexible activity execution. A dynamic business process allows to determine the execution sequence of activities at run time [33]. This implies that predefined activity sequences may weaken flexibility. Therefore, a sequential process modelling language is not expected to profoundly support the situation that certain activities are required to be executed in arbitrary orders, multiple times or even be skipped.

Support for decision logic. Decisions are essential and unavoidable in business processes. It is deterministic in the path of process execution. Hence, modelling the decision logic, including decision points, conditions and branching paths, is crucial. Moreover, there are two types of decision points, data-driven and event-driven. The former decides on the branch it takes based on the data output from the precedent activity, while the latter makes use of data from an external event. Regardless of the types, context-adaptive modelling languages are expected to provide corresponding constructs to model decision logic.

Support for routing logic. Routing logic is a representation of "workaround" in a process. It refers to the use of gateways to model the variability of a business process, hence, execution patterns of the process vary depending on the available input data or the relevant context [19].

Support for exception handling. Executions of processes may deviate due to the exceptions that greatly differ from the norm. According to [16], it is important to provide a comprehensive mechanism to define exceptional process behaviour and proper ways of handling that behaviour to achieve a complete and adequate CABP. With such mechanism, exceptions raised from changing contexts are handled without calling off the entire process or modifying the design of the whole specification. However, handlers are only specified for foreseen exceptions [38]. Unforeseen exceptions are considered as a black box, i.e. they are *non-existent* until their appearance. In this case, a flexible business process is expected to deal with these black box exceptions to ensure and maintain a proper process execution. From the modelling perspective, in addition to exception handlers, additional constructs or means are required to incorporate the support for exception handling.

3.2.3   Support for Scalability

Scalability of a process refers to its capability to expand and accommodate with growing workload due to added resources [39]. Integration of contexts into processes makes them grow rapidly. Thus, scalability is required to support the rapid growth of the models. Scalability can be split in the following two sub-requirements.

Support for creating sub-processes. Sub-processes are used to support process scalability by detailing complex activities. By using sub-processes, a simple business process can be extended to higher degree of complexity, while the main process remains abstract and clean. Sub-processes are also more reusable due to the fact that they can cover a more limited functionality, can be separated from the parent process, and can be triggered when a certain condition is satisfied or called from other processes. [29] points out that decomposition or decentralization of processes helps to increase the scalability and performance of business processes.

Support for Separation of Concerns. Complex BPs designing involves various concerns apart from major workflow. This is due to the ever-increasing process complexity and dynamic changes. Separation of these concerns decomposes the complex process such that to avoid crosscut influence of different concerns during execution. On the other hand, the process must be scalable to integrate these concerns back into the execution and further expand to include added resources. Extraction of decision logic and data modelling are examples of such concerns, for both are contextual. Hardcoding of both into the core process behaviour description may result in hyper-complex process flow and potential execution errors [35].

4 Process Modelling Notation Evaluation Using the Framework

In this section, the proposed framework is applied to evaluate to what extent BPMN, CPN, UML AD, and YAWL provide support for modelling CABPs. As such, process models of each of the four selected scenarios are constructed using each modelling notation. Figure 1 demonstrates the process model of AAL system in BPMN.

Considering that business people are the targeted end-users in the design phase, the evaluation of business notations values more the graphical representation ability, simplicity and understandability of the constructed models.

4.1 Support for Context Modelling

Support for Interoperability. YAWL supports interoperability via task decomposition, while it is limited to internal data sharing at task level. **BPMN** 2.0 supports the interoperability by using lanes and pools representing both internal and external resources. Data sharing and information exchange happen via message flows, message events, data objects and data storages. As in Fig. 1, the message sent by task "*send request for patient data*" in the STB process is received as a trigger of the smartphone process. Similar example in the remote computer system, which starts with a message start event, triggered by the reception of patient's health data. A similar mechanism as BPMN is applied in **UML AD**, where partitions are acting as lanes, accept/sent actions and data pins represent data and message flows. **CPN** does not support interoperability due to the lack of constructs.

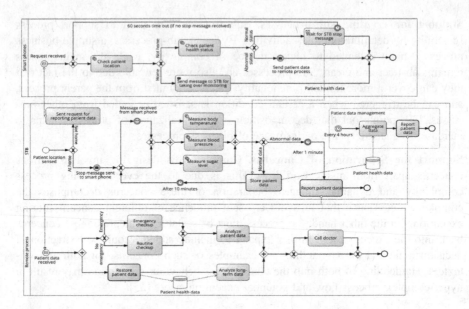

Fig. 1. Process model of AAL system in BPMN

Support for Use of External context. Except for **BPMN** 2.0, which makes use of lanes and data objects & storages to support the use of external context, none of the other three notations support this sub-requirement. In Fig. 1, the three parts of the AAL system correspond to the three resources, which are modelled as different roles participating in the process execution, represented by different pools. This also makes the process interoperable. In addition, data objects and storages are used to enable plugin of externally stored patient health data for executions of analysis tasks.

Support for Context Fusion. The fusion of contexts can be simply modelled using parallel join structure, namely, AND join which is supported by all four languages. Moreover, **YAWL** supports the fusion of context also through task decomposition. However, the limited-to-internal-data character as in interoperability applies. **BPMN** 2.0 also makes use of business rule task to support the fusion of more complicated contextual data, such as business rules. In the AAL process, the measurement of health condition is performed by a set of activities being executed simultaneously, which are enabled by using AND split. The results of these activities are synchronized by an AND join (Fig. 1).

Support for Time Constraints. Time constraints are supported by all the four languages, yet to different degrees. **YAWL** editor offers a task timer element for constructing time constraint, while it is only applicable to time-out and delay constraints on atomic manual tasks and automated tasks, respectively. **BPMN** 2.0 offers the options to model various types of time constraints through timer events, including time-out, delay, interval, and duration. Figure 1 shows different types of BPMN timers used to model time interval of ten minutes between every measurement of the health condition, as well as a one-minute time constraint before reporting the patient's abnormal health data. Moreover, a timer start event is used to trigger the event-based sub-process "patient data management", which runs every four hours. **UML AD** deploys the *hourglass* symbol to represent time events. By applying time stamps on tokens and a global clock for the whole net, **CPN** can support all types of time constraint.

4.2   Support for Flexibility and Scalability

Support for Creating sub-processes. YAWL creates sub-processes by using composite tasks, there is no distinction between types or functions of sub-processes. In addition to support for creating simple standard sub-processes, **BPMN** 2.0 extends its support for different types of sub-processes, such as compensation, loop, multiple instance and event-based sub-processes. In Fig. 1, *"Patient Data Management"* is an independent process from the main control flow, and it is modelled using an event-based sub-process, which is triggered when the condition is satisfied. In **UML AD** sub-processes are created using call behaviour action and activities. Hierarchies are used in **CPN** to decompose processes into modules to represent different levels of a CPN process.

Support for Flexible Activity Execution. To enable flexible activity execution, **YAWL** and **BPMN** use OR gateways as a solution. However, this leads to complexity and difficulty of maintenance. **BPMN** 2.0 makes use of ad-hoc sub-process to replace OR gateways and thus to avoid process errors caused by the latter [40]. However, standard **YAWL** does not provide any alternatives. In **UML AD**, there are two ways to enable flexible activity execution, either via interruptible activity region or by formulating OR gateway functions with XOR and AND gateways which results in complex process models. **CPN** does not directly support this requirement, but partial and indirect support is found through the combination of parallel and decision patterns – represented by places and transitions.

Support for Decision Logic. Simple decisions are perfectly supported by the four languages in forms of XOR-split in **YAWL** and **BPMN**, decision nodes in **UML** and formulated XOR functionality using places and transitions in **CPN**. Figure 1 shows the use of XOR-split in BPMN representing data-driven decision on which process to perform the monitoring based on the detected location. Regarding more complicated decisions which involve business rules, BPMN provides the mechanism of fusing contexts via business rule tasks. The aggregation is done in form of a decision table, which is then applied to execute complex decisions. While the definition of decision tables is not supported by BPMN 2.0 directly, compatible support is provided through the Decision Model and Notation (DMN) standard [41, 42]. In **UML AD**, for complex decisions, Object Constraint Language (OCL) is used to formulate pre- or post- conditions, constraining the possible actions of activities (Table 2).

Support for Routing Logic. In general, there are three types of routing logics, AND, XOR and OR. **YAWL** and **BPMN** both support the three types of routing behaviours. Moreover, **BPMN** provides additional gateway types with specified functionalities, like event-based gateways and complex gateways. For **UML AD**, routing logic falls into

Table 2. Evaluation of process languages on context-adaptiveness

Category	Sub-requirement	YAWL	BPMN 2.0	UML AD	CPN
Support for Context Modelling	Support for Interoperability	• Task decomposition (internal)	• Message flow • Message events • Lanes & pools • data object & storage	• Accept event & send signal action • Swimlanes • Object node & input/output pins	-
	Support for Use of External context	-	• Lanes • Data object & storage	-	-
	Support for Context Fusion	• AND join • Task decomposition (internal)	• AND join • Business rule task	• Fork and join node	• Parallel activities structure
	Support for Time Constraint	• Task timer	• Timer events	• Timer event action	• Timestamp & Global clock
Support for Flexibility	Support for Creating Sub-Processes	• Composite task	• Sub-process marker	• Call behaviour action • Activity	• Hierarchy
	Support for flexible activity execution	• OR gateway	• OR gateway • Ad-hoc sub-process • Events	• Interruptible activity region • Events	• Combination of places and transitions
	Support for Decision Logic	• XOR split • Condition	• XOR split • Business rule task	• Merge and decision node • OCL<localPrecondition> & <localPostcondition>	• Decision Structure
	Support for Routing Logic	• Task decoration	• Gateways • Events	• Merge and decision node • Fork and join node • Events	• Parallel activities structure • Decision structure
	Support for Exception Handling Foreseen	• Cancellation set	• Intermediate boundary events	• Exception handler • Interruptible activity region • Action events	• Extra transitions and places with CPN ML
Support for Scalability	Support for Creating Sub-processes	• Composite task	• Sub-process marker	• Call behaviour action • Activity	• Hierarchy
	Support for Separation of concerns	• Data separation vis XML standards	• Decision separation via business rule task	• Decision separation via OCL	-

two types, the usage of either fork and join nodes or merge and decision nodes. Either type, they refer to AND and XOR routing logic. For OR structures, the formulation applies (see 4.2 Support for Flexible Activity Execution). There are no specific constructs to directly model either of the three routing behaviours in **CPN**. However, places and transitions can be used to form corresponding routing patterns.

Support for Exception Handling. YAWL handles foreseen exceptions by implementing a cancellation set. Yet, it only covers simple exceptions like time-out of a manual task and error. The intermediate boundary events in **BPMN** 2.0 not only expand the types of possible exceptions during the execution, but also give options of handling types, interrupting or non-interrupting. Exception handlers and interruptible regions are used to provide the support for exception handling in **UML AD**. Use of extra task pattern and CPN ML language, provide **CPN** with partial support for exception handling as well. However, limitations to model exception cases in **CPN**

make the language the least favourable in this requirement. Noteworthy is that in terms of support for unforeseen exceptions, none of the four languages is competent.

Support for Separation of Concerns. UML AD and BMPN support the separation of concerns regarding the decision aspect. However, only YAWL supports data separation, as it deploys the XML-based standards for data management that can be linked to the processes.

5 Conclusion and Future Work

This paper is motivated by the growing prevalence of business process management in a rapid changing environment and its high failure rate. It focuses on the research question *"How do business process modelling languages support context-adaptive business processes?"* To answer this question, we conducted an intensive CABP related literature review, which lays a solid basis for the construction of the proposed framework. The framework consists of three categories, including in total nine sub-requirements, which are applied to evaluate the support of business process notations towards modelling context-aware processes. Moreover, this framework is evaluated through the application of different approaches in real-world scenarios using four commonly used standard business languages. An evaluation matrix is generated based on the framework to compare the support of BPMN, CPN, UML AD, and YAWL during the modelling of scenario processes. It is found that BPMN 2.0 fulfils most of the requirements among the four languages due to the wide range of elements and constructs it provides and thus it appears to be the most suitable of the four considered languages for modelling context-adaptive BP during the design phase. However, none of the other notations provide full support for modelling CABPs.

For future work, it is suggested to put more focus on the topic of context modelling in BPM since it is considered as the most important requirement in dynamic process modelling. Numerous real case studies are appearing especially due to the emergence of IoT applications. Furthermore, on top of the traditional languages, the limitations of languages towards modelling context adaptation give rise to the study of their extensions and tools, therefore, the notation extensions and the supporting tools are also worth exploring. Finally, it is worthwhile to include a more detailed empirical comparison to examine how different business languages facilitate process modelling in terms of context-adaptability.

References

1. Lu, R., Sadiq, S.: A survey of comparative business process modeling approaches. In: Abramowicz, W. (ed.) BIS 2007. LNCS, vol. 4439, pp. 82–94. Springer, Heidelberg (2007). doi:10.1007/978-3-540-72035-5_7
2. Dumas, M., La Rosa, M., Mendling, J., Reijers, H.A.: Fundamentals of Business Process Management. Springer, Heidelberg (2013)
3. Saidani, O., Nurcan, S.: Context-awareness for adequate business process modelling. In: Proceedings of the 2009 3rd International Conference on Research Challenges in Information Science, RCIS 2009, pp. 177–186 (2009)

4. vom Brocke, J., Schmiedel, T., Zelt, S.: Considering Context in Business Process Management- The BPM Process Framework. BPTrends (2015)
5. vom Brocke, J., Schmiedel, T., Recker, J., Trkman, P., Mertens, W., Viaene, S.: Ten principles of good business process management. Bus. Process Manag. J. **20**, 530–548 (2014)
6. Dey, A.K.: Understanding and using context. J. Pers. Ubiquit. Comput. **5**, 4–7 (2001)
7. Coutaz, B.Y.J., Crowley, J.L., Dobson, S., Garlan, D.: Context is key. Commun. ACM **48**, 49–53 (2005)
8. de la Vara, J.L., Ali, R., Dalpiaz, F., Sánchez, J., Giorgini, P.: Business processes contextualisation via context analysis. In: Parsons, J., Saeki, M., Shoval, P., Woo, C., Wand, Y. (eds.) ER 2010. LNCS, vol. 6412, pp. 471–476. Springer, Heidelberg (2010). doi:10. 1007/978-3-642-16373-9_37
9. Rosemann, M., Recker, J., Flender, C., Ansell, P.: Understanding context-awareness in business process design. In: Proceedings 17th Australasian Conference on Information Systems 2006 (2006)
10. Rosemann, M., Recker, J., Flender, C.: Contextualization of business processes. Int. J. Bus. Process Integr. Manag. **3**, 47–60 (2008)
11. Li, S., Xu, L.Da, Zhao, S.: The internet of things: a survey. Inf. Syst. Front. **17**, 243–259 (2015)
12. Henricksen, K., Indulska, J., Rakotonirainy, A.: Modeling context information in pervasive computing systems. In: Mattern, F., Naghshineh, M. (eds.) Pervasive 2002. LNCS, vol. 2414, pp. 167–180. Springer, Heidelberg (2002). doi:10.1007/3-540-45866-2_14
13. Saidani, O., Nurcan, S.: Towards context aware business process modelling. In: 8th Workshop on Business Process Modeling, Development, and Support, p. 9 (2007)
14. Kröschel, I.: On the notion of context for business process use. In: ISSS/BPSC, pp. 288–297 (2010)
15. Serral, E., De Smedt, J., Vanthienen, J.: Extending CPN tools with ontologies to support the management of context-adaptive business processes. In: Fournier, F., Mendling, J. (eds.) BPM 2014. LNBIP, vol. 202, pp. 198–209. Springer, Cham (2015). doi:10.1007/978-3-319-15895-2_18
16. Adams, M., Ter Hofstede, A., Russell, N., van der Aalst, W.M.P.: Dynamic and context-aware process adaptation. In: Handbook of Research on Complex Dynamic Process Management: Techniques for Adaptability in Turbulent Environments, pp. 104–136 (2009)
17. Yousfi, A., Bauer, C., Saidi, R., Dey, A.K.: UBPMN: a BPMN extension for modeling ubiquitous business processes. Inf. Softw. Technol. **74**, 55–68 (2016)
18. Meyer, S., Ruppen, A., Magerkurth, C.: Internet of things-aware process modeling: integrating IoT devices as business process resources. In: Salinesi, C., Norrie, M.C., Pastor, Ó. (eds.) CAiSE 2013. LNCS, vol. 7908, pp. 84–98. Springer, Heidelberg (2013). doi:10. 1007/978-3-642-38709-8_6
19. Ayora, C., Torres, V., Pelechano, V.: BP Variability Case Studies Development using different Modeling Approaches. pp. 1–31 (2011)
20. BÖrger, E.: Approaches to modeling business processes: a critical analysis of BPMN, workflow patterns and YAWL. Softw. Syst. Model. **11**, 305–318 (2012)
21. Jian, H.Y., Shi, X.S., Wen, S., Li, J.W.: Formal semantics of BPMN process models using YAWL. In: Proceedings - 2008 2nd International Symposium on Intelligent Information Technology Application, IITA 2008, vol. 2, pp. 70–74 (2008)
22. Lerner, B.S., Christov, S., Member, S., Osterweil, L.J., Bendraou, R., Kannengiesser, U., Wise, A.: Exception handling patterns for process modelling. IEEE Trans. Softw. Eng. **36**, 162–184 (2010)

23. Ramadan, M., Elmongui, H., Hassan, R.: BPMN formalisation using coloured petri nets. In: Proceedings of the 2nd GSTF Annual International Conference on Software Engineering & Applications (2011)

24. Geambasu, C.V.: BPMN vs. UML activity diagram for business process modeling. Acc. Manag. Inf. Syst. **11**, 637–651 (2012)

25. Vasko, M., Dustdar, S.: A view based analysis of workflow modeling languages. In: Proceedings - 14th Euromicro International Conference on Parallel, Distributed, and Network-Based Processing, PDP 2006, pp. 293–300 (2006)

26. Meyer, S., Sperner, K., Magerkurth, C., Pasquier, J.: Towards modeling real-world aware business processes. In: Proceedings of the Second International Workshop on Web of Things, pp. 1–6 (2011)

27. Dar, K., Taherkordi, A., Baraki, H., Eliassen, F., Geihs, K.: A resource oriented integration architecture for the internet of things: a business process perspective. Pervasive Mob. Comput. **20**, 145–159 (2015)

28. Ann, M., Kerryann, M.: Context-aware Process Design: Exploring the Extrinsic Drivers for Process Flexibility. vol. 26, pp. 423–436 (2005)

29. Haller, S., Magerkurth, C.: The real-time enterprise: Iot-enabled business processes. In: IETF IAB Workshop on Interconnecting Smart Objects with the Internet, pp. 1–3 (2011)

30. Alves, P., Ferreira, P.: Distributed Context-Aware Systems (2011)

31. Serral, E., De Smedt, J., Snoeck, M., Vanthienen, J.: Context-adaptive petri nets: supporting adaptation for the execution context. Expert Syst. Appl. **42**, 9307–9317 (2015)

32. Perera, C., Zaslavsky, A., Christen, P., Georgakopoulos, D.: Context aware computing for the internet of things. IEEE Commun. Surv. Tutor. **16**, 414–454 (2014)

33. Vasilecas, O., Rusinaite, T., Kalibatiene, D.: Dynamic business processes and their simulation: a survey. Databases Inf. Syst. IX, 155–166 (2016)

34. Smanchat, S., Ling, S., Indrawan, M.: A survey on context-aware workflow adaptations. In: Proceedings of the 6th International Conference on Advances in Mobile Computing and Multimedia - MoMM 2008, p. 414 (2008)

35. Vanthienen, J., Caron, F., De Smedt, J.: Business rules, decisions and processes: five reflections upon living apart together. In: Proceedings SIGBPS Workshop on Business Processes and Services (BPS 2013), pp. 76–81 (2013)

36. Eder, J., Panagos, E., Rabinovich, M.: Time constraints in workflow systems. In: Jarke, M., Oberweis, A. (eds.) CAiSE 1999. LNCS, vol. 1626, pp. 286–300. Springer, Heidelberg (1999). doi:10.1007/3-540-48738-7_22

37. Schonenberg, H., Mans, R., Russell, N., Mulyar, N., van der Aalst, W.M.P.: Process flexibility: a survey of contemporary approaches. In: Dietz, J.L.G., Albani, A., Barjis, J. (eds.) CIAO!/EOMAS -2008. LNBIP, vol. 10, pp. 16–30. Springer, Heidelberg (2008). doi:10.1007/978-3-540-68644-6_2

38. Russell, N., van der Aalst, W.M.P., ter Hofstede, A.: Workflow exception patterns. In: Dubois, E., Pohl, K. (eds.) CAiSE 2006. LNCS, vol. 4001, pp. 288–302. Springer, Heidelberg (2006). doi:10.1007/11767138_20

39. Nielsen, C., Lund, M.: The concept of business model scalability. Soc. Sci. Res. Netw. 1–20 (2015)

40. Mendling, J., Reijers, H.A., van der Aalst, W.M.P.: Seven process modeling guidelines (7PMG). Inf. Softw. Technol. **52**, 127–136 (2010)

41. OMG: Decision Model and Notation (DMN) 1.1 (2016)

42. Hasić, F., Devadder, L., Dochez, M., Hanot, J., De Smedt, J., Vanthienen, J.: Challenges in refactoring processes to include decision modelling. In: Business Process Management Workshops (2017)

Capability-Driven Digital Service Innovation: Implications from Business Model and Service Process Perspectives

Hasan Koç and Kurt Sandkuhl[(⊠)]

Institute of Computer Science, University of Rostock, 18055 Rostock, Germany
{hasan.koc,kurt.sandkuhl}@uni-rostock.de

Abstract. Today's enterprises face the need to develop user-specific solutions due to the disruptive technologies and competition in the market. Intangibility of services and service-orientation fosters creation of flexible solutions by innovating business models, service processes and service products. Capabilities are perceived as measuring indicator of service orientation in enterprises and one requirement for business model innovation. This paper investigates how design of capabilities can help enterprises to offer novel services. To do so, we analyze the degree of innovation before and after applying the capability-driven development (CDD), which is a methodological and technological enterprise modelling approach. Based on observations from two industrial cases affected from the main forces that disturb the business terrain, the paper concludes that CDD helps enterprises to innovate their digital services by causing changes mainly on business model and service process levels.

Keywords: Capability-driven development · Digital business · Digital services · Business model innovation · Service innovation · Capability modelling · Context modelling

1 Introduction

We are living in an economy that is characterized by rapid change and digitalization. The penetration of IT in our everyday life calls for a transformation from an information to a digital society. Digital economy is growing worldwide and seen as an important driver of innovation and competitiveness. Business models undergo a digital transformation to seize the opportunities provided by the current paradigms, such as Internet of Things (IoT), Sensing Enterprises and Industry 4.0 [1].

Service-oriented way of thinking in the business caused growth of the service economy, which necessarily had a vital impact on the business processes and culture of the organizations. The intangible nature of services, the pace of the disruptive technologies and competition in the market require developing customized, user-specific solutions. In a market offering services to the consumers of the digital society, the enterprises must know their digital customers, understand their preferences and are thus seeking ways that would allow them to provide them with innovative services.

G. Poels et al. (Eds.): PoEM 2017, LNBIP 305, pp. 126–140, 2017.
https://doi.org/10.1007/978-3-319-70241-4_9

Service innovation is closely related with the innovation of business models and service processes [2]. Business model innovation concerns evolving one or more components of a business model. According to one study, financial outperformers put twice as much emphasis on business model innovation as underperformers [3].

One primary requirement for business model innovation and a measuring indicator of service orientation is enterprise capabilities [4]. Seelos and Mair define business model as "a set of capabilities that is configured to enable value creation consistent with either economic or social strategic objectives" [5]. Organizational capabilities to generate innovative services are seen as a vector of competitiveness [6]. However, the relationship between business model innovation and service innovation in the context of digitalization [7] as well as the role of capabilities is under-researched. Against this background, the main research question investigated in this paper is how capability-based design can contribute to digital service innovation. Section 2 summarizes the related work in the field of service innovation, business model innovation and the role of capabilities. Then, Sect. 3 illustrates two case studies from two distinctive industries. In Sect. 4, we show how capability-based design enables digital service innovation of the aforementioned organizations, particularly by introducing changes on business model and service process levels. Section 5 discusses the findings and Sect. 6 concludes the work.

2 Related Work

2.1 Service Innovation

The rise of the service economy addresses the need of designing new organizational models to support service innovation. Increased competition, fast-paced markets and digitalization increases the pressure to generate continually new and innovative services. In the light of disruptive innovations, [8] identify three main forces that disturb the business terrain, namely "de(regulation) & trade liberalization, technology and modularity & standardized interfaces".

Service innovation is "the rebundling of diverse resources that create novel resources that are beneficial (...) to some actors in a given context" [9]. In this paper, service innovation is interpreted as the design or improvement of service concepts to satisfy unmet customer needs [2]. Different typologies and modes of service innovation are present in the literature. [10] defines four dimensions, service concept, client interface, service delivery system, and technology. [11] distinguish between four types of IT service innovations, administrative process, technological process, technological service, and technological integration innovations. Wang et al. argue in their work that service innovation embraces *business model*, *service process* and *service product innovation* [2]. The authors also investigate the dominant and supporting modes of service innovation. After analyzing a total of 69 innovation cases, they conclude that (service) product innovation rarely occurs standalone, rather it happens jointly with (service) product innovation.

In this work, we use the service innovation criteria of Wang et al. as the authors analyze various service innovation typologies and derive their framework based on the existing proposals [2]. Further, we argue that capability-based design can help enterprises to innovate their services, as a result of which business models could be changed. This view is also reflected in Wang et al.'s framework, which makes it fit for the purposes of this paper.

The distinguishing aspect of the services is that their production and delivery are simultaneous. As such, we limit the investigation in this study on the two modes, namely *business model innovation* and *service process innovation*, which are illustrated in Table 1 and explained in the next section.

Table 1. Service innovation criteria, adapted from [2]

Business model innovation	Service process innovation
Should satisfy at least one of the flowing criteria	*Should satisfy at least one of the flowing criteria*
• Substantial change in the way in which revenues and profits are earned, e.g., change of value proposition, cost structure, and revenue streams	• Significant changes in the way information is exchanged between a customer and a service provider
• Drastic change of partner/customer relationships	• Significant change of the interface between the service provider and its clients
• Can either create a new market or allow the company to enter into a totally different market	• Significant change of the back-office processes,
• Platform innovation, which builds new customer/partner relationships	• Significant change of the organizational structure

2.2 Business Model Innovation, Service Process Innovation and Capabilities

The term business model has been defined in the literature in different ways, yet the definitions seem to accentuate the quintessence and method of doing business. For instance, [12] state "a business model is the combination of 'who', 'what', 'when', 'where', 'why', 'how', and 'how much' an organization uses to provide its goods and services and develop resources to continue its efforts". [13] argue "a business model describes the rationale of how an organization creates, delivers, and captures value" Likewise, [14] interprets the business model as "the heuristic logic that connects technical potential with the realization of economic value".

The manifold definitions of the term caused problems when investigating the business model innovation aspect. Particularly, researchers and practitioners posit different views about when something is a minor business change and when it is an innovation. For instance, [15] state "innovation becomes business model innovation, when two or more elements of a business model are reinvented to deliver value in a new way". Other argue that business model innovation refers to changing at least one of a business model's constituting elements [16], the change does not need to be groundbreaking and disruptive. From a service-oriented perspective and for this paper's purposes, we position ourselves in line with the second view. We argue that business model innovation concerns changes in the way value is delivered to or co-created with the customer by means of forming new partnerships and new activities [4].

Service process innovation concerns incremental improvements to an existing delivery process which lead to new ways of meeting customer needs [17, 18]. Such processes include both service delivery activities as well as back-end tasks supporting the service delivery. Innovation in the service processes is argued to contribute to the co-production of the services and enhance the quality of the customer journey [2].

Service orientation in business models can increase competitive advantage [19] and their innovation is key to firm performance. The connection between business models and service process innovation can be strengthened with the organizational capabilities, which are perceived as "both the primary requirement for business model innovation and a measuring indicator of service orientation" [4]. Management and design of the capabilities is a promising approach to tackle the challenges of dynamic environments. One proposal in that sense is the capability-driven development (CDD) approach, which received attention in IS lately [20]. CDD approach consist of two main artefacts:

- CDD methodology. A methodology consisting of a number of upper-level method encompassing three key perspectives of organizational design – Enterprise Modeling, context modeling, and pattern modeling. Further method components concern support decision making for capability modeling and run-time adjustments modeling. CDD methodology defines a capability as "an ability and capacity that enables an enterprise to achieve a business goal in a certain context" [21]. Accordingly, a capability consists of the digital services offered to the customers, business goals that are realized by delivering this digital service as well as the potential deployment contexts of the digital services. The CDD methodology helps to systematically model those aspects from a conceptual point of view.
- CDD environment. The methodology is supported by the CDD environment, which comprises of a number of tools. Capability Design Tool (CDT) incorporates context modelling, goal modelling and business process modelling modules. Capability Context Platform (CCP) monitors the contextual values at run-time as well as a Capability Delivery Navigation Application (CNA) enables adjustments in line with the service delivery context and reusable best practices. Capability Delivery Application (CDA) retrieves adjustment information from CNA on demand or on schedule [22].

The innovation potential of CDD have been investigated in [23]. Our work follows a similar line, yet does not limit the innovation potential to business models. It rather inspects the innovation on digital services level, which requires analyzing the changes also on service process layers.

3 Application Cases

For the purposes of this study, we collected data by performing a qualitative case study, which focuses on the introduction of the CDD approach for an enhanced digital service delivery (cf. Sects. 3.1 and 3.2). To have a deeper understanding of service provision and the effects of the CDD approach in the enterprises, we elaborated the findings further by using document-centric techniques and structured interviews. The former concerns visiting the premises of the two organizations (partly in the context of a student project), modelling their way of working and analyzing the secondary data. Such data can include customer specifications, policies, guidelines, service level agreements, documents explaining the organizational processes, the structures, roles, task allocations and best practices. The interviews were performed both on executive (service manager, enter-prise architect) and operational (knowledge worker) levels [24, 25].

3.1 Utility Industry

The SIV group is a vertically integrated German enterprise that specifically serves the utility industry and is challenged by the changing regulations. The group operates in two fundamental roles in the market. As an independent software vendor (ISV), SIV.AG develops and distributes the industry-specify ERP platform kVASy®. Con-sidering the rising complexity of the market, public utilities consider outsourcing of their business processes to external service providers. In its business service provider (BSP) role, SIV Utility Services GmbH offers such services for clients running kVASy®.

This paper focuses on the business unit model of BSP, i.e. a business model defined on a specific level for business units of a corporate [26]. The key value proposition is the support of market communication, i.e. business-to-business interactions that deal with the exchange of data between market partners. Market communication requires the processing of bulk data that are transmitted from one market partner to another within a single EDIFACT-formatted file. Exchange of data may easily get into conflict with other data, which requires the initiation of a clearing procedure to complete the communication process. Currently, BSP offers clearing services with costly and manual interaction of knowledge workers. The clearing procedure is usually defined in a handling instruction, i.e. a contractual agreement specifying the clearing terms between the BSP and the client. Yet, there is no process automation nor the clearing procedures are executed in a business process management (BPM) engine. Furthermore, as the handling instructions are client-specific, the contextual aspect of its content must be continuously checked by the knowledge worker. This situation does not allow dynamic changes to service delivery (cf. Fig. 1a). Influenced mainly from the regulation and technology forces, the company needs to design innovative digital services and extend the choice space of its customers.

3.2 eGovernment

everis is a multinational consulting firm providing business and strategy solutions, application development, maintenance, and outsourcing services. The everis applica-tion case concerns the service portfolio provisioning in eGovernment sector and focuses on the services provided to municipalities, which are then used by citizens and companies. Everis has a SOA platform consisting of a service catalogue with up to 200 e-services of automated (consumed completely online), semi-automated or non-automated nature. During service provision, different factors and actors involved

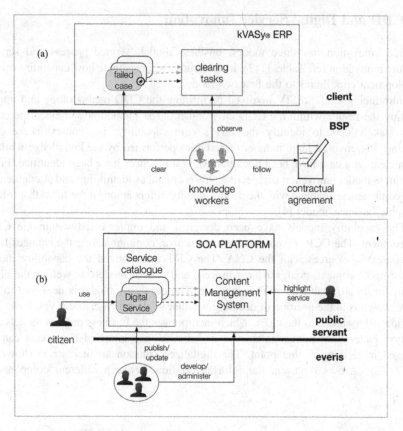

Fig. 1. Simplified business architectures in the utility (a) and eGovernment (b) cases [27]

need to be taken into account, e.g. diverse public administration's laws, regulations, calendars, types of events, weather as well as various technological tools.

This paper elaborates on the promotion of digital services in a municipality web page. Each municipality is responsible for deciding which services are offered through their home pages. Public servants in the municipality have access the to the back office applications in the SOA platform and configure them to highlight a service (cf. Fig. 1b). This example of a non-automated service is termed as service promotion. Depending on the municipality, parameters affecting service promotion may change. Currently, those parameters are managed manually; hence costs for exposing the right service is usually high, and also under-exploitation of services may occur. Motivated by the opportunities resulting from and problems created by technology forces, everis envisions designing innovative solutions that are applicable to all municipalities.

4 CDD and Digital Service Innovation

Service innovation has three modes, business model, service process and service product innovation (cf. Table 1) [2]. In this study we investigate how capability-driven development contributes to the first two modes.

Introducing CDD to SIV involved performing the CDD methodology and implementing the results within the CDD environment. The methodology helped the company stakeholders to identify the BSP's core capability, i.e. context-aware case clearing. Moreover, a large number of activities performed by the knowledge workers when clearing a case have been documented, best practices have been identified. From a business model innovation perspective, this is crucial as identifying and strengthening core competencies explain why the service quality differs amongst the firms that follow the same business model [4].

The capability models have been designed and implemented within the CDD environment. The CCP served as a business sensor, communicating the changes from the contextual sources with the CNA. The CDT incorporated the capability model consisting of context, goal, business process and pattern models as well as the algorithms for an adjustable solution at runtime. The capability model is deployed to the CNA, which is in the position of deciding whether to clear a case, and if yes, how. The solution is forwarded to the CDA, which incorporates the business process models and solution patterns. If human interaction is required, the knowledge workers can be engaged in clearing at that point. The digitalized solution architecture is shown in Fig. 2. The arrows represent the information flow between different components.

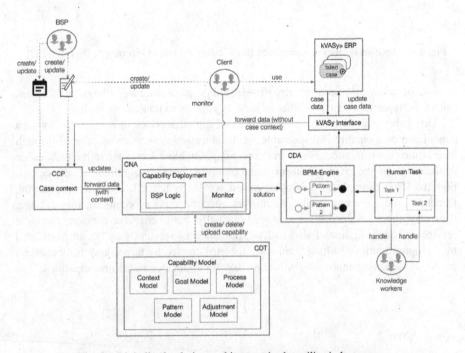

Fig. 2. Digitalized solution architecture in the utility industry case

Note that the dotted arrows represent actions performed by the participating roles as well as their results on the components.

Business model innovation in SIV group. CDD enables transferring clearing service related activities from manual to partially-automated context-aware services. By providing a multi-tenant platform, the BSP can revise its value creation and extend the choice space for its clients, for instance by allowing them to manage the contractual parameters at runtime, providing them the statistics (e.g. number of cleared cases), enabling them to monitor the current situation (e.g. open tasks). Furthermore, the key resource is not only the knowledge worker in the BSP, but also the client as the co-creator of the service, which can let SIV group to establish better customer relationships. For instance, due to performance monitoring, the client can check whether the decision to outsource/or not outsource a case was reasonable. Consequently, substantial changes on business model level is expected (cf. Table 2).

Table 2. Changes at the business model level

Model block		SIV	everis
Value propositions	Before CDD	Knowledge-worker based clearing of the exceptional messages	Service portfolio provisioning in eGovernment; deployment, management and maintenance of the SOA platform
	After CDD	Context-based clearing of the exceptional messages; Flexible contractual agreements; Monitoring of performance data (e.g. number and types of the cleared/not cleared cases)	Context-based service promotion; Integration of external service providers and citizens
Key activities	Before CDD	Message clearing, handling instruction specification (primarily driven by the BSP)	Publishing new digital services or updating existing ones
	After CDD	Key activities prior to the CDD introduction are formalized and documented. Moreover, they are now driven by both the clients and the BSP	Key activities prior to the CDD introduction are automatized and visible to all participating roles co-creating the value
Key resources	Before CDD	Knowledge-workers, know-how on legal aspects; Handling instructions; kVASy	SOA platform; Know-how on municipality properties, legal aspects; qualified employees
	After CDD	Client is also a key resource now, as it co-creates the value by configuring the parameters on the CNA; Case clearing patterns	Extended with citizens and service promotion patterns[a]
Customer segments	Before CDD	Public utilities (multi-sided as different market players are supported)	Municipalities
	After CDD	N/A	Extended with external service providers

(*continued*)

Table 2. (*continued*)

Model block		SIV	everis
Customer relationships	Before CDD	(Dedicated) personal assistance in case clearing and semi-automated services support; Service hotline & training. Depending on the contract, client may be integrated into the service creation process	Personal assistance (e.g. information exchange about the service usage); service hotline & training
	After CDD	Although personal assistance still exists, client is now heavily involved in the co-creation of the service	Increase in the rate of automated services; also service co-creation based on citizen feedback
Channels	Before CDD	Acquisition of potential clients by sales representative and events; Client-initiated request for BSP support	In-house sales force National and international projects
	After CDD	Contract templates (from the CDT) and performance data (from the CNA) allows creating additional client acquisition channels	Event-based case reporting, i.e. if the municipality did not book the capability, an email concerning the high service usage is sent [24]
Cost structure	Before CDD	Fixed, i.e. costs do not depend on the cases cleared by the knowledge worker	Fixed, i.e. costs remain same when publishing/updating a service
	After CDD	Economies of scope due to the degree of automation and the possibility to redeploy/reconfigure the capability to different clients	Economies of scope due to pre-defined parameters of municipality properties (e.g. population, size)
Revenue streams	Before CDD	kVASy is installed based on the licensing model. Clearing services are billed to the client depending on the contractual agreement	SOA Platform is deployed and managed based on the licensing model
	After CDD	Extended with effort-based model, i.e. the client is charged based on the number of cleared cases	Extended with effort-based model, i.e. upon booking the capability, client is also charged based on the number of promoted services
Key partners	Before CDD	SIV.AG; Utility market players	everis Project Management Office; Municipalities
	After CDD	N/A	N/A

[a]http://bit.ly/2jDd5gl

Service process innovation in SIV group. One substantial difference between the current and the to-be solution is that the latter transforms the informal contract attributes into machine-processable quantities. In this respect, application of CDD enables both the BSP and the client to sign in the CNA and define its own contractual parameters. Based on the altered parameters, knowledge worker can receive a more prioritized and client-independent list of clearing tasks. Hence, the application is expected to make a significant change in the interface between the BSP and the client. Furthermore, the knowledge worker will be aware of the client context and be supported with an appropriate pattern for the problem at hand. As this directly influences the clearing procedure followed by the knowledge worker, also changes in the back-office processes are envisioned.

Introducing CDD to everis concerned also application of the CDD methodology and implementing the service promotion service within the CDD environment.

Business model innovation in everis. The service promotion capability allows an automated and context-aware promotion of the most important and relevant digital services in the municipality home pages. In this way, the relevant services will be more accessible for the citizens. This causes a substantial change of the value proposition, as it is not only the SOA platform itself which is being served to the client, but also its ability to compute the most useful service at a certain point of time and to automatize its promotion process (cf. Fig. 3. The arrows represent the information flow between different components. The dotted arrows represent actions performed by the participating roles as well as the changes in the service context). As trends in the service usage are propagated to the similar municipalities, everis can extend its license-based

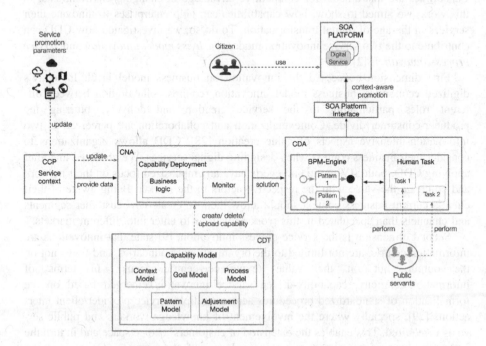

Fig. 3. Digitalized solution architecture in the eGovernment case

revenue model with and effort-based approach, where the municipalities are charged based on the number of promoted services (cf. Table 2). Based on the historical data in the CNA, the service providers can also monitor current relevant services of the municipality and adapt their services accordingly. Thus, customer segmentation in the business model is also expected to change.

Service process innovation in everis. Application of the CDD methodology has helped to understand the parameters that affect the decision of a public servant. Within the CDD environment, such parameters whether to promote a service or not could now be captured systematically, which also enables to track back the decision rationale. The innovative aspects in the service process concerned two aspects. First, the public servant's implicit knowledge is formalized as an executable business process. Necessarily, this minimized public servant's involvement degree in the promotion process. Second, the citizen feedback in social networks impacts the importance of the service, i.e. if the comments are positive, then the service could be highlighted in similar municipalities [24]. This process innovation is manifested on the key resources segment of business model.

Business models communicate the rationale of a company in doing business and can reflect service process or service product-related changes. Hence, we summarize in Table 2 how the business models can change after introducing CDD to the companies.

5   Discussion

Capabilities are instruments for competitive advantage in changing environments. In this work, we aimed to show, how capabilities can help enterprises to innovate their services in the age of digital transformation. To do so, we investigated how CDD can contribute to the two service innovation modes, *business model innovation* and *service process innovation* [2].

First dimension concerned the innovation on business model level. In today's digitized economies, business model innovation requires collaboration between different roles participating to the service creation and delivery, blurring the producer-consumer divide. Contextualization and collaboration are perceived as two information-intensive aspects of value creation [28]. CDD allows organizations to consider their business context when designing digital services. We observed that after applying CDD, both SIV group and everis have an emphasized focus on their network and co-create the value with the respective actors in the market. Being aware of their client's current business context should allow them to create new customer segments and channels than speculated in this work as well as to enter into different markets.

Second dimension is the service process innovation. [9] state that innovations are information-centric, are not limited to the organizational boundaries, and focus not on the output, but on the value (experience-centric focus). In terms of information-centricity, capability-driven service innovation emerged based on the formalization of standardized procedures across multiple service provider/client interactions [29], specially where the involvement of knowledge workers and public servants is required. This enables the extension of customers' choice space and in turn the customers become more and more co-producers of the services. Concerning the back-end tasks, providing guidelines to manage process variability, CDD helped the companies to capture and formalize their hitherto undocumented business processes, which allowed enhanced digital service delivery.

We did not perform an extensive analysis on the third mode, service product innovation. The reason behind this limitation is that the service production and consumption occurs simultaneously in the represented use cases. Moreover, Wang and colleagues identify in a study of 69 service innovation projects only 2 cases, where service product innovation takes place alone (dominant mode) [2]. In terms of service product innovation, we observed that capability-based design may enable SIV group to reposition the "MSCONS clearing" service as "Dynamic clearing center". Moreover, the ability of clients to configure the contract parameters can be applied to the existing services, e.g. accounting and billing. The services provided by the everis' SOA platform are affected by changes in requirements, environment and other aspects. Likewise, by applying CDD, everis can modify and reposition its context-dependent services. One example of this is the registration services, which enables citizens to enroll to activities online, e.g. swimming pool and marriage, as detailed in [24]. Both of the examples support the findings of Wang et al. that service product innovation and process innovation often occur jointly, and many "service product innovations are supported by an innovation in the process" [2]. On the other side, in a manufactural setting, the service product innovation might have been easier to observe, which is not represented in the two use cases.

A similar study about CDD's innovation potential has been performed in [23]. The innovation aspect in this paper concerns the digital services and investigates not only innovation on a business model level, but also on a service process level. Indeed, we share the authors' view that capability analysis could help enterprises to innovate their business models and contribute to their findings in two ways. First, although we use a different conceptualization than the authors, capability-driven design still shows potential for business model innovation. Second, by analyzing the business models and also the service processes of an enterprise from a different industry, we hope to decrease the limitation of their work.

6 Conclusion and Future Work

Due to the fast-paced changes in their environment, enterprises are seeking ways to offer user-specific value propositions to their customers. Service economy is an important determinant of economic growth and transformation. This work investigates how capability-based design can help two organizations, SIV from utility industry and everis from eGovernment sector, to innovate their digital services by innovating their business models and service processes. Both companies applied CDD in an international research project, building on which we present our research results.

To assess the impact of CDD on service innovation, we performed interviews with the business stakeholders of the companies both on management and operational level. Based on our observations from those interviews, the delta between the "as-is" and "to-be" situations documented in [27, 30] as well as the findings in [23], we performed the analysis on business model and service process levels. Conclusively, we argue that by using CDD, both companies may offer their innovative services or "capabilities" to their clients in the future. To eliminate the threat to this finding, future endeavors concern including the practitioners on validating CDD's service innovation potential.

A business model analysis can be performed on generic and specific levels. The analysis performed in this paper concerned the specific level business unit, which is usually defined for business units of a corporate [26]. The impact of CDD on other levels and their relationship with the business unit level are not analyzed. Hence, another limitation of the findings is the generalizability, which also motivates our further work in the field to applying the CDD and measure its effects on various business model levels. Still, the presented work can give significant input about how capability-driven development can pave the way to create value by extending the choice space of customers [8].

The final limitation concerns both the selection of the service innovation framework proposed by [2] as well as the exclusion of the service product innovation mode. Related work revealed other service innovation typologies, e.g. in [10] or [11]. Although these are not directly related to the innovations on business model level, future research endeavors should concern whether the application of CDD triggers service innovation from the lens of different service modes.

Acknowledgments. This work has been performed as part of the EU-FP7 funded project no: 611351 CaaS – Capability as a Service in Digital Enterprises.

References

1. Leimeister, J.M., Österle, H., Alter, S.: Digital services for consumers. Electron Mark. **24**(4), 255–258 (2014). doi:10.1007/s12525-014-0174-6

2. Wang, Q., Voss, C., Zhao, X., et al.: Modes of service innovation: a typology. Ind. Manag. Data Syst. **115**(7), 1358–1382 (2015). doi:10.1108/IMDS-03-2015-0067

3. Zott, C., Amit, R., Massa, L.: The business model: recent developments and future research. J. Manag. **37**(4), 1019–1042 (2011). doi:10.1177/0149206311406265

4. Nair, S., Paulose, H., Palacios, M., et al.: Service orientation: effectuating business model innovation. Serv. Ind. J. **33**(9–10), 958–975 (2013). doi:10.1080/02642069.2013.746670

5. Seelos, C., Mair, J.: Profitable business models and market creation in the context of deep poverty: a strategic view. Acad. Manag. Perspect. **21**(4), 49–63 (2007). doi:10.5465/AMP. 2007.27895339

6. Barlatier, P.-J., Bernacconi, J.-C., Reiter, S.: Service portfolio design for service innovation management: the case of a luxemburgish research and technology organization. In: Morin, J.-H., Ralyté, J., Snene, M. (eds.) IESS 2010. LNBIP, vol. 53, pp. 82–95. Springer, Heidelberg (2010). doi:10.1007/978-3-642-14319-9_7

7. Ostrom, A.L., Parasuraman, A., Bowen, D.E., et al.: Service research priorities in a rapidly changing context. J. Serv. Res. **18**(2), 127–159 (2015). doi:10.1177/1094670515576315

8. Keen, P., Williams, R.: Value architectures for digital business: beyond the business model. MIS Q. **37**(2), 643–648 (2013)

9. Lusch, R., Nambisan, S.: Service innovation: a service-dominant logic perspective. Manag. Inf. Sys. Q. **39**(1), 155–171 (2015)

10. Den Hertog, P.: Knowledge-intensive business services as co-producers of innovation. Int. J. Innov. Manag. **04**(04), 491–528 (2000). doi:10.1142/S136391960000024X

11. Lyytinen, K., Rose, G.M.: The disruptive nature of information technology innovations: the case of internet computing in systems development organizations. MIS Q. **27**(4), 557–596 (2003)
12. Mitchell, D., Coles, C.: The ultimate competitive advantage of continuing business model innovation. J. Bus. Strat. **24**(5), 15–21 (2003). doi:10.1108/02756660310504924
13. Osterwalder, A., Pigneur, Y., Clark, T.: Business Model Generation: A Handbook for Visionaries, Game Changers, and Challengers. Wiley, Hoboken (2010)
14. Chesbrough, H., Rosenbloom, R.: The role of the business model in capturing value from innovation: evidence from Xerox Corporation's technology spin-off companies. Ind. Corp. Change **11**(3), 529–555 (2002). doi:10.1093/icc/11.3.529
15. Lingardt, Z., Reeves, M., Stalk, G., et al.: Business Model Innovation: when the game gets tough, change the game (2009)
16. Eurich, M., Weiblen, T., Breitenmoser, P.: A six-step approach to business model innovation. IJEIM **18**(4), 330–348 (2014). doi:10.1504/IJEIM.2014.064213
17. Zomerdijk, L.G., Voss, C.A.: NSD processes and practices in experiential services*. J. Prod. Innov. Manag. **28**(1), 63–80 (2011). doi:10.1111/j.1540-5885.2010.00781.x
18. Boone, T.: Exploring the link between product and process innovation in services. In: Fitzsimmons, J.A. (ed.) New Service Development: Creating Memorable Service Experiences, pp. 92–110. Sage, Thousand Oaks (2000)
19. Peters, C., Maglio, P., Badinelli, R., et al.: Emerging digital frontiers for service innovation. Commun. Assoc. Inf. Syst. **39**(1) (2016)
20. Berziša, S., Bravos, G., Gonzalez, T.C., et al.: Capability driven development: an approach to designing digital enterprises. Bus. Inf. Syst. Eng. **57**(1), 15–25 (2015). doi:10.1007/s12599-014-0362-0
21. Grabis, J., Henkel, M., Kampars, J., et al.: Deliverable 5.3: The Final Version of Capability Driven Development Methodology: CaaS - Capability as a Service in Digital Enterprises, Collaborative Project Number 611351 (2016)
22. Koç, H., Sandkuhl, K., Fellmann, M.: Towards a flexible solution in knowledge-based service organizations: capability as a service. In: Borangiu, T., Drăgoicea, M., Nóvoa, H. (eds.) IESS 2016. LNBIP, vol. 247, pp. 100–111. Springer, Cham (2016). doi:10.1007/978-3-319-32689-4_8
23. Sandkuhl, K., Stirna, J.: Capability-as-a-service: investigating the innovation potential from a business model perspective. In: Persson, A., Stirna, J. (eds.) CAiSE 2015. LNBIP, vol. 215, pp. 137–148. Springer, Cham (2015). doi:10.1007/978-3-319-19243-7_15
24. España, S., González, T., Grabis, J., Jokste, L., Juanes, R., Valverde, F.: Capability-driven development of a SOA platform: a case study. In: Iliadis, L., Papazoglou, M., Pohl, K. (eds.) CAiSE 2014. LNBIP, vol. 178, pp. 100–111. Springer, Cham (2014). doi:10.1007/978-3-319-07869-4_9
25. Koç, H., Kuhr, J.-C., Sandkuhl, K., Timm, F.: Capability-driven development. In: El-Sheikh, E., Zimmermann, A., Jain, Lakhmi C. (eds.) Emerging Trends in the Evolution of Service-Oriented and Enterprise Architectures. ISRL, vol. 111, pp. 151–177. Springer, Cham (2016). doi:10.1007/978-3-319-40564-3_9
26. Schallmo, D.R.A.: Theoretische Grundlagen der Geschäftsmodell-Innovation – Definitionen, Ansätze, Beschreibungsraster und Leitfragen. In: Schallmo, D.R.A. (ed.) Kompendium Geschäftsmodell-innovation: Grundlagen, aktuelle ansätze und Fallbeispiele zur erfolgreichen geschäftsmodell-Innovation, pp. 1–30. Springer, Wiesbaden (2014). doi:10.1007/978-3-658-04459-6_1
27. Czubayko, U., Koç, H., Kuhr, J.-C., et al.: Deliverable 2.3: BPO Case Validation Report for the CaaS Approach: CaaS - Capability as a Service in Digital Enterprises, Collaborative Project Number 611351 (2016)

28. Lusch, R.F.: Marketing's evolving identity: defining our future. J. Public Policy Mark. **26**(2), 261–268 (2007). doi:10.1509/jppm.26.2.261
29. Barrett, M., Davidson, E., Prabhu, J., et al.: Service innovation in the digital age: key contribution and future directions. Manag. Inf. Syst. Q. **39**(1), 135–154 (2015)
30. Gonzalez, T.C., España, S., Henkel, M., et al.: Deliverable 4.4: PMO and SOA Case Validation Report for the CaaS Approach: CaaS - Capability as a Service in Digital Enterprises, Collaborative Project Number 611351 (2016)

Designing Process Architectures for User Engagement with Enterprise Cognitive Systems

Alexei Lapouchnian[1](✉), Zia Babar[2], Eric Yu[1,2], Allen Chan[3], and Sebastian Carbajales[3]

[1] Department of Computer Science, University of Toronto, Toronto, Canada
alexei@cs.toronto.edu, eric.yu@utoronto.ca
[2] Faculty of Information, University of Toronto, Toronto, Canada
zia.babar@mail.utoronto.ca
[3] IBM Canada Ltd., Markham, Canada
{avchan,sebastia}@ca.ibm.com

Abstract. Cognitive capabilities can enhance a business process by offering automated analytics-based recommendations on key decisions by applying machine learning techniques. Yet the organizational adoption of such advanced capabilities is difficult as user acceptance of advice and recommendations from an automated system requires the development of trust over time. Business processes and the processes responsible for user engagement with enterprise cognitive systems need not only to be designed, but also have to change together with the supporting processes that can emerge and evolve over a period of time to monitor, evaluate, adjust, or modify the cognitively-enhanced business processes to enable employees to adapt to the enhanced capabilities of cognitive systems. In this paper, we propose a systematic modeling approach to study and guide the design and configuration of process architectures that help enterprises implement and evolve systems with cognitive capabilities. The use of suitable enterprise modeling techniques can facilitate the exploration and analysis of obstacles to adoption and guide the systematic search for viable modes of inter-action and cooperation between a human user and a cognitive system.

Keywords: Cognitive computing · Business process management · Enterprise modeling · Enterprise cognitive systems · Business process architecture

1 Introduction

Organizations are increasingly looking to adopt and incorporate cognitive capabilities to help with decision-making tasks within the enterprise. Introducing enterprise cognitive systems (ECS) into any enterprise involves adoption challenges across multiple stakeholder and organizational perspectives. Users must learn to adapt to such systems as part of executing their business process (BP) activities, while the systems themselves have to be designed and configured as per each enterprise's unique requirements [1]. Upon reaching the desired levels of trust, confidence, accuracy, and reliability, these systems can increasingly become entrenched into the enterprise, which results in

© IFIP International Federation for Information Processing 2017
Published by Springer International Publishing AG 2017. All Rights Reserved
G. Poels et al. (Eds.): PoEM 2017, LNBIP 305, pp. 141–155, 2017.
https://doi.org/10.1007/978-3-319-70241-4_10

changes to the design and execution of business processes and the responsibilities of users in charge of these BPs [2, 3]. Enterprise cognitive systems (ECS) refer to software applications that utilize cognitive services, artificial intelligence, and machine learning techniques (among others technologies) to assist with and provide decision-making recommendations for human process participants [4]. Compared to traditional non-cognitive information systems, they do not have to be programmatically instructed to handle all future decisions and can be self-learning and self-adjusting while gradually taking on more decision-making responsibility in business processes [1].

Shifts in work allocation between human users and cognitive systems can be envisioned. They are triggered by well-defined conditions that focus on system performance, users' trust in systems' recommendations, and other important characteristics of human-system engagement. This engagement is not static. It varies over time based on not just evolving capabilities of enterprise systems, but also on user requirements and enterprise context and objectives [5]. In this paper, our view of user engagement (UE) is different from the notion of user engagement (sometimes called *customer engagement*) in marketing, which usually refers to how frequently, how long, etc. users interact with a (software) product [6]. We, on the other hand, use user engagement to describe the ways in which human users interact with enterprise cognitive systems, including the assignment of responsibilities for communication/collaboration, issues of trust, and the ability to override the system. Users' attitude towards automation in general, and the system they are interacting with in particular, can change based on the accumulated history of UE and the quality of the output the system produces – e.g., from feeling threatened, to cautiously optimistic, to wildly enthusiastic about it, and then possibly back to being cautious. These attitudes translate into different desired ways of interacting with the cognitive systems. The nature and impact of these changes to UE may not be limited to the BPs containing the decisions that cognitive systems are assisting humans decision makers with, but can also cause the introduction and modification of the additional supporting processes that monitor, evaluate, adjust, or modify the cognitively-enhanced business processes to enable humans and cognitive systems to adapt to their changing capabilities as well as business contexts and requirements. These business processes need to be studied together as a business process architecture (BPA) in conjunction with the drivers that cause shifts in user engagement and the many possible UE configurations resulting from those shifts.

2   Considering User Engagement During Business Processes Design

Recent years have seen a significant advancement in the sophistication of cognitive computing and its practical utilization in any enterprise. Maturity of cognitive computing and cognitive science is allowing for its increased penetration in the enterprise, with nearly every industry expected to be disrupted by the introduction of cognitive capabilities [8]. We use domain examples below to motivate for the approach discussed in the subsequent sections of the paper:

- Employees are responsible for repetitive execution of enterprise business processes, such as inbound and outbound customer service, processing customer-initiated loan applications, etc. Key user decisions made during process execution, while being informed by relevant data and policies, are based on experience and gut-feel, with the decision-making process considering various contextual and situational factors. As a result, the decisions may not be uniform and consistent and can vary significantly among different decision makers. Increasingly sophisticated cognitive systems can initially help their human users with recommendations for key decisions and later take complete responsibility for decision making, without the assistance or involvement of the users [9, 10]. This would, additionally, alleviate the problem of inconsistent or inaccurate decisions.
- Enterprise IT and cloud infrastructure is ever increasing in size and has stringent requirements for uptime, security, and performance while adhering to tight technology budgets. Consequently, IT departments increasingly rely on automation of key technology activities (like the overall management and monitoring of IT assets) to aid their engineering teams [11]. Cognitive systems are another tool in their overall arsenal that can take advantage of useful application and systems data to streamline deployment, orchestration, and monitoring of various technology assets [12]. By allowing such systems to take over menial and routine tasks, various technology and engineering teams can focus on higher-valued governance-related activities, resulting in the overall shift in user responsibilities and functions.
- Enterprises are typically in the business of providing services to their customers. To reduce operational costs and improve customer services, cognitive systems are increasingly being used as a front-end channel for user communication where they provide a human-like interaction experience to the end-user by utilizing a slew of cognitive capabilities. Financial and wealth management advisory services [13] or personal assistants [14] are some common applications of such systems. The concerns of end-users interacting with these cognitive systems would be different from internal enterprise users and should be considered separately when designing enterprise solutions for cognitive systems integration.

The above examples provide some interesting points to consider. From an *enterprise* and *user* perspective, users are engaging with the new types of cognitive systems being introduced while dealing with real-world business situations. Both sides (i.e., the users and the systems) need to adapt and adjust to each other and eventually converge to a workable state: the users learning to execute their assigned business processes while the systems undergoing cycles of iterative improvements to make them significantly more efficient and intelligent. Factors affecting the adoption success (of the systems by the users) may include the knowledge/skills of involved personnel, their aptitude for understanding the cognitive systems' capabilities and limitations as well as their trust in such systems, willingness to learn and adapt, attitude towards and trust in automation in general, labour relations, reward structures, business domain regulations, etc.

From a *systems* perspective, how a cognitive systems solution is accepted in an enterprise can be very specific to the situation in that organization. But even this situation will continue to evolve as the cognitive system gets better through machine learning or acquires new features, and on the side of user organization, as employees gain experience or learns new skills. Thus, enterprise cognitive systems should be capable of supporting a variety of enterprise business process configurations, with their own roles ranging from assistive, to advisory, to complete responsibility for decision making. Designers of cognitive systems cannot be expected to predict or prescribe exactly how the human side is going to use these systems.

From a *process* perspective, the impact of process-level user engagement is not limited to just direct system interactions, but includes the related processes as well. By related (or surrounding) processes we mean upstream processes that contribute in some way to the primary cognitively-enabled BP, or downstream processes that benefit from the output of the cognitively-enabled BP. These surrounding BPs too evolve in response to changes in cognitive systems' capabilities. Thus, multiple processes need to be considered for analyzing and designing user engagement. Some of these processes may operate at the transactional level while others may execute infrequently. Navigating the space of such possible process configurations that support multiple modes of decision making (from fully manual to partially autonomous to fully autonomous decision making) while considering functional and non-functional objectives of organizations and their users is difficult and may result in trial-and-error practices being employed without convergence to an acceptable solution.

Hence a large space of possible options for user engagement with cognitive systems needs to be considered, with a variety of factors and the complexity of the domain to be taken into consideration. Enterprise architects need to be prepared to help the user organization explore this space by employing techniques from their repertoire to point out the design decisions, possible alternate configurations, while considering aspects such as trust and confidence in the systems' decision-making ability, effort required to help with decision making, compliance with industry regulations and company rules, the cost of deployment, etc. Towards this end, we describe some general types of modes of user engagement suitable for different levels of cognitive sophistication in the enterprise. These lay the foundation for a systematic modeling approach (presented in the later sections) that helps model cognitively-enhanced business processes and considers the evolving needs, capabilities, and expectations in enterprises when designing and operating cognitive systems while also helping to search for workable user engagement arrangements and enabling the reasoning about why certain engagement approaches work and others do not.

3   Towards a Framework for Designing Cognitively-Enhanced Processes

In the previous sections, we highlighted the large space of possibilities for user engagement with cognitive systems that needs to be analyzed based on enterprise and user requirements, the level of trust in the system, the quality of system output, and system and user capabilities. Moreover, we stressed the fact not just the process containing the decision in question, but many additional processes can be impacted when user engagement evolves. This points to the need to model and analyze user engagement not (just) at the level of BPs, but also at the level of a BP Architecture. In this section, we outline an approach for modeling user engagement configurations at both the process and process architecture levels using an advanced BPA modeling approach.

3.1   User Engagement Actions

Let us first look at how UE can be designed from the ground up by focusing on *User Engagement Actions* (UEAs), which represent the elementary interactions that comprise UE with cognitive systems. Some are executed by human users, while others by cognitive systems. The set of these primitives that can potentially be selected for some UE configuration depends on the nature of the task that humans and cognitive systems are solving. For example, if a task is a decision to be made, then the relevant UEAs involving a human decision maker (H) and a cognitive system (C) can include the following tasks:

- *Communicate Case Data*: H communicates the details of the particular decision instance to C. Alternatively, C can obtain the relevant data itself.
- *Communicate Decision Parameters*: H communicates the decision parameters to C, including the criteria for making it, the desired confidence levels, etc.
- *Present Recommendation*: C presents the recommended decision to H. For decisions with more than two potential options (those that are non-binary), a ranked list of options may be given.
- *Approve Recommendation*: H either approves or rejects the previously presented recommendation. Variants for decisions with more than two options may include the ability for the user to pick an alternative option.
- *Explain Recommendation*: Explanation and justification of the recommendation are presented by C to H.
- *Present Decision*: C presents a previously made decision to H (or to a specially designated auditor). Variants include the presentation of batches of decisions for subsequent audits.
- *Audit Decision*: H (or a designated auditor) audits the decision previously made by C. Variants include the audit of batches of decisions.

The above is just a sample of possible actions that may exist to support interactions between humans and cognitive systems. Note that these UEAs can take many forms and employ various media. E.g., recommendations from advisors can be presented as text, voice, video, etc. The same applies to the UEAs that are executed by decision makers. In this paper, we abstract from these details.

3.2   Modeling Cognitively-Enhanced Processes

Organizations and individual decision makers will strive for UEs that reflect their changing enterprise requirements, business domain constrains, the level of trust (of both human decision makers and organizations) in analytics in general and in cognitive systems they are employing in particular, the quality and availability of relevant data, and contexts. This leads to different combinations and configurations of UEAs selected at different times. E.g., the Explain Recommendation UEA can be omitted in case of a high existing level of trust in the system while audits of system-made decisions can be added due to industry regulations. We refer to these UE configurations as User Engagement Modes (UEMs). UEMs need to evolve together with the changes in the above parameters as well as due to the feedback reflecting how they meet their objectives. Also note that for many UEAs, there exist many options about when, how frequently, etc. to execute them. E.g., decision parameters can be selected once for all instances of the decision, changed periodically, or provided for every decision instance. Recommendations can be approved per decision instance or "pre-approved" for a group or for all instances depending on the level of trust in the advisor, the similarity of the current decision instances to previous ones, etc.

Overall, we need to be able to characterize the space of alternative UE configurations reflecting the whole spectrum of UEAs for a given decision, their potential combinations, frequency and scope of their execution, and context, among other things. Standard BP modeling notations are not well equipped to represent these options. To analyze such as space, we need to take into consideration several levels (industry, organization, individual) of requirements and constraints. Further, there would be transitions across sets of UEAs due to changing enterprise requirements, contexts, etc. Also, as previously noted, changes in UE frequently affect related processes and give rise to new processes (e.g., for auditing system-produced decisions).

To address the above challenges, here we apply a previously introduced conceptual modeling framework hiBPM (for *higher-order* BPM) [15–18] for modeling user engagement processes together with organizational and automated processes that surround them and how they relate to each other. This is possible since the framework, which has BPMN as its basis, is being developed for modeling not just single BPs, but multiple BPs and their relationships, thus focusing on BPAs of organizations. Figure 1 presents a simplified BPA for a loan approval scenario, with the loan approval/rejection decision being the focus of our analysis. Figure 1 illustrates the domain-specific processes (e.g., Loan Approval and Loan Repayment), cognitive system-specific processes (e.g., Analytical Model Creation), and BPs that are part of the proposed approach for managing UE, such as UEM Selection (see Sect. 4 for further details on the method).

As part of applying hiBPM, we map UEAs into primitive process activities (referred to as *Process Elements* or PEs) in the BPA. Then, different configurations of PEs will correspond to different UEMs. The chosen set of UEAs needs to be injected into processes executed by both human decision makers and the cognitive systems. In a loan approval scenario (Fig. 1), the UEAs are modeled as shaded activities. It is not just the set of UEAs that can change, but also how these UEAs are executed, how frequently, by whom, etc. In hiBPM, PEs can be placed in various processes called *stages*, which are characterized by their execution frequencies. E.g., a decision maker (a loan officer) can supply desired decision parameters to cognitive system for each instance of a loan approval process (Fig. 1) – note the activity Communicate Decision Params in the Loan Approval process stage. This makes sense if those parameters are likely to be different for every decision instance. Alternatively, the user can preset decision parameters, which is modeled in Fig. 2A by placing the corresponding PE into the Loan Decision Config stage that is executed once for all (or some number of) loan approval

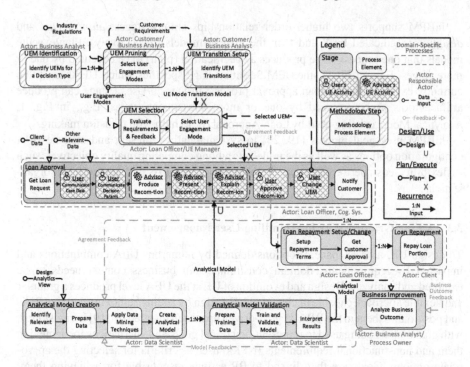

Fig. 1. BPA for a loan approval scenario with manual approval of automated recommendations.

instances (note the 1:N annotation on the outgoing flow, which indicates the recurrence relationship among stages: for each execution of the first stage, many executions of the second one are possible). This is appropriate if those parameters do not depend on the characteristics of each loan approval case. Additionally, note that stages are annotated with actors responsible for their execution and that feedback paths are also indicated to model, for instance, that users' approval/rejection of recommendations feeds back into the stages responsible for analytical model design and for UE management.

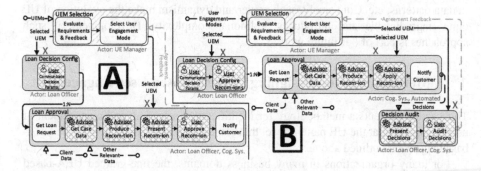

Fig. 2. HiBPM fragments showing alternative UE patterns for loan approval: (A) Preset decision parameters and no recommendation explanation. (B) Automated decision making with manual audits.

hiBPM supports two higher-order relationships among stages: *plan/execute* and *design/use* (indicated by X and U in the hiBPM models, respectively). Plan/execute models that one process stage produces a specification (plan) to be executed by one or more stages. E.g., in Fig. 1, the UEM Selection stage specifies which UEAs are to be currently executed for the loan approval process. In Design/Use, a stage can produce artifacts/tools to be (re)used by one or more subsequent stages. E.g., in Fig. 1, Analytical Model is being used by Loan Approval BP to help with decision making.

hiBPM uses goal models [19, 20] to systematically represent and analyze BPA configuration options as well as the trade-offs among competing quality objectives, such as flexibility, cost, performance, etc. for helping design BPAs that suit particular organizations.

3.3   A Fine-Grained Way for Handling User Engagement

To design UE, a large space of options defined by numerous UEA combinations and impacted by requirements, domain constraints, and business context needs to be explored and analyzed. Design and evolution of UE at the UEA level produces a granular and flexible approach capable of changing UE design by adding/removing certain UEAs and positioning them in the BPA. A goal-driven approach inspired by [19] is envisioned, with goal models being used to represent functional goals and alternatives for achieving them and non-functional requirements (NFRs) used as criteria for selecting the appropriate options. Goals are then linked to BP actions responsible for achieving them. Appropriate configurations of these actions are chosen with the help of goal reasoning algorithms based on functional and non-functional requirements and context. Using this approach improves transparency and predictability since goal models are human-readable.

Similarly, methods based on declarative process modeling [21] or AI-type planning can be used. These approaches would support the dynamic identification of new UE configurations based on changing goals and contexts. These capabilities match cognitive systems' self-adaptation and self-learning capabilities and their support (with the appropriate feedback) for handling previously unidentified conditions, unexpected changes in data patterns, etc. Conversely, such power and dynamism make the evolution of UE quite unpredictable and introduces additional complexity. Development of such approaches is part of our future work.

4   A Methodology for Designing Pattern-Based User Engagement

This section presents a methodology for identification, selection, and management of user engagement at the UE pattern level that can be used as an alternative to the UEA-based approach outlined above.

For many organizations in many business domains, the fine-grained UEA-based approach described in Sect. 3.3 might be overly complex while at the same time lacking in transparency and predictability and providing more flexibility than required. This points to the need for a simpler approach for well-known decision types and for organizations requiring more transparency and predictability in their users' engagement with cognitive systems. One way to address this issue is to propose an coarser-grained approach focusing on UEMs rather than UEAs. In such an approach, given a type of a decision problem, a set of UEMs, each representing a typical UE pattern – a tried-and-tested selection of UEAs and their allocation to the appropriate process stages – is identified. Since finer-grained adjustments (at the UEA level) are not possible, the identified set of UEMs captures the space of UE configurations completely. Such an abstraction reduces the number of options for UE, thus simplifying its management at runtime while also providing more transparency and predictability. Moreover, important types of decision problems can be analyzed ahead of time and the relevant set of UE patterns can be identified for them, to be reused by many enterprises. This supports organizations that may be cautious in relation to cognitive technology and automation in general and simplifies the adoption of cognitive systems in general.

Given some organization, a cognitive system, and a problem at hand (i.e., a decision to be made), how do we design and manage UE in this context? The solution should be a method that takes into consideration organizational goals as well as personal goals of the users involved in decision making, constraints originating within the enterprise and coming from the business domain, and various contexts. For instance, for loan approval, some of these constraints might be the need to either manually approve or audit all recommendations made by automated systems (as illustrated by all the user engagement configurations shown in Figs. 1 and 2). Moreover, a method for managing user engagement needs to support its evolution.

Below we present the steps of the method for designing and evolving UE at the UEM level. Note that with the help of hiBPM, UE management processes can be represented in the same model as runtime domain-specific BPs, such as those involved in loan approvals (see Fig. 1).

Step 1: UE Pattern Identification (See UEM Identification stage in Fig. 1). This step is typically done more rarely than the following steps. This is captured by the recurrence relationship (1:N) the stage has with the subsequent stages. Here, UE patterns are designed using goal-driven analysis techniques available in the hiBPM approach [15, 16] and then empirically validated. Given high-level quality objectives, appropriate UE patterns are identified for particular types of decisions (e.g., approve/reject vs. that with a higher number of possible choices). For instance, for an approval type decision (i.e., with only *yes/no* options), some of the UE patterns that can be identified include:

- *P1: Supervised learning.* Decisions are made by a human decision maker while an enterprise cognitive system (ECS) monitors his work. ECS uses case data, context, and the decision outcome as the input to a supervised learning algorithm.
- *P2: ECS as an Advisor.* Human decision maker makes the decisions while ECS's recommendations are presented as advice.
- *P3: Human approval of ECS's decisions.* ECS's recommendations are approved or rejected by human decision maker (per decision instance) – e.g., see Fig. 1.
- *P4: Human is informed of decisions by ECS.* A human decision maker is informed of ECS's decisions (per instance).

- *P5: ECS's decisions with (batch) human audits*. Humans audit ECS's decisions periodically (once per N number of decision instances, once in a certain time interval, etc.) – see Fig. 2B as an example.
- *P6: ECS's decisions with human audits on request*. Humans can audit ECS's recommendations whenever they wish.
- *P7: ECS's decisions with automated self-audits*. Humans are not involved by default, but can review automated self-audits.

In Figs. 1 and 2, selected UE patterns are evident from the UEAs (shown as shaded activities) that are present in the Loan Approval process. Variations of the above patterns with slightly different UEA arrangements are possible. In Fig. 1, one can see that the decision maker (a loan officer in this case) communicates case data and decision parameters within the Loan Approval stage (i.e., for every instance of that loan approval decision), indicating that volatility is expected in these areas. Upon presenting its recommendation, a cognitive system explains it to the user. This indicates that the loan officer does not yet fully trust the system. It is a variant of the UE pattern P3.

Step 2: UE Pattern Pruning   (See UEM Pruning stage in Fig. 1). To further customize user engagement, the set of UE patterns identified in Step 1 *can* be pruned based on particular organization's and/or user's requirements and constraints. E.g., in some domains and/or organizations, audit of decisions may be mandatory and only the patterns containing the audit UEAs will be selected. This step of the approach is normally executed for every decision problem to select the set of UE patterns available for each decision that requires cognitive system assistance.

Step 3: UE Pattern Transition Setup   (See UEM Transition Setup in Fig. 1). Here, we switch our attention to the dynamic aspect of UE and model its possible evolution trajectories by specifying transitions between UE patterns triggered based on a certain level of trust in the system (e.g., Fig. 2A shows the UE pattern missing the task Explain Recommendation, perhaps due to a high level of user trust in a cognitive system), a certain quality of recommendations (recent recommendations of lower quality may warrant a reduction of automation level and the shift, say, from automated decision making to cognitive systems only providing advice to humans). This step is usually run once per decision problem instance – e.g., for a particular loan approval BP.

Context change may also trigger a transition to a different UE pattern – e.g., a significant shift in the properties of decision instances compared to the dataset on which the analytical model was trained can cause a selection of a more conservative (less-automated) UE pattern until the model has been retrained. Quality requirements and organizational or problem domain constraints will affect the transitions as well. Similarly, the ability to manually trigger transitions or override automatically triggered transitions, which puts humans in control of the automation, is important as trust plays a crucial role in UE. All of this helps with transparency and predictability in UE evolution. While this approach can only handle predefined conditions and evolution trajectories since they are explicitly defined upfront, all methodology steps can be re-run when needed. Thus, UEM Identification and UEM Transition Setup can be re-executed to update the set of UE patterns and/or to change the transitions among them. This produces a potentially new output to be reused in the subsequent stages in the hiBPM model.

Statecharts are used to define possible UE transitions, with states representing UE patterns and transitions referring to the possible UE evolution paths. Figure 3 shows a statechart capturing one possible UE evolution specification using the patterns discussed in Step 1 and modeled as states in the model. Transition labels specify conditions that trigger changes in the active UE configurations. E.g., once the analytical model is trained in P1, the UE state changes to P2 where a cognitive system is acting as an advisor to humans. Then, once its recommendations are deemed to be of high quality, the system starts making decisions and applying them with human approval (P3). If a change in business context is detected in the states P2-P4, the supervised learning UEM (P1) is activated. Greyed out states (P5) are those removed in Step 2 of the approach.

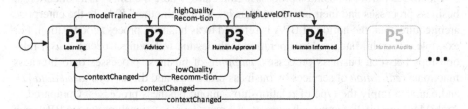

Fig. 3. An abstract statechart illustrating UEM transitions.

Step 4: UE Pattern Selection (See UEM Selection in Fig. 1). In this step, a process running concurrently with the BP containing the decision (Loan Approval in our examples) monitors the various parameters through feedback (focusing on decision quality, etc.), evaluates triggers, and drives the appropriate changes in user engagement. It uses a model like the one in Fig. 3 to enact UE changes. Looking at the hiBPM model in Fig. 1, we see that UEM Selection *executes* the transitions *planned* by UEM Transition Setup(thus, the plan/execute relationships between these BPA stages). Moreover, UEM Selection itself implements the chosen UE pattern by instantiating the appropriate stages and instructing which UEAs to execute (also modeled by plan/execute stages). Different UE patterns create different BPA variations, as evident from the comparison of Figs. 1, 2A and B.

Figure 2A and B give examples of the range of options for specifying UE, showing both the set of UEAs and their positioning in the BPA. Figure 2A is a fragment BPA illustrating a UE pattern where decision parameters are preconfigured (see the separate Loan Decision Config stage), no recommendation explanation is provided, and manual UE pattern change is no longer available (compared to Fig. 1). Figure 2B shows a fully automated loan approval process. There, Approve Recommendation is executed in the stage prior to Loan Approval, indicating that cognitive system's recommendations are approved for a certain time frame or number of decision instances, thus stressing the high level of trust in the system. Note that this "pre-approval" is about system recommendations and is different from the domain-specific action of pre-approving loans.

5 Related Work

Decision making and decision theory are much-studied areas in psychology and having an understanding of the deliberation process and the outcome can help in designing artificial cognitive systems that emulate a human decision-making process. Rational and descriptive approaches to decision-making and judgements are discussed in [22], including how decisions can be reached by deliberating among complex alternatives while considering emotions. Actors may not always invoke an optimum logic to select the best alternative within a set of possibilities, but rather have preferential solutions to a problem based on prior experience; this selection of a solution as part of routinized decision making is a component of an ongoing learning and evolving process [23].

Within any enterprise, there exist multiple business processes that can be collectively considered as part of a business process architecture, where the BPA "is a collection of business processes and their interdependencies with each other" [24]. In the enterprise architecture area, the notion of BPA is referred to as business process cooperation. For example, in ArchiMate, such cooperation includes the following aspects: *causal* relationships between business processes, *mapping* of business processes onto business functions, *realization* of services by business processes, and the *use of shared data* [7], and can also imply the type of relationships among business processes. Compared to ArchiMate, our hiBPM approach supports the meta-level relationships among BPs, such as plan/execute, which helps integrate multiple levels of processes into BPAs. For instance, it supports the modeling of UE evolution.

Cognition is the process by which "an autonomous system perceives its environment, learns from experience, anticipates the outcome of events, acts to pursue goals, and adapts to changing circumstances" [25]. The impact of cognitive computing on business process management (BPM) is covered in [26] where multiple types/levels of business processes are discussed – transaction-intensive, judgement-intensive, and design & strategy support processes – resulting from the incorporation of cognitive capabilities within an enterprise and how cognitive processes enablement can be attained.

Human-Computer Interaction (HCI) involves the study of the communication of information and data between a human user and a computer through an interface, using various modes and mechanisms such as input/output peripheral devices, voice, text, sound, gesture control etc. [27]. HCI aims to greatly improve the experience of the user interaction by leveraging the principles of information design, interaction design and sensorial design [28]. We approach the problem of user engagement with machines differently in that we consider the shifts in user approaches for decision making (as part of a routine business process execution) that are caused by changes in the design and implementation of cognitive systems.

Agent-Oriented approaches to software engineering provide design and implementation guide for software agents that need to demonstrate autonomous behaviour and social ability while responding (both proactively and reactively) to changing environmental stimuli [29]. Software agents need to have intentions, beliefs and mental states based on which they'd plan, negotiate and perform actions which are deduced rather than programmatically executes. In this paper, we considered cognitive systems with much less social ability compared to a typical software agent. The body of research on agents and multiagent systems can provide a wealth of techniques and ideas for handling user engagement with cognitive systems.

6   Conclusions and Future Work

This paper focuses on the issues of designing and configuring BPAs where user engagement with enterprise cognitive systems is considered. Such user engagement needs to take into consideration trust in the systems' decision-making abilities, organizational and user requirements and constraints, and evolving business and technological context. A UEM – a way a human interacts with a cognitive system – and the BPA implementing it are not static and must evolve since the above parameters are also dynamically changing. To support the design and evolution of UE, user engagement actions were proposed as the building blocks of UE. A systematic model-driven approach based on the hiBPM BPA modeling framework is outlined. This framework is utilized for modeling the space of UE options through multiple levels of process modeling, higher-level relationships between business processes, and other advanced features. Although not illustrated in this paper, to analyze the space of options, hiBPM's requirements-driven techniques focusing on reasoning about objectives, alternative solutions, and trade-offs can be utilized.

This approach is a starting point for the development of a comprehensive method aimed at simplifying enterprise adoption of advanced cognitive systems by enabling the systematic design of UE with such systems based on organizational, social, and technical needs and constraints and supporting the ongoing evolution of such engagements driven by changes in these parameters. Overall, this method is aimed at supporting a systematic and controlled introduction of automation into organizations. Among other things, future research in this area will focus on the following:

- As stressed in the paper, the issue of trust if of paramount concern when it comes to user engagement. We plan to investigate how to incorporate the analysis and evaluation of trust into our approach together with the identification of various UEAs aimed specifically at establishing, maintaining, and increasing trust.
- Introduction of cognitive systems in enterprises usually results in increasing automation and thus causes changes in responsibility assignments among humans and automated systems. We plan to study this dimension of change in more detail while focusing on the social and organizational impact of such changes.
- We plan to focus on more complex types of decisions/recommendations (compared to the approve/reject type discussed in this paper) and identify new sets of UEAs and UE patterns as well as the typical transitions among these patterns for those decision types. Moreover, the we plant to develop the corresponding BPAs for those UE configurations to simplify the adoption of cognitive systems by enterprises,
- We would also like to concentrate on a more thorough modeling and analysis of feedback in the context of user engagement and on identifying the typical metrics and triggers to be used in specifying UE evolution.

- While we are building on the foundation of goal and process modeling many features of the proposed approach are novel and need to be further studied, implemented, and validated.

At present, we are working with a large enterprise software provider and aim to introduce the proposed approach into its business process management offering and subsequently validate it in real-world engagements.

Acknowledgement. This work was partially funded by IBM Canada Ltd. through the Centre for Advanced Studies (CAS) Canada (Project #1030).

References

1. Ogiela, L., Ogiela, M.R.: Advances in Cognitive Information Systems, vol. 17. Springer, Heidelberg (2012)
2. Muir, B.M.: Trust between humans and machines, and the design of decision aids. Int. J. Man Mach. Stud. **27**(5–6), 527–539 (1987)
3. Lee, J.D., See, K.A.: Trust in automation: designing for appropriate reliance. Hum. Factors **46**(1), 50–80 (2004)
4. Schatsky, D., Gurumurthy, R.: Cognitive Technologies – Applying Machine Intelligence to Traditional Business Problems. Deloitte University Press (2015). https:// dupress.deloitte.com/dup-us-en/focus/signals-for-strategists/trends-cognitive-technology-business-issues.html. Accessed
5. Hull, R., Nezhad, H.R.M.: Rethinking BPM in a cognitive world: transforming how we learn and perform business processes. In: La Rosa, M., Loos, P., Pastor, O. (eds.) BPM 2016. LNCS, vol. 9850, pp. 3–19. Springer, Cham (2016). doi:10.1007/978-3-319-45348-4_1
6. O'Brien, H.L., Toms, E.G.: What is user engagement? A conceptual framework for defining user engagement with technology. J. Assoc. Inf. Sci. Technol. **59**(6), 938–955 (2008)
7. ArchiMate 3.0 Specification. http://pubs.opengroup.org/architecture/archimate3-doc/. Accessed
8. Chui, M.: Artificial intelligence the next digital frontier?, McKinsey and Company Global Institute (2017). https://www.mckinsey.de/files/170620_studie_ai.pdf. Accessed
9. Bond, A.H., Gasser, L. (eds.): Readings in Distributed Artificial Intelligence. Morgan Kaufmann, San Mateo (2014)
10. Kushniruk, A.W.: Analysis of complex decision-making processes in health care: cognitive approaches to health informatics. J. Biomed. Inform. **34**(5), 365–376 (2001)
11. Cherubini, G., Jelitto, J., Venkatesan, V.: Cognitive storage for big data. Comput. Mag. **49**(4), 43–51 (2016)
12. Talia, D.: Towards internet intelligent services based on cloud computing and multi-agents. In: Gaglio, S., Lo Re, G. (eds.) Advances onto the Internet of Things. AISC, vol. 260, pp. 271–283. Springer, Cham (2014). doi:10.1007/978-3-319-03992-3_19
13. Benjamin, B., Burrowes, K., Gemes, A., Hogan, A., Lenzhofer, A., Ong, J., Spellacy, M.: Sink or swim: Why wealth management can't afford to miss the digital wave. Strategy & PwC (2016). https://www.strategyand.pwc.com/media/file/Sink-or-swim.pdf. Accessed
14. Myers, K., Berry, P., Blythe, J., Conley, K., Gervasio, M., McGuinness, D.L., Morley, D., Pfeffer, A., Pollack, M., Tambe, M.: An intelligent personal assistant for task and time management. AI Mag. **28**(2), 47–61 (2007)

15. Lapouchnian, A., Yu, E., Sturm, A.: Re-designing process architectures towards a framework of design dimensions. In: IEEE 9th International Conference on Research Challenges in Information Science (RCIS 2015), pp. 205–210. IEEE (2015)

16. Lapouchnian, A., Yu, E., Sturm, A.: Design dimensions for business process architecture. In: Johannesson, P., Lee, M.L., Liddle, Stephen W., Opdahl, Andreas L., López, Ó.P. (eds.) ER 2015. LNCS, vol. 9381, pp. 276–284. Springer, Cham (2015). doi: 10.1007/978-3-319-25264-3_20

17. Lapouchnian, A., Yu, E.: Exploiting emergent technologies to create systems that meet shifting expectations. In: 24th Annual International Conference on Computer Science and Software Engineering, pp. 371–374. IBM Corporation (2014)

18. Babar, Z., Lapouchnian, A., Yu, E.: Modeling DevOps Deployment Choices Using Process Architecture Design Dimensions. In: Ralyté, J., España, S., Pastor, Ó. (eds.) PoEM 2015. LNBIP, vol. 235, pp. 322–337. Springer, Cham (2015). doi:10.1007/978-3-319-25897-3_21

19. Lapouchnian, A., Yu, Y., Mylopoulos, J.: Requirements-driven design and configuration management of business processes. In: Alonso, G., Dadam, P., Rosemann, M. (eds.) BPM 2007. LNCS, vol. 4714, pp. 246–261. Springer, Heidelberg (2007). doi: 10.1007/978-3-540-75183-0_18

20. Lapouchnian, A., Yu, Y., Liaskos, S., Mylopoulos, J.: Requirements-driven design of autonomic application software. In: IBM CAS Conference (CASCON) (2006)

21. De Giacomo, G., Dumas, M., Maggi, F.M., Montali, M.: Declarative process modeling in BPMN. In: Zdravkovic, J., Kirikova, M., Johannesson, P. (eds.) CAiSE 2015. LNCS, vol. 9097, pp. 84–100. Springer, Cham (2015). doi:10.1007/978-3-319-19069-3_6

22. Hastie, R., Dawes, R.M.: Rational Choice in an Uncertain World: The Psychology of Judgment and Decision Making, 2nd edn. Sage Publishing, Thousand Oaks (2010)

23. Betsch, T., Haberstroh, S., Hohle, C.: Explaining routinized decision making: a review of theories and models. Theory Psychol. **12**(4), 453–488 (2002)

24. Eid-Sabbagh, R.-H., Dijkman, R., Weske, M.: Business process architecture: use and correctness. In: Barros, A., Gal, A., Kindler, E. (eds.) BPM 2012. LNCS, vol. 7481, pp. 65–81. Springer, Heidelberg (2012). doi:10.1007/978-3-642-32885-5_5

25. Vernon, D.: Artificial Cognitive Systems: A primer. MIT Press, Cambridge (2014)

26. Hull, R., Nezhad, H.R.M.: Rethinking BPM in a cognitive world: transforming how we learn and perform business processes. In: La Rosa, M., Loos, P., Pastor, O. (eds.) BPM 2016. LNCS, vol. 9850, pp. 3–19. Springer, Cham (2016). doi:10.1007/978-3-319-45348-4_1

27. Dix, A.: Human-computer interaction. In: Liu, L., ÖZsu, M.T. (eds.) Encyclopedia of Database Systems, pp. 1327–1331. Springer, Boston (2009). doi: 10.1007/978-1-4899-7993-3_192-2

28. Shedroff, N.: Information interaction design: a unified field theory of design. In: Information Design, pp. 267–292 (1999)

29. Bresciani, P., Perini, A., Giorgini, P., Giunchiglia, F., Mylopoulos, J.: Tropos: an agent-oriented software development methodology. Auton. Agent. Multi-Agent Syst. **8**(3), 203–236 (2004)

An Analysis of Enterprise Architecture for Federated Environments

Niklas Lindström[1], Björn Nyström[2], and Jelena Zdravkovic[2(✉)]

[1] HSB Stockholm, Fleminggatan 41, Stockholm, Sweden
niklas.lindstrom@hsb.se
[2] Department of Computer and Systems Sciences, Stockholm University, Kista, Sweden
{bjny7070,jelenaz}@dsv.su.se

Abstract. The challenge of business and IT-alignment has been a major concern for IT managers over the last few decades, as an increased congruence between the two aspects improves effectivity and results in organizations. Enterprise Architecture (EA) addresses the alignment by providing a holistic model-based view of the organization. However, previous research has revealed some generic discrepancies in prominent EA frameworks regarding their support towards more decentralized organizational structures. Following a case study research of a federated organization this paper analyzes in depth The Open Group Architecture Framework (TOGAF) EA framework, and based on identified discrepancies how it should be extended to provide an adequate support. By enabling the establishment and maintenance of a federated EA, the proposed extension should further increase the business and IT-alignment for federated organizations.

Keywords: Enterprise Architecture · TOGAF · Organizational structure

1 Introduction

A major concern for IT managers during the last few decades has been business-IT alignment [1, 2]. The emergence of the global and increasingly complex organizational environments has entailed a wider use of decentralized structures within them. Decentralization allows organizations to encounter some of the past decade's most important business concerns, including cost reduction, productivity, agility, and time to market [3]. However, the alignment can become increasingly difficult when utilizing a decentralized structure due to the decision-power being pushed out into the organization, increasing the challenge of moving in a unanimous direction [4, 5]. Research has shown that an organization with effective alignment between business and IT outperform non-aligned organizations in both turnover and growth [2, 6, 7].

To solve the alignment problems, there are multiple theoretical approaches available. Earlier research has presented approaches such as developing a digital business strategy [6, 8], following IT governance models [9], and implementing enterprise architecture frameworks [7]. Enterprise Architecture (EA) is a comprehensive framework that links an enterprise's main components, e.g. business strategy and goals, processes,

G. Poels et al. (Eds.): PoEM 2017, LNBIP 305, pp. 156–170, 2017.
https://doi.org/10.1007/978-3-319-70241-4_11

information systems and infrastructure [10], providing a holistic, model-based blueprint of the enterprise. EA frameworks used in today's organizations are mostly The Open Group Framework (TOGAF) [11], Federal Enterprise Architecture (FEA) [12], Department of Defense Architecture Framework (DoDAF) [13], British Ministry of Defense Architecture Framework (MODAF) [14], and NATO Architecture Framework (NAF) [15]. Sandkuhl et al. [16] mention that TOGAF is more widely used across multiple branches than the other frameworks previously named. According to The Open Group's blog [17], the amount of TOGAF certified people across the globe has now exceeded 60 000, compared to 7000 the year 2011 and 13 000 during the year 2013 which gives an indication of its fast-paced growth.

By combining business strategy and goals, processes, and information systems in an enterprise and not solely focusing on specific aspects (such as strategy or IT governance), it should be possible to solve the business-IT alignment problem. However, previous research has shown that there are discrepancies between the EA and its possibility to solve major CIO concerns, such as decision support for issues related to the IT organization and estimating and managing costs [18]. Furthermore, Speckert et al. [19], argue that EA frameworks do not support decentralized organizational structures. Combined with [20] stating that the frameworks were initially developed focusing on a centralization of IT and management; it entails an emergence of problems such as governance and decision-making irregularities in decentralized organizations.

The paper presents a case study research conducted in a large Swedish company in the real estate business domain. The research critically analyzed TOGAF and the way of working in the organization. Using the elicited knowledge, it attempted to highlight insufficiencies of TOGAF in contrast to the identified federated structural aspects of the organization, and suggest potential improvements. The results should facilitate further harmonization between EA and federated organizations as well as it should increase the business-IT alignment of organizations with similar characteristics.

The paper is organized as follows: Sect. 2 presents a brief overview of EA and TOGAF, different organization structures, and related works. Section 3 describes the organization of the case study, while Sect. 4 provides research results in details. Section 5 follows with a discussion of the results, and Sect. 6 provides concluding remarks as well as relevant directions for further research.

2 Background

2.1 EA, TOGAF

Situated at the level of an enterprise, EA regards an interconnected overarching set of methods, principles, and models utilized in the development and implementation of an enterprise's organizational structure, business processes, information systems, and infrastructure, attempting to align business with IT [21]. Because developing an EA generates a significant number of architectural components, e.g. artefacts, dividing the EA into different architecture layers provides a structure among the components and reduces the number of elements residing in the same model. TOGAF is an EA framework created by The Open Group [22] defining a subset of architecture layers: Business

Architecture; Information System Architecture (including Data- and Application Architecture); and Technology Architecture. Furthermore, the framework enables the inclusion of other architectural styles, such as Security Architecture and Service Oriented Architecture (SOA). TOGAF is divided into six parts, and each part is accounted for as a main component: Architecture Development Model (ADM), ADM Guidelines and Techniques, Architecture Content Framework, Enterprise Continuum and Tools, Reference Models and Architecture Capability Framework. Below we describe the framework's essences relevant for the results of the study.

ADM describes a process for developing and managing the TOGAF core [11]; the process is repeatable and an iterative cycle for building and transforming the organization. Figure 1 below visualizes the ADM process, with the circles representing the main phases A-H and a continuous Requirements Management phase, and the arrows representing the flow of artefacts between the phases.

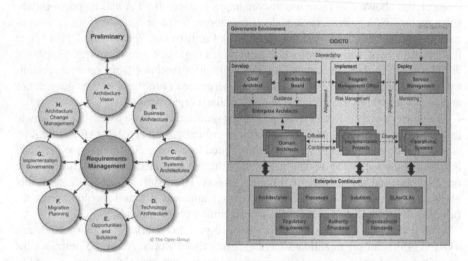

Fig. 1. TOGAF's ADM process (left) and Architecture Governance Framework [11]

Architecture Capability Framework presents support to establish, operate and control at the enterprise level the architecture function according to the organization structure, business processes, roles, responsibilities, and skills, controlled at the enterprise level [11]. Two vital concepts involving the implementation, development, and governance of the EA, is Architecture Governance and Architecture Board, both positioned in the Architecture Capability Framework. The concept of Architecture Governance [11, Chap. 50] includes a framework and guidelines regarding architecture governance. TOGAF suggests that architecture governance could be practiced in four separate domains, including corporate, technology, IT, and architecture governance. In turn, each domain and their area of responsibility may exist in multiple levels within the whole enterprise. The Architecture Governance Framework is shown in Fig. 1.

To increase the success rate of architecture's governance, TOGAF suggests the implementation of an Architecture Board. The concept of Architecture Board [11, Chap.

47] refers to a cross-organization group overseeing the implementation of the architecture strategy. Its main responsibilities include providing the basis for all decision-making regarding the various architectures, enforcing architecture compliance, and ensuring compliance and adherence with specified Architecture Contracts, which details joint requirements regarding the architectures. TOGAF suggests that the Architecture Board should consist of four or five members.

2.2   Organizational Structure

Enterprise activities are often grouped into subdivisions - departments, such as marketing, sales, manufacturing. The capabilities, responsibilities, and interconnection of the various subdivisions are defined in enterprise's organizational structure referring to *the formal configuration between individuals and groups regarding the allocation of tasks, responsibilities, and authority within the organization* [23, p. 1]. Furthermore, [24, p. 451] states that organizational structure shapes an ecology of distinct frames that exist at the level of organizational subunits. Organizations can be distinguished from a few different dimensions [23], where the relevant for this study is *The Type of Decentralization*, referring to where decisions in the organization are conducted.

Deciding upon the degree of decentralization in an organization can be a difficult task. Typically, different organizations, although facing similar conditions and environment, will choose different settings of decentralization, as described in [25]. In Fig. 2, three main kinds of organizational structures are visualized, including (a) Centralized, (b) Federated, and (c) Decentralized. The circle shaped forms in the figure represent various subunits of the organization, and the archs refer to the steering forces of decision-making power and authority.

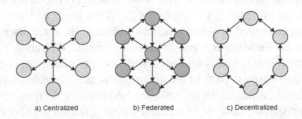

a) Centralized   b) Federated   c) Decentralized

Fig. 2.   Three types of organizational structure

A centralized structure induces that the steering forces flow from a center unit towards the various subunits, and with a decision-making process where all authority and power resides within one center, e.g. a top management group or one specific individual, providing a tight type of structure with increased coordination and supervision [26]. A federated structure, similarly to the centralized approach, contains a center; however, the steering forces between the center and subunits are bidirectional and exist between the subunits, making the central unit informal. A federated structure consists of multiple (semi-)autonomous subunits sharing a common mission and purpose. Usually, the subunits together share the control of the central body, and each subunit enters the larger association voluntarily. A decentralized structure contains no central unit, i.e. authority and decision power are shared among organizational subunits [26].

Utilizing a centralized structure implies that all decisions are founded on knowledge relying on the central unit. However, by moving towards a more decentralized approach, decisions can be made by people with increased knowledge regarding the specific area of business. Decentralization suits situations when sufficient knowledge to support the decision-making process is too cumbersome to transfer or when cognitive limitations exist in the central unit. Furthermore, decentralization enables quicker adoption to local dynamic environments by reducing steps in the decision-making process, and it contributes to stimulating creativity and innovation [26]. According to [27], a trade-off exists between knowledge transfer costs and control costs. Larger organizations with expanding potential facing volatile and unstable environments tend to generate more specialized knowledge that is increasingly difficult to transfer to decision makers, thus making decentralization a more appropriate approach. Furthermore, according to [25], a more decentralized structure induces better alignment between the subunits' ideas and their environment, although at the cost of reduced learning and improvement between subunits.

2.3   Related Work

A significant amount of research has been conducted in the area of business-IT alignment and EA, however, the articles related in the same context as ours – decentralization issue, are very few. [27] emphasizes that the frameworks were initially developed focusing on a centralization of IT and central management, entailing emergence of problems such as governance and decision-making irregularities due to the characteristics of non-centralized organizations. In an article by Lindström et al. [18], a survey was conducted concluding that the available EA frameworks fulfill the needs and solve problems in theory, but when compared to actual practical problems, there are discrepancies. The survey indicated that the major concerns of Chief Information Officers (CIOs) in Sweden are to decrease the cost of business-related elements e.g. personnel, increase the interplay between the IT and business parts of the organization, provide technological solutions supporting the business part of the organization, and improve the quality of IT systems along with decreasing the costs of IT related elements. The survey revealed that some of the available EA frameworks provide insufficient support to solve the top concerns of the CIOs, and the authors suggested further harmonization between the concerns and EA framework's foci is needed. Similar conclusions were derived in [16, 17] stating that discrepancies between TOGAF and the federated organizational structure exist. Speckert et al. [19] addressed the challenge of EA for decentralized organizations by investigating and concluding that commonly utilized EA frameworks need to be extended to support such organizations (included even FEA, which despite the recognition of individual units prescribes standards that are to be followed throughout the organization limiting thus flexibility and opinions of the units). However, as for the aspect of solving the identified problems, the results of this paper differ. [19] suggests a more theoretical solution, by utilizing peer production in the matters of decision making and governance within EA. The developed artefact of this study is closer aligned to the practical operational conduct of federated organizations and thus in more depth reflecting the characteristics of such organizations. Therefore, the results comprise increased alignment between EA, in particular TOGAF, and federated organization's actual way of working.

3 Business Case

The business case regards a federated Swedish organization concerned in developing, building and managing real estate. The organization consists of multiple semi- autonomous subunits. They are autonomous in the sense of having their customer base, deciding upon what services they provide, and having full ownership of their economy (Fig. 2). 28 federated units share a common mission and a purpose defined at a national level. The enterprise is owned by its members and can be split into two parts, national level, and regional level (Fig. 3).

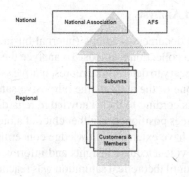

Fig. 3. The organizational structure of the enterprise

At the regional level, the core business is executed. The autonomous subunits own the deliverables and the results that are produced. To be a member of the enterprise/ federation organization, a membership is needed, as well as compliance with company's regulations. The structure and operational concepts deciding how the subunits conduct and manage their internal business is solely decided upon within each subunit without the interference of external actors.

At the national level, there exists coordinating and supporting functions. The National Association is the owner of the company brand and it is responsible for the company's vision, public appearances that regard national statements, as well as all political involvement. AFS is the internal business support organization (swe. Affärsstöd) merging the IT infrastructure and digital services of the federated organization into one company to achieve synergy effects. This for example implies that different IT functions already existing within the federated organization have been combined into one starting thus to provide a centralized IT service. AFS works with joint processes and approaches that the subunits within the federated organization decide upon. Based on the needs of the federated organization, new solutions are developed with the goal to be competitive as well as customized towards the federated subunits' needs. This implies that all necessary joint solutions, whether they are IT- or business oriented, are developed, delivered and maintained by AFS. However, being autonomous, it is not mandatory for any subunit of the federated organization to purchase joint solutions.

Merging of multiple processes and infrastructure into one has entailed several problems. AFS has centralized the IT infrastructure, while applications and IT decisions are still decentralized. Business needs in the federated organization are identified through a longer development process, which increases the time to market and decision-making times. The CIO of AFS has therefore requested an analysis of how the concept of EA, and more specifically TOGAF, could solve important practical problems within the organization such as lack of integration schemes, guidelines regarding data-handling, architectural and platform documentation, and other, while at the same time fully adhering to the established federated structure and way of working.

4   Case Study Results

4.1   Data Collection and Analysis

The case study combined document-readings (internal-business) and semi-structured interviews as the main data collection methods. To analyze the way of working through the interviews, it was necessary to determine a representative sampling. Since the organization is well known to one of the authors, the purposive sampling was used, i.e. the respondents were picked according to their knowledge regarding the organization and its operations. The employees positioned as either chief of a business unit or supporting functions were deemed to have extensive knowledge concerning the organization, and thus they were able to provide adequate insights and information. Data collection and sampling were conducted until theoretical saturation was reached, i.e. when the analysis of new data solely contributed to the confirmation of previously derived insights, which was achieved after 8 interviews.

The analysis has resulted in a thematic map consisting of the key concepts reflecting the federated organization's ways of working (Fig. 4).

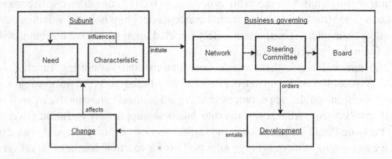

Fig. 4. Thematic map from the study analysis

Subunit. The federated organization consists of multiple subunits. The subunits are fully autonomous economic powers in charge of day-to-day operations, inferring a complete control and decision mandate, except for certain guidelines and policies specified on the national level. Induced by the autonomous nature of the subunits, the federated organization lacks a joint business strategy. The concept denoted Characteristics is coupled to every Subunit and influence its Needs. Some examples of Characteristics is the size (number of employees), turnaround, economic strength, amount of members/ customers, business units, way of working, local competition. Various characteristics infer different needs, such as larger subunits having an expanded need for automation due to the increased demand for employees in non-automated processes. The subunits of the federated organization have different needs, which can be either unique or shared with other subunits. The subunits desire to have their needs solved by joint solutions, but not all unique needs in a subunit can be addressed, inducing complications for the subunits and the federation. Furthermore, investing in information systems is expensive, and the subunits will not survive the market competition if they keep moving in separate directions. Developing joint solutions that work for all subunits is more efficient. To gather the proposals for the development of joint solutions and to allow each subunit to voice their opinion, the federated organization has developed and implemented a way of working, further described as Business Governing.

Business governing.   The concept embraces the way of taking federated business decisions by combining Networks, Steering Committees and Board. The business governing function in the federated organization embraces all matters, whether they are IT-related or business-related. The business decisions are empowered, either through AFS that develops IT solutions to support the business, or through the networks handling strictly business-oriented matters, such as policy updates. Each core business area within the federated organization has its own Network. The networks are populated by representatives from the subunits working in the relevant business areas. By introducing the concept of networks, the federated organization has simplified the subunits possibility to voice their opinion and to further increase the anchoring of proposed ideas, boosting the persuasive force of steering in a common direction. The concept of network acts as an interface towards the subunits to ensure their possibility to fulfill their democratic rights. The Steering Committee is democratically chosen and populated directly from the network representatives. By further aggregating the networks into smaller groups, proposals can be prioritized and discussed in a democratic matter, while also reducing the number of stakeholders involved, which could otherwise distort the attention towards the holistic progress of the federated organization. The steering committees could be described as filters percolating the proposals and forwarding prioritized proposals to the board. The Board is populated by business manager representatives from the subunits. The board's task is to assess the proposals received from the steering committee. In the assessment process, the board will check adherence with the federated organization deciding whether the proposal would induce a positive or negative outcome not solely for individual subunits. An idea assessed and accepted by the board will eventually lead to development.

Development.   The development of common solutions within the federated organization entails multiple constraints, problems, and considerations. The various Characteristics and Needs of the individual Subunits and the great span of differentiation among them produce a challenging way of creating common solutions, as it requires various reorganizations in the subunits and control over employees, process descriptions, which is a big job especially for larger subunits. The maturity level regarding the subunits ability to receive and utilize solutions further infers problems to the development process, as although subunits may require the specific common solutions, their ability to receive and utilize it correctly could be cumbersome. Furthermore, multiple subunits possess existing individual solutions, which affect the outcome and their interest in newly developed common solutions. Additionally, a major concern regarding the development process involves financing, as it is voluntary for the individual subunits to participate and purchase the common solutions. The development phase is initiated by a pilot study, which involves a group of subunit business representatives deemed as experts within their respective fields. The finalized pilot study suggests a solution (whether the solution is bought on the market or self-developed) with complete pricing including user-support, system administration, future adjustments, etc. AFS presents the solution to all the subunits, which then have a choice to buy the solution, or not. In the development process, when attempting to solve a common need shared throughout the whole company, a lack of requirements exists. Often, subunits, as well as AFS, will have separate information systems that need to be integrated with the new joint solution. There is an identified discrepancy between the documentation of requirements from the development unit that eventually hands over the responsibility to the IT governance unit, causing an inadequate and complicated workflow.

Change. The Change represents how the development of joint solutions affects the subunits and federation. The subunits' capability to receive created joint solutions greatly varies, inducing implications in the implementation process, i.e. how receivable the change is in the specific subunit. This is due to the subunits' different existing solutions, maturity levels (resource pool, commitment, knowledge, etc.), local strategies, and characteristics. Hence, change management is of great importance and it can become a major concern for producing desired outcomes of the common solutions. Furthermore, it is of great importance to persuade as many subunits as possible with the necessity for change in order to decrease the overall costs and simplify future development.

4.2   Business Case and TOGAF

In this section, the derived and analyzed way of working in the federated organization is compared to relevant propositions and concepts from TOGAF. The ADM process is the heart of TOGAF, providing a method for developing and managing the EA lifecycle. However, due to the generic level of the ADM process and its main components such as Architecture Capability Framework being in the focus of this study, i.e. their insufficiencies in the support, TOGAF lacks customization towards organizations of various structures, such as federated organizations.

According to the Architecture Governance, the successfulness of the architecture function requires certain organizational structures, processes, roles, and responsibilities. The organizational structures and roles are clearly defined within the ramification of a centralized organization. However, TOGAF provides less or nearly no support regarding decision-making power and mandate to organizational structures not utilizing a centralized, hierarchical structure.

Set in contrast to the federated organization's way of working, some areas of concern can be identified. In the federated organization, the concept of an enterprise-wide control system trying to control adherence to the common strategy, would be neglected due to the autonomous nature of the subunits and the fact that no party within the federated organization could possibly hold that type of mandate. Requirements produced within the federated organization require increased involvement of subunits in order to boost the anchoring, such as IT-security aspects for example. The Requirement Managements phase is a major component inside the ADM process. Its main objective is to ensure that requirements are available and managed throughout the whole ADM process and all of its relevant phases. However, TOGAF does not mention within the different phases how the requirements should be collected and prioritized except that the prioritization should be conducted according to the architecture vision.

The concept of Architecture Board is according to TOGAF a key success factor of Architecture's governance. Compared to the federated organization's way of working, multiple concerns can be identified. The suggested size of 4–5 members, would neglect the subunits' possibility to voice their opinion, as 10 members would not be able to handle a large quantity of subunits, inducing a decreased level of anchoring regarding proposals. Furthermore, as the Architecture Board is a major part of the Architecture Governance, and the fact that it should act as a top management type of group controlling adherence and compliance regarding the EA, it would be neglected in the federated organization due the autonomous state of the subunits. Furthermore, controlling adherence to the architecture vision could be problematic, as there is no authority holding the ability to supervise the subunits' actions.

Considering the concepts of Change and Development derived in the analysis of the interviews in comparison to the proposed relevant concepts of TOGAF, the identified problems involves the areas of governing and decision-making. The proposed relevant areas regarding change and development in TOGAF, stating what is needed to solve the practical problems of an organization, such as documentation and integration, is deemed appropriate for various organizational structures. However, the areas of how it should be implemented and maintained could become problematic, as mentioned previously in this section. As mentioned controlling adherence to the architecture vision could be problematic, as there is no authority holding the ability to supervise the subunits' actions.

Concluding, a gap exists between TOGAF's proposal for having a governing body (architecture board, architecture governance), and the ability for a federated organization to have a governing body that is formed according to the TOGAF documentation. TOGAF does not provide necessary details to support federated organizations. Any provided guideline or examples involve a centralized way of working, such as illustrated Architecture Governance and Architecture Board. From an enterprise-wide organizational viewpoint, this approach of working is not feasible nor supportive to a federated organization.

4.3 Proposal

The main requirement of the proposed solution is to support federated organizations to implement and maintain an EA such as TOGAF by adding an extension according to the specifics of the federated organizational structure characteristics as it is earlier described. Two main alternatives excelled from the generated ideas that were discussed:

Alternative 1: Design an entity (conceptual) model representing an organizational structure that will serve as an alternative to the Architecture Board, i.e. an extension to the Architecture Capability Framework [11, Chap. 45]. The organizational structure will provide guidelines to the decision and governing aspects of an EA, and support the implementation and maintenance of an EA in federated environments.

Alternative 2: Design a method for supporting an organizational structure change in the federated organizations using TOGAF. The artefact would provide guidelines on how the federated organization should restructure in order to adhere to the concepts of TOGAF, and thus enable a successful transition into utilizing the framework.

Selecting alternative 2 would result in an organization-specific solution, requiring possibly major restructuring within the enterprise, which in turn would substantially affect the organization's way of working. In addition, the foundation of the enterprise is of greater importance than any framework, as it has been developed and refined over a significant period. The selection of alternative 1 is further validated by the fact that it would result in a more generalized solution, i.e. trying to fit TOGAF onto the organization rather than the opposite. The resulting conceptual model will contribute to federated organizations' ability to adhere and include all relevant subunits, allowing increased anchoring of proposals throughout the whole enterprise.

In Fig. 5, the proposed solution (artefact) of alternative 1 is presented. The circles of the figure represent the entities of the model. The cardinality of the specific entity is inferred by the amount of circles, i.e. multiple circles imply a higher quantity of the entity. The arrows in Fig. 5 refer to how the various entities are related.

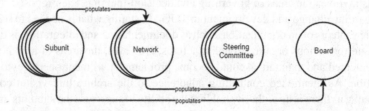

Fig. 5. The proposed artefact – an extension to support federated organizations

The *Subunits* are completely autonomous and control day-to-day operations. They generate their own revenue, and are enabled to produce ideas commonly influenced by specific needs and characteristics for new developments. The *Network* is populated by representatives from the *Subunits*. Each core business area within the federated organization has its own *Network*. The *Steering Committee* is democratically chosen from the *Network*, by the *Network* representatives, in order to prioritize the ideas. The *Board* consists of business manager representatives from the *Subunits* in order to accept or decline ideas imparted from the *Steering Committees*.

In the model, subunits influence all aspects of business development. The subunits populate the networks, which in turn populate the steering committees. Furthermore, the subunits also populate the board. The selection of representatives for the steering committee is performed utilizing a democratic process, while each subunit decides on their representative on their own. By involving the subunits in every area and aspect of the decision making process, an increased anchoring of proposals can be reached. Increased anchoring and subunit involvement provides greater possibility of convincing subunits to steer in a common direction, benefiting the federated organization as a whole.

The proposed model can be positioned as an extension within the Architecture Governance Framework (Fig. 1, right). The governance framework is a part of the over-arching Architecture Capability Framework, which is an integral part of successfully operating an architecture function within the enterprise. As an extension of the Architecture Governance Framework, the artefact will be seen as an alternative solution, replacing the CIO/CTO function and the Architecture Board. The artefact is not contradicting or refining any other concepts proposed in TOGAF; in the ADM process or the content meta-model.

5 Discussion of Results

In this section, an example of a theoretical case utilizing the designed and developed artefact will be compared to the current TOGAF recommendations. The theoretical case starts with the emergence of multiple needs in the subunits of a federated organization, and ends with an enterprise-wide impact. In Table 1, the managing of the needs by TOGAF and the proposed solution is presented.

The main goal of implementing a framework such as TOGAF is to optimize an enterprise's capability to support change and to increase the successfulness in delivering business strategy. Its popularity on the market is a sign that it supports that capability. However, while using examples of typical centralized organizational structures and the broad generalization given in the framework, it needs to be expanded to giving examples for other organizational structures. In organizations that are not centrally controlled, the decision mandate of what and how something should be done cannot be given to only one group. The solution that is proposed should be seen as an extension or alternative to TOGAF's Architecture Board [11], and as such will affect the Architecture Governance and Requirements Management.

The problem is not unique to the examined organization's domain. There are multiple businesses in Sweden, both public and private, facing the same governance and alignment problems. The decision rights are decentralized while the IT is attempting to be centralized and the whole organization uses a federated structure. One could always argue that all companies are unique depending on the granularity. However, this study approaches the federated characteristics and business procedures with a holistic view. Thus, this proposal is a representative for generalization towards larger federated organizations.

Table 1. Theoretical case comparison

Theoretical case phase	TOGAF	Solution artefact
Gather needs	No guidance stating how to collect needs emerging from various sources	The needs of a particular subunit are presented to networks represented by the subunits of the federated organization allowing for the gathering of other subunits' similar needs
Prioritize needs	No guidance stating how to identify and prioritize needs other than conducting a gap analysis detailing benefits and drawbacks	Prioritization is performed by the steering committee, populated by the subunits. In turn, this allows for increased subunit involvement. Furthermore, this enables prioritized solutions to satisfy a majority of the needs rather than what is most beneficial towards one specific unit or enterprise
Control holistic adherence	Suggests the utilization of an Architecture Board in charge of controlling the holistic adherence of solutions	Utilizing the artefact, the concept denoted Board (Fig. 5) handles the adherence controlling. The board increases the enterprise-wide involvement as it is populated by subunits
Solution acceptance	Using the stated recommendations, the final solution suffer from decreased enterprise-wide acceptance. Multiple steps in the process from needs to solution entails top-management decision and decreased involvement of the subunits of the federated organization	As the artefact ensures involvement of subunits throughout the whole process, the proposed solution will have increased enterprise-wide acceptance, and further the solution will satisfy a majority of the subunits' needs

6   Concluding Remarks

The paper presented a case study research conducted in a large Swedish company in the real estate business domain. It contrasted TOGAF's concepts and methods related to governance with the way of working in the federated organization of the case study. Using the elicited knowledge from organization's experts, it emphasized insufficiencies of TOGAF to support the identified federated structural aspects of the organization, and suggest potential improvements. In particular, the concepts regarding governing and decision making in TOGAF, including but not limited to Architecture Governance,

Architecture Board, and Requirements Management, would be neglected in a federated organization due to the autonomous state and quantity of various subunits.

The resulting solution, with similar areas of impact as the Architecture Board proposed by TOGAF, is aimed to act as a support to guide federated organizations when implementing and maintaining an EA, such as TOGAF. By ensuring the involvement of all relevant subunits, and further increasing the anchoring of proposals throughout the organization, the artefact could increase the alignment between business and IT.

The presented solution should be of a particular interest for the case organization, as it was produced utilizing its own structure and the way of working as a model. Large federated organizations would also benefit from the result as it could provide guidance and increased success rate when implementing TOGAF.

To further confirm the validity and control the functionality of the presented solution, it should be tested in an actual practical case involving a federated organization and their implementation of TOGAF. Secondly, as the artefact was derived utilizing only one specific federated organization, future research should involve multiple federated organizations in order to increase the credibility of the results and to further contribute to an increasingly generalized conclusion. Thirdly, as this research involved a federated organization not utilizing TOGAF, it would be of interest to analyze a federated organization working with TOGAF to identify concrete practical problems in their day-to-day business. The focus towards TOGAF can be a hindrance when researching concerns that focus on organizational forms and concepts. Finally, a research direction of interest includes analysis for supporting customers' preferences [28] in different organizational forms.

References

1. Luftman, J., Ben-Zvi, T.: Key issues for IT executives 2011: cautious optimism in uncertain economic times. MIS Q. Executive **10**(4), 203–212 (2011)
2. Silvius, A.J.G., de Waal, B., Smit, J.: Business and IT alignment; answers and remaining questions. In: PACIS 2009 Proceedings (2009). http://aisel.aisnet.org/cgi/viewcontent.cgi?article=1044&context=pacis2009
3. Luftman, J.: Assessing Business-IT Alignment Maturity. Commun. Assoc. Inf. Syst. **4**(1), December 2000
4. Kearns, G.S., Sabherwal, R.: Strategic alignment between business and information technology: a knowledge-based view of behaviors, outcome, and consequences. J. Manag. Inf. Syst. **23**(3), 129–162 (2006)
5. Tarigan, R.: An Evaluation of the relationship between alignment of strategic priorities and manufacturing performance. Int. J. Manag. **22**(4), 586–597 (2005)
6. Chan, Y.E., Reich, B.H.: IT alignment: what have we learned? J. Inf. Technol. **22**(4), 297–315 (2007)
7. Chan, Y.E., Huff, S., Barclay, D., Copeland, D.: Business strategic orientation, information systems strategic orientation, and strategic alignment. J. Inf. Syst. Res., 125–150, June 1997
8. Bharadwaj, A., Sawy, E., Pavlou, O., Venkatraman, N.: Digital Business Strategy: Toward a Next Generation of Insights. Social Science Research Network, Rochester, NY, SSRN Scholarly Paper ID 2742300, June 2013

9. Weill, P.: Don't just lead, govern: how top-performing firms govern IT. MIS Q. Executive **3**(1), 1–17 (2004)
10. Sessions, R.: A Comparison of the Top Four Enterprise-Architecture Methodologies, May 2007. https://msdn.microsoft.com/en-us/library/bb466232.aspx
11. TOGAF® 9.1. http://pubs.opengroup.org/architecture/togaf9-doc/arch/
12. FEA Consolidated Reference Model Document Version 2.3. https://www.fsa.usda.gov/Assets/USDA-FSA-Public/usdafiles/SDLC-non-secure/Enterprise-Architecture-Program-/Training/Docs/FEA
13. DODAF - DOD Architecture Framework Version 2.02 - DOD Deputy Chief Information Officer. http://dodcio.defense.gov/Library/DoD-Architecture-Framework/
14. MOD Architecture Framework - GOV.UK. https://www.gov.uk/guidance/mod-architecture-framework
15. UK Ministry of Defense. Proposed NAF v4 Meta-Model (MODEM). NATO Architecture Framework v4.0 Documentation (2013). http://nafdocs.org/modem
16. Sandkuhl, K., Stirna, J., Persson, A., Wiotzki, M.: Enterprise Modeling: Tackling Business Challenges with 4EM Method. Springer, Heidelberg (2014)
17. TOGAF 9.1 | The Open Group Blog. https://blog.opengroup.org/tag/togaf-9-1/
18. Lindström, Å., Johnson, P., Johansson, E., Ekstedt, M., Simonsson, M.: A survey on CIO concerns-do EA frameworks support them? Inf. Syst. Front. **2006**(8), 81–90 (2006)
19. Speckert, T., Rychkova, I., Zdravkovic, J., Nurcan, S.: On the changing role of enterprise architecture in decentralized environments: state of the art. In: 17th IEEE International Enterprise Distributed Object Computing Conference Workshops, pp. 310–318 (2013)
20. Rabelo, R.J., Noran, O., Bernus, P.: Towards the next generation service oriented enterprise architecture. In: IEEE 19th EDOC Workshop, pp. 91–100 (2015)
21. Jonkers, H., Lankhorst, M., ter Doest, H., Arbab, F., Bosma, H., Wieringa, R.: Enterprise architecture: management tool and blueprint for the organization. J. Inf. Syst. Front. **8**(2), 63–66 (2006)
22. Leading the development of open, vendor-neutral IT standards and certifications | The Open Group. http://www.opengroup.org/
23. Lunenberg, F.C.: Organizational structure: Mintzberg's framework. Int. J. Scholar Acad. Intellect. Divers **14**(1) (2012)
24. Jacobides, M.J.: The inherent limits of organizational structure and the unfulfilled role of hierarchy: lessons from a near-war. J. Organ. Sci. **18**(3), 455–477 (2007)
25. Chang, M.H., Harrington, J.E.: Centralization vs. decentralization in a multi-unit organization: a computational model of a retail chain as a multi-agent adaptive system. J. Manag. Sci. **46**(11), 1427–1440 (2000)
26. Mintzberg, H.: The Structuring of Organizations: A Synthesis of the Research. Prentice-Hall, Michigan (1979)
27. Christie, A., Joye, M., Watts, R.: Decentralization of the firm: theory and evidence. J. Corp. Financ. **9**(1), 3–36 (2003)
28. Svee, E.-O., Giannoulis, C., Zdravkovic, J.: Modeling business strategy: a consumer value perspective. In: Johannesson, P., Krogstie, J., Opdahl, A.L. (eds.) PoEM 2011. LNBIP, vol. 92, pp. 67–81. Springer, Heidelberg (2011). doi:10.1007/978-3-642-24849-8_6

From Indicators to Predictive Analytics: A Conceptual Modelling Framework

Azadeh Nasiri[1,2,3], Soroosh Nalchigar[3], Eric Yu[3], Waqas Ahmed[1,2(✉)],
Robert Wrembel[1], and Esteban Zimányi[2]

[1] Institute of Computing Science, Poznan University of Technology, Poznań, Poland
robert.wrembel@cs.put.poznan.pl
[2] Department of Computer and Decision Engineering,
Université Libre de Bruxelles, Brussels, Belgium
{waqas.ahmed,ezimanyi}@ulb.ac.be
[3] Department of Computer Science, University of Toronto, Toronto, Canada
{nazadeh,soroosh,eric}@cs.toronto.edu

Abstract. Predictive analytics provides organisations with insights about future outcomes. Despite the hype around it, not many organizations are using it. Organisations still rely on the descriptive insights provided by the traditional business intelligence (BI) solutions. The barriers to adopt predictive analytics solutions are that businesses struggle to understand how such analytics could enhance their existing BI capabilities, and also businesses lack a clear understanding of how to systematically design the predictive analytics. This paper presents a conceptual modelling framework to overcome these barriers. The framework consists of two modelling components and a set of analysis that systematically (1) justify the needs for predictive analytics within the organisational context, and (2) identify the predictive analytics design requirements. The framework is illustrated using a real case adopted from the literature.

Keywords: Conceptual modelling · Predictive analytics · Goal-oriented requirements engineering

1 Introduction

Data analytics is defined as the discovery of meaningful patterns in data [1]. While descriptive analytics provides insights about the past and current business performance, predictive analytics answer what will happen in the future [2]. Results from such analytics trigger proactive actions towards achieving organisational objectives in an optimal and timely fashion [3,4]. Despite the importance of predictive analytics, only 13% of the organisations utilize it [5]. According to Gartner, over 70% of organisations still use only the traditional business intelligence (BI) which provides descriptive insight by means of indicators. Indicators are measurements that quantify the fulfilment of the business goals. The insights obtained via indicators are retrospective, and answer questions what happened

© IFIP International Federation for Information Processing 2017
Published by Springer International Publishing AG 2017. All Rights Reserved
G. Poels et al. (Eds.): PoEM 2017, LNBIP 305, pp. 171–186, 2017.
https://doi.org/10.1007/978-3-319-70241-4_12

or what is currently happening in terms of goal fulfilment. However, today's fast-paced business environment demands actionable insights to make real-time optimization adjustments to the business goals. In this regard, descriptive insights provided by indicators should be evolved to future-oriented actionable insights which is provided by predictive analytics.

While many businesses have already invested in BI systems, they are struggling to understand how predictive analytics could enhance their existing BI capabilities. The effective use of predictive analytics requires business stakeholders (1) to identify how to move from descriptive insight to an actionable insight that could answer why and where in the organisations to use predictive analytics, and (2) to identify the important design requirements of predictive analytics from data and computational perspectives.

Conceptual modelling techniques can potentially provide great value towards the effective use of data analytics solutions [6]. Research efforts in this domain have addressed a wide range of data-intensive problems in business domains, from data warehousing [7,8] to business intelligence [9,10] to advanced analytics [11,12]. The existing conceptual modelling approaches do not address challenges such as: How to obtain the right predictive analytics requirements from available descriptive insights? How to make analytics design choices such as what are the available prediction strategies to address the problem at hand and what are the potential algorithms and data asset to focus on?

Consider a retailer from the fashion industry that already uses a descriptive BI system tracking the fulfillment of the business goals. The BI system reveals often deficiency in the inventory-related goals. The insight has driven the retailer to improve the replenishment of the inventory to increase the fulfillment chance of the corresponding goals. It has been decided to estimate the demand and replenish the inventory based on that. The estimation needs to utilize predictive analytics. The challenge is that the retailer does not know how to drive the estimation of demand that responds to the current goal deficiency captured by the traditional BI system. Besides, to support the estimation by predictive analytics, the retailer does not know how to make analytics design choices such as what in the business domain or in its environment drives the demand? What are the potential algorithms and data to use?

This paper presents a conceptual modelling framework to overcome the barriers to adapt predictive analytics in organisations. The framework consists of two modelling components: (1) the Context Modelling that extends the Business Intelligence Model (BIM) language [9] to support moving from descriptive insight to an actionable insight (provided by predictive analytics), (2) the Analytics Design Alternatives Modelling that adapts the i* framework [13] to support designing the predictive analytics. Furthermore, we present a set of analyses to capture the modelling components from the methodological perspective. The framework is applied to a real case prepared from the literature. Section 2 explains the motivation case from the literature. Section 3 provides an overview of the modelling components and a metamodel of the framework. Section 4 represents the framework which is applied on the motivation case. Section 5 reviews the related works and finally, Sect. 6 concludes the paper.

2   A Motivating Case

In this section, we elaborate on the example from the fashion industry. A retailer orders a certain amount of products from manufacturers and put them in the inventory to meet consumer demands. There are trendy and functional products. Trendy products are sold through the fast fashion retailing process which involves 20 short selling seasons in a year. There is no chance to buy them when a season is over. Functional products are sold through a traditional process with two selling seasons in a year. The retailer wants to improve the replenishment of the inventory by predicting the customer demands and for that, aims at building a predictive analytics solution. We first describe how the BI system of the retailer is set up without use of predictive analytics.

The retailer has already invested in a BI system to track the fulfillment of its business goals by monitoring of various indicators benefiting from the BIM modelling framework. *BIM* is a goal-oriented modeling language that assists enterprises to keep track of their performance and sense how well they are doing with regard to their strategic goals. Modelling with BIM involves building a *goal model* which consists of business concepts such as *strategies, business processes, indicators* and *influences*. A detailed introduction of BIM is beyond the scope of this pape (refer to [9] in order to use BIM for enterprise modelling). Using BIM, the retailer has formalised the strategies which have been further decomposed into lower level business goals. The relevant business processes, tasks, and resources have been assigned to each business goal to fulfill it. In Fig. 1, the business strategy of *To meet consumer demand* is decomposed into business goals namely, *To increase reliability* and *To increase responsiveness*. The first goal is achieved by executing the *Traditional retailing process*. The second goal is achieved by executing the *Fast fashion retailing process* through which the *trendy products* are sold.

Indicators are associated with each business goal to quantify its fulfilment. For example, in Fig. 1, *Functional products sale missed* is an indicator that measures the amount of unfulfilled demand due to the insufficient product in the inventory. This indicator quantifies the achievement of goal *To avoid under stocking*. At run-time, each indicator obtains its current value from the data sources to which it is linked to. The current value is typically compared with a target, threshold and the worst value. The result of this comparison is visually expressed for business users by color. Depends on the current value at the given time, indicators fall into a green, a yellow, or a red state. The green, yellow and red state of an indicator means that the associating goal is fulfilled, partially fulfilled, or not fulfilled, respectively. At a given time, the state of the various indicators provides a descriptive insight over the current performance of the retailer in terms of goal fulfillment. The insight is historically-oriented and reflects which business goals have been already fulfilled and which are still unfulfilled. However, it does not deal with the desired outcome in terms of goal fulfillment.

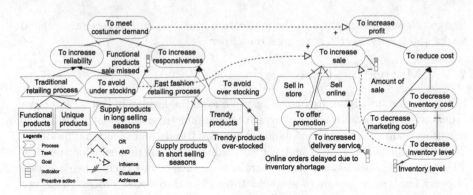

Fig. 1. An excerpt of the BIM schema of the retailer. (Color figure online)

The retailer has recently observed inventory-related indicators often in the yellow or red state representing deficiencies in the fulfillment of associating goals. To deal with that, the inventory replenishment should be improved. For that, a predictive analytics solution is needed that estimates the customer demand and based on that the inventory is replenished. The objective of the predictive analytics is to improve the replenishment in a way that the fulfilled goals (with green indicator state) are kept as they are while the fulfillment chance of the deficient goals (with yellow or red indicator state) is increased.

Although BIM simplifies interpreting the descriptive insight over the fulfillment of inventory-related goals using indicators, it does not support a future-oriented insight over the demand that improves the fulfillment chance of unfulfilled goals. To provide an actionable insight using BIM, there are business and analytics-related challenges. We will go through them in the next two paragraphs. The challenges addressed are synthesized from the literature [14].

Regarding the business challenges, the first issue is to deal with the goals in conflict. It means that the efforts to make one goal fulfilled might negatively impact the fulfillment of another goal. For example, *To decrease the inventory level* which saves inventory cost might negatively impact *To increase sale* because of the insufficient stock to meet demand. The retailer does not know how to effectively replenish the inventory that decreases the cost while meeting the demand. Moreover, the business goals are achieved through different business processes and target various products and services. The retailer needs to take different initiatives when improving the fulfillment of one goal to another. For example, *To avoid over-stocking* is achieved by *Fast fashion retailing process* by which trendy products are sold. To improve such goal the replenishment of *Trendy products* should be improved. Whereas, *To avoid under-stocking* the replenishment of *traditional products* should be addressed with a different replenishment frequency than *Trendy products*. Besides, goal fulfillment undergo changes over time as a result of dynamics in internal and external business environment. For example, *To avoid over stocking* which was fulfilled awhile ago happened to be unfulfilled now because of a sudden drop in sales. Therefore, depending on which inventory-related goals are unfulfilled and which one is met at given time, the different replenishment and accordingly the different demand estimation is required. It is challenging for the retailer to know how to replenish the inventory that responds to goal deficiencies in an optimal and timely fashion. To conclude, the challenge is to align the predictive analytics that supports the estimation of demand with the descriptive insight provided in BIM.

Along with business challenges to replenish the inventory, there are also challenges to design the predictive analytics for estimating the demand of products There are different domain-dependant ways to estimate the demand. For example, for trendy products, the retailer deals with the demand of new products which is different from traditional products with a history of sales. To estimate the demand for trendy products, one way is to run a pre-test sale and based on the consumer response, forecast the demand. The other ways are to estimate the demand based on the sale of similar products previously sold, based on user-generated content on social media, or based on weather forecast, etc. Moreover, each way can involve various data as well as various computational techniques. It is challenging for the retailer to make critical choices to design a predictive analytics that supports the estimation of demand. In Sect. 3 we introduce new business and analytics-related concepts to make it easier for the retailer to address the above-mentioned challenges.

3 The Proposed Framework

The proposed framework consists of two components to augment the BIM framework, namely, Context modelling and Analytics design alternatives modelling. The former justifies the rationale behind the predictive analytics solutions. The latter focuses on how to design the predictive analytics solutions. Next, we explain each component in detail.

3.1 Context Modelling

This part aims to justify the need for predictive analytics. This component systematically aligns the predictive analytics with the descriptive insight provided by the indicators in BIM. To support and facilitate this alignment, a set of concepts are introduced and captured in the extended BIM schema using the new notations illustrated in Fig. 3. The concepts are defined as follows:

Optimization goal represents an intention to make a balance among a set of goals that are possibly in conflict. The goals influenced by an optimization goal, called **influenced goals**, have indicators that evaluate to which degree they are fulfilled whereas, optimization goal has no clear-cut fulfillment level. It is considered to be sufficiently fulfilled if all associating goals are fulfilled.

Indicator state depicts visually the performance level of an indicator at run-time using green, yellow and red colors. The colors simplify the interpretation of the fulfillment of the goal. The performance level is obtained from the current value (comes from data sources) of an indicator compared with a target, threshold, and the worst value [10]. Green, yellow, and red are interpreted as the fully fulfilled, the partially fulfilled, and the unfulfilled goal, respectively.

Business situation is a meaningful combination of indicator states appeared over a group of indicators (belong to the influenced goals of an optimization goal) in a snapshot from BIM at run-time. This combination includes at least one yellow or red indicator state.

Forward-looking insight contributes to satisfy an optimization goal by studying the future. It determines what to know about the future that helps to improve the fulfillment of the goals influenced by an optimization goal. It aims to increase the fulfillment chance of the goals with the yellow or red indicator state while to keep the goals with the green indicator state as they are. There are three main attributes: focus as a target object of the forward-looking insight, the coordinate as a perspective of the forward-looking insight over the focus, and time window as a time frame covered by the forward-looking insight. The time window attribute has three types of short-term, mid-term, and long-term whose time horizon can be defined by users, e.g., up to a month, a year, etc.

Proactive action represents an action triggered as a result of a forward-looking insight. It serves to be prepared or intervened in advance to increases the fulfilment chance of deficient goals.

3.2 Analytics Design Alternatives Modelling

This modelling component aims to answer how to design a predictive analytics that supports a certain forward-looking insight. Here, the objective is to systematically capture the requirements that are central to designing a predictive analytics, based on the business analysis provided by the context modelling. Using the goal modelling part of the i* framework, a goal model is constructed to explore the alternative ways to design predictive analytics. Each alternative is composed of a set of design requirements. To do so, we introduce a set of new concepts adapted from the i* framework as applied to the domain of predictive analytics. These concepts are generally categorised into analytics goals, tasks, soft-goals, and analytics resources. An analytics goal represents the intention to extract insight from data. An analytics task is a set of computational steps necessary to achieve an analytics goal. An analytics resource is the data required to perform an analytics task. An analytics soft-goal [11] is a quality that should sufficiently hold when aiming to achieve an analytics goal or performing an analytics task, or using an analytics resource. A brief description of the new concepts is given below (some of the concepts such as prediction top goal, algorithm, and constraint are adopted from the approach proposed in [11]).

Prediction top goal is an analytics goal with emphasis on prediction. It represents an intention to forecast the future value of an object of interest in the business domain [11]. Each prediction top goal is assigned a prediction type as: predicting a continuous attribute, predicting a sequence, etc. This concept is visualised by the i* notation to describe a goal with a horizontal line at the top.

Prediction strategy is a type of analytics goal that represents an intention to forecast the object of interest using another object. It aims to look for the possible objects from the business domain or its environment that could relate to the object of interest to forecast. This concept is visualised by the i* notation to describe a goal with one horizontal line at the top and one at the bottom.

Exploration task is an analytics task that addresses the procedure to fulfill a prediction strategy. It captures the steps required to derive the forecast of the object of interest from another object. This concept is visualised by the i* notation to describe a task with a horizontal line at the top.

Computation task is an analytics task that represents the computation aspect of an exploration task by assigning a mining technique. Mining techniques include: clustering, classification, etc. This concept is visualised by the i* notation to describe a task with one horizontal line at the top and one at the bottom.

Algorithm is an analytics task that represents how to perform a computation task using computer. Therefore, this concept addresses the computer understandability of the computation task. This concept is visualised by the i* notation to describe a task with one horizontal line at the top and two at the bottom.

Variable is an analytics resource that deals with the data used to perform a computation task which can be structured data or unstructured data. Structured data could be coming from data warehouses which has fact and dimension. Unstructured data takes a form such as text, audio, etc. This concept is visualised by the i* notation to describe a resource with a horizontal line at the top.

Constraint is an analytics soft-goal that represents business, computation or data limitations to deal with when designing a predictive analytics. This concept denotes a constraint type such as data constraint and business constraint.

3.3   Metamodel

The concepts introduced in the framework are described and the relationships between them are captured using a metamodel. The metamodel aims to provide an overall perspective over the concepts. The attributes captured in the classes embody the important information to collect for each concept. In Fig. 2 the metamodel is captured using a UML class diagram. In the figure, the concepts introduced for the Context modelling are distinguished from the one in the Analytics design alternatives modelling with a gray shadow on the background.

4   Illustrative Example

In this section, we apply the framework on the motivating case. Figure 3 illustrates the context modelling. The purpose of this modelling is to facilitate the elicitation of the predictive analytics requirements that is responsive to the descriptive insight provided by indicators. It ensures that deficiencies in the goal fulfilment are addressed effectively. The context modelling uses the notions of optimization goal, indicator state, business situation, proactive action and forward-looking insights to align the fulfillment of business goals and the predictive analytics solution (new concepts are highlighted by purple in Fig. 3).

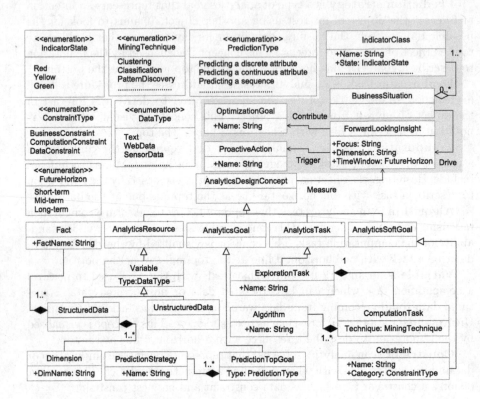

Fig. 2. Metamodel for concepts involved to adapt predictive analytics

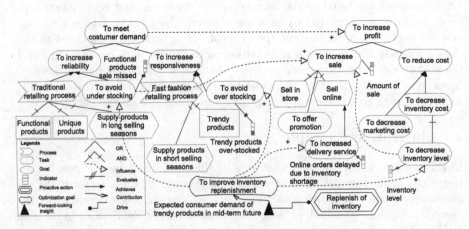

Fig. 3. An excerpt of the context modelling to improve the inventory replenishment. (Color figure online)

The model in Fig. 3 shows that *To improve inventory replenishment* is an example of an optimization goal which influences various business goals such as *To increase sale*, *To decrease inventory level*, *To avoid under stocking*, etc. Such goals are influenced goal which some of them might be in conflict such as *To increase sale* and *To decrease inventory level*. At run time, the color of the indicator of an influenced goal visually expresses to which degree the goal has been fulfilled. Figure 3 represents the *Functional product sale missed* indicator as green which is an example of the indicator state. It means that the *To avoid under stocking* goal has been fulfilled. However, at the same time, *Trendy product over stocked* and *Inventory level* have the red and yellow that represents unfulfillment and partially fulfilment of associating goals, respectively. The combination of [green: *Functional products sale missed*, yellow: *Trendy product over stocked*, red: *Inventory level*] captures an example of a business situation that the retailer faces at the given time. Such business situation requires a forward-looking insight over demand in the context of trendy products which is replenished weekly.

Figure 3 captures a forward-looking insight over *The expected consumer demand for trendy products in the mid-term future horizon* that helps to increase the chance of unfilled goals by triggering the right proactive action of *Replenish of inventory*[1]. At some other point of time the business situation might change to the combination of [green: *Inventory level*, yellow: *Functional product sale missed*, red: *Amount of sale*] which is captured by BIM at run-time. This business situation motivates a different forward-looking insight of *The expected consumer demand for functional products in the long-term future horizon*.

By modelling optimisation goal and its influence to other goals, the areas that need support from analytics insights are represented. By capturing the business situation composed of indicator states, the connection between the predictive analytics and the descriptive insight provided by indicators are ensured. The forward-looking insight concept secures the relatedness and alignment of the predictive analytics to the current business situation in terms of goal fulfilment. It frames what is the subject of interest to be estimated by predictive analytics as a result of indicator state. Besides, the concept helps business users to make sense of predictive analytics within organisational context. This facilitates triggering the right proactive action that aims to increase the fulfillment chance of goals.

Figure 4 illustrates the Analytics design alternatives modelling. The purpose is to capture the alternative ways to design the analytics that supports the forward-looking insight. A goal model is developed for each insight that captures the design alternatives in terms of prediction top goal, prediction strategies, exploration tasks, computation tasks algorithms, data variables, and constraints.

In Fig. 4, *To forecast demand for trendy products in mid-term future horizon* is an example of a prediction top goal. To achieve this goal, there are various prediction strategies which specifies a domain-dependent way to estimate the demand for trendy products. Trendy products are new products for which there

---

[1] The concepts of forward-looking insight and proactive actions captured in BIM will have the temporal attribute of expiration at run time. The instances of these concepts will be automatically expired and replaced when the business situation change.

is no historical sale data. Therefore the estimation of demand might rely on weather condition, user's comments on the social media, a pilot sale of the new product. Some of these factors such as pilot sale are under the control of the business while some others such as weather condition are not. In this regard, the prediction top goal is decomposed into *To forecast based on controlled factors* and *To forecast based on uncontrolled factors* which are the examples of a prediction strategy to take. The model in Fig. 4 illustrates the further decomposition of prediction strategies. There are various domain-dependent ways to accomplish *To forecast based on controlled factors*. For example, *To forecast based on pre-sale test* is a way that relates the demand for the trendy products to the sale data of the pilot sales. To achieve the latter prediction strategy, the retailer selects some stores and sells the new trendy products for a short period to test how consumers respond to the new products. Then, the sales of the test period is being used to predict the demand across all stores.

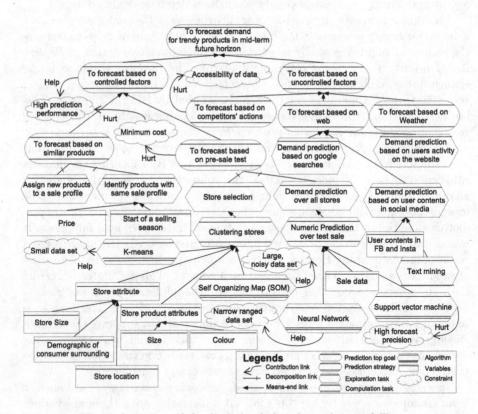

Fig. 4. A portion of the Analytics design alternatives modelling

The model in Fig. 4 shows that *To forecast based on pre-sale test* requires to take two courses of actions *Select stores* and then *Forecast demand over all stores*[2]. These tasks are the examples of a exploration task that is necessary to accomplish a prediction strategy. The tasks address the steps of a procedure to drive the prediction of the object of interest from other objects in the business domain or its environment. To accomplish *Select stores*, a computation task needs to be applied which is *Cluster stores*. There are also computer understandable algorithms to accomplish a computation task. For example, *K-Means* is an algorithm to address the *Cluster stores*. We remark that computation task, and algorithm do not necessarily address forecasting. For example, *Select stores* is only a step to fulfill a prediction strategy that forecast the demand for trendy products based on the pre-sale technique. It should not be mistaken that *Select stores*, alone, represents a task to perform the forecast. The same case applied to computation task, and algorithm.

Figure 4 also shows that the *Store selection*, as a computation task, can be either performed over the *Store attributes* including *Store location, Store size, etc* or over the *Store products attributes* such as *Size* and *Colour*. These are the examples of variables to use in a predictive analytics. Figure 4 also represents some of the constraints to fulfill a goal or perform a task or use a resource in the goal model. For example, *Low-cost prediction* is a constraint to take into account to design a predictive analytics that supports a certain forward-looking insight. The constraints guide to choosing a certain alternative among analytics goals, tasks, or resources. For example, *Limited accessibility to data* might be considered to choose the alternative of *To forecast based on competitor's action* when the competitor's information is not available.

By modelling prediction top goal, the objective of a forecast to support a forward-looking insight is specified. A prediction top goal connects the analytics design concepts with the business concepts captured in BIM. Modelling the prediction strategy ensures that all of the possible drivers in the business environment are taken into accounts when designing a predictive analytics. The exploration task makes it explicit how to relate and drive the forecast of the object of interest from another object. The computation task clarifies the quantitative aspect of relating the object of interest to forecast to other objects using a certain data mining technique. The quantitative aspect of the forecast is further clarified by the algorithms that are understandable by computers. Modelling the variables gives the possibility to explore the data set where an algorithm can be performed on to run the forecast. It makes sure that the data asset are used effectively. Modelling the constraints simplify to make analytics design choices.

5   Analysis with the Proposed Framework

The proposed framework suggests five type of analyses which support the framework from a methodological perspective. Each analysis provides a set of steps required to systematically build the models discussed in Sect. 3.

---

[2] To capture the order of analytics tasks, readers can refer to proposals in the literature to deal with the temporal aspects of goal models.

The Insight analysis aims to drive a forward-looking insight from a descriptive insight provided by the indicators in BIM. It systematically captures the Context modelling by eliciting the concepts of optimisation goal, indicator state, business situation, forward-looking insight, and proactive action. The Analytics goal analysis, Analytics task analysis, Analytics resource analysis, and Analytics soft-goal analysis aim to design a predictive analytics that supports the forward-looking insight. The Analytics goal analysis systematically elicits and captures the prediction top goal and prediction strategy concepts in the Analytics design alternatives modelling. The Analytics task analysis elicits the tasks required to accomplish the analytics goals. It systematically captures the exploration task, computation task, and algorithm concepts in the Analytics design alternatives modelling. The Analytics resource analysis elicits the analytics resources to perform analytics tasks by systematically capturing the variable concept in the Analytics design alternatives modelling. The Analytics soft-gaol analysis elicits the analytics soft-goals by systematically capturing the constraints concepts in the Analytics design alternatives modelling. The analyses are described as follows:

(1) **Insight analysis:** Identify an optimization goal and represent it using the new notation in the BIM schema developed for monitoring purposes. Then, identify which business goals of BIM are influenced by the optimisation goal and name these as influenced goals. Next, link the optimization goal with the corresponding influenced goals by means of a influence link of BIM. After that, identify the meaningful business situations. To do so, analyse the indicators associated with the influenced goals at the run-time. Determine which meaningful combination of color over various indicators in a snapshot of BIM would shape a meaningful business situation that needs an improvement. Various combinations of indicator states constitute various business situations. Afterwards, translate each business situation into a forward-looking insight that aims to keep the green states of the influenced goal as they are and improve the yellow and red states to green. Furthermore, define precisely the insight by specifying the attributes of focus, dimension, and time window (indicators with a red or yellow state can provide a guide). Next, capture the forward-looking insight in the BIM with the new notation introduced and link it with the optimization goal using a contribution link of the BIM language. Identify the proactive action triggered by the forward-looking insight and capture it in BIM. Also connect the proactive action to the forward-looking insight using the new link drive.

(2) **Analytics goal analysis:** Start by developing a goal model for each forward-looking insight identified in the insight analysis. To do so, represent a prediction top goal that addresses an intention to design a predictive analytics in order to support the forward-looking insight. Define the prediction top goal based on the attributes of the forward-looking insight. Then, identify prediction type by denoting the predicting a discrete variable or predicting a continues variable etc. Next, decompose the prediction top goal into prediction strategies. Determine the strategies to drive the forecast from the objects in the business domain or its environment. Decompose prediction strategies till a certain object is determined.

(3) **Analytics task analysis:** Analyse the lowest level goal of the prediction strategies in order to identify the tasks to achieve them. Determine the exploration tasks which relates the object of interest to forecast to an object in the business or its environment to drive the predictive analytics. Link the exploration tasks to the corresponding prediction strategy using decomposition links or means-end links. Next, decompose each task until it is not possible to address the computation aspect of the task by a mining technique. Then, capture a computation task that addresses the mining technique and link it to the corresponding exploration task using a means-end link. Afterwards, capture the alternatives of machine understandable algorithms to perform a computation task. Link the algorithms to the corresponding computation tasks with a means-end link. Refer to data mining catalogue introduced in [11] to see how to assign algorithms to a computation task. While exploration tasks and computation tasks are defined at business level, the algorithms address a generic concept in the advanced analytics domain. It is important to note that exploration task, computation task, and algorithm, individually, do not necessarily address forecasting. Instead, they represent a task in a prediction procedure that aims to forecast the target object.

(4) **Analytics resource analysis:** Analyse the exploration task in order to find a relevant data set to perform the computation task. Capture the variables representing the data set and link the variable with a means-end links to the corresponding exploration task. Next, decompose variables if it is necessary. Also, determine the attribute of fact and dimensions if the variables are accessed from a data warehouse repository. Determine the form of the data set if the variables are accessed from a source of unstructured data by denoting audio, text, etc.

(5) **Analytics soft-goal analysis:** Identify the constraints that should be taken into account when designing a predictive analytics. Capture the constraints in the goal model. Identify analytics goals, tasks, and resource that contribute to each constraint[3]. Link the analytics goals, analytics tasks or analytics resources to constraints that contribute to satisfice the constraints by means of the contribution links of the i* framework. Next, link the constraints among each other when satisfying one affects the other. Such links guide (or restrict) the selection among alternatives of analytics goals, tasks, and resources captured in the goal model. Next determine the attribute of constrain type by specifying business constraint, data constraint, or computation constraint.

6   Related Work

Conceptual modelling research plays a critical role in addressing challenges of designing and implementing data-intensive solutions in business domains [15]. The work in [11] proposes a modelling framework for requirements analysis and design of business analytics solutions. It captures analytics requirement in terms of business goals, decision goals and questions goals and connects them to advanced analytics system design. The main difference of this work is that the

---

[3] Satisficed means sufficiently satisfied and it is taken from the definition of the soft goal in the i* framework.

predictive analytics requirements are derived from descriptive analytics sensed from indicators states, whereas in [11] requirements derived from business goals. It is also different in that it focuses on the predictive type of analytics and captures requirements in terms of forward-looking insight. The approach in this paper can take advantage of the algorithms catalogue in [11] to support the analyses. In [16] authors extend the notion of indicators into measures, key performance indicators, and key result indicators and use that to drive data mining (e.g., time series analysis). The work in this paper is different as it captures the analytics solutions design and associated trade-offs.

Previous research also provides modelling support for design and development of BI systems. The work in [17] uses a goal-oriented approach to derive the analytics requirements as a form of reports demanded by business users and then defines the relation of the analytics component with other BI components such as data warehouse, indicators, data sources, and ETL at macro level. There are frameworks [9,10,18] that discuss indicators as a BI component used to track enterprise performance. These approaches model indicators as a BI components in relation to business concepts, such as goals, processes, and roles in both formal [18] and semi-formal [9,10] ways. Indicators in their approach are captured to provide a descriptive insight over the business goal fulfillment. The framework in this paper extends the BIM language [9] with forward-looking insight to reveal predictive analytics requirements and connects them to a solution design.

Another body of related work proposes conceptual modelling approaches for requirements design of data warehouses [19]. For example, the work in [7] proposes GRAnD as a goal-oriented approach for requirement analysis of data warehouses. The work in [20] proposes the Goal-Decision-Information (GDI) model from requirements analysis of data warehouses. The work in this paper is different in that it aims to support designing the predictive analytics solutions that generate forward-looking insights, as opposed to descriptive analytics.

7   Conclusion and Future Work

In this paper, we presented a conceptual modelling framework to adopt predictive analytics in organisations. In the future, we plan to enrich the presented framework to cover all the steps of the design science methodology [21] including: problem motivation, objectives of a solution, design and development, demonstration, evaluation, and communication. We have already represented the business and technical challenges of adopting predictive analytics in organisations. The objective is to develop a dedicated requirements engineering (RE) framework by which a predictive analytics is effectively and efficiently adopted to enhance the organisational performance. The design artefact which we represented in this paper is a model-based RE framework demonstrated with the help of an inventory problem. The in-depth evaluation of the framework is going to be represented in the future work. For the evaluation, we are conducting a case study in which business users from various domains are utilizing the proposed framework. Besides, the design and development step of the design science methodology which involves creating the artefact is still an ongoing work. In this step, we are extending the framework to quantitatively measure the influence of the predictive analytics on the business goals. Moreover, we are also precisely representing the temporal aspect of the BIM schema at the run time. We also plan to develop tools that support the framework.

References

1. Vaisman, I., Zimányi, E.: DW Systems: Design and Implementation (2014)
2. Sharda, R., Delen, D., Turban, E.: Business Intelligence: A Managerial Perspective on Analytics. Prentice Hall Press, Upper Saddle River (2013)
3. Evans, J.R.: An exploratory study of performance measurement and relationships with performance results. J. Oper. Manag. **22**(3), 219–232 (2004)
4. Parmenter, D.: Key Performance Indicators: Developing, Implementing, and Using Winning KPIs. Wiley, Chichester (2015)
5. Oestreich, T.W.: Gartner magic quadrant for BI and analytics platforms (2016)
6. Storey, V.C., Song, I.: Big data technologies and management: what conceptual modeling can do. Data Knowl. Eng. **108**, 50–68 (2017)
7. Giorgini, P., Rizzi, S., Garzetti, M.: GRAnD: a goal-oriented approach to requirement analysis in data warehouses. Decis. Support Syst. **45**(1), 4–21 (2008)
8. Tryfona, N., Busborg, F., Borch, C.: starER: a conceptual model for DW design. In: Proceedings of International Workshop on Data Warehousing and OLAP, pp. 3–8 (1999)
9. Horkoff, J., Barone, D., Jiang, L., Yu, E., Amyot, D., Borgida, A., Mylopoulos, J.: Strategic business modeling: representation and reasoning. Softw. Syst. Model. **13**(3), 1015–1041 (2014)
10. Pourshahid, A., Amyot, D., Peyton, L., Ghanavati, S., Chen, P., Weiss, M., Forster, A.: Business process management with the user requirements notation. Electron. Commer. Res. **9**(4), 269–316 (2009)
11. Nalchigar, S., Yu, E., Ramani, R.: A conceptual modeling framework for business analytics. In: Comyn-Wattiau, I., Tanaka, K., Song, I.-Y., Yamamoto, S., Saeki, M. (eds.) ER 2016. LNCS, vol. 9974, pp. 35–49. Springer, Cham (2016). doi:10.1007/978-3-319-46397-1_3
12. Nalchigar, S., Yu, E.: Conceptual modeling for business analytics: a framework and potential benefits. In: Proceedings of International Conference on Business Informatics (CBI), vol. 1, pp. 369–378. IEEE (2017)
13. Yu, E.: Modelling strategic relationships for process reengineering (2011)
14. Nenni, M., Giustiniano, L., Pirolo, L.: Demand forecasting in fashion industry: a review. Int. J. Eng. Bus. Manag. **5**, 37 (2013)
15. Storey, V., Trujillo, J., Liddle, S.: Research on conceptual modeling: themes, topics, and special issues. Data Knowl. Eng. **98**, 1–7 (2015)
16. Maté, A., Trujillo, J., Mylopoulos, J.: Key performance indicator elicitation and selection through conceptual modelling. In: Comyn-Wattiau, I., Tanaka, K., Song, I.-Y., Yamamoto, S., Saeki, M. (eds.) ER 2016. LNCS, vol. 9974, pp. 73–80. Springer, Cham (2016). doi:10.1007/978-3-319-46397-1_6
17. Burnay, C., Jureta, I.J., Linden, I., Faulkner, S.: A framework for the operationalization of monitoring in business intelligence requirements engineering. Softw. Syst. Model. **15**(2), 531–552 (2016)

18. Popova, V., Sharpanskykh, A.: Modeling organizational performance indicators. Inf. Syst. **35**(4), 505–527 (2010)
19. Nasiri, A., Wrembel, R., Zimányi, E.: Model-based requirements engineering for data warehouses: from multidimensional modelling to KPI monitoring. In: Jeusfeld, M.A., Karlapalem, K. (eds.) ER 2015. LNCS, vol. 9382, pp. 198–209. Springer, Cham (2015). doi:10.1007/978-3-319-25747-1_20
20. Prakash, N., Gosain, A.: Requirements driven data warehouse development. In: Proceedings of International Conference on CAiSE, vol. 252 (2003)
21. Peffers, K., Tuunanen, T., Rothenberger, M., Chatterjee, S.: A design science research methodology for information systems research. J. Manag. Inf. Syst. **24**(3), 45–77 (2007)

Product Life-Cycle Assessment
in the Realm of Enterprise Modeling

Mario Nolte[✉] and Monika Kaczmarek-Heß

University of Duisburg-Essen, Essen, Germany
{mario.nolte,monika.kaczmarek}@uni-due.de

Abstract. 'Sustainable development' is perceived as a topic of steadily increasing importance. At its core lies a tension between the goals of economic growth and protection of environmental quality. As organizations have a direct impact (e.g., through their production processes) on the sustainability of a society and the planet as a whole, ensuring their sustainable development is crucial. In this paper, we argue that the sustainable development of organizations may be positively influenced by increasing organizations' awareness of environmental impact of their products. Therefore, to support the assessment of environmental impact of product systems, based on ISO 14040, we design a domain-specific modeling method *ImpactM* as part of the Multi-perspective Enterprise Modeling (MEMO) approach. We evaluate it against identified requirements as well as using an exemplary scenario.

Keywords: Sustainable Development · LCA · MEMO

1 Introduction

At the core of *sustainable development* (SD) lies a tension between the goals of economic growth and protection of environmental quality; and a resulting need to achieve a balance among the environmental, economic, and social aspects [1,2]. As organizations are part of economy, thus through their choices of, e.g., raw materials, manufacturing process, suppliers, geographic locations; organizations "contribute to the sustainability or unsustainability of a society and the planet as a whole" [1, p. 113]. Indeed, many decisions made by enterprises have causes or consequences that extend beyond the here-and-now of the original question and the decision-maker, and affect the whole supply chain. E.g., a choice between a plastic and a paper bag influences not only material suppliers upstream, but also waste managers downstream, the production chain, or not-directly involved stakeholders (e.g., fishermen who have to tackle with the plastic waste [3]).

In order to support the SD of organizations, there is a well-recognized need to increase the organization's awareness of the environmental impact of their products [4,5]. It thus follows that there is a need to collect and use within the decision processes the relevant information on potential impacts caused by

G. Poels et al. (Eds.): PoEM 2017, LNBIP 305, pp. 187–202, 2017.
https://doi.org/10.1007/978-3-319-70241-4_13

all activities needed to produce a certain product or a type of a product [5, pp. 185–187]. This information should be captured in such a way that would, among others, allow to: (1) increase the transparency of the consequences of the decisions made, (2) increase the understanding of possible impact, (3) foster communication between the organizational stakeholders involved in the decision making process, and (4) account for various perspectives on an enterprise and consider them in an integrated manner [4,6,7].

In this paper, we propose to apply conceptual modeling in general, and enterprise modeling in particular, in order to reach the above aims. Enterprise modeling (EM) supports sense-making of an organization and thus, focuses on the construction and application of conceptual models to describe, analyze, and (re-)design different aspects of an enterprise action system and information system [8,9]. In opposition to the pure textual form that may be used to collect, aggregate and represent information on the environmental impact of products and services, we argue that *conceptual models* can be used to express information in a more structured manner which is considered to better support understanding [10] and be more comprehensible to involved actors [11, p. 93].

The main goal of our research is thus to develop a modeling method supporting an assessment of potential environmental impact of enterprises and their products. Since the highest enterprise's impact results from the production and the consumption of products, we focus on the products life-cycle analysis, i.e., on the Life-Cycle Assessment (LCA) method. LCA provides a structured, comprehensive perspective to quantify material and energy flows and their associated emissions in the life-cycle of products (i.e., goods and services from cradle-to-grave) so that whole product systems are considered [12,13].

We follow a design-oriented research strategy [14] and contribute a modeling method *ImpactM* that aims at providing a benefit to organizations by supporting their product life-cycle analysis taking into account the sustainability related aspects. To design the postulated method we follow the approach proposed by [15]. Here, we focus on three main resulting artifacts: identified requirements, abstract syntax of proposed language, and its exemplary application.

The paper is structured as follows. First, the concepts of SD and LCA are discussed. Then, the requirements towards a modeling method are identified and used to discuss the existing approaches. Next, a meta model is presented and evaluated as well as an outlook on future steps is given. The paper concludes with final remarks considering assumptions and limitations of the method proposed.

2   Sustainable Development and Life-Cycle Assessment

The term *sustainability* in the context of environmental aspects can be traced back to 1791 when Hans Carl von Carlowitz used it to argue that the amount of lumbered wood should be in accordance with the rate of growth of the forest [16, pp. 105–106]. The term's current prominence was given by the Brundlandt commission that defined *sustainable development* as a "development that meets the needs of the present without compromising the ability of future generations

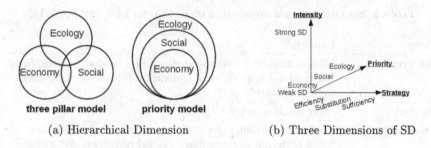

(a) Hierarchical Dimension   (b) Three Dimensions of SD

Fig. 1. Dimensions of sustainable development

to meet their own needs" [17, p. 41]. Although this understanding seems to be commonly accepted, it remains unclear how the idea can be conceptualized. Thus, SD is considered to be a *contested concept* [18]: whereas a distinct discourse can clearly be identified, SD's conceptions, goals and their operationalisations are unclear and juxtaposing [19].

To provide a guiding orientation for situating and evaluating our work in the context of SD we build on three dimensions: hierarchy, intensity and strategy (Fig. 1b), which we also later use to position our work. The 'hierarchical dimension' refers to the aspect already mentioned: that an ecologic system is a precondition for any social system, which in turn itself is a precondition of any economic system. In literature this dimension is represented either as a *Priority Model* or *Three Pillar Model* (cf. Fig. 1a). The 'intensity dimension' concerns the substitutability of natural and man-made resources. While the *weak sustainability* assumes that it is possible to substitute natural resources through man-made resources [20, p. 11], the *strong sustainability* is more pessimistic about possible substitutions and sets natural resources as a precondition for any human activity. The strong sustainability results in several rules like, e.g., an *assimilation rule* requiring that "waste emissions rates should equal the natural assimilative capacities of the ecosystem into which the wastes are emitted" [21, p. 2]. Finally, the third dimension refers to 'strategic options' guiding possible actions related to SD. Here the *efficiency strategy* asking for more efficiency in production processes (e.g., less waste material while keeping the production output) seems to be intuitive at first glance. But since this strategy might result in a *rebound effect*, where savings for one product may lead to a higher consumption in total [22, 23, pp. 96–100], other options are needed. Beside a *substitution strategy* where certain products should be substituted by products with the same functionality (e.g., plastic bags through linen bags), a *sufficiency strategy* is proposed asking for a behavioral change in production and consumption processes that result in a self-limitation of consumers.

Life-Cycle Assessment (LCA) and ISO 14040: LCA is a well established method to collect information about environmental impact of products and services [12, 13]. With respect to SD it allows at least to satisfy the efficiency strategy by capturing current consumption of raw material [12]. LCA, although

Table 1. Selected concepts proposed in ISO 14040 for LCA [24, pp. 7–14]

Term	Definition
Life cycle	"Consecutive and interlinked stages of a product system, from raw material acquisition or generation from natural resources to final disposal" [p. 7]
Product	"Any goods or service" [p. 8]
Productsystem	"Collection of unit processes with elementary and product flows, performing one or more defined functions, and which models the life cycle of a product" [p. 11]
Sys. boundary	"Set of criteria specifying which unit processes are part of a product system" [p. 11]
Functional unit	"Quantified performance of a product system for use as a reference unit" [p. 10]
Unitprocess	"Smallest element considered in the life cycle inventory analysis for which input and output data are quantified" [p. 12]
Impactcategory	"Class representing environmental issues of concern to which life cycle inventory analysis results may be assigned" [p. 13]
Categoryendpoint	"Attribute or aspect of natural environment, human health, or resources, identifying an environmental issue giving cause for concern" [p. 12]

having some limitations (e.g., subjectivity and uncertainty regarding interrelationships of ecological causes and effects [25]), is considered to be the best available instrument for "evaluating the potential environmental impacts of manufacturing processes or products from cradle-to-grave" [12, p. 223]. An important step to consolidate LCA procedures or methods was the development of international standards ISO 14040 [26] and ISO 14044 [24], which contributed to LCA's acceptance [27] and development of LCA software [28].

The application of LCA is based on several concepts (cf. Table 1), and is guided by four main phases [24]: (1) goal and scope definition, (2) life-cycle inventory analysis, (3) life-cycle impact assessment, and (4) interpretation. Those phases should allow to assess environmental impact in an iterative process, which should be guided by seven main LCA principles defined within ISO 14040 [26, pp. 14–15]. Firstly, a *life-cycle perspective* (**P1**) postulates accounting for "the entire life cycle of a product, from raw material extraction and acquisition, through energy and material production and manufacturing, to use and end of life treatment and final disposal" [24]. Secondly, LCA has an *environmental focus* (**P2**) (economic and social aspects are outside of its scope). The basis of LCA is a *relative approach* making use of a *functional unit* (**P3**). The latter quantifies the intended use of certain product systems (e.g., four cups of coffee per day over a period of four years), which allows to normalize assessment data so that different product systems can be compared regarding their impacts (e.g., amount of CO_2 produced by a product system of a push-through pot or of a fully automated coffee machine). To contribute to the comprehensiveness and consistency of the analysis, an *iterative approach* (**P4**) should be followed. To ensure a proper interpretation of results, *transparency* (**P5**) in executing LCAs should be ensured. Next, LCA postulates *comprehensiveness* (**P6**) and thus, tries to consider all relevant aspects of natural environment, human health and resources, in order to identify potential trade-offs. Finally, LCA promotes *priority of scientific approach* (**P7**), thus, decisions are preferably based on natural science.

3   Goals and Requirements

Goals and main scenarios: To support the organizations' SD, as outlined in Sect. 1, the proposed method should allow to collect, document, aggregate and present data about potential environmental impacts of products along their entire life-cycle. Because of the contesting interpretations of SD, the method should not provide a solution on its own, but it should allow to collect and document a potential environmental impact within models which can be used in the form of diagrams for discursive decision making.

Exemplary use scenarios that should be supported by the method correspond to the phases proposed by ISO 14040 (cf. Sect. 2). First, the *Goal and Scope Definition* (Scenario 1) is performed during workshops, where different stakeholders prepare LCA for a product. It is done by setting the goal and scope of LCA and collecting information about all activities which need to be performed inside and outside of the company to produce, use and dispose or recycle the product. Using a model, those activities are assigned to different life cycle steps of the product system. Annotating the activities' accomplishments will allow in the next step to be more specific about potential impacts (e.g., considering the energy mix of a specific country). Furthermore, using the model, the stakeholders document the boundary of the system and assumptions related to certain activities.

In a second step *Life-cycle inventory analysis* (Scenario 2) detailed information about material flows (e.g., amount of material or energy consumption) is collected, calculated or estimated per activity documented in the first step. While in some cases concrete measurements are available, in others not all information will be directly available or accessible, so that a supporting model should provide concepts that allow to document calculations, estimations, data sources and of course the amount and type of a typical material flow and impact (e.g., CO_2 emission, water consumption). To ensure a better traceability and a proper interpretation of the results (cf. P6), it might be necessary to decompose the activities into more detailed ones and to document assumptions taken.

Life-cycle Impact Assessment (Scenario 3): Because some material flows might have impacts that go beyond their emission or consumption, *characterization models* are developed allowing asserting specific *impact categories* representing classes of environmental issues of concern (e.g., global warming potential, stratospheric ozone depletion [29]). In such models material flows of chemical substances are related to impact categories by numerical characterization factors. A supporting diagram in this phase allows to visualize such characterization models by relating chemical substance using its characterization factor to the impact category and resulting impacts (e.g., carziogenic impact of ozone depletion). Annotating sources or attributes indicating the acceptance of an impact, helps also in the next step interpret and evaluate the results of LCA.

Finally, *Interpretation* (Scenario 4) requires support for the assessment and interpretation of the results. Here decision makers have to assess and evaluate all gathered information (e.g., regarding its appropriateness) and to compare it to alternatives (e.g., by using functional units, cf. P3). For this purpose models may be used to (1) present aggregated information about environmental impacts and related data sources, as well as (2) document whether an element of the product system was assessed. Presenting impacts related to a specific locality allows arguing about environmental aspects with local stakeholders.

Resulting Requirements: To support the goal and the mentioned scenarios, first, *the method should allow for the calculation, analysis and documentation of material flows and potential environmental impact of a product along its entire life-cycle* (**R1**). Using the concepts described in Table 1 allows to benefit from the existing knowledge and link to the terminology that potential-users are familiar with. Thus, *the method should account for the main concepts of ISO 14040* (**R2**). In addition, as presented in Sect. 2, the concept of strong sustainability requires avoiding the consumption of non-renewable resources and using renewable ones only as much as they grow again. Thus, to allow assertions on the strong or weak sustainability of a product, *it should be possible to differentiate between the consumption of renewable and non-renewable resources* (**R3**).

As in only rare cases own measurements of environmental impact are available, *it should be possible to identify information on environmental effects which is not based on own measurements and such information should be accompanied by notes on data sources, calculations and justifications* (**R4**). While the latter information refers to the type level (e.g., average amount of waste water produced), an own measurement can be related to an instance as well. Thus, *the modeling method needs to account for both type and instance level information* (**R5**). Furthermore, reuse and calculation of impact data should be supported, thus, *the method should provide means for deriving data based on the model or obtaining data from other data sources* (**R6**).

While conceptual models of one specific product system might support an efficiency strategy, the substitution strategy requires to compare impacts of different product systems which provide the same functionality. Thus, *the method should allow for comparing different product systems, by relating to the same functional unit* (**R7**). This leads as well to the need to set a boundary for LCA, therefore *the method must allow to justify and document deliberately excluded information on environmental impacts* (**R8**). To assess the local impact of a product system, *the method should allow to assign environmental impacts to local areas* (**R9**). Because most environmental impacts might be based on estimations and historical data, *the method needs concepts which allow to evaluate* *the appropriateness of data used* (**R10**), e.g., locality and time of referred data used for calculations. Finally, because the knowledge on environmental impacts is increasing or changing, *the method should be open to new findings on cause-effect relationships* (**R11**).

Fullfilment of the requirements by existing EM approaches: A number of modeling languages and methods to model an enterprise and its architecture exist. Examples encompass ArchiMate [30], Architecture of Integrated Information Systems (ARIS) [31], 4EM [9] and Multi-Perspective Enterprise Modeling (MEMO) [8]. These methods are based on different modeling foundations and assumptions, and define different sets of modeling concepts for describing selected facets of organizations. Although all of them, on a high level, support a structured description of enterprises, those approaches are quite different as they have been developed with different purposes and goals in mind [32].

To answer a question whether the existing EM approaches fulfill the identified requirements, we consider two aspects: (1) the scope of information required and (2) required expressiveness of the language architecture. Regarding the former, as LCA, to our best knowledge, has not been defined as one of the scenarios to be supported by any of EM approaches [32], it is not surprising that they do not account for the main concepts required for the LCA analysis (except for *Product*). Therefore, to reach the defined goals and benefit in the analysis from the concepts allowing to describe the enterprise action system and information system, it is necessary to extend an already existing EM method with relevant concepts. To select the candidate for extensions, the requirements regarding the expressiveness need to be considered.

Based on the requirements, an approach is needed that would, among others: (1) support definition of semantically rich concepts, i.e., account for attributes, both on the type and instance level, (2) distinguish between different types of attributes (derived, obtained), and (3) provide a rudimentary support for calculations and analysis. Most of the existing approaches however, on purpose, provide a rather generic set of concepts, without attributes (e.g., ArchiMate), and mostly on the type level, thus, representing the information required is not straightforward possible. The exception is MEMO, whose language architecture not only supports definition of semantically rich concepts, but also allows for differentiating instance and type levels, which allows to consider measured data of a specific product in instance level diagrams, while estimated and calculated data can be assigned to the type level [8]. Although the support for calculations as such is not provided, we chose MEMO as point of departure for our work.

4   ImpactM: Abstract Syntax

Modeling Guidelines Followed: MEMO includes an extensible set of modeling languages, which are defined within a multi-layer language architecture [8] and specified using the MEMO Meta Modeling Language (MML [33]). This architecture adheres to the meta modeling paradigm [8], thus, the abstract syntax of the modeling language is defined in the form of a meta model (M_2) containing definitions of meta classes, their attributes and relations (i.e., language specification). A meta model is instantiated to create models at the type level (M_1) (i.e., language application). MML, when compared to other meta modeling languages provides additional language constructs allowing to express, e.g., intrinsic attributes and relations (instantiated only on the instance level and not on the type level), obtainable and derivable attributes (attributes which can be derived from other attributes within the same model or are obtainable from external sources), or language level types (instantiated on the type level, but no further, visualized with a grey background of the concept's name) [33].

Defining a meta model requires making a number of decisions, among others, (1) whether a concept should become part of a language at all, (2) whether a concept should be part of language specification (i.e., be a meta type, M_2 level) or part of language application (i.e., a type, M_1 level), and (3) which attributes of which types as well as which relations with which cardinalities should be defined. To support decision-making process and ensure the desired quality of the developed meta model, the guidelines proposed in [34] have been applied.

Design Decisions and Main Concepts: The meta model of the proposed language is shown in Fig. 2. Apart from the specification of concepts, it shows exemplary constraints defined using the Object Constraint Language (OCL) [35].

We used the discussed scenarios to identify relevant attributes and relations of rather generic ISO 14040 concepts. In this context, a design decision needed to be made regarding the language level applicable to the identified attributes. While in most cases users might model a typical product system by using average values, it seems also desirable to use single measurements to improve the quality of resulting LCA (cf. R5). Thus, we decided to assign concepts related to average data (e.g., calculations and related data sources) to the type level, and to introduce within meta classes intrinsic attributes which allow to capture concrete instances of a product system and related measurements. This instance data can be used on the type level to derive average values. The average values may be also obtained from external data sources (cf. R6).

This allows, e.g., to gather data on a certain `ProductSystem` with a specific `SerialNumber` in the intrinsic attribute `measuredAmount` of `SubstanceAmount`. An average value can be derived based on the instance-level data and represented within the relevant type-level concept as `avgAmount`. This average amount needs to be qualified through a `name` and `unit`, which are modeled by using the concept `SubstanceFlow`, which can also be amended with additional chemical information. Since `avgAmount` might be also based on a `Calculation`, which itself might refer to data sources like `Literature` and be based on an `Assumption`, we provide concepts allowing to trace and evaluate the appropriateness of calculations (cf. R10). These concepts are defined as language level types since the information they capture refers to a typical substance flow of a product system.

To enable a more differentiated analysis, we introduce a dedicated concept for `Transportation` with a set of attributes providing information relevant for environmental impacts. In addition, accounting for this concept allows language

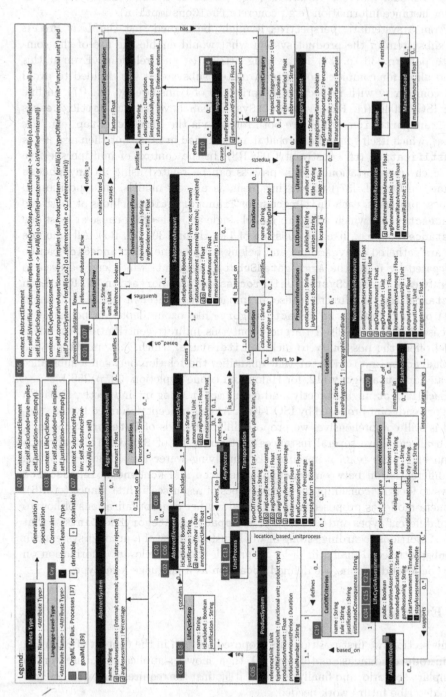

Fig. 2. A meta model of ImpactM

users to model different variations (e.g., means of transportation, cf. R7) or gather instance information (e.g., concrete `fuelConsumption`).

From a systematic perspective, it might be argued that the *Unit Process* is a subsystem of the product system what would enable the use of the composite pattern [36, p. 239] for reusing attributes and relations. Even if this would allow for complex models with nested subsystems, we decided to avoid such complexity with respect to the principle of transparency (cf. P7). In line with ISO 14040 (cf. R2), a `ProductSystem` can have several `UnitProcesses` and `Transportations` which are both related via the `LifeCycleStep` (e.g., *use phase*), which itself can indicate that it `isExcluded` in LCA, but then also needs a `justification` (cf. constraint C03; R8). In the context of multiperspective EM, each transportation or unit process can be related using an `AnyProcess` (defined in OrgML [37]) to existing business process models. In opposition to business processes, each `UnitProcess` or `Transportation` includes at least one `ImpactActivity`, which allows to model single activities that cause at least one `SubstanceFlow`, e.g., like the emission of 1 kg Halon 1301 (cf. R1). All amounts that are gathered as `avgAmount` and belong to the same `SubstanceFlow` can be aggregated by using the `AggregatedSubstanceAmount`, which can be used to quantify each `ProductSystem`, `UnitProcess` or `Transportation` (cf. R1). Each `SubstanceFlow` can directly cause an impact (like cancer in the case of Halon 1301) or contribute to an `ImpactCategory` (like ozone depletion potential in the case of Halon 1301). To argue about this indirect contribution, the meta model offers the possibility to include `Literature`, which, e.g., might provide the `CharacterizationFactor` that quantifies the relation between a substance and an `ImpactCategory` (12, for Halon and ozone depletion [38, p. 259]).

Each `Impact` might directly, and each `ImpactCategory` indirectly, impact a category endpoint proposed by ISO 14040. As this concept described by the standard is still comprehensive, we propose different kinds of `CategoryEndpoints`, which all can have several instances that might be of `StrategicImportance` for an enterprise (e.g., a specific lake supplying water for a brewery). While the differentiation between `RenewableResource` and `NonRenewableRessource` allows to identify consumption of both types of resources at first glance (cf. R3), the meta model as proposed here will need further conceptualizations of how to relate different types and instances of an `Impact` to `CategoryEndpoints` so that sound assertions regarding strong or weak sustainability of a product system can be substantiated. Finally, in order to provide location relevant information on the type-level diagrams, we defined `Location` as a language level type.

5   Evaluation

In this section, we first position our proposed method in the context of SD using the introduced dimensions (cf. Sect. 2), then show its applicability based on an exemplary scenario, and finally, evaluate it against the requirements which allows us to describe future work needed.

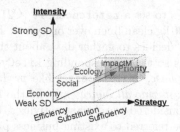

Fig. 3. ImpactM located in the possible dimension of SD (Color figure online)

Positioning ImpactM: With respect to the 'priority dimension', due to selecting ISO 14040 as a foundation for our work, the method supports ecological aspects only. Regarding the 'intensity dimension', the method might support both a weak and strong SD, however additional work is required to allow for addressing the assimilation rule. Therefore, we mark this dimension with a decreasing color gradient (Fig. 3). While an *efficiency strategy* can clearly be supported in the 'strategy dimension' through documenting current consumptions to assess the efficiency of used substances, a *substitution strategy* might be supported by the use of the functional unit. A *sufficiency strategy* however, can only be supported indirectly by providing information about a possible impact that might be used to change behavior of different stakeholders like customers.

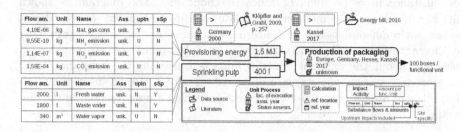

Fig. 4. An exemplary diagram to support inventory analysis

Exemplary Application: The application builds on the scenarios as described in the third section. A hotel manager is interested in comparing the environmental impacts of two laundry detergents for internal purposes. For the purpose of a better traceability, the accomplishment of LCA is set as a goal and mandated to the *Corporate Social Responsibility* department (CSR; e.g., by instantiating an EngagementGoal of MEMO GoalML [39], which related to a LifeCycleAssessment and is assigned to the UnitOfWork *CSR department*). To set the goal and the scope of LCA, CSR instantiates the meta class LifeCycleAssessment by providing among others values for the intendedApplication and the goalReasoning. Because the environmental impacts of two detergents should be compared, comparativeAsserstions is set to *true*, which enforces to set a `referenceUnit` (C21) while instantiating a `ProductSystem` (e.g., 1000 kg clean linen over one year). To learn about as many impacts as possible, CSR decides to gather data about the production, use and disposal of the detergents so that corresponding `LifeCycleSteps` are instantiated. In the *production phase*, `UnitProcesses` like *production of packaging* or *production of surfactants, mixing all ingredients* and the `Transportation` *delivery to the laundry*, are considered as relevant activities. Internal unit processes and transportation can be referred to existing business process models by using the meta type `AnyProcess`. Because the waste water treatment in the use phase is the same for both detergents and cannot be influenced, this Unit Process is marked as `isExcluded` by providing a corresponding `justification`. Now for each `UnitProcess` or `Transportation` data of related `ImpactActivities` with their `SubstanceFlows` is gathered. Figure 4 shows a diagram where impact relevant data is gathered for the `UnitProcess` of *production of packaging*. Please note that the concrete syntax as suggested by the legend is only preliminary.

Beside gathering and documenting all data and calculations for each unit process, the diagram type proposed here allows to answer analytical questions, which concern appropriateness of the data (e.g., suitable time and locality, data sources used) by assessing calculations or comparing the location of execution of a unit process and data used for the calculation. Furthermore, the status of the assessment can be set by using the attribute `statusAssessment`.

After documenting the first activities with the corresponding `Substance Flows`, CSR is using different data sources to determine potential impacts of substance flows on different kinds of `Endpoints`. The diagram as shown in Fig. 5 allows the modeler to relate a direct `Impact`, or to depict other environmental issues of concern by relating an `ImpactCategory` over a `CharacterizationFactorRelation` to a `SubstanceFlow`. It provides an overview about the different kinds of impacts caused by the substances used in a product system, the strength of contribution of a specific substance to an impact, and used literature to trace assertions which are represented in the diagram.

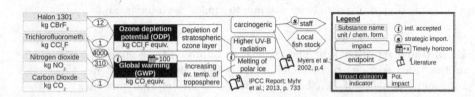

Fig. 5. An exemplary diagram to support impact assessment

Fulfillment of Requirements and Future Work: The result of the evaluation of the proposed method using the requirements presented in Sect. 3 may be found in Table 2. As indicated not all of the requirements are fulfilled to the

Table 2. Fulfillment of requirements

R	Ev	Comment
R1	●	Offering the language user meta classes which provide attributes for calculating, documenting and presenting different material flows and related environmental impacts throughout different life cycle steps allows him analyzing a product for impacts along its life cycle.
R2	◑	Choosing ISO 14040 allowed to build on many terms of the standard and to refine them for purpose of conceptual modeling. Beside additional concepts that were derived from our design decisions other concepts of the standard were integrated or refined, e.g., an intermediate product is built in the method proposed as SubstanceFlow. Because concepts like allocation and related operations are not considered, further work is needed.
R3	◑	Associating SubstanceFlow with its related amounts to resources (e.g., NonRenwableResource) on instance level allows for limited assertions regarding strong or weak sustainability. As calculation procedures on type level are not specified, a further work is needed.
R4	●	By proposing meta classes that allow for documented and transparent calculations of environmental effects the LCA can be produced in a traceable way.
R5	◑	The MEMO language architecture allowed assigning concepts and attributes to type and instance levels. Considerations for some concepts indicate however that another language architecture might be more appropriate (e.g., refining a product like discussed in [41, p. 321]).
R6	●	The MEMO MML allows to indicate that data is derived or obtained from other sources.
R7	●	Setting the attribute comparativeAssertion of LifeCycleAssessment indicates a comparative LCA. This requires a user to set the attribute typeOfReferenceUnit of ProductSystem to *functional unit* and choose for all product systems the same referenceUnit (cf. C21)
R8	●	Using the attribute isExcluded in several meta classes allow modelers to indicate that information was excluded on purpose. Constraints (e.g., C02) enforce the modeler to provide a justification in those cases.
R9	◑	Each Impact can be assigned to a CategoryEndpoint which itself can be assigned to a Location. The design decisions here indicate however, that other conceptions might be needed to relate impacts to local areas.
R10	●	Setting the attribute statusAssessment allows a user to indicate the evaluation and appropriateness of data used.
R11	●	Instead of proposing certain impacts or impact categories to a user, the language proposes corresponding meta classes which allow to specify own cause-effect relationships.

Legend: ○– not fulfilled; ◑– partly fulfilled; ●– fulfilled

satisfactory extent. Taking that into account, aside of developing a concrete syntax, two main streams of our future work may be distinguished. The first one relates to the scope of information captured (cf. R2, R3, R9). Namely, there are few concepts, like, e.g., *endpoint* or *resource* which require more structured conceptualization. Here representations used in existing LCA software [28] might provide a good starting point. In addition, social aspects could be integrated to the life-cycle perspective built into ImpactM (cf., TracyML, [40]).

The second stream relates to the language architecture followed (cf. R5). Here, the application of MEMO MML allowed to take advantage of the intrinsic features and relations, and thus, to refer to the instance level. However, we faced a challenge connected with, on the one hand, the type differentiation pertaining to the restrictions given by the type/instance dichotomy and the semantic differences between instantiation and specialization, cf. [41], and on the other hand, a need to support a number of different calculations, preferably by different model elements. Therefore, considering the limitations imposed by the language architecture which is based on a fixed amount of levels and based on the semantics of dominant object-oriented programming, as a next step we undertake an attempt to apply a multilevel modeling language like, e.g., FMML^x with an integrated programming and modeling environment [41]. Changing the language architecture should also allow for an integration of the proposed method with existing LCA software tools and relevant databases.

6   Conclusions

In this paper we have shown how conceptual modeling in general, and enterprise modeling in particular, can be used to support the organizations' SD by collecting and presenting information about potential environmental impacts of product systems along their life-cycle. While the exemplary application of *ImpactM* in the last section indicated the general usage of such a method, the evaluation revealed the need for further work encompassing (1) refinement of concepts and (2) investigating the potentials of multilevel modeling. Furthermore, the positioning of *ImpactM* within the selected dimensions of SD (cf., Fig. 3) indicated that further work is needed to fully address them.

Beside that, following Hovorka et al. [42], further limitations need to be accounted for, which are connected with conducting research in the area of environmental sustainability. Those limitations are, e.g., boundary issues or uncertainty regarding ecological causes and effects which are, on the one hand, inherent to LCA itself [25], and on the other, result out of the vagueness of the SD topic, which might lead to opportunistic self-representations in the name of transparency while generating opacity [43,44]. Especially the last point raises questions how conceptual modeling can be used to improve the transparency of organizations and it is to be covered by our future work as well.

References

1. Diesendorf, M.: Models of sustainability and sustainable development. IJARGE **1**(2), 109–123 (2001)
2. Jabareen, Y.: A new conceptual framework for sustainable development. Environ. Dev. Sustain. **10**(2), 179–192 (2008)
3. Eriksen, M., Lebreton, L.C.M., Carson, H.S., Thiel, M., Moore, C.J., Borerro, J.C., Galgani, F., Ryan, P.G., Reisser, J.: Plastic pollution in the world's oceans: more than 5 trillion plastic pieces weighing over 250,000 tons afloat at sea. PloS one **9**(12), e111913 (2014)
4. Giddings, B., Hopwood, B., Brien, G.O.: Environment, economy and society: fitting them together into sustainable development. Sustain. Dev. **196**, 187–196 (2002)
5. Melde, T.: Nachhaltige Entwicklung durch Semantik, Governance und Management. Springer, Wiesbaden (2012)
6. Melville, N.: Information systems innovation for environmental sustainability. MIS Q. **34**(1), 1–21 (2010)
7. Bass, S., Prescott-Allen, R., Carew-Reid, J., Dalal-Clayton, B.: Strategies for National Sustainable Development. Earthscan Publications Limited, London (2013)
8. Frank, U.: Multi-perspective enterprise modeling: foundational concepts, prospects and future research challenges. SoSyM **13**(3), 941–962 (2014)
9. Sandkuhl, K., Stirna, J., Persson, A., Wißotzki, M.: Enterprise Modeling: Tackling Business Challenges with the 4EM Method. Springer, Berlin (2014)
10. Thalheim, B.: The science and art of conceptual modelling. In: Hameurlain, A., Küng, J., Wagner, R., Liddle, S.W., Schewe, K.-D., Zhou, X. (eds.) Transactions on Large-Scale Data- and Knowledge-Centered Systems VI. LNCS, vol. 7600, pp. 76–105. Springer, Heidelberg (2012). doi:10.1007/978-3-642-34179-3_3

11. Wolff, F.: Ökonomie multiperspektivischer Unternehmensmodellierung. Gabler, Wiesbaden (2008)
12. Chang, Y.-J., Neugebauer, S., Lehmann, A., Scheumann, R., Finkbeiner, M.: Life cycle sustainability assessment approaches for manufacturing. In: Stark, R., Seliger, G., Bonvoisin, J. (eds.) Sustainable Manufacturing. SPLCEM, pp. 221–237. Springer, Cham (2017). doi:10.1007/978-3-319-48514-0_14
13. Finkbeiner, M.: The international standards as the constitution of life cycle assessment: the ISO 14040 series and its offspring. In: Klöpffer, W. (ed.) Background and Future Prospects in Life Cycle Assessment. LCTCWLCA, pp. 85–106. Springer, Dordrecht (2014). doi:10.1007/978-94-017-8697-3_3
14. Österle, H., Becker, J., Frank, U., et al.: Memorandum on design-oriented information systems research. EJIS **20**, 7–10 (2011)
15. Frank, U.: Outline of a Method for Designing Domain-Specific Modelling Languages. ICB Research Report 42, University of Duisburg-Essen, Essen (2010)
16. Von Carlowitz, H.C., von Rohr, J.B.: Sylvicultura oeconomica. Otto Wigand, Leipzig (1732)
17. Brundtland Comission: Our common future. Technical report, Oxford University Press, Oxford (1987)
18. Jacobs, M.: Sustainable development as a contested concept. In: Dob, A. (ed.) Fairness and Futurity: Essays on Environmental Sustainability and Social Justice, pp. 21–45. Oxford University Press, Oxford (1999)
19. Gallie, W.B.: Essentially Contested Concepts. In: Meeting of the Aristotelian Society, vol. 56, pp. 167–198. The Aristotelian Society, London (1956)
20. Solow, R.M.: The economics of resources or the resources of economics. In: Gopalakrishnan, C. (ed.) Classic Papers in Natural Resource Economics, pp. 257–276. Palgrave Macmillan, London (1974)
21. Daly, H.E.: Toward some operational principles of sustainable development. Ecol. Econ. **2**, 1–6 (1990)
22. Grunwald, A.: Nachhaltigkeit, 2nd edn. Campus Verlag, Frankfurt (2012)
23. Otto, S., Kaiser, F.G., Arnold, O.: The critical challenge of climate change for psychology. Eur. Psychol. **19**(2), 96–106 (2014)
24. ISO: DIN EN ISO 14044 - Umweltmanagement - Ökobilanz - Anforderungen und Anleitungen (2006)
25. Adensam, H., Ganglberger, E., Gupfinger, H., Wenisch, A.: Wieviel Umwelt braucht ein Produkt?. Österreichisches Ökologie Institut, Wien (2000)
26. ISO: DIN EN ISO 14040 - Umweltmanagement - Ökobilanz - Grundsätze und Rahmenbedingungen (2009)
27. Finkbeiner, M., Inaba, A., Tan, R., Christiansen, K., Klüppel, H.J.: The new international standards for life cycle assessment: ISO 14040 and ISO 14044. Int. J. Life Cycle Assess. **11**(2), 80–85 (2006)
28. Seto, K.E., Panesar, D.K., Churchill, C.J.: Criteria for the evaluation of life cycle assessment software packages and life cycle inventory data with application to concrete. Int. J. Life Cycle Assess. **22**(5), 694–706 (2017)
29. Stranddorf, H.K., Hoffmann, L., Schmidt, A.: LCA technical report: impact categories, normalization and weighting in LCA. Update on selec. EDIP97-data (2005)
30. The Open Group: ArchiMate 2.1 Specification: Open Group Standard. The Open Group Series. Van Haren, Zaltbommel (2013)
31. Scheer, A.W.: ARIS - Modellierungsmethoden, Metamodelle, Anwendungen, 4th edn. Springer, Heidelberg (2001)

32. Bock, A., Kaczmarek, M., Overbeek, S., Heß, M.: A comparative analysis of selected enterprise modeling approaches. In: Frank, U., Loucopoulos, P., Pastor, Ó., Petrounias, I. (eds.) PoEM 2014. LNBIP, vol. 197, pp. 148–163. Springer, Heidelberg (2014). doi:10.1007/978-3-662-45501-2_11
33. Frank, U.: The MEMO Meta Modelling Language (MML) and Language Architecture, 2nd edn. ICB Research Report 43, University of Duisburg-Essen, Essen (2011)
34. Frank, U.: Some guidelines for the conception of domain-specific modelling languages. In: Nüttgens, M., Thomas, O., Weber, B. (eds.) Proceedings of EMISA 4th International Workshop, LNI, vol. 190, pp. 93–106. German Informatics Society, Bonn (2011)
35. Warmer, J.B.: The Object Constraint Language: Getting Your Models Ready for MDA, 2nd edn. Addison-Wesley, Boston (2003)
36. Gamma, E., Helm, R., Johnson, R., Vlissides, J.: Entwurfsmuster. Addison-Wesley, München (2011)
37. Frank, U.: MEMO Organisation Modelling Language (2): Focus on Business Processes. ICB Research Report 49, University of Duisburg-Essen (2011)
38. Klöpffer, W., Grahl, B.: Ökobilanz (LCA). Wiley-VCH, Weinheim (2009)
39. Overbeek, S., Frank, U., Köhling, C.: A language for multi-perspective goal modelling: challenges, requirements and solutions. CSI **38**, 1–16 (2015)
40. Fritsch, A., Betz, S.: TracyML Specification. Working Paper 1.0, Karlsruhe Institute of Technology, Karlsruhe (2016)
41. Frank, U.: Multilevel modeling. BISE **6**(6), 319–337 (2014)
42. Hovorka, D.S., Labajo, E., Auerbach, N.: Information systems in environmental sustainability: of cannibals and forks. In: vom Brocke, J., Seidel, S., Recker, J. (eds.) Green Business Process Management, pp. 59–72. Springer, Heidelberg (2012). doi:10.1007/978-3-642-27488-6_4
43. Gray, R., Milne, M.: Sustainability reporting: who's kidding whom? Chart. Account. J. N. Z. **81**(6), 66–70 (2002)
44. Christensen, L.T., Cheney, G.: Peering into transparency: challenging ideals, proxies, and organizational practices. Commun. Theor. **25**(1), 70–90 (2015)

Towards Reasoning About Pivoting in Startups and Large Enterprises with i*

Vik Pant[1(✉)], Eric Yu[1,2], and Albert Tai[3]

[1] Faculty of Information, University of Toronto, Toronto, Canada
vik.pant@mail.utoronto.ca, eric.yu@utoronto.ca
[2] Department of Computer Science, University of Toronto, Toronto, Canada
[3] Hypercare, Toronto, Canada
albert@hypercare.ca

Abstract. Many start-ups fail, or are abandoned, due to flawed reasoning underpinning their products, business models, and engines of growth. Similarly, many strategic initiatives in large enterprises fail, or are decommissioned, because they are predicated on faulty assumptions that do not comport with reality. The lean start-up and lean enterprise approaches encourage decision makers to test their fundamental hypotheses and effect strategic pivots to identify new and superior fundamental hypotheses. This paper presents a model-based approach to support reasoning about strategic pivoting. It outlines key constructs from the i* modeling language that can be used to model various pivot types. Experience with a real-life application provided a preliminary validation about the benefits of modeling to support pivoting. The case study demonstrated how this approach can be used to compare alternatives for pivoting as well as to generate further ideas for alternative pivots.

Keywords: Enterprise modeling · Startup · Entrepreneurship · Pivoting

1 Introduction

Modern enterprises operate in dynamic environments where technologies and relationships undergo rapid and continual shifts. This requires enterprises of all sizes to assess and adapt their fundamental hypotheses on an ongoing basis. Changes to an enterprise's product, business model, or engine of growth that are catalyzed by disproving of their fundamental hypotheses are referred to as pivots [1–3]. Pivoting is useful for effecting strategic redirection in many situations such as when new competitors enter the market; novel substitute products are launched; key suppliers exit the market; technologies disrupt an industry; as well as when laws and regulations are changed. Due to high opportunity costs of scarce resources – mistakes and errors by an enterprise, within a competitive industry that is undergoing disruption, can be fatal. Pivoting can help enterprises of all sizes to validate their assumptions, logics, and hypotheses.

A catalog of ten types of pivots was identified and popularized by Reis [1] (Table 1). In this paper, we follow the naming and description of pivot types by Reis [1].

G. Poels et al. (Eds.): PoEM 2017, LNBIP 305, pp. 203–220, 2017.
https://doi.org/10.1007/978-3-319-70241-4_14

Table 1. Catalog of ten common types of pivots (Source: Adapted from Reis [1])

Pivot	Meaning
Zoom-in	Functionality that was formerly a single feature becomes the whole product
Zoom-out	All the functionality in a product is considered insufficient for meeting the requirements of a customer segment and thus it is assimilated into another product whereby the original product becomes a feature in the larger product
Customer segment	The functionality in a product meets the needs of a certain customer segment that is different from the customer segment that it was targeted to and thus that product is positioned to a customer segment whose needs its satisfies
Customer need	The original need of a customer segment that a product is designed to meet is recognized to be less important than another need for that customer segment and thus the product is changed to meet the other more important need of that customer segment
Value capture	An enterprise changes the way by which it captures value from its product such as by monetizing features individually or commercializing functionality holistically
Engine of growth	An enterprise changes its growth strategy by focusing on different ways of growing market share, increasing revenues, and boosting margins
Platform	A product is turned into a platform where other enterprises can also offer their products or conversely a platform on which other enterprises offer their products is changed into a product
Business architecture	An enterprise changes from a margin business to a volume business or conversely from a volume business to a margin business
Channel	An enterprise changes its sales distribution channel as well as process to take its products to market more effectively
Technology	An enterprise changes the technology underlying an existing solution in order to benefit from better price or performance

Ries [1] promotes the notion of Lean Startup [2] which encourages decision-makers at startup companies to pivot their products, business models, or engines of growth if tests disprove their fundamental hypotheses. He [1] notes that "Lean Startup approach can work in any size company, even a very large enterprise, in any sector or industry." Owens and Fernandez [3] relate the principles of Lean Startup to large enterprises by promoting the notion of Lean Enterprise. They assert that executives of large corporations should adopt the practices of startup entrepreneurs to innovate more productively [3]. Humble et al. [4] share this view and encourage the application of lean approaches for managing enterprises of all sizes. They argue that lean approaches typify scientific and systematic problem exploration and solution experimentation to arrive at better decisions and judgement [4]. Edison [5] proposes a conceptual framework for implementing the Lean Startup approach within an established corporation to manage the venturing process. Gbadegeshin and Heinonen [6] studied the relevance of the Lean approach in the context of small and midsize enterprises (SMEs).

Ries [1] argues that a start-up or corporate venture may need to pivot multiple times and may also need to execute multiple pivots quickly. Pivoting affects an enterprise in significant ways because it establishes new fundamental hypotheses for its products, business model, and engines of growth [1]. Thus, the stakes are high if an organization executes an incorrect pivot or executes a required pivot incorrectly. However, there is a dearth of enterprise modeling (EM) support for evaluating or designing strategic pivots in enterprises. A structured and systematic approach for analyzing pivots can be valuable for decision-makers in startups as well as large enterprises because it can help them to identify and generate relevant pivots as well as ways of implementing those pivots successfully.

We present an EM approach that supports the representation of pivoting in a systematic and structured manner. We discussed the concept of pivoting and its relevance for startups and large enterprises. We outlined ten archetypes of pivoting from the Lean Startup approach [1]. We propose generic pattern models and offer abstract representations of select archetypes of pivoting from this catalog. In the main section, we present a model showing various types of pivoting options that are available to a healthcare software (mobile application) startup. We also share the results from validating our approach for modeling of pivoting. We indicate research in the EM literature that pertains to modeling of strategic management concepts. We conclude by noting our key findings as well as laying out future work related to this line of research.

2 Towards Modeling Pivoting in Startups and Large Enterprises with i*

EM research on pivoting in startups and large enterprises is sparse. However, EM researchers have proposed several approaches for representing and reasoning about business strategy. Kim et al. [14] offer a modeling approach to represent a value chain of a virtual enterprise. Giannoulis et al. [15] present a unified language for modeling of strategy maps. Pant and Yu [16] propose preliminary models of coopetition between organizations as well as competition driven by contention over resources. Cardoso et al. [17] proffer methodological guidelines and a hierarchical architecture to model various kinds of goals in organizations. Svee et al. [18] associate the concept of consumer value to strategy maps and balanced scorecards (SMBSC). Pijpers et al. [19] apply a value modeling language, e3Value, to demonstrate the alignment between the organizational strategies of an Internet company and its information system. This paper presents an innovative EM approach for expressing the impacts of the external aspects of an enterprise (such as its relationships) on its internal facets (such as its objectives and alternatives).

Johannesson [20] notes that enterprise models can be of many types such as value, process, and goal models. Value modeling languages are useful for articulating economic transactions such as monetary exchanges. Process modeling languages are useful for representing workflows such as sequences of activities. Goal modeling languages are relevant for depicting graphs of intentionality. Additionally, actor-oriented modeling languages are relevant for expressing dependencies between actors. Some key criteria for modeling pivoting can be extracted from Table 1.

Then the sufficiency of typical value, process, goal, and actor modeling languages for meeting those criteria can be preliminarily evaluated. This extraction of requirements and preliminary appraisal of EM languages is based upon the intuitions and experiences of the authors.

An examination of Table 1 reveals that the key requirements for modeling of pivoting include the ability to represent the concepts of value (e.g., economic, non-economic), resources (e.g., data, physical), stakeholders (e.g., enterprise, customers), objectives (e.g., goals and qualities), and relationships (e.g., between stakeholders). Additional requirements for modeling of pivoting includes the ability to depict hierarchies (e.g., of needs, requirements, offerings), alternatives (e.g., choices, options), impacts (e.g., consequences, outcomes), conditionality (e.g., prerequisites, obligations), and temporality (e.g., time, sequence). By reducing pivoting to these constructs it is possible to select an EM language that is suitable for modeling pivoting. An EM language for modeling of pivoting needs to be expressive with respect to these constructs.

Different EM languages satisfy various abovementioned requirements for modeling of pivoting. Value modeling languages typically focus on the portrayal of value (e.g., objects, exchanges, etc.) as well as stakeholders (e.g., actors, customer segments). However, they do not cover the objectives of the stakeholders or their relationships that are not directly value-oriented. Process modeling languages generally focus on the depiction of activity flows at operational or tactical levels rather than strategic levels where pivoting occurs. They usually depict associations between stakeholders in transactional terms rather than relational terms.

Goal modeling languages typically focus on the objectives (functional and non-functional requirements) of a stakeholder as well as on alternatives (operationalizations) and their impact (contributions) on objectives. Actor-oriented modeling languages focus on the expression of relationships between stakeholders. They are useful for showing the alternatives and resources that are available to stakeholders for pursuing their objectives. None of the widely-used EM languages directly satisfy each of the abovementioned requirements for modeling of pivoting.

In this paper, we adopt i* for representing distinct types of pivots in startups and large enterprises because it meets many of the criteria for modeling pivoting that are listed above. i* is a goal- and actor-oriented socio-technical modeling language [8]. It can be used to express stakeholders as distinct actors, objectives as goals and softgoals, relationships as dependencies between actors and resources as physical or data entities. Additionally, it supports Means-ends decomposition to show alternatives, contribution links to show impact of alternatives on quality objectives, and label propagation to show goal satisfaction or denial. Core i* does not support the articulation of conditionality and temporality. Overall, i* is suitable for modeling pivoting because startups and large enterprises are fundamentally human enterprises (i.e., socio-technical entities) that exist at the confluence of people, process, technology, and organization.

The key elements of i* are actors, goals, tasks, resources, and softgoals. An actor is an entity comprising the characteristics of autonomy, sociality, intentionality, strategic reflectivity, abstract/physical identity, contingent boundary, and pursuit of rational self-interest [9]. A goal is a state of affairs in the world that an actor wishes to achieve, a task is an alternate way of achieving an end, a resource is a physical or data entity that is required for completing a task, and a softgoal is a quality objective that is considered to be achieved or denied solely from the perspective of an actor. i* is explained in [10].

The primary relationship types in i* include means-end decomposition, task-refinement, and dependencies. Means-end decomposition links a goal with any of the tasks that can be used to achieve it. A goal can be achieved through the achievement of any of the tasks that are associated with it. Task-refinement links a task with its components such as sub-goals, sub-tasks, sub-softgoals, and resources wherein each of the components need to be satisfied for that task to be completed. Inter-actor dependencies link an actor that depends (i.e., depender) on another actor (i.e., dependee) for something (i.e., dependum). These types of relationships in i* support the depiction of strategic rationale (SR) of an actor as well as its strategic dependencies (SD) with other actors.

The characteristics of i* that make it useful for expressing and evaluating pivoting in startups include means-ends reasoning; task-refinement and elaboration; inter-actor dependencies; distinction between concrete/abstract actors (i.e., agents, roles, positions); and actor associations. Additionally, the semantics and notation of i* are helpful for articulating and analyzing pivoting requirements that are listed above. Figures 1, 2 and 3 present i* SR diagrams representing abstract patterns for four types of pivots. Core requirements for modeling each type of pivot as well as the corresponding features of i* are discussed below.

- **Zoom-in/Zoom-out:** Modeling zoom-in/zoom-out pivots requires the ability to show products on offer as well as bundles of those products on offer. Representing a zoom-in pivot requires the ability to express products in a bundle being offered by themselves. Conversely, expressing a zoom-out pivot requires the ability to depict multiple products being combined and offered as an amalgamated bundle. Zoom-in/zoom-out pivots can be shown in i* via means-end decomposition and task-refinement. Figure 1 presents abstract i* models of Zoom-in/Zoom-out pivots. As shown in Fig. 1, a focal actor's product/service features can be represented as goals that can be chained in a hierarchy of tasks, sub-goals, and sub-tasks such that a higher-level goal represents composition and aggregation of features and functions. Similarly, a lower level sub-goal represents decomposition and refinement of higher level goals (i.e., features). Goals and tasks are interleaved to show the purpose of a feature (i.e., goal) as distinct from its implementation (i.e., task). In Fig. 1a, upward pointing arrows depict examples of zoom-out pivoting while, in Fig. 1b, downward pointing arrows represent examples of zoom-in pivoting. The inability to represent temporality in i* hampers the expression of time-dependent aspects (e.g., factors that can accelerate/decelerate a zoom-in/zoom-out pivot) of the model.

- **Customer Segment:** Central to the modeling of customer segment pivots is the ability to show distinct stakeholders (e.g., enterprise, customer) and their relationships. Representing a customer segment pivot requires the ability to express a shift from one objective of the enterprise to another and the impact of that shift on customer segments. Value propositions for the customer segments can be represented as goals/softgoals that are mapped to the customer segments via inbound dependency links from the enterprise. Similarly, the objective that the enterprise

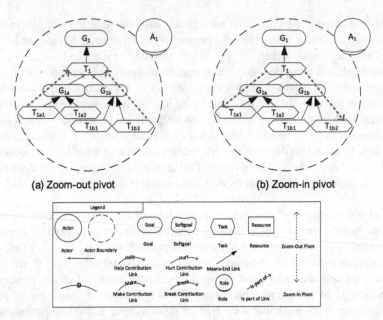

Fig. 1. Abstract i* model of (a) Zoom-out and (b) Zoom-in pivots

wishes to achieve (e.g., payment) by serving its intended customer segment can be depicted as outbound dependency links from the enterprise. Value propositions are depicted as goal/softgoal dependencies because they can be satisfied by various kinds of value exchanges. i* models can be used to show objectives that are satisfied by different types of value exchanges. This approach to modeling is complementary to modeling of value exchanges (e.g., via e3Value) because this higher level depiction provides the rationale behind value exchanges that can be represented in more detail in value exchange models.

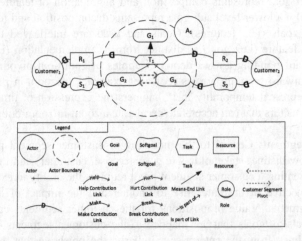

Fig. 2. Abstract i* model of customer segment pivot

As shown in Fig. 2, two customer segments can be shown as distinct actors with specific dependencies on the enterprise. An enterprise (A_1) has two distinct customers (*Customer$_1$* and *Customer$_2$*). It can satisfy the dependum (S_1) of *Customer$_1$* via its value proposition (G_2) or it can satisfy the dependum (S_2) of *Customer$_2$* via its value proposition (G_3). When the enterprise (A_1) decides to switch the customer segment that it wishes to serve (i.e., from *Customer$_1$* to *Customer$_2$* or vice versa) then it can do so by switching the value proposition that it delivers to the intended customer segment (i.e., from S_1 to S_2 or vice versa). The inability to express conditionality in i* hinders the depiction of enabling/disabling mechanisms (e.g., factors that can impel/impede a customer segment pivot) in the model.

- **Customer Need:** A modeler needs to show the objectives of various stakeholders (e.g., enterprise, customer) for modeling customer need pivots. Representing a customer need pivot also requires the ability to express a shift from one objective of the enterprise to another for serving different needs of its customer. This can be expressed in i* by modeling the intentional structures of multiple actors as well as dependencies between those actors. Specific value propositions for a customer can be represented as softgoals and can be mapped to the particular goals of a customer via inbound dependency links from the enterprise. Similarly, the objective that the enterprise wishes to achieve (e.g., payment) by serving an intended customer need can be depicted as outbound dependency links from the enterprise. Since the same product can be offered for different customer needs under different terms and conditions – rather than offering products an enterprise offers value propositions with respect to distinct customer needs.

As shown in Fig. 3, two customer needs can be shown as distinct goals with specific dependencies on the enterprise. An enterprise (A_1) has a customer (*Customer*) with two distinct needs (G_5 and G_6). It can satisfy the dependum (S_1) of *Customer* via its value proposition (G_2) or it can satisfy the dependum (S_2) of *Customer* via its value

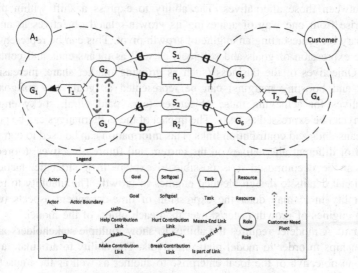

Fig. 3. Abstract i* model of customer need pivot

proposition (G_3). When the enterprise (A_1) decides to switch the customer need that it wishes to serve (i.e., from G_5 to G_6 or vice versa) then it can do so by switching the value proposition that it delivers to the intended customer need (i.e., from G_2 to G_3 or vice versa). A focal actor's decision to execute a customer need pivot must consider the impact of that pivot on its own targets and not be motivated merely by a desire to meet additional or different customer requirements. The inability to depict quantities in i* hampers the representation of economic topics (e.g., reason for offering one value proposition over another) in the model.

Similar abstract patterns for remaining pivot types as well as instantiated examples of these decontextualized representations were omitted from this paper due to space constraints.

- **Value Capture:** The ability to show distinct options of achieving specific objectives and the opportunity costs of each option are necessary for modeling value capture pivots. Representing a value capture pivot requires the ability to depict change in the objectives of the focal enterprise from one way of achieving its value capture objectives to another. This can be represented in i* via means-end decomposition and task-refinement as well as contribution links. A product's features as well as their respective value inputs to the revenue stream can be represented as softgoals. These features and value inputs can be related to each other via contribution links. Equally importantly, the impact of features on value inputs of other features can also be related via contribution links. This information can be used to compare groups of features to evaluate the optimal bundles of features for achieving the value capture goals of the business. The inability to perform quantitative reasoning in i* can encumber the analysis of economic actions (e.g., amounts of value captured through various activities might be different) with the model.

- **Engine of Growth:** Modeling engine of growth pivots requires the ability to show distinct alternatives for achieving various growth-related objectives and the trade-offs between those alternatives. The ability to express a shift within the focal enterprise from one way of achieving its growth-related objectives to another is necessary for representing an engine of growth pivot. This can be represented in i* via the expression of goals and softgoals as well as means-ends and contribution links. Objectives of the business (such as growing market share, increasing revenues, and boosting margins) can be represented as goals and softgoals. The alternatives for achieving those objectives (e.g., paid, viral, sticky engines of growth) can be expressed as tasks. The impact of these alternatives can be portrayed via means-ends and contribution links. This information can be used to compare the impact of different alternatives on the current and future objectives. Moreover, as tasks can be decomposed it is possible to explore their strategic, tactical, and operational details to design blended engines of growth. The inability to represent temporality in i* may deter the expression of time-dependent aspects (e.g., are certain engines of growth faster/slower than each other) of the model.

- **Platform:** A modeler requires the ability to show multiple stakeholders and their relationships in order to model platform pivots. The ability to articulate a change from one objective of the focal enterprise to another as well as the impact of that change on its stakeholders is needed to represent a platform pivot. This can be depicted in i* via strategic dependencies between different types of actors (such as customers, brokers, resellers, co-sellers, etc.). In the case of a product, the relationship between the focal actor (i.e., business) and the customer can be shown via direct dependencies. Here, the customer depends on the business directly to meet its product needs while the business depends on the customer directly to meet its economic needs. However, in the case of a platform, customer and the partners can have direct or indirect dependency relationships with the business which is the platform operator. Here, the customer depends on the other actors (i.e., partners) directly or indirectly to meet its product needs while the partners also depend on the customer directly or indirectly to meet their economic needs. This information can be used to analyze whether more of its own objectives are served when it functions as a product vendor or as a platform operator. The inability to perform quantitative analysis in i* can hinder the comparison of product- or platform-orientation (e.g., amounts of value generated by product and platform might be different) via the model.

- **Business Architecture:** The ability to show the goals of a focal enterprise is a starting point for modeling business architecture pivots. Representing a business architecture pivot requires the ability to express a change from one goal of a focal enterprise to another as well as the impact of that change on its various needs. This can be shown in i* via the use of goals and softgoals as well as means-ends and contribution links. The objectives of a business architecture (e.g., maximize quantity, maximize price) can be represented as goals as well as softgoals. The impact of different alternatives for achieving those objectives can be compared using means-ends and contribution links. This information can be used to analyze the impact that each alternative has on the currently selected objective and the prospective candidate objective. The current alternative may be equally suitable for serving both the present and future objectives or it may only be suitable for either of these in which case other alternatives may need to be considered. The inability to perform quantitative reasoning in i* can hamper the evaluation of various objectives of the enterprise (e.g., amounts of value created by price or quantity maximization might be different) from the model.

- **Channel:** A modeler requires the ability to show stakeholders as well as their relationships to model channel pivots. A channel pivot entails a shift within from one goal of the focal enterprise to another as well as the impact of that shift on other stakeholders (e.g., customers, distributors, etc.). This can be depicted in i* by articulating strategic dependencies between different types of actors such as customers, brokers, resellers, co-sellers, etc. A channel can be depicted as the chain of dependencies from a focal actor (i.e., business) to a customer. Dependencies between the business and its customers without any intermediary actors can be thought of to constitute a direct channel. Whereas, if the business and its customers have dependencies with mutual intermediaries but not each other – then these can be regarded as constituting an indirect channel. This information can be used to reason about whether the benefits of using intermediaries (e.g., business softgoals of revenue scaling, market penetration, etc.) are outweighed by the vulnerabilities of a hold up problem. The inability to express conditionality in i* can hinder the expression of enabling/disabling mechanisms (e.g., factors that can support/undermine a channel pivot) in the model.

- **Technology:** The ability to show the goals of relevant stakeholders (i.e., enterprise, customer) as well resources (e.g., hardware, software) is necessary for modeling technology pivots. A technology pivot changes the mechanisms that are required to better serve the needs (e.g., innovation, differentiation) of a focal enterprise. This can be modeled in i* via softgoals, tasks, resources, and contribution links. Technology alternatives can be represented as tasks as well as its resources and product features can be depicted as softgoals. The impacts of alternate technologies on product features can be shown via contribution links. Substitutive technologies (i.e., those that can be used to do the same thing) can be identified by finding tasks with similar contribution links to common softgoals. The impacts of different technologies on the overall bundle of features can be used to select the future technology. The additional softgoals that are supported by the future technology compared to the past technology can be regarded as sustaining innovation. Resources can be used to show the building blocks of technology alternatives. The inability to represent temporality in i* may deter the expression of time-dependent aspects (e.g., can certain technologies be commercialized/monetized sooner/later than others) of the model.

3 Case Study: Instant Messaging Application for Healthcare Practitioners

To test the use of i* modeling to support pivoting, we applied i* modeling to a real life case study. The case concerns a software startup in Toronto that is facing pivoting decisions. The company offers an instant messaging service to healthcare practitioners. Its Founder and CEO is the third co-author of this paper. Models were constructed in collaboration with the CEO of the company. They were elaborated by the first author in consultation with the CEO and were also validated by the CEO.

The main stakeholders in this case study are the messaging service provider (i.e., vendor), managers of a healthcare facility (i.e., administrators), and practitioners at that facility (i.e., end users). The vendor offers an instant messaging service that is used by doctors via a mobile app. The need for such a mobile app exists because some healthcare facilities do not offer an instant messaging system to doctors while some offer a system albeit one that is inconvenient, complicated, or impractical for use by doctors. As a workaround, many doctors use public consumer mobile apps for communication (e.g., WhatsApp, Dropbox) that is non-compliant with privacy policies.

3.1 Considerations Relating to the Use of Instant Messaging Services

Doctors that use publicly available instant messaging services can be categorized into three groups. These include plain text messaging users, multimedia messaging users, and power users. Plain text messaging users use the short messaging service

(SMS) built into their mobile phones to send and receive text messages. Multimedia messaging users exchange photos, videos, and audio via public consumer chatting tools (e.g., Skype, Viber, etc.) on their smartphones. Power users share data from medical systems (e.g., patient records, pharmaceutical reports, etc.) via public consumer tools (e.g., Dropbox, Slack, etc.) on their tablets. The usage of these tools is non-compliant with privacy regulations. Each category of users has different requirements for instant messaging services that correspond with their usage scenarios.

This heterogeneity of messaging tools within a healthcare facility creates many redundancies and inefficiencies for the doctors that use them. This also exposes administrators of those healthcare facilities to legal risks and uncertainties due to potentially non-compliant behavior. For example, in terms of users, a doctor may need to install multiple messaging apps on a mobile device to communicate with other doctors that use those specific apps. Similarly, messages sent in one app may not be compatible with other apps and this may slow down knowledge sharing. With respect to healthcare administrators, confidential data about patients or proprietary details about the organization can be accidentally disclosed and unintentionally exposed. Leakage of sensitive content can make administrators vulnerable to legal liabilities as well as diminish the reputation and goodwill of their institution.

This reasoning suggests that, an instant messaging service must meet the needs of many stakeholders to be accepted by the administrators and adopted by the medical practitioners in a healthcare facility. In some cases, these needs may converge such as in the case of quick delivery of messages because that is a feature that users would like and a function that the administrators would approve of. However, in many cases, these needs may be contradictory or even mutually exclusive. For example, users may want a service that can be used to engage in free flowing "off the record" watercooler discussions that are outside the purview of administrators. However, administrators may demand a service that supports logging of all messages for monitoring compliance with relevant statutes and auditing abidance with pertinent protocols. Designing an instant messaging service that satisfies such an intricate latticework of requirements, encompassing those from users and administrators, is a complex undertaking.

Additionally, while satisfying the requirements of users and administrators, the provider of an instant messaging service must also fulfil its own requirements. For example, the provider may wish to grow its revenues, generate margins, and run on income rather than investments. The achievement of these objectives is necessary if the instant messaging service is to become self-sufficient, sustainable, and solvent. This added set of requirements further obscures and obfuscates the design of an instant messaging service. However, an approach for systematic and structured representation and reasoning about the diverse intentions of myriad parties, and the relationships between them, can be helpful for elaborating and refining such a design.

3.2   Towards Modeling Select Pivots in Instant Messaging Service

It is imperative for the decision makers at the startup, that is the subject of this case, to spend its marketing and sales (M&S) budget properly. It operates with limited financial resources and thus its operational goals include economizing as well as increasing its return on M&S expenses. It dedicates the bulk of its M&S budget towards segmenting the market, targeting buyers based on their personas, and positioning its service in a way that is appealing to those personas.

The goal of its M&S activities is to encourage its prospects and intended customers to try and buy its instant messaging service. This is a resource intensive endeavor because it requires the company to research the market, identify buyer/user personas, elicit requirements for each persona, prioritize and target personas, build value propositions for selected personas, and advertise their service to chosen personas.

Positioning value propositions to selected personas is an example of a niche strategy and is attractive for companies with limited budgets because their financial resources might be insufficient for targeting the whole addressable market. This is also a productive approach because by using it a company can build concentrated value propositions that focus on the specific needs of chosen buyers/users.

These are more likely to result in engagement than generic advertising claims that are not directed at anyone in particular. The main personas of interest to this startup include administrators of healthcare facility including Chief of Medical Staff (CMS), Chief Privacy Officer (CFO), and Chief Technology Officer (CTO) as well as intended users of this service which include users of plain text messaging, users of multimedia messaging, and power users. Each of these personas have different requirements including some that conflict.

Figures 1a and b present partial i* SR diagrams of instant messaging service provider. Figure 1c presents an enlarged view of a section of Fig. 1b to draw attention to the representation of pivots. The overall model is spread over two diagrams (Figs. 1a and b) to simplify visual presentation. The dashed lines in the bottom left corner of Fig. 1a and top right corner of Fig. 1b can be linked during interpretation to obtain a full depiction of this model. As these figures show, the instant messaging service provider has a choice of positioning its value propositions to administrators of healthcare facilities (i.e., sell its enterprise tier) or its intended users which are medical practitioners (i.e., market its basic tier). To drive adoption among its target user community, this company must cater to their needs. At the same time, to get acceptance to deploy its service in a healthcare delivery facility, this company must also meet the requirements of the administrators of that facility. This startup has two possible go-to-market strategies which are top-down (market to users and then create an organic demand for acceptance) and bottom-up (sell to administrators and then require adoption by users). Since this startup has a limited M&S budget it can only adopt one of these strategies in at the beginning (i.e., target either user or administrator persona). If needed, this startup can implement a customer segment pivot to focus on the other persona after testing its fundamental hypotheses underlying the originally chosen persona.

Figure 4 shows customer segment pivots using a dashed arrow. The dashed arrow shows that the Messaging Service Provider can switch from offering its value proposition from enterprises to users or vice versa. By analyzing the contribution links to its softgoals the Messaging Service Provider can assess the impact of such a pivot on its quality objectives. It can also review the impact of its customer segment pivot on the dependums that are satisfied for various stakeholders through label propagation. For example, if the Messaging Service Provider pivots from its approach of Market to users

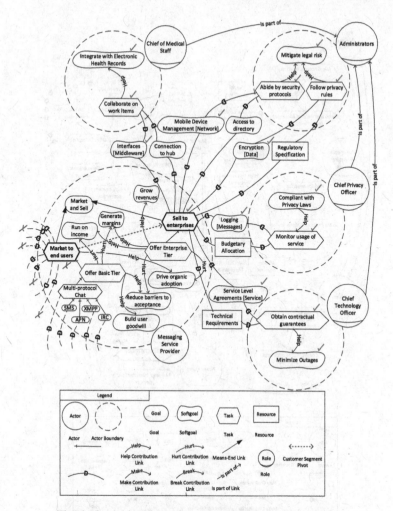

Fig. 4. Partial i* SR diagram of messaging service provider

to Sell to enterprises then it must focus on its service features such as data encryption, message logging, service level agreement, and mobile device management.

Figure 5 shows zoom-out/zoom-in pivots while Fig. 6 shows customer need pivot using dashed arrows. The downward dashed arrow in Fig. 5 shows that the Messaging Service Provider can switch from offering its XMPP application within a multi-protocol chat service to offering it as a standalone application (i.e., zoom-in pivot). Conversely, the upward dashed arrow in Fig. 5 shows it can merge that XMPP application into a multi-protocol chat service rather than offering it as a stand-alone application (i.e., zoom-out pivot). XMPP is typically used on Android OS and can be delivered in a dedicated application for those devices or bundled with other protocols in a multi-protocol chat service.

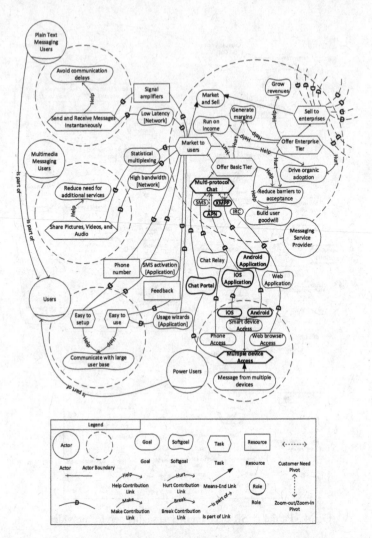

Fig. 5. Partial i* SR diagram of messaging service provider

The dashed arrow in Fig. 6 shows that the Messaging Service Provider can switch from offering an SMS compatible application to offering an APN compatible application. By changing the protocol that is supported by its application the Messaging Service Provider can change which customer need is met by that application (i.e., customer need pivot). Power users that wish to access a chat relay using their phone are not able to do so if the SMS protocol is not supported. However, power users that wish to use iOS devices for chatting are able to do so if the APN protocol is supported. This shows that product/service choices made by the Messaging Service Provider impact the needs of the customers that are served by those products/services.

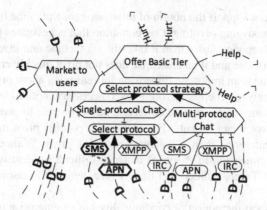

Fig. 6. Partial extended i* SR diagram of messaging service provider

4 Discussion

In this paper, we asserted that modeling can be used by decision makers in enterprises to represent and reason about the fundamental hypotheses underlying products, business model, and engines of growth. Despite the ubiquity and impact of pivoting in the industry there is a shortage of EM support for design and support of pivoting. Therefore, a structured and systematic EM approach for reasoning about pivoting can be a valuable tool for decision support within enterprises. This is also because the absence of such an approach can expose decision makers at startups to risks and costs from mistakes and omissions.

We proposed a model-based approach for modeling of pivoting and validated it in a mobile app startup. The Founder and CEO of the software startup that is featured as the case study in this paper noted that modeling of pivoting supported his decision-making in four main ways which include: (1) comparing pivoting options in an objective and unbiased manner, (2) contrasting existing pivoting alternatives as well as generating new options for pivoting, (3) planning/forecasting empirical tests of pivots before committing to them, and (4) grouping pivoting advice from mentors and advisors into themes of recommendations and suggestions.

He noted that he found many aspects of i* modeling to be supportive of pivoting. These include the ability to represent the concepts of resources, stakeholders, objectives, and relationships. Additional requirements for modeling of pivoting includes the ability to depict value, conditionality, and temporality. i* was able to meet many of these requirements fully or partially and a few of these requirements none at all. The only addition to i*, in this paper, was the use of the dashed arrows for indicating the transition from Before (As-is) to After (To-be) configurations. The analysis was provided based on the underlying concepts of pivoting and the model was annotated with dashed arrows to highlight pivots. Without extending i* it was demonstrated that i* could provide various analytical capabilities to reason about pivoting.

i* was found to be limited in three main respects with respect to modeling of pivoting. These are its inability to support temporal, conditional, and quantitative reasoning. i* does not support the notion of relative or absolute time but both concepts can be relevant in analyzing pivoting. One condition that necessitates pivoting is when an enterprise spends money faster than it takes in via income and investments. This is referred to as its burn rate and if an enterprise does not pivot quickly enough then it can go bankrupt. So, time is an important dimension for reasoning about pivoting because it can be used to analyze whether pivoting is a necessary option for an enterprise. Moreover, the amount of time that an enterprise has to be able to pivot can determine which type of a pivot it can execute. For example, a product pivot may take more or less time for an enterprise than a customer segment pivot. Without being able to represent the time dimension in i* means that it is difficult to identify which of these pivots are viable. Tropos offers real-time linear temporal reasoning support by extending i* [11].

i* does not support the notion of conditionality but an enterprise may only be able to execute a pivot after certain requirements are met. Without being able to show the preconditions for pivoting it can be difficult to fully understand the feasibility of pivoting. One or more pivots might be prerequisites for a particular type of pivot. Therefore, an enterprise may need to execute a combination of pivots albeit in a certain order. For example, an enterprise may first need to implement a zoom out pivot in order to implement a customer need pivot or it may need to execute a platform pivot in order to implement a customer segment pivot. Without being able to represent such conditions in i* means that it is difficult to show the prerequisites of pivots. Some researchers have combined BPMN and i* to depict conditionality in process flows [12].

i* does not support quantitative reasoning but it can be relevant in analyzing pivoting. Reasoning about certain types of pivots is especially dependent on the concept of economic value. These include business architecture pivot, value capture pivot, and engine of growth pivot. In each of these pivots, different economic objectives are evaluated in quantitative terms. For example, they may need to exactly measure the attainment of numerical targets (e.g., revenue, margin). While the attainment of these metrics can be represented in i* in binary terms (i.e., as goals), their partial attainment cannot be depicted practically. Without being able to reason about quantitative aspects of pivoting in i* means that it is difficult to analyze the economic impact of certain types of pivots in a precise manner. Goal-oriented requirements language (GRL), which is a derivative of i*, offers various types of quantitative reasoning support [13].

5   Conclusion and Future Work

This paper provided an overview of modeling pivoting by startups and large enterprises. It proposed EM requirements for key types of pivots. It also presented abstract patterns and decontextualized representations of select pivot types and applied some of these to a case study. Experience with a real case study provided validation about the benefits of modeling to support pivoting. Future work on this research will include the validation and verification of this approach in the industry. Early validation will be conducted via published case studies of pivoting by startups and large enterprises. Subsequent verification will be performed via empirical case studies in partnership with startup entrepreneurs and decision-makers at large enterprises. A focus of this verification will be on the usefulness of this EM approach for entrepreneurs and decision-makers within startups and large enterprises as well as consultants and advisors that are commissioned to guide and monitor strategic pivots in a variety of enterprises. We will consider extending i* to address more fully the needs for pivoting (e.g., quantitative, temporality, conditionality, etc.). However, we wish to do so by balancing richness and complexity in our models of pivoting.

References

1. Ries, E.: The Lean Startup: How Today's Entrepreneurs Use Continuous Innovation to Create Radically Successful Businesses. Crown Publishing Group, New York (2011)
2. Blank, S.: Why the lean start-up changes everything. Harv. Bus. Rev. **91**(5), 64–68 (2013)
3. Owens, T., Fernandez, O.: The Lean Enterprise: How Corporations Can Innovate Like Startups. Wiley, Hoboken (2014)
4. Humble, J., Molesky, J., O'Reilly, B.: Lean Enterprise: How High Performance Organizations Innovate at Scale. O'Reilly Media, Inc., Sebastopol (2014)
5. Edison, H.: A Conceptual framework of lean startup enabled internal corporate venture. In: Abrahamsson, P., Corral, L., Oivo, M., Russo, B. (eds.) PROFES 2015. LNCS, vol. 9459, pp. 607–613. Springer, Cham (2015). doi:10.1007/978-3-319-26844-6_46
6. Gbadegeshin, S.A., Heinonen, L.: Application of the Lean Start–up technique in commercialisation of business ideas and innovations. Int. J. Bus. Manag. Res. **43**(1), 1270–1285 (2016)
7. Barjis, J.: Enterprise, organization, modeling, simulation: putting pieces together. In: Proceeding of EOMAS (2008)
8. Yu, E.: Agent-oriented modelling: software versus the world. In: Wooldridge, M.J., Weiß, G., Ciancarini, P. (eds.) AOSE 2001. LNCS, vol. 2222, pp. 206–225. Springer, Heidelberg (2002). doi:10.1007/3-540-70657-7_14
9. Yu, E.: Agent orientation as a modelling paradigm. Wirtschaftsinformatik **43**(2), 123–132 (2001)
10. Yu, E.S., Mylopoulos, J.: Understanding "why" in software process modelling, analysis, and design. In: Proceedings of 16th International Conference on Software Engineering (ICSE 2016), pp. 159–168. IEEE (1994)
11. Castro, J., Kolp, M., Mylopoulos, J.: Towards requirements-driven information systems engineering: the Tropos project. Inf. Syst. **27**(6), 365–389 (2002)
12. Koliadis, G., Vranesevic, A., Bhuiyan, M., Krishna, A., Ghose, A.: Combining i* and BPMN for business process model lifecycle management. In: Eder, J., Dustdar, S. (eds.) BPM 2006. LNCS, vol. 4103, pp. 416–427. Springer, Heidelberg (2006). doi:10.1007/11837862_39
13. Mussbacher, G.: Aspect-oriented user requirements notation: aspects in goal and scenario models. In: Giese, H. (ed.) MODELS 2007. LNCS, vol. 5002, pp. 305–316. Springer, Heidelberg (2008). doi:10.1007/978-3-540-69073-3_32
14. Kim, C.H., Son, Y.J., Kim, T.Y., Kim, K., Baik, K.: A modeling approach for designing a value chain of virtual enterprise. Int. J. Adv. Manuf. Technol. **28**(9–10), 1025–1030 (2006)
15. Giannoulis, C., Petit, M., Zdravkovic, J.: Towards a unified business strategy language: a meta-model of strategy maps. In: van Bommel, P., Hoppenbrouwers, S., Overbeek, S., Proper, E., Barjis, J. (eds.) PoEM 2010. LNBIP, vol. 68, pp. 205–216. Springer, Heidelberg (2010). doi:10.1007/978-3-642-16782-9_15

16. Pant, V., Yu, E.: Coopetition with frenemies: towards modeling of simultaneous cooperation and competition among enterprises. In: Horkoff, J., Jeusfeld, M.A., Persson, A. (eds.) PoEM 2016. LNBIP, vol. 267, pp. 164–178. Springer, Cham (2016). doi:10.1007/978-3-319-48393-1_12

17. Cardoso, E., Mylopoulos, J., Mate, A., Trujillo, J.: Strategic enterprise architectures. In: Horkoff, J., Jeusfeld, M.A., Persson, A. (eds.) PoEM 2016. LNBIP, vol. 267, pp. 57–71. Springer, Cham (2016). doi:10.1007/978-3-319-48393-1_5

18. Svee, E.-O., Giannoulis, C., Zdravkovic, J.: Modeling business strategy: a consumer value perspective. In: Johannesson, P., Krogstie, J., Opdahl, A.L. (eds.) PoEM 2011. LNBIP, vol. 92, pp. 67–81. Springer, Heidelberg (2011). doi:10.1007/978-3-642-24849-8_6

19. Pijpers, V., Gordijn, J., Akkermans, H.: Aligning information system design and business strategy – a starting internet company. In: Stirna, J., Persson, A. (eds.) PoEM 2008. LNBIP, vol. 15, pp. 47–61. Springer, Heidelberg (2008). doi:10.1007/978-3-540-89218-2_4

20. Johannesson, P.: The role of business models in enterprise modelling. In: Krogstie, J., Opdahl, A.L., Brinkkemper, S. (eds.) Conceptual Modelling in Information Systems Engineering, pp. 123–140. Springer, Heidelberg (2007). doi:10.1007/978-3-540-72677-7_8

Evolution Models for Information Systems Evolution Steering

Jolita Ralyté[✉] and Michel Léonard

Institute of Information Service Science, University of Geneva, Geneva, Switzerland
{jolita.ralyte,michel.leonard}@unige.ch

Abstract. Sustainability of enterprise Information Systems (ISs) largely depends on the quality of their evolution process and the ability of the IS evolution steering officers to deal with complex IS evolution situations. Inspired by Olivé [1] who promotes conceptual schema-centric IS development, we argue that conceptual models should also be the centre of IS evolution steering. For this purpose we have developed a conceptual framework for IS evolution steering that contains several interrelated models. In this paper we present a part of this framework dedicated to the operationalization of IS evolution – the evolution metamodel. This metamodel is composed of two interrelated views, namely structural and lifecycle, that allow to define respectively the structure of a particular IS evolution and its behaviour at different levels of granularity.

Keywords: Information systems evolution · IS evolution steering · IS evolution structure · IS evolution lifecycle · IS evolution impact

1 Introduction

No matter the type and the size of the organization (public or private, big or small), sustainability of its Information Systems (ISs) is of prime importance to ensure its activity and prosperity. Sustainability of ISs largely depends on the quality of their evolution process and the ability of the officers handling it to deal with complex and uncertain IS evolution situations. There are several factors that make these situations complex, such as: proliferation of ISs in the organization and their overlap, independent evolution of each IS, non-existence of tools supporting IS evolution steering, various IS dimensions to be taken into account, etc. Indeed, during an IS evolution not only its information dimension (the structure, availability and integrity of data) is at stake. IS evolution officers have also to pay attention to its activity dimension (the changes in enterprise business activity supported be the IS), the regulatory dimension (the guarantee of IS compliance with enterprise regulation policies), and the technology dimension (the implementation and integration aspects).

In this context, we claim that there is a need for an informational engineering approach supporting IS evolution steering, allowing to obtain all the necessary

© IFIP International Federation for Information Processing 2017
Published by Springer International Publishing AG 2017. All Rights Reserved
G. Poels et al. (Eds.): PoEM 2017, LNBIP 305, pp. 221–235, 2017.
https://doi.org/10.1007/978-3-319-70241-4_15

information for an IS evolution at hand, to define and plan the evolution and to assess its impact on the organization and it ISs. We found the development of such an approach on conceptual modelling by designing a conceptual framework for IS evolution steering. Some parts of this framework were presented in [2,3]. In this paper we pursue our work and present one of its components – the operationalization of the IS evolution through the metamodel of IS Evolution.

The rest of the paper is organized as follows: in Sect. 2 we overview the context of our work – the conceptual framework that we are developing to support the IS evolution steering. Then, in Sect. 3, we discuss the role and principles of conceptual modelling in handling IS evolution. In Sects. 4 and 5 we present our metamodel formalizing the IS evolution, its structural and lifecycle views, and illustrate their usage in Sect. 6. Section 7 concludes the paper.

2   Context: A Framework for IS Evolution Steering

With our conceptual framework for IS evolution steering we aim to face the following challenges: (1) steering the IS evolution requires a thorough understanding of the underpinning IS domain, (2) the impact of IS evolution is difficult to predict and the simulation could help to take evolution decisions, (3) the complexity of IS evolution is due to the multiple dimensions (i.e. activity, regulation, information, technology) to be taken into account, and (4) the guidance for IS evolution steering is almost non-existent, and therefore needs to be developed.

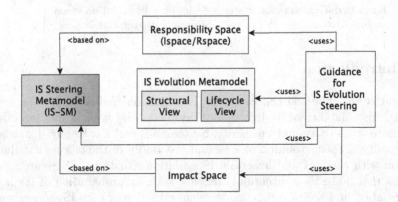

Fig. 1. Conceptual framework for IS evolution steering

As shown in Fig. 1, the framework contains several components each of them taking into account a particular aspect of IS evolution steering and considering the evolution challenges listed above. Let us briefly introduce these components.

The *IS Steering Metamodel* (*IS-SM*) is the main component of the framework having as a role to represent the IS domain of an enterprise. Concretely, it allows to formalize the way the enterprise ISs are implemented (their structure in terms of classes, operations, integrity rules, etc.), the way they support enterprise business and management activities (the definition of enterprise units, activities, positions, business rules, etc.), and how they comply with regulations governing these activities (the definition of regulatory concepts, rules and roles). Although IS-SM is not the main subject of this paper (it was presented in [2,3]), it remains the bedrock of the framework, and is necessary to be presented for better understanding other models and illustrations. IS-SM is also the kernel model for implementing an Informational Steering Information System – ISIS. ISIS is a meta-IS for steering enterprise IS (IS upon ISs according to [4]). While enterprise ISs operate at business level, ISIS performs at the IS steering level. Therefore, we depict IS-SM in Fig. 2 mainly to make this paper self-explanatory, and we invite the reader to look at [5] for further details.

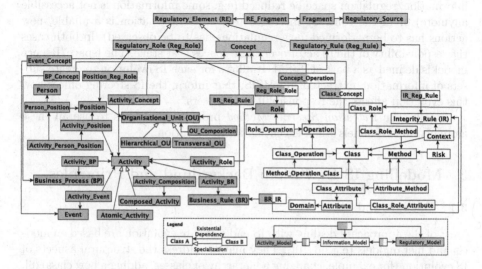

Fig. 2. Simplified version of IS-SM. The right part (in white) shows the information model generic to any IS implementation, the left part (in red) represents enterprise business activity model, the top part (in grey) represents the regulatory model governing enterprise business and IS implementations. The multi-coloured elements represent pivot elements allowing to interconnect the information, activity and regulation models, and so, to capture how ISs support enterprise activities and comply with regulations. (Color figure online)

The role of the *Evolution Metamodel* is to specify IS changes, and to assist the IS steering actor responsible for performing these changes. This metamodel comprises two interrelated views: structural and lifecycle. While the former deals with the extent and complexity of the IS evolution, the later supports its planning and execution. The Evolution Metamodel is the main subject of this paper, and is detailed in the following sections.

The *Impact Space* component provides mechanisms to measure the impact of IS changes on the enterprise IS, on the business activities supported by these

ISs, and on the compliance with regulations governing enterprise activities. The impact model of a particular IS evolution is defined as a part of the IS-SM including the IS-SM elements that are directly or indirectly concerned by this evolution. An IS-SM element is directly concerned by the evolution if its instances undergo modifications, i.e. one or more instances of this element are created, enabled, disabled, modified, or deleted. An IS-SM element is indirectly concerned by the evolution if there is no modification on its instances but they have to be known to make appropriate decisions when executing the evolution.

The *Responsibility Space* (*Ispace/Rspace*) component [3] helps to deal with responsibility issues related to a particular IS evolution. Indeed, each IS change usually concerns one or several IS actors (i.e. IS users) by transforming their information and/or regulation spaces (Ispace/Rspace). An IS actor can see her information/regulation space be reduced (e.g. some information is not accessible anymore) or in the contrary increased (e.g. new information is available, new actions has to be performed, new regulations has to be observed). In both cases the responsibility of the IS actor over these spaces is at stake. The Ispace/Rspace model is defined as a part of IS-SM. It allows for each IS evolution to create subsets of information, extracted from ISIS, that inform the IS steering officer how this evolution affects the responsibility of IS users.

Finally, the *Evolution Steering Method* provides guidelines to use all these aforementioned models when executing an IS evolution.

3   Modelling IS Evolution: Background and Principles

3.1   Background

Most of the approaches dealing with IS and software evolution are based on models and metamodels (e.g. [6–10]). They mainly address the structural aspects of IS evolution (for example, changing a hierarchy of classes, adding a new class) [6], model evolution and transformations [7], and the traceability of changes [9,10]. They aim to support model-driven IS development, the automation of data migration, the evaluation of the impact of metamodel changes on models, the development of forward-, reverse-, and re-engineering techniques, the recording of models history, etc. The importance and impact of model evolution is also studied in [11] where the authors stress that understanding and handling IS evolution requires models, model evolution techniques, metrics to measure model changes and guidelines for taking decisions.

In our work, we also claim that the purpose of conceptual modelling in IS evolution steering is manifold, it includes the understanding, building, deciding and realising the intended IS changes. As per [12], the notion of IS evolution has to be considered as a noun and as a verb. As a noun it refers to the question "what" – the understanding of the IS evolution phenomenon and its properties. While as a verb, it refers to the questions "how" – the theories, languages, activities and tools which are required to evolve a software. Our metamodel for IS evolution steering (see Fig. 1) includes two complementary views, namely structural and lifecycle view, and so serves to cope with complex IS artefacts, usually having multiple views.

Models are also known as a good support for taking decisions. In case of IS evolution, usually, there are several possible ways to realise it, each of them having a different impact on enterprise ISs and even on its activities. Taking a decision without any appropriate support can be difficult and very stressful task. Finally, with a set of models, the realisation of IS evolution is assisted in each evolution step and each IS dimension.

3.2   Principles of IS Evolution

The focus of the IS evolution is to transform a current IS schema (ASIS-IS) into a new one (TOBE-IS), and to transfer ASIS-IS objects into TOBE-IS objects. We use ISIS (see the definition in Sect. 2), whose conceptual schema is represented by IS-SM (Fig. 2), as a support to handle IS evolution. Indeed, ISIS provides a thorough, substantial information on the IS structure and usage, which, combined with other information outside of ISIS, is crucial to decide the IS evolution to pursue. Furthermore, ISIS is the centre of the management and the execution of the IS evolution processes both at the organizational and informatics levels. So, one main principle of IS evolution is always to consider these two interrelated levels: the ISIS and IS levels with their horizontal effects concerning only one level, and their vertical effects concerning both levels. In the following, to make a clear distinction between the IS and ISIS levels, we use the concepts of "class" and "object" at the IS schema level, and "element" and "instance" at the ISIS schema level.

IS evolution is composition of transformation operations, where the most simple ones are called atomic evolution primitives. Obtaining an initial list of atomic evolution primitives for an IS and its ISIS is simple: we have to consider all the elements of the ISIS schema, and, for each of them, all the primitives usually defined over an element: Search, Create, Read, Update, Delete (SCRUD). In the case of IS-SM as ISIS schema, there are 53 elements and so, 265 atomic evolution primitives. Since the aim of the paper is to present the principles of our framework for IS evolution steering, we simplify this situation by considering only the most difficult primitives Create and Delete. Nevertheless, there are still 106 primitives to be considered. The proposed conceptual framework for IS evolution steering is going to help facing this complexity.

4   Structural View of IS Evolution

An IS evolution transforms a part of the ASIS-IS *ISP* into *ISP'*, which is a part of the TOBE-IS, in a way that the TOBE-IS is compliant with:

- the *horizontal perspective*: the instances of the new ISIS and the objects of TOBE-IS validate all the integrity rules defined respectively over ISIS and TOBE-IS;

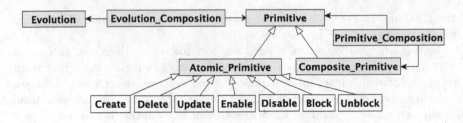

Fig. 3. Structural view of the IS evolution

- the *vertical perspective*: the TOBE-IS objects are compliant with the instances of the new ISIS.

In a generic way, we consider that an overall IS evolution requires to be decomposed into several IS evolutions, and so the role of the structural IS evolution model view (shown in Fig. 3) consists in establishing the schema of each IS evolution as a schema of composition of evolution primitives defined over IS-SM to pursue the undertaken IS evolution.

An evolution primitive represents a kind of elementary particle of an evolution: we cannot split it into several parts without loosing qualities in terms of manageable changes and effects, robustness, smartness and performances, introduced in a following paragraph. The most basic evolution primitives are the atomic evolution primitives: some of them, like Create, Delete and Update, are classic, since the other, Enable, Disable, Block, Unblock are crucial for the evolution process.

4.1   Atomic Evolution Primitives

Since the ISIS schema (i.e. IS-SM) is built only by means of existentially dependencies[1], the starting point of the IS evolution.decomposition is very simple – it consists of a list of atomic primitives: *create, delete, update, enable, disable, block* and *unblock* an instance of any IS-SM element. We apply the same principle at the IS level, so the IS schema steered by ISIS is also built by using only existential dependencies. Moreover, an instance/object is existentially dependent on its element/class.

These atomic primitives determine a set of possible states that any ISIS instance (as well as IS object) could have, namely *created, enabled, blocked, disabled*, and *deleted*. Figure 4 provides the generic life cycle of an instance/object.

Once an instance is created, it must be prepared to be enabled, and so to be used at the IS level. For example, a created class can be enabled, and so to have objects at the IS level, only if its methods validate all the integrity rules whose

---

[1] A class C2 is existentially dependent on the class C1, if every object o2 of C2 is permanently associated to exactly one object o1 of C1; o2 is said to be existentially dependent on o1. The existential dependency is a transitive relation. One of its particular cases is the specialization.

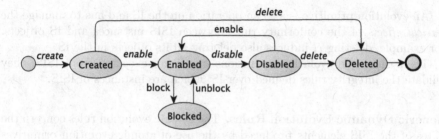

Fig. 4. Lifecycle of an instance of any element from IS-SM

contexts contain it. A created instance can be deleted if it belongs to a stopped evolution.

Enabled instances are disabled by an evolution when they do not play any role in the targeted TOBE-IS. They are not deleted immediately for two reasons: the first one concerns the fact that data, operations, or rules related to them, which were valid before the evolution, still stay consistent for situations where continuity is mandatory, for instance due to contracts. The second one concerns the evolution itself: if it fails, it is necessary to come back to the ASIS-IS, and so, to enable again the disabled instances.

Enabled instances are blocked during a phase of an evolution process when it is necessary to avoid their possible uses at the IS level through objects and/or execution of operations. At the end of this phase they are unblocked (re-enabled). For instance an activity (an instance of the element Activity) can be blocked temporary because of the introduction of a new business rule. Finally when an instance is deleted, it disappears definitively.

4.2   Robust Generic Atomic Evolution Rules

The generic atomic evolution rules must be validated to assure the consistency of the evolution process. Indeed each atomic evolution primitive has effects on other elements than its targeted elements. For example, deleting an integrity rule has effects on the methods of several classes belonging to the context of this integrity rule. Below, we present two kinds of generic atomic evolution rules: the first concerns the horizontal and vertical evolution effects, while the second deals with the dynamic effects.

Evolution Effects Horizontally and Vertically. An evolution primitive is firstly an atomic operation on the ISIS. So, it must verify the integrity rules defined over the IS-SM model to manage the *horizontal effects*. For example, if an instance cl of the element Class is deleted, then all the instances clo_i of the element Class_Operation related with cl must be deleted due to the existential dependency between these two elements (see Fig. 2).

An evolution primitive is also an operation on the IS and has to manage the *vertical effects* of the conformity rules between ISIS instances and IS objects. For example, deleting *cl* induces also deleting all its objects in the IS.

Then, since the evolution operations on IS are executed from ISIS, they validate the integrity rules defined over IS, which are instances of ISIS.

Generic Dynamic Evolution Rules. The generic evolution rules concern the states of the ISIS elements produced by the use of atomic evolution primitives (Fig. 4): created, enabled, blocked, disabled, deleted, and especially the interactions between instances of different elements in different states. They must be observed only at the ISIS level.

Some generic rules concerning the states "created" and "deleted" are derived directly from the existentially dependencies. Considering the element *Einf* depending existentially on the element *Esup*, any instance of *Einf* may be in the state "created" only if its associated instance *esup* of *Esup* is in the state "created", and it must be in the state "deleted" if *esup* is in the state "deleted".

The generic rules concerning the states "blocked" and "disabled" require to consider another relation between the IS-SM elements, called "determined by", defined at the conceptual level and not the instance level. An element *Esecond* is strictly/weakly determined by the element *Efirst* if any instance *esecond* to be exploitable in IS must/can require to be associated to one or several instances *efirst*.

Then there is the following generic dynamic rule: any instance *esecond* must be in the state disabled/blocked/deleted if at least one of its *efirst* is in the state respectively disabled/blocked/deleted.

For instance, the element Operation is *strictly determined by* the element Class, because any operation to be executed at the IS level must be associated to at least one class (see Fig. 2). Then, if an operation is associated to one class in the state disabled/blocked, it also must be in the state disabled/blocked, even if it is also associated to other enabled classes.

The element Integrity_Rule is *weakly determined by* the element Business_Rule because integrity rules are not mandatory associated with a business rule. In the same way, all elements, like Class, associated with the Regulatory_Element are weakly determined by it, because their instances are not mandatory associated to an instance of Regulatory_Element.

Considering the following elements of the IS-SM models (see Fig. 2): Person, Position, Business_Process (BP), Activity, Business_Rule (BR), Role, Operation, Class, Integrity_Rule (IR), Regulatory_Element (RE), here is the list of relations *strictly determined by* (=>): BP => Activity, BR => Activity, Operation => Class, Operation => IR, IR => Class. The list of the relations *weakly determined by* (->) (in addition to the aforementioned ones with the Regulatory_Element) is: IR -> BR, IR -> RE, Class -> RE, Operation -> RE, Role -> RE, BR -> RE, Activity -> RE, Position -> RE, Event -> RE, BP -> RE.

Robustness. Every aforementioned evolution primitive is *robust* if it manages all its horizontal and vertical effects and respects all the generic dynamic evolution rules. The use of only existential dependencies at the both levels, IS and ISIS, in our approach, facilitates reaching this quality. Nevertheless, at the IS level, such an approach requires that the whole IS schema (including static, dynamic and integrity rule perspectives) must be easily evolvable, and the IT system supporting the IS (e.g. a database management system) must provide an efficient set of evolution primitives [13].

4.3   Composite Evolution Primitives

The composite primitives are built by a composition of the atomic ones (Fig. 3). They are necessary to consider IS evolution at the management level [3], but also for informational and implementation purposes. For instance, replacing an integrity rule by a new one can be considered logically equivalent to delete it and then to create the new one. But this logic is not pertinent if we consider the managerial, IS exploitation and implementation perspectives. It is much more efficient to build a composite evolution primitive "replace" built from the atomic primitives "create" and "delete".

A composite evolution primitive is robust, if it manages all its horizontal and vertical effects and respects all the generic dynamic evolution rules.

4.4   Managerial Effects

The managerial effects consider the effects of the IS evolution at the human level, and so concern the IS-SM elements Role, Activity, Position and Person. The evolution steering officers have to be able to assess whether the proposed evolution has a harmful effect on organization's activities or not, and to decide to continue or not this evolution. The evolution primitives are *smart* if they alert these levels by establishing a report of changes to all the concerned roles, activities, positions, and persons. To do that, they will use the responsibility space (Fig. 1) with its two sub-spaces: its informational space (Ispace) and its regulatory space (Rspace). This part was presented in [3]. Below in the paper, all primitives are smart.

5   Lifecycle View of IS Evolution

Evolution of an information system is generally a delicate process for an enterprise for several reasons. First, it cannot be realized by stopping the whole IS because all the activities supported by IS should be stopped and this situation is unthinkable in most cases. Second, it has impacts, especially on actors and on the organization of activities. It can even induce the need for reorganizing the enterprise. Third, it takes time and often requires to set up a process of adaptation to the changes for all concerned actors to enable them to perform their activities. Moreover, it concerns a large informational space of IS-SM and requires to be decomposed into partial evolutions called sub-evolutions. So, it requires a coordination model to synchronize all processes of these sub-evolutions as well as the process of the main evolution. Furthermore, it is a long process, with an important number of actors who work inside the evolution process or whose activities are changed by the evolution. Finally, most evolutions of ASIS-IS into TOBE-IS are generally nearly irreversible, because it is practically impossible to transform back TOBE-IS into ASIS-IS at least for two main reasons: (1) some evolution primitives, used by the evolution, can be irreversible themselves (e.g. the case of an existing integrity rule relaxed by the evolution), and (2) actors, and even a part of the enterprise, can be completely disoriented to go back to TOBE-IS after all the efforts they have done to adapt to ASIS-IS. So, a decision to perform an evolution must be very well prepared to decrease the risks of failure. For this purpose, we explore a generic lifecycle of an evolution, first at atomic primitive level, then at composite primitive level and finally at evolution level.

An atomic primitive can be performed stand-alone in two steps: (1) preparation and (2) execution or abort. They are defined as follows:

- *Preparation*: prepares the *disabling list* of ISIS instances and IS objects to be disabled if success, the *creating list* of ISIS instances and IS objects to be created if success, the list of reports of changes, and the blocking list of ISIS instances;
- *Execution*: sends the reports of changes, blocks the concerned IS parts, disables/creates effectively contents of the disabling/creating lists, then unblocks the blocked IS parts.

The work done at the preparation step serves to decide whether the primitive should be executed or aborted. Finally, the execution of the primitive can succeed or fail. For example, it fails if it cannot block an IS part. As an example let us consider the deletion of a role: its creating list is empty and its disabling list contains all the assignments of operations to this role. Blocking these assignments signifies these operations cannot be executed by means of this role during the deletion of the role. It can fail if an IS actor is working through this role.

In the case of the atomic evolution primitive "Create an instance Cl of Class", the preparation step defines:

- how to fill the new class with objects,
- how to position it in the IS schema by linking Cl to other IS classes by means of existential dependencies,
- how to alert the managers of Role, Operation and Integrity_Rule about the Cl creation.

Besides, it is important to create together with Cl its methods and attributes, and even the association classes between Cl and other IS classes. For that, we need a more powerful concept, the composite evolution primitive, as presented below.

A composite primitive is composed of other composite or atomic primitives, which builds a hierarchy of primitives. The top composite primitive is at the

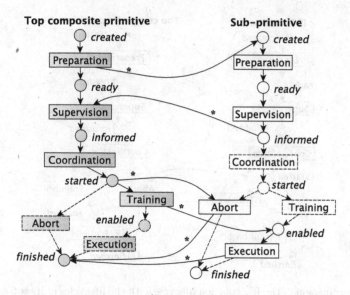

Fig. 5. Coordination of the lifecycle of a composite primitive (left) with the lifecycles of its sub-primitives (right); * indicates multiple transitions, dashed lines indicate that the step is under the responsibility of the lower or upper level model.

root of this hierarchy; the atomic primitives are at its leaves. Every composite primitive has a supervision step, which controls the execution of all its sub-primitives. Only the top composite primitive has in addition a coordination step, which takes the same decision to enable or abort for all its sub primitives in the hierarchy. The main steps of a composite primitive life cycle are:

- *Preparation*: creates all direct sub-primitives of the composite primitive;
- *Supervision*: determines the impacts and the managerial effects from the enabling lists and the creating lists established by the sub-primitives;
- *Coordination*: takes the decision of enabling or aborting primitive processing and transmits it to the sub-primitives;
- *Training*: this is a special step for the top primitive; it concerns training of all actors concerned by the whole evolution. This step is performed thanks to the actors' responsibility spaces.

The top composite primitive is successful if all its sub-primitives are successful; it fails if at least one among its sub-primitives fails. The life cycle of the atomic primitives must be adapted by adding the abort decision and by taking into account that enable/abort decisions are made by a higher level primitive. Figure 5 illustrates the co-ordination between the composite primitive lifecycle and its sub-primitive lifecycle.

Thus, from the atomic evolution primitive "Create Class" we build the composite evolution primitive "C-Create Class" with the following sub-primitives:

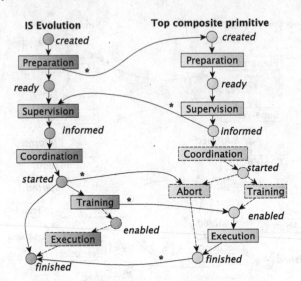

Fig. 6. Coordination of the IS evolution lifecycle with the lifecycles of its top composite primitives

- Create Class, which is used to create the intended class *Cl* and also all the new classes to associate *Cl* with other classes, as mentioned previously,
- Create Class_Concept, Create Class_Attribute,
- if necessary, Create Attribute, and Create Domain,
- C-Create Method with its sub-primitives Create Method and Create Attribute_Method.

Let us now look at the lifecycle of an entire evolution, which is a composition of primitives. During the processing of an evolution, the *preparation* step consists in selecting the list of composite primitives, whose processing will realize this evolution. Then, from the impacts and the managerial effects determined by the supervision steps of these composite primitives, the *supervision* step of the evolution determines a plan for processing these primitives. It decides which primitives can/must be executed in parallel and which in sequence. Next, the *coordination* step launches processing of primitives following the plan. After analyzing their results (success or failure), it decides to launch other primitives and/or to abort some of them. Finally, the evolution is finished and it is time to assess it. Indeed, the evolution processing transforms the enterprise and its ways of working, even if processing of some composite primitives fails. Due to the important complexity, it seems important to place the *training* step at the evolution level and not at the level of composite primitive. Of course, the training step of a composite primitive must be realized before its execution. But, in this way, it is possible to combine training steps of several composite primitives into one, and to obtain a more efficient training in the context of the evolution. Figure 6 shows the coordination between the lifecycles of IS evolution and its top composite primitives.

6   Illustrating Example

To illustrate our approach, we use the example of a hospital. Figure 7 depicts a small part of the kernel of its IS schema. In this example we will consider:

- one organizational unit: the general medicine department,
- two positions: the doctor and the nurse,
- two activities of a doctor: a_1 concerning the care of patients (visit, diagnostic, prescription) and a_2 concerning the management of the nurses working in her team.

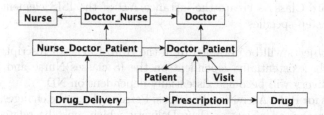

Fig. 7. A small part of the ASIS-IS schema of the hospital

To illustrate an evolution case, let us suppose that now our hospital has to apply new rules for improving patients' safety. To this end, each doctor will be in charge to guarantee that nurses of her team have sufficient competences for administrating the drugs she can prescribe. So, the IS of the hospital must evolve, especially by introducing new classes: Nurse_Drug that associates a nurse with a drug for which she is competent according to her doctor, and Doctor_Drug that associates a doctor with a drug that she can prescribe. The TOBE-IS schema is shown in Fig. 8.

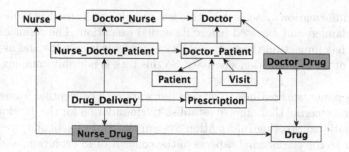

Fig. 8. A part of the TOBE-IS schema of the hospital

The IS evolution is then composed of 2 top composite primitives, one around Doctor_Drug (DD), the other one around Nurse_Drug (ND). The first one is built from the composite primitive C-Create Class to create the instance *DD* of the ISIS element Class. Its preparation step specifies:

- the DD objects will be obtained from the ASIS-IS class Prescription;
- DD will be existentially dependent on the IS classes Doctor and Drug, and Prescription will become existentially dependent on DD and no more directly dependent on Drug;
- the alerts for Role, Activities, Positions, Persons about the changes, especially in the creation an object of Prescription, which in TOBE-IS must be related to a DD object;
- creation of DD objects, creation or modification of roles for reaching them;
- the blocking list for its execution, which includes Doctor, Drug and Prescription.

The second composite primitive is built from the composite evolution primitive C-Create Class to create the instance *ND* of the ISIS element Class. Its preparation step specifies:

- the ND objects will be obtained from the ASIS-IS class Prescription;
- ND will be existentially dependent on the IS classes Nurse and Drug, and Drug_Delivery will become existentially dependent on ND;
- the alerts for Role, Activities, Positions, Persons about the changes, especially in the creation an object of Drug_Delivery, which must be related to a ND object;
- creation of ND objects, creation or modification of roles for reaching them;
- the blocking list for its execution, which includes Nurse, Drug and Drug_Delivery.

In the case of this example, the execution process of the IS evolution after the training of involved actors is simple: to execute the top evolution composite primitives related to Doctor_Drug and then to Nurse_Drug.

7   Conclusion

Handling information systems evolution is a complex task that has to be properly defined, planned and assessed before its actual execution. The result of each IS evolution has impact on the sustainability on organization's ISs and also on the efficiency of the organization's activity. So this task is not only complex but also critical.

In this paper, we continue to present our work on a conceptual framework for IS evolution steering that aims to establish the foundation for the development of an Informational Steering Information System (ISIS). In particular, we dedicate this paper to the engineering aspects of the concept of IS evolution, and present its metamodel, which is one of the components in our framework (Fig. 1).

The role of the IS Evolution Metamodel consists in supporting the operationalization of the IS evolution. Therefore, it includes two views: structural and lifecycle. The structural view allows to progressively decompose a complex IS evolution into a set of atomic primitives going trough several granularity levels of composite primitives. The obtained primitives as robust because they follow generic evolution rules and take into account horizontal and vertical effects on

ISIS and IS. They are also smart because they pay attention to the managerial effects of IS evolution at the human level. The lifecycle view helps to operate IS evolution at its different levels of granularity by providing a set of models and rules for progressing from one step to another.

To complete our framework for IS evolution steering we still need to define the Impact Space component that will provide mechanisms to measure the impact of IS evolution and to take decisions accordingly. With the IS Evolution Metamodel we have prepared the basis for developing the detailed guidance for IS evolution steering, which will complete our work on this conceptual framework.

References

1. Olivé, A.: Conceptual schema-centric development: a grand challenge for information systems research. In: Pastor, O., Falcão e Cunha, J. (eds.) CAiSE 2005. LNCS, vol. 3520, pp. 1–15. Springer, Heidelberg (2005). doi:10.1007/11431855_1
2. Opprecht, W., Ralyté, J., Léonard, M.: Towards a framework for enterprise information system evolution steering. In: Frank, U., Loucopoulos, P., Pastor, Ó., Petrounias, I. (eds.) PoEM 2014. LNBIP, vol. 197, pp. 118–132. Springer, Heidelberg (2014). doi:10.1007/978-3-662-45501-2_9
3. Ralyté, J., Opprecht, W., Léonard, M.: Defining the responsibility space for the information systems evolution steering. In: Horkoff, J., Jeusfeld, M.A., Persson, A. (eds.) PoEM 2016. LNBIP, vol. 267, pp. 179–193. Springer, Cham (2016). doi:10.1007/978-3-319-48393-1_13
4. Le Dinh, T.: Towards a new infrastructure supporting interoperability of information systems in development: the information system upon information systems. In: Konstantas, D., Bourrières, J.P., Léonard, M., Boudjlida, N. (eds.) Interoperability of Enterprise Software and Applications, pp. 385–396. Springer, London (2006). doi:10.1007/1-84628-152-0_34
5. IS-SM: IS-SM. http://cui.unige.ch/~ralyte/ISIS/IS-SM.html
6. Pons, C., Kutsche, R.D.: Model evolution and system evolution. In: V Congreso Argentino de Ciencias de la Computacion (CACIC 1999), Universidad Nacional del Centro de la Provincia de Buenos Aires, Argentina (1999)
7. Burger, E., Gruschko, B.: A change metamodel for the evolution of MOF-based metamodels. In: Modellierung. LNI, GI, vol. 161, pp. 285–300 (2010)
8. Aboulsamh, M.A., Davies, J.: Towards a model-driven approach to information system evolution. In: Song, W., et al. (eds.) ISD 2009, pp. 269–280. Springer, New York (2009). doi:10.1007/978-1-4419-7355-9_23
9. Kchaou, D., Bouassida, N., Ben-Abdallah, H.: A MOF-based change meta-model. In: The 13th International Arab Conference on Information Technology (ACIT 2012), Zarq, Jordan, pp. 134–141 (2012)
10. Ruiz Carmona, L.M.: TraceME: traceability-based method for conceptual model evolution. Ph.D. thesis. Universitat Politecnica de Valencia (2016)
11. Lehman, M., Fernández-Ramil, J.C.: Software Evolution. Wiley, Hoboken (2006)
12. Lehman, M.M., Ramil, J.F., Kahen, G.: Evolution as a noun and evolution as a verb. In: Workshop on Software and Organisation Co-evolution (SOCE 2000) (2000)
13. Andany, J., Léonard, M., Palisser, C.: Management of schema evolution in databases. In: VLDB 1991, pp. 161–170. Morgan Kaufmann (1991)

Toward GDPR-Compliant Socio-Technical Systems: Modeling Language and Reasoning Framework

Marco Robol[✉], Mattia Salnitri, and Paolo Giorgini

University of Trento, Trento, Italy
{marco.robol,mattia.salnitri,paolo.giorgini}@unitn.it

Abstract. Privacy is a key aspect for the European Union (EU), where it is regulated by a specific law, the General Data Protection Regulation (GDPR). Compliance to the GDPR is a problem for organizations, it imposes strict constraints whenever they deal with personal data and, in case of infringement, it specifies severe consequences such as legal and monetary penalties. Such organizations frequently are complex systems, where personal data is processed by humans and technical services. Therefore, it becomes fundamental to consider privacy from the social perspective when designing such system, i.e., when relations between different components are specified. This is, indeed, also specified in the GDPR, which encourages to apply privacy-by-design principles. This paper proposes a method to support the design of GDPR compliant systems, based on a socio-technical approach composed of a modeling language and a reasoning framework.

Keywords: Privacy · Socio-technical systems · Requirement engineering · Modeling languages · Automated reasoning

1 Introduction

Privacy is a central aspect for citizens and it is strongly safeguarded in most countries all over the world. The European Union (EU) has recently developed a privacy law, the General Data Protection Regulation (GDPR) [2], with the aim to equalize privacy safeguard and constraints among all EU member states. All organizations that operate with personal data of EU citizens must be compliant with the GDPR, otherwise, they may occur into legal punishments and monetary penalties. Such organizations are frequently socio-technical systems, i.e., they are composed by people and machines that interact and share personal data of citizens to achieve their objectives. For example, an hospital is considered a socio-technical system since doctors provide medical treatments to patients, they use a database service to store medical record of patients and they use televisit

© IFIP International Federation for Information Processing 2017
Published by Springer International Publishing AG 2017. All Rights Reserved
G. Poels et al. (Eds.): PoEM 2017, LNBIP 305, pp. 236–250, 2017.
https://doi.org/10.1007/978-3-319-70241-4_16

systems to visit patients remotely. Given the complexity of such systems, privacy has to be considered since from design phase, indeed also the GDPR incentives the principle of privacy-by-design, and privacy analysis should includes not only the technical aspects but also the social aspects, i.e., the interactions and the dependencies between people and machines.

The literature offers many approaches to support the principle of privacy-by-design. Design strategies are proposed in [8] as a guide to the main Privacy Enhancing Technologies (PETs) and patterns. In [6], data minimization concept is proposed as the fundamental aspect of privacy-by-design practices. In [11], two different approaches are proposed to privacy: (i) privacy-by-policy, based on the principle of fair information practices; and (ii) privacy-by-architecture, based on the concept of data minimization. There are also attempts to handle security at design-time an that consider the social aspects of organizations. A socio-technical approach to security, that considers a system as a composition of autonomous actors each with its own goals, is adopted by SI* [3], a security requirement engineering framework that extends i^* to handle security concepts. The Socio-Technical Security (STS) [1] adopts a socio-technical approach to support the design of secure systems. It handles only the confidentiality aspect of privacy, globally seen as an aspect of security.

As far as our knowledge goes, no privacy-oriented modeling languages have been proposed that consider privacy aspects during the design of socio-technical systems. In particular, current state-of-art modeling languages and methods lack of specific concepts and relations that can be used to specify requirements and constraints expressed by privacy regulations, such as the GDPR, and verify the compliance of organizations.

In this paper, we propose a modeling framework inspired by the privacy-by-design principle to support the design of GDPR compliant systems. The method is a revision of the STS method [1]: it extends STS-ml, the goal based modeling language provided in STS, with privacy-oriented concepts such as personal data, user consent, legal basis, and the legal figures of data controller and data processor. The extension of STS-ml provided in this paper is supported by a reasoning method to verify model properties expressing privacy policies derived by legal constraints.

The paper is structured as follows. A baseline section explains the STS method, after having introduced a case study. Section 3 presents our proposed method: we define new constructs for the STS-ml language. Section 4 presents the automated reasoning support framework. A related work section presents the main works in the field. The paper ends with some considerations on the obtained results and then general conclusions are drawn.

2   Baseline

The research work described in this paper is based on STS [1] and extends it with privacy-specific concepts, in particular the legal aspects introduced by the GDPR [2]. This section introduces a case study about the medical domain and the STS method.

2.1 Case Study

We consider a case study about the health-care services, focusing on patients data. Particularly, we will focus on the management of patient medical history by the national health-care system and the production of analysis report by private analysis laboratories. Medical data vary from medical analysis results to diagnosis, medical history of the patient, medical prescription, or report. Parties include private organizations, family doctor, the national health-care system, hospitals, and regional health-care services companies.

The case study will focus on the Trentino's health-care services organization, Azienda Provinciale per i Servizi Sanitari (APPS). APSS offers the medical performance through the national health-care system and private medical services organizations. The main hospital in Trento is the S. Chiara, which has a very complex organizational structure with different responsibility figures, such as, director, surgery doctor, nurse, and many others.

2.2 Socio-Technical Security Method

STS [1] is a method for the design of secure complex systems. Complex systems can be modeled as socio-technical system, where a composition of autonomous actors, machines and humans, depend one to another to achieve objectives. STS adopts a socio-technical approach to handle security by considering the system as a whole, and focusing on social aspects among the participants. The method is composed by a goal-based modeling language and a supporting tool with automated reasoning capabilities.

STS-ml is the formally defined language provided by the STS method. It is a goal-based modeling language that relies on the concept of intentional actor and focuses on dependencies among them, in terms of goals delegation and documents transmission. Distinct aspects of the same model are represented in three separate views, with a different diagram in each of them. The rest of the section explain STS-ml in using the case study.

Figure 1 shows an example of STS model. Example of diagrams in the three views of STS are showed in the left part of the Figure. The right part shows a legend of STS graphical notation.

Actors are modeled in the **social view**, each with a set of objectives, called goals, and a set of documents they can use. In the top left part of Fig. 1 is represented the social view diagram of an example of socio-technical system taken from the case study. Goals can be delegated among actors and documents can be transmitted. In the example, patient delegates the goal medical prescription to family doctor, who receives a diagnosis document from private company doctor. Goals can be AND- or OR-decomposed in sub-goals and can depends on a document in terms of reading, editing, or production. As represented in the model, the doctor need to read the document containing the diagnosis, in order to prescribe a medication to the patient.

STS allows to identify information: intangible assets that represent pieces of knowledge relevant for the actors of the system, for example, medical records.

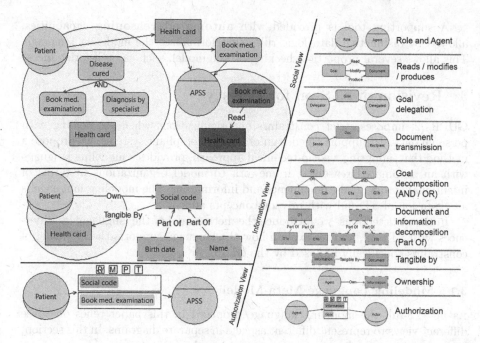

Fig. 1. STS model

Information is modeled in the **information view**, where it is possible to specify the respective owners, the composition of these information with respect to other information, and the documents that make them tangible. An example of information view diagram is showed in the middle left part of Fig. 1. Every document is possessed only by an actor, who can use them to accomplish goals, but can also be transmitted and used by others, as modeled in the social view. For example, Health Card is a document possessed by the patient that makes tangible his social code. The social code information is composed by information about his name and birth.

In order to process a document (read, modify, or produce), actors must be either the owners of the contained information, or be authorized by the owners. Authorizations are represented in the **authorization view** and are identified by: the sender, the addressee, the information, and the goals for which the information can be used. For example, the patient authorizes the APSS to read his social code within the context of booking a medical examination. An example of an authorization view diagram is showed in the bottom left part of Fig. 1.

In STS, actors are distinguished into **roles and agents**. An agent is a participant known to be in the system already at design time, for example the APSS in Fig. 1, while a role represents an actor or a class of actors identifiable by a common behavior, for example the director of the S. Chiara Hospital or the Patient of Fig. 1. Agents can eventually play several roles and roles can be eventually played by several agents.

A supporting tool is provided with **automated reasoning** capabilities, allowed by disjunctive data logic rules that formalizes the modeling language. This allows several properties checking on the model, such as, well-formedness.

3   Revision of STS-ml for Privacy

GDPR [2] imposes strict constraints on organizations whenever dealing with personal data. To support the design of GDPR-compliant systems, we propose a method that, adopting a socio-technical approach, provides a modeling language with an automated reasoning framework to model organizations in terms of intentional actors, goals, documents and information. The modeling language is an extension of STS-ml with privacy concepts added.

In the next sections, we introduce the meta-model of the language, its differences with STS-ml, and we explain how the language supports the modeling of constraints specifically imposed by the GDPR.

3.1   Modeling Language Meta-Model

As in STS-ml, the modeling language proposed in this paper relies on three different views to represent different aspects in separate diagrams. In this section, we present the modeling language proposed in this paper.

Figure 2 shows the meta-model of the social view, where actors are represented with their goals and documents. Relationships between actors are also showed in terms of goal delegation and document transmission. The elements of agent and role, which remains the same as in STS-ml, here are omitted from the meta-models for simplicity.

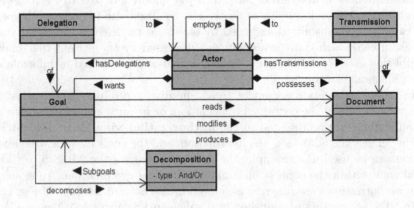

Fig. 2. Meta-model of the social view of the modeling language

Figure 3 shows the meta-model of the information and authorization views. The left part of Fig. 3 is the meta-model of the **information view**, where information are represented with their owners and are associate with the documents

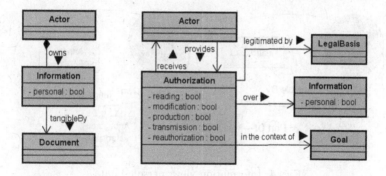

Fig. 3. Meta-model of the information and authorization views

that makes them tangible. The right part of Fig. 3 represents the meta-model of the **authorization view**.

With respect to STS-ml, the modeling language proposed in this paper, focusing on privacy, permits to represent the fundamental concept of **personal data**, as an information. In the meta-model in Fig. 3, a boolean attribute discriminates a personal data from an information. In the revisited language, we also included the **employment** relationship, which is defined from actor to actor. It is used to distinguish third party actors from actors within the same organization. This aspect is fundamental when considering laws and the constraints that they impose on organizations, as in the case of privacy laws. To represent the legal aspects of privacy, we also allow to specify the **legal basis** needed to legitimate the processing of a document revealing personal data. The legitimation relationship is defined between a legal basis and an authorization.

3.2   Representing GDPR Principles

The method proposed in this paper takes into account legal aspects of privacy, to support the representation of social constrains imposed by privacy laws, such as, the GDPR [2]. In this section, we shows how it is possible to represent GDPR constrains in the modeling language.

The modeling language already supports the representation of **personal data**, which in the GDPR are defined as information that is possible to relate to an identified or identifiable natural person, where an identifiable natural person is one who can be identified, directly or indirectly, in particular by reference to an identifier such as a name, an identification number, location data, an online identifier or to one or more factors specific to the physical, physiological, genetic, mental, economic, cultural or social identity of that natural person. Figure 4 shows an example of a diagram where a small letter P in the top right angle of the information identify it as a personal data.

A **natural person** is an individual human being who has its own legal personality. The language does not explicitly support the concept of natural person but only the ones of agent and role, which represent active participants of the

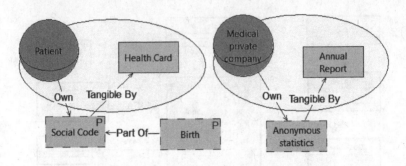

Fig. 4. Information view: personal data

socio-technical system and can be either machines, organizations, or humans, indeed natural persons. For example, APSS is an agent and represents an organization, while patient is a role and represents a class of participants which is a class natural persons.

Data subject is defined as the natural person the data are about. While to data subjects are always granted the right of being in control of their personal data, there are exceptions as in the case of under-aged people, where personal data are under the control of parents or tutors. The modeling language does not explicitly support the concept of data subject but only the one of data owner.

The GDPR identifies two types of responsibilities among the parties (actors) involved in every processing of personal data: controller and processor. GDPR is primarily imposed on **data controller**, who has the primary responsibility for compliance. **data processor**, instead, has limited responsibilities, acting on behalf of the controller by means of a written contract. Employees of data controller or data processors are not to be considered data processors on their own. In the modeling language we identify these two figures by defining direct or indirect authorizations. Data controllers are identified by a direct authorization by the owner, while data processors are identified by an indirect authorization (re-authorization) done by the data controller.

We distinguish among authorizations given to a third party and internal authorizations given to an employee with an apposite relationship defined between actors that identifies employers and employees actors: the **employment relationship**. The employment relationship is modeled in the social view. Figure 5 shows the employment relationship between medical private company and private company doctor.

The GDPR requires a **legal basis** for every lawful processing of personal data. The language allows to model the legal basis needed to legitimate the transmission and the processing of personal data; it also allows to adopt one of them in each authorization involving personal data. The GDPR defines a set of legal basis however, it allows EU member states to define further legal basis. For the above reason, the modeling language described in this paper does not provide a set of predefined legal basis but allows to specify them in a simple and minimalistic way, where all legal basis are represented in a list and each on

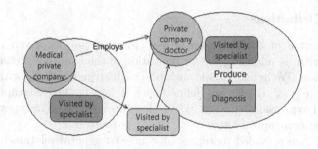

Fig. 5. Social view: employment

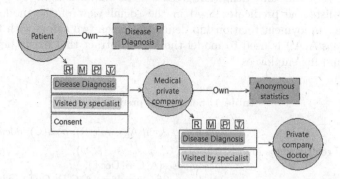

Fig. 6. Authorization view: legitimation

them is provided with a name and a textual description. Figure 6 shows a legal basis provided in the context of the authorization that includes personal data between patient and medical private company.

4   Automated Reasoning Support

Models are an approximation of the world represented in a structured form. Modeling languages should be enough simple to be understandable by non-expert users but, as the models start growing, they could became complex. Automated reasoning can support the designer in the identification of potential inconsistencies in the models, conflicts, and violation of properties.

The formal specification of the language includes constraints on the composition of the model, so that well-formedness can be automatically checked by automated reasoning. This is useful to avoid inconsistencies in the models, such as, cyclical delegations or chains of employment. The formalization allows for a flexible specification of further properties that can be automatically verified, such as, constraints introduced by the GDPR.

In this section, we give a formalization of the language by providing a set of rules that can be automatically verified, then we show how it is possible to formally represent GDPR constraints, so to automate their verification.

4.1 Core Definitions

The formalization of the language is a revision of the one given by Dalpiaz et al. in [1], with, in addition, the formalization of the concepts presented in the previous section. We define atomic variables with strings in italic with a leading capital letter (e.g., G, I); sets are defined with strings in the calligraphic font for mathematical expressions (e.g., $\mathcal{G}$, $\mathcal{J}$); relationship are defined in typewriter style with a leading non-capital letter (e.g., wants, possesses).

Predicates are provided to represent concepts, general relationships among them, intentional relationships, and social relationships. For those inherited from STS-ml we kept the same definition given by STS-ml authors in [1].

Table 1 lists the predicates used in the social view of the modeling language. The employment relationship defined between two actors with the predicate $employs(A, A')$ is used to model the legal contract that exists between an employer and his employees.

Table 1. Social view predicates

Concepts	$actor(A)$, $agent(Ag)$, $role(R)$, $goal(G)$, $document(D)$
Intentional relationships ($\mathcal{JRL}$)	$wants(A, G)$, $possesses(A, D)$, $decomposes(A, G, \mathcal{S}, DecT)$, $reads/modifies/produces(A, G, D, OpT)$ (where $OpT \in \{R, M, P\}$ and $DecT \in \{and, or\}$)
Social relationships ($\mathcal{SR}$)	$plays(Ag, R)$, $delegates(A, A', G)$, $transmits(A, A', D)$, $employs(A, A')$

Table 2 lists the predicates used in the information view of the modeling language. Personal data are a subclass of information and are represented with the predicate $personalData(I)$.

Table 2. Information view predicates

Concepts	$information(I)$, $personalData(I)$
Relationships	$owns(A, I)$, $makes\text{-}tangible(I, D)$, $part\text{-}of\text{-}i(I_1, I_2)$, $part\text{-}of\text{-}d(D_1, D_2)$

Table 3 lists the predicates used in the authorization view of the modeling language. The predicate $legalBasis(LB)$ models a law, or a law article, that can be used to legitimate something (e.g. explicit consensus legitimates the processing of personal data). The predicate $legitimates(LB, autorises)$ specifies the legal basis used to legitimate an authorization that includes some processing of personal data. For example, in Fig. 6 the consensus is used to legitimate the authorization for the processing of disease diagnosis provided by patient to medical private company.

Table 3. Authorization view predicates

Concepts	$legalBasis(\mathsf{LB})$
Social relationships ($\mathcal{SR}$)	$authorises(\mathsf{A}_1, \mathsf{A}_2, \mathcal{I}, \mathcal{G}, \mathcal{P}, \mathsf{TrAuth})$ (where $\mathcal{P} = (\{R, M, P, T\} \cup \{\overline{R}, \overline{M}, \overline{P}, \overline{T}\})$ and $\mathsf{TrAuth} \in \{and, or\}$)
Relationships	$legitimates(\mathsf{LB}, authorises)$

Definition: Actor Model. An actor model AM is a tuple $\langle \mathsf{A}, \mathcal{G}, \mathcal{D}, \mathcal{G}_{\mathcal{IRL}}, \mathcal{D}_{\mathcal{IRL}} \rangle$, where A is an actor, $\mathcal{G}$ is a set of goals, $\mathcal{D}$ is a set of documents, $\mathcal{IRL}$ is a set of intentional relationships. We denote the set of actor models as $\mathcal{AM}$.

Actor Model Well-Formedness. An actor model $\mathsf{AM} = \langle \mathsf{A}, \mathcal{G}, \mathcal{D}, \mathcal{G}_{\mathcal{IRL}}, \mathcal{D}_{\mathcal{IRL}} \rangle$ is well-formed if: (i) for each each intentional relationship $\mathsf{IRL} = decomposes(\mathsf{A}', \mathsf{G}, \mathcal{S}, \mathsf{DecT})$ in $\mathcal{IRL}, \mathsf{A}' = \mathsf{A}$, and both G and all goals in $\mathcal{S}$ are in $\mathcal{G}$; and (ii) for each intentional relationship $\mathsf{IRL} = reads/modifies/produces(\mathsf{A}', \mathsf{G}, \mathsf{D}, \mathsf{OpT})$ in $\mathcal{IRL}, \mathsf{A}' = \mathsf{A}$, $\mathsf{G} \in \mathcal{G}$, and $\mathsf{D} \in \mathcal{D}$.

Definition: Model. We tie together all the elements in the social, information, and authorization views to define a model. A model M is a tuple $\langle \mathcal{AM}, \mathcal{SR}, \mathsf{IM} \rangle$ where $\mathcal{AM}$ is a set of actor models, $\mathcal{SR}$ is a set of social relationships, and IM is an information view model. Definition 3 lays down the constraints on the well-formedness of a model.

Model Well-Formedness. A model $\mathsf{M} = \langle \mathcal{AM}, \mathcal{SR}, \mathsf{IM} \rangle$ is well-formed if:

1. social relationships are only over actors with models in $\mathcal{AM}$;
2. only leaf goals are delegated; for each $delegates(\mathsf{A}, \mathsf{A}', \mathsf{G})$ in $\mathcal{SR}$, there is an actor model $\langle \mathsf{A}, \mathcal{G}, \mathcal{D}, \mathcal{G}_{\mathcal{IRL}}, \mathcal{D}_{\mathcal{IRL}} \rangle$ in $\mathcal{AM}$ such that $\mathsf{G} \in \mathcal{G}$ and there is no decomposition of G in $\mathcal{IRL}$;
3. delegated goals appear in the delegatee's actor model: $\forall delegates(\mathsf{A}, \mathsf{A}', \mathsf{G})$ in $\mathcal{SR}$, there is an actor model $\langle \mathsf{A}, \mathcal{G}, \mathcal{D}, \mathcal{G}_{\mathcal{IRL}}, \mathcal{D}_{\mathcal{IRL}} \rangle$ in $\mathcal{AM}$ s.t. $\mathsf{G} \in \mathcal{G}$;
4. the transmitter must possess the document for the document transmission to take place: for each $transmits(\mathsf{A}, \mathsf{A}', \mathsf{D})$ in $\mathcal{SR}$, there is an actor model $\langle \mathsf{A}, \mathcal{G}, \mathcal{D}, \mathcal{G}_{\mathcal{IRL}}, \mathcal{D}_{\mathcal{IRL}} \rangle \in \mathcal{AM}$ s.t. $\mathsf{D} \in \mathcal{D}$. An actor possesses a document if:
   - it has the document since scratch: $possesses(\mathsf{A}, \mathsf{D}) \in \mathcal{IRL}$, or
   - it creates the document, i.e., $\exists \mathsf{G} \in \mathcal{G}.wants(\mathsf{A}, \mathsf{G}) \wedge produces(\mathsf{A}, \mathsf{G}, \mathsf{D}) \in \mathcal{IRL}$, or
   - there is an actor A'' such that $transmits(\mathsf{A}'', \mathsf{A}, \mathsf{D}) \in \mathcal{SR}$.
5. transmitted documents appear in the receiver's actor model: $\forall transmits(\mathsf{A}', \mathsf{A}, \mathsf{D}) \in \mathcal{SR}, \exists \mathsf{AM} = \langle \mathsf{A}, \mathcal{G}, \mathcal{D}, \mathcal{G}_{\mathcal{IRL}}, \mathcal{D}_{\mathcal{IRL}} \rangle \in \mathcal{SR} | \mathsf{D} \in \mathcal{D}$;
6. authorizations are well-formed if: $\forall authorizes(\mathsf{A}', \mathsf{A}, \mathcal{I}, \mathcal{G}, \mathcal{OP}, \mathsf{TrAuth}) \in \mathcal{SR}$, there must be at least one information entity specified ($| \mathcal{I} | \geq 1$), and at least one prohibition or permission is specified;

7. delegations have no cycles: for each $delegates(A, A', G)$ in $\mathcal{SR}$, there is no A'' such that $delegates(A'', A, G)$ in $\mathcal{SR}$ or $delegates(A'', A, Gi)$ in $\mathcal{SR}$, where Gi is a descendant of G in the goal tree of A'';
8. part-of relationships (either over information or documents) have no cycles;

Definition: Authorization Closure. Let $M = \langle \mathcal{AM}, \mathcal{SR}, \mathsf{IM} \rangle$ be a well-formed model. The authorization closure of $\mathcal{SR}$, denoted as $\triangle_{\mathcal{SR}}$, is a superset of $\mathcal{SR}$ that makes prohibitions explicit, when no authorization is granted by any actor. Formally: $\forall A, A'$ with an actor model in $\mathcal{AM}, \forall owns(A, \mathsf{I}) \in \mathcal{SR}$.

$\neg \exists A''.authorises(A'', A', \mathcal{I}, \mathcal{G}, \mathcal{OP}, \mathsf{TrAuth}) \in SR$ where $\mathsf{I} \in \mathcal{I} \rightarrow$ $authorises(A, A', \mathsf{I}, \mathcal{G}', \overline{\mathcal{OP}}, \mathsf{false}) \in \triangle_{\mathcal{SR}}$ where $\mathcal{G}'$ is the set of goals of A'

Definition: Authorizations Conflict. Two authorizations: $authorises(A_1, A_2, \mathcal{I}_1, \mathcal{G}_1, \mathcal{OP}_1, \mathsf{TrAuth}_1)$, and $authorises(A_3, A_2, \mathcal{I}_2, \mathcal{G}_2, \mathcal{OP}_2, \mathsf{TrAuth}_2)$ are conflicting if and only if they both regulate the same information ($\mathcal{I}_1 \cap \mathcal{I}_2 \neq \emptyset$), and either:

- $\mathcal{G}_1 \neq \emptyset \wedge \mathcal{G}_2 = \emptyset$, or vice versa; or,
- $\mathcal{G}_1 \cap \mathcal{G}_2 \neq \emptyset$, and either: $\exists OP.OP \in \mathcal{OP}_1 \wedge \overline{OP} \in OP_2$; or $\mathsf{TrAuth}_1 \neq \mathsf{TrAuth}_2$.

4.2 Verification of Policies Properties

The formal definition of a modeling language allows for automated reasoning over the models, such as, the verification of model properties. In this section, we show how it is possible to formally represent some of the social constraints imposed by the GDPR and automatically verify them. An automated verification of the constraints presented later in this Section is not to be intended sufficient for a system to be compliant with the GDPR, but more as a support in the analysis of the compliance of complex systems with the GDPR.

Employment. Under the GDPR, organizations and employers have different responsibilities with respect to their employees, for what concerns the processing of personal data. To identify employers and employee, the modeling language supports the employment relationship, which can be defined only between actors within the same organization, and, more in particular, always from the employer to all his employees, so to avoid chains of employments and circular relationships.

Formally, employment relationship is defined among two actors, an employer and an employee, where it must be valid that: (i) each employer can have several employees and cannot be employed; and (ii) each employee can have only one employer and no employee: $\forall A, A'$, with an actor model in $\mathcal{AM}$, $\forall\ employs(A, A') \in \mathcal{SR}, \neg \exists A'' \neq A$ s.t. $employs(A'', A) \vee employs(A', A'') \vee employs(A'', A')$.

This policy specify the impossibility to define chains of employment relationships, so to avoid model inconsistencies, with respect to the legislation. For example, if we model the APSS as employer of doctors and nurses, and the APSS director as employer of nurses, we would have an inconsistent model. Automated reasoning can support the designer in the detection of this violation.

Data Controller. Under the GDPR, for every processing of personal data done by other subjects other then the data owner, it is always required to identify a data controller. In the language, the processing of personal data, or more generally of information, is represented by either: (i) the intentional relationship *read/modify/produce(*A,G*),D,OpT* defined from a goal (in some actor's scope) to a document; or (ii) the social relationship *transmits*(A, A', D) defined between two actors. Both of these relationships are valid only in the cases of: (i) an authorization allows for them; or (ii) the actor processing the data (reading, modifying, producing, or transmitting it) is the owner of the information itself. Formally: $\forall I$, *reads/modifies/produces*(A, G, D, OpT).*makes-tangible*(I, D) $\implies$ *owns*(A, I) $\vee$ $\exists authorises$($A', A, \mathcal{I}, \mathcal{G}, \mathcal{OP}$, TrAuth).OpT $\in \mathcal{OP}, G \in \mathcal{G}, I \in \mathcal{I}$.

The GDPR requirement of having a data controller for every processing of personal data, can be supported by automated reasoning on the social relationship of authorization. In the language, the data controller is the direct addressee of the authorization provided by the data owner, or its employer (if exists). Since an authorization is always needed in the case of information processed by someone different from the owner himself, if a data controller is missed, an authorization violation can be detected by automated reasoning, and the system designer can be notified. For example, in the model represented in Fig. 5 the goal visited by specialist produces the document diagnosis, which makes tangible personal data. This is a personal data processing and the GDPR requires for it a data controller. Figure 6 shows the authorization given by the data owner to the company for the disease diagnosis information in the context of visited by specialist, this authorizations identify the company as the data controller for this data processing. If this authorization had been missed, a data controller would not have been specified as required by the GDPR.

Legitimation. The GDPR imposes on organizations to have a valid legal basis for every processing of personal data or sharing with a third party (e.g. explicit consensus or contractual necessity). For example, when the Santa Chiara hospital transmits a document containing personal information of a patient to the APSS, the hospital needs to provide a lawful basis, such as, an explicit consensus of the data owner, in order to legitimate the authorization to the APSS.

Formally, for each authorization that includes a personal data, provided to an actor who is not in the same organization of the provider itself (from the employer to an employee, or from an employee to the employer, or among employees within the same organization), it is necessary to specify the legal basis used to legitimate the authorization. Formally: $\forall authorises$($A, A', \mathcal{I}, \mathcal{G}, \mathcal{OP}$, TrAuth)$|$ $\neg employs$(A, A')$\wedge \neg employs$(A', A)$\wedge \neg \exists A''.employs$($A'', A$)$\wedge employs$($A'', A'$) $: \exists I \in \mathcal{I}.personalData$($I$) $\rightarrow \exists LB.legitimates$($LB$, *authorises*)

In the case of complex scenarios, the number of authorizations can increase a lot and could became difficult to identify the authorizations that includes personal data and that are not between members of the same organization. The automated reasoning feature can support the designer in the identification of this critical subset of authorization, for which it is required to provide a legal basis. For example, in the medical domain, many information are personal data but not all authorizations are defined between members of different organizations, so we could need help to identify them. For example, Fig. 6 shows two different authorizations, the one on the left, from patient to medical private company, requires a legal basis because it includes the personal data disease diagnosis and is defined between the data owner and a different actor. The authorization on the right part of Fig. 6 is about the same personal data of above, but it is defined between actors within the same organization, so it does not requires any legal basis.

5   Related Work

In this section, we compare with other works about privacy requirements engineering, privacy enhancing technologies and automated reasoning applied to modeling languages.

Hoepman et al. in [8] identify eight privacy design strategies to help IT architects to support privacy by design early in the software development life cycle. The work has been done when data protection regulation in EU was only a proposal, but the ideas of privacy by design and by default were already there. The work reviews the mains available PETs and patterns, but focuses more on the design of a system by providing design strategies. The work does not provide a concrete method for a specific privacy legislation but try to define high level strategies to adopt at the very beginning of system design.

Gurses et al. in [6] provide an overview of privacy-by-design practices, inspired by policy makers but expressed from an engineering perspective. They present two case studies focusing on the aspect of data minimization, trying to demonstrate its importance in the concept of privacy-by-design.

Spiekermann et al. in [11] try to introduce the privacy domain to engineers, by providing a concrete privacy-friendly systems design guidance. The work examines effects on user behavior of three types of system operations, data transfer, storage, and processing. The authors develop guidelines for building privacy-friendly systems, distinguishing two approaches: privacy-by-policy and privacy-by-architecture, where the former relies on the principle of fair information practices and the latter on data minimization concept. In the GDPR these two concepts are both central but there are also other aspects that are not taken into consideration by this work, such as legal responsibilities.

Guarda et al. in [5] present a technological interpretation of legal aspects of privacy for the development of requirement engineering methods. The authors recognize the legal perspective as the leading one important for privacy. They do not propose any method or language but provide an overview of privacy aspects to be taken into consideration by designing methods for privacy-aware systems. The work is antecedent to the GDPR and it is therefore based on the previous EU Directive, the 95/46/EC.

Kalloniatis et al. in [9] present PriS, a security requirement engineering method that, focusing on privacy aspects, incorporates privacy into the system design process. By considering privacy requirements as organizational goals, PriS uses the concept of privacy-process pattern for describing the impact of privacy onto the organizational processes. The work provide an effective method but does not take into consideration any legal aspect.

Qingfeng et al. in [7] present a privacy goal-driven requirements modeling framework to support the design of a Role-Based Access Control (RBAC) system. The work proposes a solution to define low-level access control policies given privacy requirements. The proposed framework addresses a single aspect of privacy, without supporting other privacy-enhancing practices or legal aspects.

Van Lamsweerde et al. in [12] propose automated analysis features to support requirements engineering methods in managing conflicts and applying design principles. Giorgini et al. in [4], introduce automated reasoning feature in order to identify conflicts among goals in the Tropos method.

Giorgini et al. in [3] presents SI*, a security requirement engineering framework that extends i^* [13][1] to handle security concepts. The work does not focus specifically on privacy but handles security aspects by providing a goal modeling language to identify dependencies between actors.

6   Conclusions and Future Work

We have proposed a method for supporting the implementation of systems compliant with the GDPR. More in particular, we have defined a goal-based modeling language, an extension of STS-ml, that allows to model social aspects of the GDPR, such as, the relationship between data subjects, data controllers, data processors, employer, and employees, in the context of personal data processing. We also showed how it is possible to use the modeling language to formally represent and automatically verify privacy policies.

Future work includes the extension of the framework with a business process language, to allow a more detailed specification of the social aspects represented in the language. A further formalization of the language will be needed to specify other constrains imposed by the GDPR. We also plan to develop a tool to support the method, by extending the STS-tool presented in [10]. It will feature automated reasoning capabilities and it will support the user in the identification of inconsistencies and in the verification of other users policies. The tool will also generate, in an automated fashion, documents which report the information and diagrams specified for a system in a format understandable to non STS-ml experts.

---

[1] i^* is a modeling framework that uses the concepts of actors, goals, tasks, and resources to define dependencies between actors.

References

1. Dalpiaz, F., Paja, E., Giorgini, P.: Security Requirements Engineering: Designing Secure Socio-Technical Systems. MIT Press, Cambridge (2016)
2. Regulation (EU) 2016/679 of the European Parliament and of the Council of 27 April 2016 on the protection of natural persons with regard to the processing of personal data and on the free movement of such data, and repealing Directive 95/46/EC (General Data Protection Regulation). Official Journal of the European Union L119/59, May 2016. http://eur-lex.europa.eu/legal-content/EN/TXT/?uri=OJ:L:2016:119:TOC
3. Giorgini, P., Massacci, F., Mylopoulos, J., Zannone, N.: Modeling security requirements through ownership, permission and delegation. In: Proceedings of the 13th IEEE International Conference on Requirements Engineering, pp. 167–176. IEEE (2005)
4. Giorgini, P., Mylopoulos, J., Sebastiani, R.: Goal-oriented requirements analysis and reasoning in the tropos methodology. Eng. Appl. Artif. Intell. 18(2), 159–171 (2005)
5. Guarda, P., Zannone, N.: Towards the development of privacy-aware systems. Inf. Softw. Technol. 51(2), 337–350 (2009)
6. Gürses, S., Troncoso, C., Diaz, C.: Engineering privacy by design (2011)
7. He, Q., Antón, A.I., et al.: A framework for modeling privacy requirements in role engineering. In: Proceedings of REFSQ, vol. 3, pp. 137–146 (2003)
8. Hoepman, J.-H.: Privacy design strategies. In: Cuppens-Boulahia, N., Cuppens, F., Jajodia, S., Abou El Kalam, A., Sans, T. (eds.) SEC 2014. IAICT, vol. 428, pp. 446–459. Springer, Heidelberg (2014). doi:10.1007/978-3-642-55415-5_38
9. Kalloniatis, C., Kavakli, E., Gritzalis, S.: Addressing privacy requirements in system design: the PriS method. Requirements Eng. 13(3), 241–255 (2008)
10. Paja, E., Dalpiaz, F., Poggianella, M., Roberti, P., Giorgini, P.: Specifying and reasoning over socio-technical security requirements with STS-tool. In: Ng, W., Storey, V.C., Trujillo, J.C. (eds.) ER 2013. LNCS, vol. 8217, pp. 504–507. Springer, Heidelberg (2013). doi:10.1007/978-3-642-41924-9_45
11. Spiekermann, S., Cranor, L.F.: Engineering privacy. IEEE Trans. Software Eng. 35(1), 67–82 (2009)
12. Van Lamsweerde, A., Darimont, R., Letier, E.: Managing conflicts in goal-driven requirements engineering. IEEE Trans. Software Eng. 24(11), 908–926 (1998)
13. Yu, E.: Modelling Strategic Relationships for Process Reengineering: Social Modeling for Requirements Engineering 11 (2011)

Development of Capability Driven Development Methodology: Experiences and Recommendations

Janis Stirna[1(✉)], Jelena Zdravkovic[1], Jānis Grabis[2], and Kurt Sandkuhl[3]

[1] Department of Computer and Systems Sciences, Stockholm University,
PO Box 7003, 164 07 Kista, Sweden
{js, jelenaz}@dsv.su.se
[2] Institute of Information Technology, Riga Technical University, Kalku 1, Riga, Latvia
grabis@rtu.lv
[3] Institute of Computer Science, Rostock University, 18051 Rostock, Germany
kurt.sandkuhl@uni-rostock.de

Abstract. The field of Information Systems (IS) and Enterprise Modeling (EM) is continuously striving to address the challenges of the practice by developing new methods and tools. This paper presents experiences and lessons learned from the Method Engineering of the Capability Driven Development (CDD) methodology. The CDD methodology supports organizations operating in dynamic environments and integrates EM with information system (IS) development taking into account changes as the application context. The main focus is on presenting the CDD meta-model and the associated development activities as well as sharing the experience and recommendations for developing similar methods and tools.

Keywords: Enterprise modeling · Meta-modeling · Method engineering · Capability Driven Development

1 Introduction

Information Systems (IS) have to dynamically adapt to new and unexpected, often drastic, business opportunities and threats. To respond to this challenge of continuous adaptation, the EU FP7 project "Capability as a Service in digital enterprises" (CaaS) [1] developed a methodology for capturing and analyzing the influence of the business application context on the IS using the notion of capability. Capability is generally seen as a fundamental abstraction to describe what a core business does [2]. For instance, *"an ability and a capacity for an enterprise to deliver value, either to customers or shareholders, right beneath the business strategy"* [3], or *"the ability of one or more resources to deliver a specified type of effect or a specified course of action"* [4]. The CaaS project has developed an integrated methodology for context-aware business and IT solutions: *Capability Driven Development* (CDD). It consists of a modeling language and guidelines for the way of working. The areas of modeling performed as part of CDD are Enterprise Modeling (EM), context modeling, variability modeling, adjustment algorithms, and patterns for capturing best practices. The development of the CDD

G. Poels et al. (Eds.): PoEM 2017, LNBIP 305, pp. 251–266, 2017.
https://doi.org/10.1007/978-3-319-70241-4_17

methodology followed principles defined during analysis of use case requirements and documented in [5]:

- The CaaS project should not develop a single methodology mandatory for all business cases, but a reference methodology for using in majority of cases and pathways of extending the reference methodology to proprietary methodologies.
- All concepts of the methodology should be based on a common meta-model.
- The CDD methodology should not be a monolithic block but component-oriented to allow flexible use of selected method components depending on the intentions of an organization and a particular development situation.
- Integration of existing methods or method components should be given preference before substituting them with new.
- The CDD methodology is to be supported by the CDD Environment, a part of which is the *Capability Design Tool* (CDT) implemented in Eclipse.

The objectives of this paper are (i) to report on the process that led to development of the CDD methodology, (ii) to share the experiences method development, and (iii) to formulate a set of guidelines for development of EM methods.

The research approach followed the principles of design science [8] consisting of several design and evaluation cycles. The proposed CDD methodology has been applied and validated in 4 use case companies of the CaaS project.

The rest of the paper is organized as follows. Section 2 presents the research approach taken, while Sect. 3 gives a background to method development. The process of method development that took place is presented in Sect. 4 while the CDD meta-model and the CDD process is summarized in Sect. 5. Section 6 presents the experiences and recommendations for method development, while Sect. 7 summarizes and provides concluding remarks.

2   Research Methodology

Within IS engineering, Design Science Research (DSR) is a problem-solving paradigm which aims to resolve problems by creating innovative scientific artifacts through development- and evaluation cycles within an operating context (organizational domain, social setting, environment, etc.) [8]. The creation of artifacts evolves iteratively and incrementally through a research process and results in a practical solution; the essential activities of the process concern the explication of the problem, an outline of the artifact with the related requirements, artifact's design and development, as well as its demonstration, evaluation, and communication.

Our research concerns the CDD methodology as the main *design artifact*, for enabling IS development to capture changes in business context through variability terms and to accordingly adapt using adjustment algorithms. This design artifact is composite because the components of the methodology, e.g. the meta-model, are also design artifacts. Furthermore it is closely related to another design artifact of the project – the CDD Environment. This paper presents the experience of applying the DSR paradigm to the development CDD methodology and environment. The DSR process of constructing the artifact according to needs of multiple stakeholders was iterative and incremental. Participatory modeling workshops, focus-groups sessions, and questionnaires were the main techniques used for requirements elicitation. The artifact was developed and validated during a number of design cycles, notably, two cycles of initial feasibility design and analysis [5], three parallel cycles of application of the methodology at the use case companies leading to the reference CDD methodology [6], followed by a number of design-validation cycles for development of extensions of the methodology (available from [1]).

3 Background to Method Development

Method engineering (ME) is *the engineering discipline to design, construct and adapt methods, techniques and tools for the development of information systems* [9]. One of the first efforts in modeling of modeling methods (meta-modeling) was proposed by [10] and development of customizable tools for supporting various modeling approaches (meta-tools) by [11]. The main motivation was to search and adopt or tailor existing methods, as well as, to develop a new method by designing its modeling language, way of working, and tool support. The efforts concentrating on tool support became known as Computer Aided Method Engineering, c.f. [12, 13].

The need to adapt methods and tools according to organizational needs has been addressed by Situational Method Engineering (SME) [14]. Recently it has been systematically presented in [15]. In a nutshell, SME is an ME approach that includes all aspects of creating, using and adapting an IS development method based on local conditions. This is achieved by designing method parts, i.e. method chunks [16], supporting the realization of some specific IS development activity as well as by tailoring by extracting a set of appropriate method parts assessed based on local situational factors (e.g. the business sector, or size of the business). Each method part is represented according to a same template and adheres to a unique meta-model.

Another practicable ME approach was proposed in [17]; it sets a high attention on the elaboration of method parts such as the procedures for meta-modeling, i.e. for choosing appropriate concepts for inclusion.

Since the CDD methodology aimed for creating a new method for IS development based on the notion of capability because any similar has not existed, the core concern was to correctly identify the main method parts and their relevant concepts. For that reason, the approach described in [17] has been chosen. It proposes that methods are to be described in terms of the following aspects:

- *Purpose* every method component has to clearly state its purpose, e.g. what modeling or problem-solving task it supports. Furthermore, a method usually describes the procedure for the modeling task from a particular perspective (e.g. business goals, process), which influences what is considered important when following the procedure. This perspective should also be stated explicitly.
- *Overview* to method components describes the relationships between the individual method components, i.e. which components are to be used and under what conditions, as well as the sequence of the method components (if any).

- *Method component* defines in operational terms what are the modeling language (in terms of concepts and notation) and procedure to be used. The *concepts* specify what aspects of reality are regarded as relevant in the modeling process, i.e. what is important and what should be captured a model. These relevant concepts and their relationships should be named in the method component and explained if necessary. The *procedure* describes how to identify the relevant concepts in a method component. It may also state prerequisites, resources, input, output, and tool support. In some cases it includes guidelines of modeling and assessing model quality. The *notation* specifies how the result of the procedure is to be documented, i.e. the graphical symbols, providing appropriate representation for each concept and for the relationships between them.
- *Forms of cooperation* many modeling tasks require a range of specialist skills or cooperation between different stakeholder and developer types, i.e. roles in the project. The skills and roles are described along with the responsibilities and the forms of cooperation, e.g. who will take responsibility for each task or method component, will it be participatory or analyst-driven modeling.

The conceptualization of the relevant aspects is an important concern when designing method components. This is typically done using meta-modeling to specify a modeling language in a declarative manner, to generate a tool for its support. A key challenge is to organize ME and tool development in such a way that it is based on common modeling constructs and structure. In this regard MOF meta-modeling architecture [18] defining four modeling layers – from M3 (meta-meta model layer) to M0 (instance layer). Modeling languages are typically specified at M2 (meta-model layer). Once they are used to describe models reflecting reality, M1 model layer is populated. When the models at M1 level are instantiated M0 level is reached.

The CDD methodology has been defined by an M2 model, and as we show in Sect. 5, we have obtained it starting from a conceptual M2 model to enable communication as well as to reach the agreement for the meta-model requirements among the methodology's stakeholders.

4 Overview of the Process of Method Development

The following phases of method development took place: (i) requirements elicitation and analysis of the business motivators; (ii) method development first iteration – base line methodology, (iii) second iteration of method development, focusing on fine-tuning the base line methodology and the creation of regular CDD methodology as well as elaborating method extensions; (iv) integration of the method extensions and packaging for exploitation – final version of the CDD methodology.

4.1 Requirements Elicitation

The motivation for the CDD methodology development was analyzed in the initial requirements elicitation phase of the project. This was done by interviews with the use case companies, survey with a large number of external companies, as well as by several iterations of methodology development and capability designs for the four use case companies in order to validate the initial versions of the modeling language. This allowed us to elaborate the overall goals (see Fig. 1) and requirements for the CDD methodology, define an initial conceptual meta-model for representing capability designs, and to outline method components. Results of this work are reported in [5].

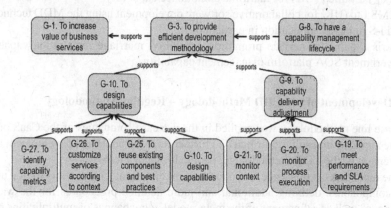

Fig. 1. A goal model fragment for the CDD methodology, adapted from [5]

4.2 Development of the of the CDD Methodology – Base Line

The CDD methodology defines both aspects that comprise a modeling methodology – (1) *the modeling language* in terms of concepts, relationships, and notations used to represent the modeling product, i.e. the models of capability designs created, and (2) the way of working, the procedures and tools used, to arrive at a capability design of good quality i.e. *the modeling process*. The CDD methodology consists of a number of inter-linked method components [6] described according to the framework of [17].

The CDD method components were divided into *upper-level method components* and *method extensions*. At this stage the upper-level components were designed according to the requirements and business goals elicited in the previous phase and the initial versions were documented. The resulting methodology was denoted, *base line methodology* and it included the following components:

- *Capability Design Process.* It describes an overview on how to design capabilities by using process models, goal models and other types of models.
- *Enterprise Modeling.* The component guides the creation of enterprise models that are used as input for capability design. We have incorporated the 4EM approach to for the purpose of this component.
- *Context Modeling.* It describes the method components needed for analyzing the capability context, and the variations needed to deal with variations.
- *Reuse of Capability Design.* This component contains guidelines for the elicitation and documentation of patterns for capability design.
- *Run-Time Delivery Adjustment.* For development of capability runtime adjustments including implementation of capability delivery adaptation algorithms.

The base line methodology was applied and validated by application in the following use case companies:

- SIV AG (Germany) for business processes outsourcing (BPO) and execution capability.
- Fresh T Limited (UK) for maritime compliance capability.
- CLMS Ltd (UK) for collaborative software development using the MDD technology and i-Symbiosis application in particular.
- Everis (Spain) for service promotion capability, marriage registration capability, government SOA platform management capability.

4.3   Development of the CDD Methodology – Regular Methodology

The base line methodology was applied in the use case companies of the CaaS project and the application results contributed to further improvements and development of the next version of the CDD methodology, denoted *regular methodology*.

The main tasks at this stage was development of new subcomponents for the upper-level components, defining additional and more detailed procedures for the ways of working, as well as refinement of the meta-model, e.g. changes of multiplicities representing model integrity rules, and introducing new components needed for representing information needed by the newly developed method subcomponents. In addition, *method extensions* addressing specific business challenges to which the regular methodology can be applied were developed as part of the process of applying the base line methodology (c.f. [1]). The main purpose with the method extensions is to broaden the range of problems to which CDD can be applied. There following method extensions were developed:

- The *Capability Ready Business Services* covers the transition from textual instructions and activity descriptions to process models. With this extension many more BPO services can be designed as capabilities.
- The *Prepare Local and Global Optimization* improves service delivery by balancing the local optimization of services provided to a client and global optimization from a Business Service Provider (BSP) perspective.
- The *Evolutionary Development of Business Information Exchange Capability* helps organizations to develop capabilities in the case when pre-existing capability delivery solution must be tailored to the needs of a new client.
- The *Integration of CDD and MDD* for analyzing the potential for integrating MDD and CDD concepts. MDD is sharing a common ground with the CDD approach because both use models for analysis and design.
- The *Analysis of Capability Relationships* is proposing an analysis of capability relationships and mapping capabilities to delivered services including those offered by external partners.
- The *Predictive analysis* describes capability delivery adjustment using predicted context values to attain proactive behavior.
- The *Capacity evaluation* evaluates capability delivery capacity requirements to determine capability's suitability to context ranges.

4.4 Development of the Final Version of the CDD Methodology

At this stage the upper level method components and method extensions had been applied and tested in several iterations in the use case companies and hence were considered relatively stable, i.e. only minor refinements to the documentation were performed, e.g. for eliminating redundancies and inconsistencies in the documentation, improving the understandability of the definitions.

Considering the project's aim to deliver a method for practical use, an additional method component to *Support Executive Decision Making* for the adoption of CDD in organizations. This method component defines the steps for CDD adoption as well as specifies the organizational roles needed for its successful and long-term use. The final version of the CDD methodology is reported in [19].

CDD was also analyzed with respect to the current EM and Enterprise Architecture contributions that include the concept of capability for similar purposes [20].

5   Overview of the CDD Meta-model

For the purpose of providing background, this section briefly presents the Capability Meta-model and the CDD way of working, the two aspects to which the experiences and lessons learned are related. The theoretical and methodological foundations for CDD are provided by the conceptual *core CaPability Meta-model* (CPM) in Fig. 2, c.f. [6] for details. CPM was developed on the basis of requirements from the industrial project partners and related research. It has three main sections:

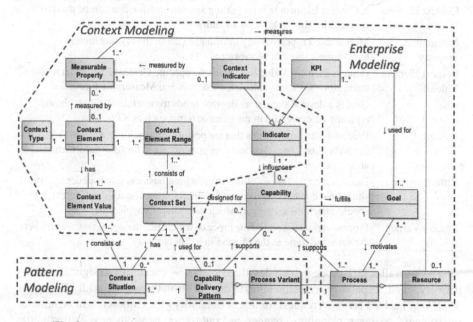

Fig. 2. A core meta-model for supporting Capability Driven Development [5]

(a) *Enterprise model* representing organizational designs with Goals, KPIs, Processes (with concretizations as Process Variants) and Resources;
(b) *Context model* represented with Context Set for which a Capability is designed and Context Situation at runtime that is monitored and according to which the deployed solutions should be adjusted. Context Indicators are used for measuring the context properties (Measuring Property); and
(c) *Patterns and variability model* for delivering Capability by reusable solutions for reaching Goals under different Context Situations. Each pattern describes how a certain Capability is to be delivered within a certain Context Situation and what Processes Variants and Resources are needed to support a Context Set.

Note that this is a simplified version of the CPM showing the key components of CDD; the version including definitions of components and associations is available in [19] (Table 1).

Table 1. Concepts of the core capability meta-model

Concept	Description
Capability	Capability is the ability and capacity that enable an enterprise to achieve a business Goal in a certain context (represented by Context Set)
KPI	Key Performance Indicators (KPIs) are measurable properties that can be seen as targets for achievement of Goals
Context Set	Context Set describes the set of Context Elements that are relevant for design and delivery of a specific Capability
Context Element Range	Context Element Range specifies boundaries of permitted values for a specific Context Element and for a specific Context Set
Context Element	A Context Element is representing any information that can be used to characterize the situation of an entity
Measurable Property	Measurable Property is any information about the organization's environment that can be measured
Context Element Value	Context Element Value is a value of a specific Context Element at a given the runtime situation, calculated from several Measurable Properties
Goal	Goal is a desired state of affairs that needs to be attained. Goals should typically be expressed in measurable terms such as KPIs
Process	Process is series of actions that are performed to achieve a result. A Process supports Goals, has input and produces output in terms of information and/or material
Pattern	Patterns are reusable solutions for reaching business Goals under specific situational contexts. The context defined for the Capability (Context Set) should match the context in which the Pattern is applicable
Process Variant	Process variant is a part of the Process, which uses the same input and delivers the same outcome as the Process in a different way

The overall CDD process includes three cycles – capability design; capability delivery; and capability refinement/updating. It usually starts with *Enterprise Modeling*, i.e. by a business request for a new capability - the request might be initiated by strategic business planning, changes in context, or new business opportunities requiring reconfiguration of existing or the creation of, e.g. new goals, business processes. This is followed by *capability design* – a formalized definition of requested capabilities and of relevant contexts, linking with relevant capability delivery patterns, as well as with supporting IT applications. The designed capability is then deployed and executed which is denoted by *capability delivery*.

6   Experiences of the CDD Methodology Development

This section presents our findings in terms of development of the CDD methodology and Environment.

6.1   Iterative and Incremental Development of the Meta-model

The work started by iterative development of the CPM in Fig. 2. It was used throughout the methodology development process. At first it presented the overall vision of the project consortium, the main components of a capability design, such as, capability, context, KPI, business process, which became clear in the early stages of the project. This was then validated in several iterations of, first instantiating the CPM, c.f. [5], and later applying to model the capability designs of the use case companies. All components in the meta-model had a textual description according to the following fields, compo-. nent's name, description, purpose explaining why it should be used, associations including their purpose, and attributes.

There were four major versions of the CPM (Fig. 3) based on the initial version of the CDD methodology as well as 4EM that provided a core set of EM concepts. The initial CPM was developed prior to considering use cases, documented in [21]. It introduced concepts distinctive to capability, namely, context, indicators, patterns, and variants.

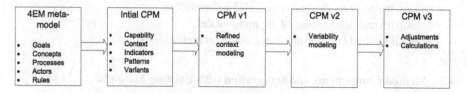

Fig. 3. Evolution of the CPM

The first CPM development iteration within the project focused on the refinement of the existing concepts. This was based on high-level use case requirements for CDD. Initial capability models were developed as instantiations of the CPM. These capability models were further elaborated during analysis and design of the use cases, and this information was used in the second version. The main group of concepts added concern variability modeling as the use case partners found it important to represent contextual causes of variability in their capability models.

The next use case development stage focused on the actual implementation and delivery of capabilities and the CPM was extended to represent capability delivery aspects, which are the main executable parts of the capability design. The concepts of calculations and adjustments were added [22]. The former concerns transformation of contextual and performance data into context elements and indicators while the latter concerns definition of the capability delivery adaptation logics.

In addition to the aforementioned iterations and the use case validations, further refinements were introduced after interactions with the CDD Environment development team. Some modeling components were difficult to understand by some method and tool developers in the project and discussing them from the point of view of meta-model and creating examples of capability models based on the meta-model proved useful. The most frequent changes were of multiplicities representing integrity constraints of the CDD methodology. There was a need to balance capability analysis and high level design needs with capability implementation and delivery needs. It was decided that the CPM v1 is used to communicate capability design concepts to business owners and analysts, while elements representing implementation details are defined in a separate view of the capability model (CPM v3).

Meta-modeling was instrumental to the process of designing method components with a clear purpose and precise semantics. This process was iterative during which CPM constructs and definitions were discussed in the method developer team to reach common understanding. A notable characteristic of CDD in comparison with other methods is that the same meta-model components are used by a considerably large number of method components and extensions. E.g. the constructs related to context modeling are used by almost all methodology components.

Development of all new method components started with the inclusion of the new modeling components in the CPM, which included certain restructuring and defining links to the existing components.

In summary, the following recommendations can be formulated:

– Develop the meta-model in design-validate iterations;
– Develop textual descriptions of the meta-model;
– Relate all method components to the common meta-model.

6.2   Method Components and Integration with Existing Methods

One of the initial decisions of methodology development was to base the CDD on existing methods and method components. The concept of method component proved to be very suitable because it allowed the development of support for the core tasks of CDD concurrently and in a modular fashion based on common principles.

It was assumed that capability design is based on EM and the CPM contains elements commonly used in EM. Hence, it was decided to incorporate an existing EM approach for the CDD tasks that are aligned to EM tasks. The 4EM approach was chosen because of three primary reasons: (1) 4EM sub-models are similar to method components and they are suited for modeling the perspectives of an organizational design (goals, business rules, process, concepts, actors and IS requirements) that are relevant for capability design, (2) the 4EM meta-model is formally defined, and (3) two of 4EM developers and authors of [7] participated the CDD method development.

Once the initial assessment of the suitability of 4EM was done, we investigated how the elements in the CPM correspond to the elements of the 4EM sub-models. Figure 4 depicts this on a conceptual level with the dashed links showing the correspondence between the modeling perspectives of CDD and 4EM. The links show which sub-models of CDD can be supported by 4EM in the way that they use and where needed extend the 4EM models.

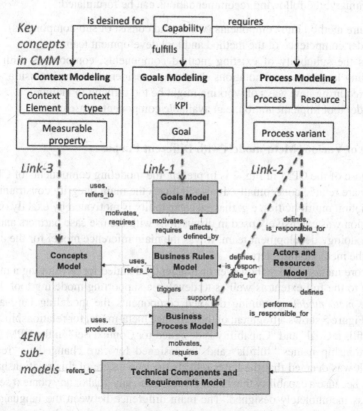

Fig. 4. Alignment of sub-models of capability meta-model and 4EM framework

Link-1: CPM goals and KPIs represent the intentional dimension of capability design and they correspond to the 4EM Goals Model components, namely, goal, problem, opportunity, cause, and relationships, namely, supports, hinders, and AND and OR refinement. Hence 4EM Goals Model was incorporated in CDD.

Link-2: Capability design is specified in terms of business process, process variants and resources, which can be addressed by 4EM Business Process Model and Actors and Resources Model. However, considering that the use case companies were more acquainted with the BPMN and that CDD Environment was developed in the Eclipse

Environment for which there was an available BPMN plug-it it was decided to use BPMN instead, which considerably reduced the implementation costs of the tool.

Link-3: CPM constructs for representing capability context, such as context element, context indicator, and measurable property define properties of things and phenomena, which makes them, in principle, appropriate for modeling with the 4EM Concepts Model. However, analyzing the use case requirements led to a conclusion that a specific modeling guidance is needed and it was decided to develop a dedicated modeling component and a distinct notation for context modeling.

In summary, the following recommendations can be formulated:

– Structure method into components (which and consist of sub-components);
– Consider competence of the method and tool development team;
– Assess the suitability of existing method components; components with similar modeling languages and notations should be considered for the inclusion, components requiring new ways of working might be too difficult to include;
– Consider tool implementation, e.g. available components, ease of use.

6.3   Use of Various Meta-models with Different Purposes

The purpose of the CPM in Fig. 2 is to present the modeling components of CDD and how they are related conceptually. It also includes the main integrity constraints based on association multiplicities, e.g. that each capability is motivated by exactly one goal. This version was extensively used in discussions with the use case partners and within the methodology development team. It was the main reference model for the development of the methodology steps.

The core meta-model, is however insufficiently detailed for developing a modeling language to the full extent as well as to develop a supporting modeling tool. Hence a *language meta-model* containing detailed components the modeling language was created. Figure 5 shows a fragment of the language meta-model for relationships "Capability fulfills a Goal" and "Capability is designed for Context Set" in the CPM (Fig. 2). The relationship names "fulfills" and "is designed for" are changed to "requires", because it was deemed that the latter reflects the true nature of this relationship more precisely because a capability that is not associated to any goal or any context set would be seen as incompletely designed. The main difference between the language meta-model and core meta-model is that associations and association roles are modeled as classes to specify which association types are permitted between which modeling component types. The language meta-model was developed analytically – by considering the purpose of each component in the CPM and how it could be represented by a modeling language taking the constructs and notation of 4EM a starting point. The resulting meta-model was also useful in discussions between method developer and tool developer teams. It was later extended to represent information needed for other parts of the CDD methodology, such as variables and calculations for adjustment algorithms, which were not part of the modeling language but were needed for capability monitoring at runtime.

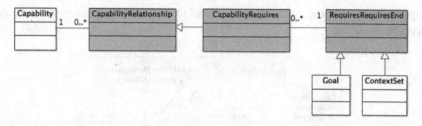

Fig. 5. A fragment of the language meta-model showing Capability relationships with Goal and Context Set

The CPM represented integrity and quality constraints assumed to be useful in the CDD methodology, e.g. each capability requires exactly one context set. This, however, does not take into account temporal states of the model, i.e. in an incomplete model, once a capability is placed in a model it will exist without a link to a context set until such a context set is created and an association to it is defined.

The language meta-model essentially served as the reference point for development of the CDD Environment, but it was not useful for conceptual discussions, e.g., when developing the different method components. Referring to MOF levels of meta-models, the language meta-model followed the principles of M2 level, while Ecore (meta-model of the Eclipse Modeling Framework) provided M3 level components.

In summary, the following recommendations can be formulated:

- Develop several meta-models in parallel – core meta-model for discussions and method development and language meta-model for tool development
- Assess integrity constraints and quality criteria built in the meta-model.

6.4 Development of the CDD Environment

The language meta-model was subsequently implemented in the CDD Environment consisting of a number of components (see Fig. 6). *Capability Design Tool (CDT)* is an Eclipse based graphical modeling tool for supporting the creation of models according to the capability meta-model. It supports the CPM and its modeling notation. *Capability Navigation Application (CNA)* uses capability models to monitor the capability context by receiving the values of measurable properties (MP) and handle run-time adjustments. CNA manages information at run-time defined according to the meta-model. *Capability Context Platform (CCP)* distributes internal and external context information to the CNA. It aggregates MPs into context elements for models in CDT; it provides runtime values for external context elements (external data providers - Internet, other organizations, individuals); it also allows defining new context elements based on the existing MPs, and specifying KPIs based on MPs for monitoring. *Capability Delivery Application (CDA)* represents the business applications that are used to support the capability delivery. This can be a custom-made or configured, e.g. an ERP, system. The CNA communicates or configures the CDA to adjust for changing contexts during capability design and delivery. It also receives MP values from the data providers internal to the organization. *Capability Pattern Repository (CPR)* stores reusable capability designs.

It supports the part of the capability meta-model that is related to patterns and business processes.

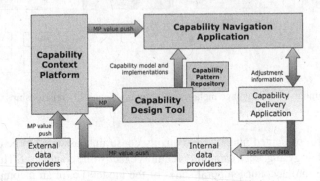

Fig. 6. Components of the CDD Environment

The case of developing the CDD Environment differs from the more traditional cases of developing tool support for modeling methods where a modeling language is implemented only in a modeling tool. Because the CDD environment also included other components, for example, the parts of the meta-model related to runtime monitoring and adjustments had to be supported by other components of the CDD environment. Similarly, the CCP was used for monitoring measurable properties and context elements that had to be structured according to the meta-model. To simplify deployment of the CDD environment, a cloud-based version of the environment was also created supporting the final version of the methodology. Virtual instances of CDT, CCP, and CNA are hosted on the common Apache CloudStack platform and CDT was made accessible using web browser by means of desktop virtualization.

In summary, the following recommendations can be formulated:

- Use the language meta-model for tool development
- Include in the meta-model components that are not modeled in a traditional way, such as for runtime data, adjustments
- Consider that the meta-model will be used even outside the modeling tool
- Use cloud based tools and services to support deployment

7   Concluding Remarks

The process of CDD methodology development followed the principles of DSR. The main focus in this paper has been set on the development of the modeling language using meta-modeling with a particular effort on integration with concepts of the 4EM approach and on supporting the development of a modeling tool. A number of experiences and recommendations have also been presented. The CDD methodology and environment have been validated in real life capability design projects at four use case companies as part of design-evaluation cycles of the project. The presented recommendations are by no means exhaustive and more work on collecting such experiences from other ME projects should be devoted.

References

1. EU FP7 CaaS Project: Capability as a Service for digital enterprises, proj. no. 611351. http://caas-project.eu/
2. Ulrich, W., Rosen, M.: The business capability map: building a foundation for business/IT alignment. In: Cutter Consortium for Business and Enterprise Architecture (2012)
3. OPENGROUP TOGAF - enterprise architecture methodology, version 9.1 (2012). http://www.opengroup.org/togaf/
4. UK Ministry of Defence: NATO Architecture Framework v4.0 Documentation (2013). http://nafdocs.org/modem
5. Bērziša, S., et al.: Deliverable D1.4: Requirements specification for CDD, FP7 proj. 611351 CaaS (2014). http://caas-project.eu/deliverables/
6. Bērziša, S., et al.: Deliverable 5.2: The initial version of capability driven development methodology, FP7 proj. 611351 CaaS (2015). doi:10.13140/RG.2.1.2399.4965
7. Sandkuhl, K., Stirna, J., Persson, A., Wißotzki, M.: Enterprise Modeling – Tackling Business Challenges with the 4EM Method. Springer, Heidelberg (2014). doi: 10.1007/978-3-662-43725-4. ISBN 978-3-662-43724-7S
8. Hevner, A.R., March, S.T., Park, J., Ram, S.: Design science in information systems research. MIS Q. **28**(1), 75–105 (2004)
9. Brinkkemper, S.: Method engineering: engineering of information systems development methods and tools. Inf. Softw. Tech. **38**(4), 275–280 (1996)
10. Smolander, K.: OPRR: a model for modelling systems development methods. In: Lyytinen, K., Tahvanainen, V.-P. (eds.) Next Generation CASE Tools. IOS Press, Amsterdam (1991)
11. Bergsten, P., Bubenko, J., Dahl, R., Gustafsson, M.R., Johansson, L.A.: RAMATIC - A CASE Shell for Implementation of Specific CASE Tools. SISU, Stockholm (1989)
12. Marttiin, P., Harmsen, F., Rossi, M.: A functional framework for evaluating method engineering environments: the case of Maestro II/Decamerone and MetaEdit+. University of Jyväskylä (1996)
13. Kelly, S.: Towards a comprehensive MetaCASE and CAME environment: conceptual, architectural, functional and usability advances in MetaEdit+. Ph.D. thesis, University of Jyväskylä, Finland (1997)
14. Brinkkemper, S., Saeki, M., Harmsen, F.: Meta-modelling based assembly techniques for situational method engineering. Inf. Syst. **24**(3), 209–228 (1999)
15. Henderson-Sellers, B., Ralyté, J., Ågerfalk, P.J., Rossi, M.: Situational Method Engineering, pp. 1–274. Springer, Heidelberg (2014). doi:10.1007/978-3-642-41467-1. ISBN 978-3-642-41466-4
16. Ralyté, J., Backlund, P., Kühn, H., Jeusfeld, M.A.: Method chunks for interoperability. In: Embley, D.W., Olivé, A., Ram, S. (eds.) ER 2006. LNCS, vol. 4215, pp. 339–353. Springer, Heidelberg (2006). doi:10.1007/11901181_26
17. Goldkuhl, G., Lind, M., Seigerroth, U.: Method integration: the need for a learning perspective. IEEE Proc. Softw. **145**(4), 113–118 (1998)
18. OMG: OMG Meta Object Facility (MOF) Core Specification, Ver. 2.5 (2015)
19. Grabis, J., Henkel, M., Kampars, J., Koç, H., Sandkuhl, K., Stamer, D., Stirna, J., Valverde, F., Zdravkovic, J.: D5.3 The final version of Capability driven development methodology, FP7 proj. 611351 CaaS. doi:10.13140/RG.2.2.35862.34889

20. Zdravkovic, J., Stirna, J., Grabis, J.: A comparative analysis of using the Capability notion for congruent business and information systems engineering. CSIMQ (10), 1–20 (2017). https://doi.org/10.7250/csimq.2017-10.01

21. Stirna, J., Grabis, J., Henkel, M., Zdravkovic, J.: Capability driven development – an approach to support evolving organizations. In: Sandkuhl, K., Seigerroth, U., Stirna, J. (eds.) PoEM 2012. LNBIP, vol. 134, pp. 117–131. Springer, Heidelberg (2012). doi: 10.1007/978-3-642-34549-4_9

22. Grabis, J., Kampars, J.: Design of capability delivery adjustments. In: Krogstie, J., Mouratidis, H., Su, J. (eds.) CAiSE 2016. LNBIP, vol. 249, pp. 52–62. Springer, Cham (2016). doi: 10.1007/978-3-319-39564-7_5

Management Structure Based Government Enterprise Architecture Framework Adaption in Situ

Meri Katariina Valtonen(✉)

University of Jyväskylä, Jyväskylä, Finland
mi.katariina.valtonen@jyu.fi

Abstract. The fragmentation of the public sector makes it difficult to manage strategically and architecturally as a whole. Enterprise Architecture (EA) is considered as an improvement to that. Architectural modeling and visualization of the general management strategy plans along with parallel database development in a local government forms the primary data in the longitudinal case study using Action Design Research Method. To find a proper organizational fit for the EA framework in public sector, we reflect on how the current state architectural descriptions got organized in situ in a deep corporate hierarchy, and what were the emerging management needs in re-organizing the content of the descriptions. We suggest the EA framework in public sector as a strategic corporate management tool. As for the current state EA descriptions, we propose implementing the framework not as a static, but as a dynamic data model of the current management structures.

Keywords: Government enterprise architecture · Framework adaption · Strategy architecture · Action design research

1 Introduction

Public sector changes are trending toward privatizations, cost savings, e-government, and private sector management practices [1]. Today's challenges like mergers, corporate governance, and new business models are due [2]. Public sector is formed of organizations of high complexity. When silo-thinking among public organizations is added [3], consequences follow, e.g., e-government efforts end up sparsely structured and basing on ad hoc cooperation [4].

Enterprise architecture (EA) emerges as a promising tool for change and coherency management in public sector [5–7]. We refer to the public sector use of the EA tool as *Government Enterprise Architecture, GEA* [5]. EA is defined as 'analysis and documentation of an enterprise in its current and future states from an integrated strategy, business, and technology perspective' [8]. It provides people at all organizational levels a meaningful frame that allows understanding of the enterprise [9]. Any conscious change of a complex entity requires descriptions as a starting point to shed light on its components and their relationships [10]. The description models for architecting an enterprise are typically organized in an *EA framework*, e.g., in

G. Poels et al. (Eds.): PoEM 2017, LNBIP 305, pp. 267–282, 2017.
https://doi.org/10.1007/978-3-319-70241-4_18

[10, 11]. *EA method* comprises the EA framework, models, developing process and roles, etc. [12]. The present study focuses on the EA framework adaption in situ.

An organization who starts using the EA tool usually adopts a particular EA framework, either an existing or a customized one [13]. No method is suitable as such but rather needs adaption to the situational need [14]. *Method adaption* means customization of a method for a certain use, e.g., for an industry, organization or a project [15]. To select an EA method for the customization is not straightforward [16] due to the difference in approaches, scope and purpose [17], see different approaches e.g., in [18–20]. Some organizations adapt a known framework, whereas others develop their own, possibly based on others [6]. In public sector, all these approaches seem to be used [21]. A framework is not necessary, since EA is adopted without a framework, too [6]. Some approaches are even listed as 'ontology frameworks' in [22], not displaying the categories of EA models but rather focusing on the relationships of the EA descriptions and their contents, e.g., in [23, 24].

Assuming that no GEA framework is fit to adopt as such in the complex public sector, we are concerned, how to adapt GEA framework for the current state descriptions in a public corporation. Coherency of an organization means that the parts of it have logical, orderly and consistent relations to the whole [7]. We assume that the up-to-date current state GEA descriptions could support achieving the coherency of the public organization. We aim at the adaption principles of the GEA framework for the current state GEA management. This is done by analyzing, how the current state architectural descriptions got organized in a deep corporate hierarchy, and what management requirements emerged in re-organizing the content of the descriptions. Architectural modeling and visualization of the strategic plans along with the parallel database development yield the primary data of the study. The report is part of a longitudinal case study in Finnish local government using *action design research*, ADR [25] from 2008 to 2015. It presents the reflection and learning of the ADR cycles in the city. The case study composes an abductive evaluation of former findings in Finnish state government [26]. Previously resulted propositions are reconsidered based on the artifact building and organizational intervention.

The results suggest the current state GEA framework as a dynamic data model of the management structures of the adopting corporation. The limitations, as to generalizability of the results are due to one case organization and one architectural viewpoint. As a longitudinal study with several artifact iterations and levels of data collection, we wish to present preliminary suggestions for the current state GEA framework adaption. Related literature is described in Sect. 2, the case organization in Sect. 3, the propositions for the evaluation and the research methodology in Sect. 4, along with the strategy architecture development. Section 5 describes findings, Sect. 6 discusses the implications and limitations, and Sect. 7 concludes.

2   Related Works: Enterprise Architecture Frameworks

Enterprise Architecture, EA, as the analysis and documentation of the enterprise [8], is dependent on the architectural representations, i.e., *EA descriptions,* that display the enterprise structures and functions in the current or target state as pictures, diagrams, lists, etc., [11, 27]. Each type of EA description - *EA model* - is preferably based on a commonly agreed modeling notation and practice. EA models are traditionally enlisted in an EA framework, e.g., [8, 11, 28]. A framework signifies a skeletal structure, a frame containing something, or a set of frames [29]. We denote *EA framework* as a container of EA models and connected information, typically including classifications. In 'traditional EA approach' [30] EA frameworks are typically 2- or 3-dimensional matrices or cubes, e.g., in [10, 31] or [8, 28, 32]. We use the term *EA grid* synonymous to EA framework, and *GEA grid* to governmental one.

The dimensions of the EA grid vary in the suggested frameworks and other comprehensive works [11, 28, 32, 33]. There seems not to be a general opinion on how many dimensions the EA grid should include and what these dimensions should signify. Convergence seems clear of the dimension called *EA layers* [34] or *EA viewpoints* [35]. We use these terms synonymously. EA models are typically categorized in the EA layers of Business, Information, Systems, and Technology Architectures, (BA, IA, SA, TA), e.g., in [11, 31]. Simon et el. [34] have categorized a vast amount of EA studies based on their focus on one or more of the four aforementioned layers. These four EA layers seem to be identifiable in most EA grids one way or another. In some frameworks, strategy descriptions are included in the BA layer [11], some grids explicate *Strategy* as a separate layer [8, 28, 33], and some call it *Business motivation,* including the strategy concepts such as mission, vision, goals and objectives [36]. When any of these layers is documented in an organization, it may alone produce a set of co-dependent descriptions. For example, the *strategy architecture* in a hierarchical organization comprises institutionalized strategy goals as hierarchies of descriptions [33]. That is as laborious job per se to produce [37].

Beyond the EA layers, suggestions of the following dimensions vary. Typical options for the second and third dimensions are the organization structure or lines of business [8], the abstractions level of the models [8, 38] or the system life-cycle [32]. By using the word *EA grid dimension* it is emphasized here that the conception of the EA framework dimensions is not settled. In addition to the aforementioned 2–3 dimensions as 'x-, y-, and z-axes', we shall suggest that there might be more dimensions for the current state GEA management in situ.

Many authors signify the EA evolvement for new purposes [6, 17, 39]. In [6], EA is seen as an advanced development tool for information systems engineering from 80's, an enhanced information management tool by 2000, and a promising future tool for strategic business management by 2020. It is titled as a tool for solving business questions as 'only abstract representation of the entire enterprise' [39]. Lapalme [17] shares EA evolvement in three purposes 1. the business-IT alignment, 2. the organizational integration for enterprise coherency, and 3. the adaptive co-evolution of the organization with its environment. The EA grid scope seem to appear in different variations differentiated by the EA purpose. In [17], for enterprise IT architecting, e.g. [40], for enterprise integration, e.g., [19], and for co-evolution [20]. In the last example [20], the EA grid's scope may evolve when the EA maturity of the deploying organization grows. Hoogervorst and Dietz [41] emphasize the importance of identifying the future system that is to be architected, and then defining the EA grid accordingly. However, achieving the coherent fit of the EA grid with the future system to be architected is seen meager by them [41]. Beyond the aforementioned traditional grids, there are other types of frameworks which are not literally frameworks in the sense of a 2–3-dimensional grid [22]. Instead of an explicitly defined grid, they offer EA principles, modeling rules and standardizations, e.g., [23, 24]. When standardized diagrams become 'data with well-defined structures and meanings' and represent the facts and concepts behind the picture [24], the descriptions form more structural dataset than traditional figures, enabling searches and reconstructions, e.g., in [24, 42].

There is a challenge in the EA literature for more case studies to bridge the theoretical foundations and practical work [30, 34]. A mature theory to tie-in the variety of EA frameworks is called for [8]. There is 'no generally accepted theory, recommendations or standard of the EA framework, even though such one is included in numerous EA works of governmental institutions, standards bodies, academia, and practitioners' [34]. Partly this may be, because the EA concept has evolved in purpose and scope. However, this raises up the question, whether the EA framework as the classification of the EA models has anything to do with the practical EA description in situ. In the case study, we are drilling in the development of the current state GEA descriptions for the strategy architecture. Certain organizational classifications for the current state GEA description contents arise, and propound to reformulate the GEA grid adaption propositions.

3   The Case Organization

The study connects to GEA adoption in Finnish public sector, where state government and local government co-exist [43]. *State government* comprises 12 ministries that draft legislation and steer their branches with the help of around fifty specialized central agencies. The regional and local state services are governed by approx. two hundred regional state agencies. *Local government* consists of circa 300 municipalities. Municipalities are self-governing units by Constitution, with the right to tax the residents. The services are further dispersed locally in the town areas. State and local government develop the public services together. Similar organizational trends can be perceived in both, e.g., corporatizations.

The case organization in the study is a municipality corporation in Finland, the city of Kouvola. The city was formed in 2009 in a merger of six municipalities and three municipal joint organizations. By 2015, the city had more than 90,000 citizens on the area of 3,000 km^2, 6,500 city employees, and annual expenditure of 0.5 G€. The provided services were education from nursery to secondary school, health care up to a district hospital, business support services for entrepreneurs and farmers, social and legal services of citizens, water supply and sewerage, as well as the planning, building and maintenance of land, city infrastructure and town buildings. This resulted in deep hierarchies in *administrative organization* with multiple *organizational actors* such as the sectoral domains, central management (CM), and in-house enterprises. CM tasks were shared to corporate executives (CxO) and their units. The *political organization* comprised city council, board and 19 sub-boards in 2009. Since beginning, the new city was in continuous change. After starting as a 'purchaser-provider organization' in 2009, it was changed gradually to process organization. Some management levels appeared purely administrative due to vast service catalogues, service groupings, as well as both geographical and governmental oversight tasks. Accordingly, the administrative levels were diminished. Gradual outsourcing of prominent business areas was apparent as they were exposed to market competition. These drivers resulted in three major organizational changes in 2011, 2013, and 2015.

4   Application of the Action Design Research

Finland has been launching GEA since 2006, and after that it has established its role by Information Management Act 2011. The effort has yielded a common GEA method [38], where the GEA grid forms a central part, cf. [16, 26, 44].

The report presents a reflection and learning phase of the *Action Design Research ADR* [25] as part of a longitudinal case study in City of Kouvola in 2008–2015. The city needed novel management tools in the merger. Case study results from the state government were deployed, i.e., the GEA grid adaption model, *Geagam* [26]. Geagam was subdued to abductive evaluation in the City of Kouvola. *Abductive logic of reasoning* forms a 'process of discovery', where inferences are drawn to the best explanation when the phenomenon under study is investigated with wider sets of data [45]. This is particularly effective for evaluating the findings of new phenomena [45]. The research setting is figured in Fig. 1. With the insight of the CxOs, a city specific GEA grid adaption model was constructed and applied in two ADR research cycles as *Kouvola Geagam*. These *alpha* and *beta versions* included GEA method objectives and inherent adaption principles [46, 47]. Kouvola Geagam was included in GEA governance model of the

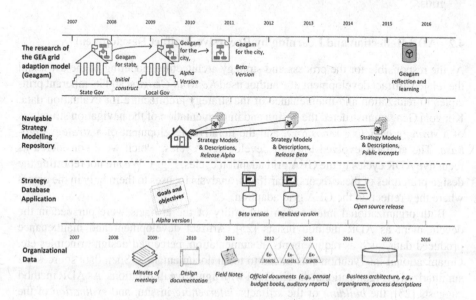

Fig. 1. The research setting for GEA framework adaption

town, and admitted as strategy framework by city board. Propositions under evaluation are explicated in Sect. 4.1. The ADR reflection techniques are described in Sect. 4.2, and the development of the strategy architecture artifacts in Sect. 4.3.

4.1 Geagam Propositions

GEA grid adaption model, *Geagam*, presents of a set of typified EA grids for the public sector organization types in Finland. The model was initially constructed using state government as the unit of analysis [26]. Kouvola Geagam followed presenting the set of GEA grids in the local government context [46, 47]. The new context provided new findings of the GEA grid adaption especially for the required EA layers [46, 47]. For the ADR learning and reflection phase at hand, the inherent adaption principles in [26, 46, 47] were subjected to textual analysis to explicate the propositions for evaluation. By excerption and categorizing, the suggested principles in-between the Geagam constructs were triangulated and enforced. For the study, we chose the most significant propositions enforced by the traditional assumptions of the 2- and 3-dimensional EA frameworks. Administrative organization hierarchy was suggested to display as the description levels (rows) of the adopted GEA grids. The political decision levels were mapped to these administrative levels. GEA grid viewpoints as columns of the GEA grids were suggested to cover the concern areas of the CxOs as *expanded EA layers*.

Propositions: GEA descriptions of a complex public corporation are to be organized in static GEA grids with two dimensions, those being

1. the administrative levels as the description levels of the GEA grids, and
2. the central management concern areas as the expanded EA viewpoints of the GEA grids.

4.2 ADR Reflection and Learning by Recursive Artifact Development

As the responsible for the process and strategy architecture modeling of the town and the related artifact development, the author used *Kouvola Geagam* and its inherent principles to realization and maintenance of the strategy architecture for evaluation data. Kouvola Geagam instructed the design and implementation of the navigation structures of a *strategy modeling repository*, and the iterative development of a *strategy database*. The artifacts evolved through development cycles, which were considered as recursive ADR cycles to the GEA grid adaption cycles, Fig. 1. We are not reporting the design principles of these recursive artifacts, analysis focuses to them only in the extent where they reflect on the GEA grid adaption.

Both organizational intervention and utility of the artifacts were pursued in the development as ADR method insists [25]. Artifact development and maintenance produced data, such as requirements, documentation, perceived design principles etc. Organizational intervention was traced to town documentation. Such data sources are summarized as organizational data in Fig. 1 with figurative illustrations. As ADR method suggests [25], the *building* of the artifacts, *intervening* in situ, and *evaluation* of the innovations were interlinked and mutual. Central and sectoral management insights were continuously perceived in regular meetings during the development. CxOs were keen on the applicability of the tools in their management role. The annual city audit process took official stance on the prevailing strategy planning principles. User experiences and feedback were gained from the sectoral management. The author acted as principal designer and researcher in the design of the Kouvola Geagam, and the recursive strategy artifacts.

We reflected on the Geagam propositions based on the artifact building and organizational intervention in situ. The propositions were submitted to the evaluation by analyzing the *recursive artifacts* as 'wider set of data', as abduction logic presumes [45]. This was done by analyzing, how the current state strategy architecture descriptions got organized in a deep corporate hierarchy during organizational changes, and what were the emerging management needs in re-organizing the content of these descriptions. Based on the analyses, a revised explanation of GEA grid adaption is proposed for current state GEA management.

4.3   Strategy Architecture Development

Next, the strategy artifacts, their premises and development are described along with the data analysis. Town strategy was institutionalized by strategic planning [48], as instantiations of the town strategy goals by each organizational actor and relevant administrative levels. The strategic planning was updated annually as a part of the budgeting process. In 2009, no systematic long term expressions could be perceived in strategic planning. Strategy visualization and modeling were unknown. There was no information systems support for strategic planning beyond text editing. No adequately specific solution was found in the market either. Goal and objectives, as well as follow-up information were given point-like by actors. This yielded unstructured institutionalization and incoherent implementation of the town strategy.

Strategy discourse was facilitated by GEA practices and tools. Strategy modeling practices were developed along the *strategy-modeling repository*. Secondly, the strategy information management was developed as an in-house *strategy database*. The artifacts were introduced to the central and sectoral managers. The first yielded the visualized

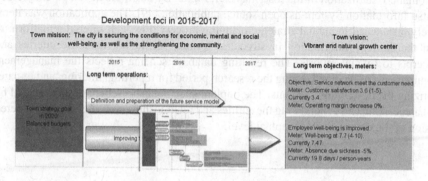

Fig. 2.   *Strategy modeling repository*: Road map for mayor, in budget book in 2015

long term objectives and operations as road maps (Fig. 2), the latter, the structural data for the same (Fig. 3). The development of the strategy artifacts was parallel for practical reasons, carrying a vision of a united system though.

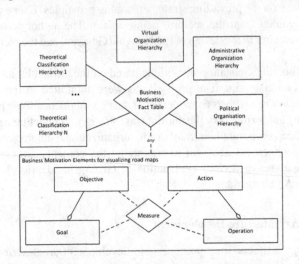

Fig. 3. *Analysis results:* Business motivation elements classified by management structures

Strategy modeling repository. A process modeling tool was deployed for the strategy modeling in a cyclic manner. The town strategy goals were institutionalized as objectives, measures, and related operations as *strategy road map*, of the description owner, Fig. 2. Optional actions maps were further navigable from this picture, as (not clear) in Fig. 2. By 2015, the repository consisted sets of road maps along administrative hierarchy, yielding 'a hierarchical set of descriptions', as *strategy architecture* [33]. The navigation structures of the different repository versions were at the focus of our data analysis, and they were compared to organigrams, process architectures, and suggested GEA grid dimensions.

Strategy database application. The development of the strategy database aimed at automatic visualization of the road maps, cf. Fig. 2. By 2014, the development yielded Ratsu Information System as open source publication [49]. The application was iteratively introduced in annual strategic planning process, Fig. 1. It offered a platform to test the strategy information in structural format, facilitating database queries and excerpts to official reports. The resulting database schema reflects the management requirements as emerged during the research period for reporting, filtering, and re-categorizing the description contents. The implemented database schema was analyzed by re-categorizing and generalizing the entities and relationships, to achieve a reconsidered vision of the database at conceptual level.

5   Findings About GEA Grid Dimensions in Situ

During the development of the strategy modeling repository, we discovered that the tabular data given by managers could be automatically visualized as road maps, and thus leverage on everyday governance as suggested in [7]. This launched the design and implementation of the strategy database with a normalized database schema [49].

The database covered the basic entities that are depicted in Fig. 3 as business motivation elements, such goals, long-term objectives and operations, measures and actions as the refinements of the operations. Business motivation (BM) is used from [36] as one of the 'building blocks' of EA [8]. The conceptual diagram inside the rectangle is figurative, since the BM model was not at the focus of our analysis. Instead, based on the reverse engineering and database schema abstractions, *categorizing dimensions* of the BM elements were identified. Figure 3 illustrates the results as a conceptual diagram of a data-warehouse. BM is related to the categorizing dimensions via a fact table that can be instantiated for any BM element.

The conceptual model in Fig. 3 illustrates the management structures that dictated the management information needs. They are signified as a star-model dimensions for organization hierarchies and a theoretical classification. In our data, all the categorizing dimensions could be hierarchical, and most were. The dimensions also could have relations to each other [49]. There were three types of organization hierarchies. *Administrative organization* refers to line hierarchy of the corporation and its organizational actors. *Political organization* denotes the hierarchical structure of the city council, board, and subordinate boards. *Virtual organization* comprised strategic and political development efforts, e.g., cross-sectoral or cross-agency policy programs, e.g., enforced by the state government or law. In the municipality, these were typically governed by a virtual organization. As one example, the environmental program was one of our pilots when introducing the strategy artifacts. *Theoretical classification hierarchy* refers to the theoretical management classification in use, with possible sub-classes. The number is not limited, some examples are the strategy viewpoints, the EA layers, quality management viewpoints, and various other classifications for various purposes, either district or nation wide. Next, the Geagam propositions (from Sect. 4.1) are reflected based on the strategy architecture data.

5.1   From Classifying GEA Models to Classifying the GEA Model Elements

EA models are typically enlisted in EA grid. Our propositions in Sect. 4.1 suggested *static GEA grid* with two dimensions as 'GEA model container'. The proposed GEA grid dimensions were the administrative levels, and the expanded EA viewpoints achieved by expanding the business architecture layer to its subparts with the stakeholders.

The assumption in 2009 was that it would be enough to classify the business motivation elements firstly according to the administrative organization, and secondly according to the expanded EA viewpoints. The expanded Kouvola Geagam viewpoints were 1. Operational Environment, including strategies, 2. Service & Customer, 3. Information & Data, 4. Personnel, 5. Systems & Technology, and 6. Finance [47]. In the first development cycle of the strategy modeling repository, CxOs corporately produced the road maps for each of these Kouvola Geagam viewpoints. The road maps for the six partial architectures composed kind of crystallized sub-strategies to town strategy. As for the sectoral management, they depicted their road maps for each of the administrative levels without including this classification to Kouvola Geagam viewpoints. However, the sectoral outputs were of interest to CxOs and virtual organizations' managers, because both had a synthetizing role to the whole. The interests focused on particular objectives, e.g., the chief human resource officer (CHRO) was keen to report the objectives and operations of the human resource (HR) development from the road maps of other managers. Thus, very soon the need to re-organize the road map contents emerged.

During the development cycles, instead of one organization hierarchy, three of them emerged. Also organizational classifications were multiple, even though two of them, the EA and the strategy viewpoints had already been converged as one. Consequently, we provided in the strategy database the three organization structures, and a dimension table for any management classification. The ability to select the description contents dynamically by user was provided.

Based on the strategy artifact development for strategy architecture management, the classification of the strategy descriptions into static grids with 2 dimensions showed inadequate at least for their contents. The strategy model elements were classified in the relational database, to enable the re-organization of the description contents by different areas of concern. As a generalization, this could be done to EA descriptions of the other partial architectures too (such as BA, IA, SA, TA). Why CHRO should not be interested in HR related process phases, objects, etc.? We contemplate it inadequate to classify the current state GEA model elements in 2-dimensional frameworks. A similar kind of argument is presented for the GEA models as an implication and a 'best explanation' [45], in Sect. 6.

5.2   From Description Levels to Multiple Management Hierarchies

We proposed the administrative levels of a public corporation as one GEA grid dimension in Sect. 4.1. This was implemented in both of the strategy artifacts. Strategy descriptions hierarchy followed the administrative hierarchy. Notification of the line organization seemed an essential management requirement. The organizational rules may have had effect on that, since the objectives and measures were required at the top administrative levels in the annual budgeting and strategic planning process.

Strategy architecture modeling supported dependencies between the administrative levels in the deep line hierarchy. The administrative managers insisted strategic representations of the subunits under them. E.g., the team of the mayor prioritized and picked the most important objectives of the sectoral and central management road maps into the budget book, as illustrated in Fig. 2. It seemed that a description becomes strategic only after strategic way of processing. Two road maps seemed similar by notation, but the other had been processed strategically and the other not. Strategic descriptions sprang up by prioritizing, synthesis, summing, mean values, or iterating in top-down and bottom-up workshops between administrative levels.

5.3 From GEA Layers to Multiple Theoretical Classifications

Very typically EA grids refer to conventional BA, IA, SA, and TA layers. We proposed in Sect. 4.1, that the CM concern areas should be supported by expanding EA viewpoints in the adapted GEA grid. Figure 3 shows one theoretical classification entity for the *expanded GEA layers* of Kouvola Geagam (listed in Sect. 5.1).

To support the CM concerns, we made an attempt to combine the EA and strategy viewpoints by converging them into one classification. This classification was used for both GEA management and strategy planning purposes. CxO were in the practitioner role both while creating Kouvola Geagam, and in strategy modeling. The first strategy descriptions in 2009 were corporately produced by CxO's. They followed the expanded GEA layers, and were close to the CM units' division as a result but not enough. They could not serve as corporate 'sub-strategies', because CxOs had difficulties to differentiate their 'own' objectives from others'. Accordingly, the next strategy modeling repository version was organized along the CxO roles. In different ADR cycles of the strategy artifacts, no one-to-one relationship between the extended GEA viewpoints (EA + strategy) to prevailing CM functions were reached. This would have required organizational changes, which were not due. This is not necessarily to be aimed either, since theoretical classification is not same as management functions. If CxO roles cannot be mapped to an existing classification, CM functions could be implemented as another one for reporting needs.

As a generalization, we suggest, that any theoretical classification used in the adopting public organization could be presented as a dataware dimension. EA and strategy viewpoints integration could in principal work, since both are theoretical classifications. However, this presumes agreement in the adopting corporation, and in the research society. Next, the findings are discussed and generalizations propounded.

6 Discussion

We suggested in the results that classification of the current state GEA model elements should situationally reflect the prevailing real-world management structures of an adopting public organization. This is illustrated in Fig. 4(a) as a conceptual data-warehouse model. The management structures refer to prevailing organization structures or theoretical classifications as described in Sect. 5. Their amount

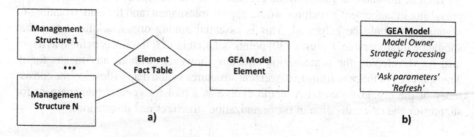

Fig. 4. (a) Generalization of the results as a conceptual model (b) GEA model class

is situational as indicated in Fig. 4(a) by 1…N. The possible practical implications are discussed in Sect. 6.1, and the theoretical ones, the validity and reliability in Sect. 6.2.

6.1   Practical Implications: Dynamic Hypercube for As-is GEA Management

The as-is, or the current state GEA management of a public corporation could benefit of a dynamic hypercube implementation, based on the proposed generalizations in Fig. 4. *The GEA Model* Class in Fig. 4(b) comprises the attributes 'model owner' and 'strategic processing' manner. It relates to many GEA Model Elements (not drawn into Fig. 4). *Model owner* refers to the unit of the adopting organization, which is responsible for the development and maintenance of the model notation and instantiation in situ. For example in our case, the responsible unit was sought and officially named for the process modeling. *Strategic processing* of the strategy road map was described in Sect. 5.3, e.g., as the synthesis and prioritization of the descriptions. Both of the exemplary attributes of the GEA model are dependent on the organizational hierarchies. GEA model entity could thus also benefit from a similar fact table as we proposed for the GEA Model Element in Fig. 4(a). GEA model associations to management structures could also be further added and differentiated. For example in the strategy database, the strategy model elements were associated to management structures via association types *owner*, and *report*.

Relating the GEA models and model elements situationally to management structures would presume hypercube data-warehouse implementation. This type of development of the current state GEA management would open chances to almost unlimited implications. Here we are restricted to mention just few. Any GEA model contents could be refreshed according to user preferences (e.g., categorized by the chosen management structures), as suggested in Fig. 4(b) by the class functions 'ask parameters' and 'refresh'. Organization types in a public corporation could be implemented as a categorizing dimension with associations to any GEA model as a recommended on for that organization type. The static 2-dimensional grids for any organizational actor could be excerpted in real-time by chosen dimensions. Even if the hypercube implementation was not on tap, for an enterprise architect entering in a public organization to implement the current state descriptions, he could anticipate the interests of the various stakeholders by identifying the situational management structures of the organization as *enterprise* (architecture) *dimensions*.

If GEA information followed the prevailing management structures real-time, the prevailing management structures would appear transparent, and the understanding of organization could be enhanced. This is essential among organizational actors that should be interoperable. Kotusev [30] points out, that in [23] the EA is defined as a tool also for developing the organization structure, however, without any means for it. Transparency of the prevailing management structures would help to develop the consistency of the organization. GEA would evolve as a tool for general management for supporting the rationalization of the organization structures and dimensions.

6.2   Theoretical Implication: Differentiating Current and Target State GEA Fit

Typically, in the EA theory, no specific difference is made between the current or target state use of an EA framework. The results here incline to differentiate the GEA methodology for current state and target state GEA management. The current state grid would 'fade out' to become dimensions in a data-warehouse. If the current state GEA management evolved into this direction, it might shift the GEA grid notion towards adaptive EA frameworks [23, 24], and closer to practice of using 'no grid' [6]. According to Buckl et al. [42], the EA grids are often too abstract for real use as such, or too massive and large for practical deployment. They [42] present paths and dependencies of EA models for rearranging them according to management requirements. Our results have resemblances also to model driven architecture [24], which also presumes presenting model and model element dependencies.

Discussing the target state EA grid adaption is beyond the paper. However, the situational EA grid adaption by Hoogervorst and Dietz [41] might suit for the target state GEA development. Kotusev [30] classifies EA management methods as traditional, rigid ones, e.g., in [8, 10, 11, 28], and to more flexible ones concentrating more on the target state EA development, e.g., in [18]. Even though his literature analysis concerns basically IT architecture management methods, the results might be considered indicative to our suggested theoretical implication about separating the adaption principles for GEA grid in the current and target states.

Reliability and validity. The generalization in Fig. 4 is presented with the humble notion, that it is restricted to primary data concerning the strategy architecture development. A municipality is an extraordinary case organization for public administration studies. It has a wide geographical service outlet, multiple service domains, deep hierarchies at least in a dual organization, various enterprise forms, and typically a separate corporate management. As such, it shares structural analogies with the state government. However, one case, principally one researcher, and a single partial architecture set limitations to the generalizability. Consequently, the results cannot be validated based on this study, even though according to the observations, the management requirements for re-organizing the descriptions contents seemed to hold for other architectural viewpoints too. The construction of the artifacts is also never subject independent. Their interpretation as the primary data source is therefore challenging. In the study, the use of recursive artifacts exponentiates the challenge. The development of the artifacts and minutes of the workshops and meetings were submitted to participants. The arguments are also based on conceptual models to make the inferences transparent and arguable. The strategy artifacts and excerpts were published for reliability in [49], and in annual budget and audit books. The results can still be considered initial, typically abductive logic.

7   Conclusions

We described the reflection and learning of an action design research case study in a Finnish city corporation. Government enterprise architecture (GEA) framework adaption guided the development of the strategy architecture. GEA framework adaption principles were evaluated and reconsidered based on that work. As a generalization of the results, we proposed implementing GEA framework as a dynamic data model of the prevailing management structures for the current state GEA. This would facilitate deeper understanding of organization structures, and enhance the GEA method use as a strategic general management tool in public sector.

We reflected on traditional EA framework assumptions, critically questioning the concepts of a given framework and its dimensions. The results imply the current state GEA implementation as a dynamic hypercube along management structures in situ. The suggested approach comes close to model and content driven EA approaches. We acknowledged the restrictions of the study, as for the generalizability of results. Accordingly, we call for further constructive case studies on the GEA framework adaption, differentiated for current state GEA management and situational target state GEA development. GEA tool development as data-warehouses seems a fruitful area to study. Many more research areas can be perceived, e.g., how to automatically visualize the GEA descriptions for each model type, and how to gather the needed tabular information, and classify it according to management structures.

Acknowledgements. To the staff of University of Jyväskylä, City of Kouvola, Kalibu Academy, the friends and family, and anonymous reviewers of Poem 2017 and Tear 2016, Finnish Education Fund and The Nyyssönens' Fund. Soli Deo Gloria!

References

1. Cordella, A.: E-government: towards the e-bureaucratic form? J. Inf. Technol. **22**(3), 265–274 (2007)
2. Op't Land, M., Proper, E., Waage, M., Cloo, J., Steghuis, C.: Enterprise Architecture: Creating Value by Informed Governance. Springer, Berlin (2009). doi:10.1007/978-3-540-85232-2
3. Lankhorst, M., Bayens, G.: A Service-oriented reference architecture for e-government. In: Saha, P. (ed.) Advances in Government Enterprise Architecture, pp. 30–55. IGI Global, Hershey (2009)
4. Hjort-Madsen, K., Burkard, J.: When enterprise architecture meets government: an institutional case study analysis. J. Enterp. Architect. **2**(1), 11–25 (2006)
5. Saha, P.: Advances in Government Enterprise Architecture. IGI Global, Hershey (2009)
6. Ahlemann, F., Stettiner, E., Messerschmidt, M., Legner, C.: Strategic Enterprise Architecture Management: Challenges, Best Practices, and Future Developments. Springer Science & Business Media, Heidelberg (2012). doi:10.1007/978-3-642-24223-6
7. Doucet, G., Gøtze, J., Saha, P., Bernard, S.: Coherency Management: Architecting the Enterprise for Alignment, Agility and Assurance. AuthorHouse, Bloomington (2009)
8. Bernard, S.A.: An Introduction to Enterprise Architecture. AuthorHouse, Bloomington (2012)
9. Strano, C., Rehmani, Q.: The profession of enterprise architect. J. Enterp. Architect. **1**(1), 7–15 (2005)
10. Zachman, J.A.: Enterprise architecture: The issue of the century. Database Programming and Design **10**(3), 44–53 (1997)
11. The open group: TOGAF® 9 Jan 2011. http://pubs.opengroup.org/architecture/togaf9-doc/arch/index.html. Accessed 22nd Oct 2015

12. Leist, S., Zellner, G.: Evaluation of current architecture frameworks. In: Proceedings of the 2006 ACM Symposium on Applied Computing. ACM (2006)

13. Armour, J., Kaisler, S.H., Liu, S.Y.: Building an enterprise architecture step by step. IT Prof. 1(4), 31–39 (1999)

14. Brinkkemper, S., Lyytinen, K., Welke, R.J. (eds.).: Method Engineering: Principles of Method Construction and Tool Support: In: Proceedings of the IFIP TC8, WG8.1/8.2 Working Conference on Method Engineering, 26–28 August 1996, Atlanta, USA. Chapman & Hall, London (1996)

15. Leppänen, M.: An ontological framework and a methodical skeleton for method engineering: a contextual approach. University of Jyväskylä (2005)

16. Hirvonen, A., Pulkkinen, M., et al.: Selection criteria for enterprise architecture methods. In: Proceedings of European Conference on Information Management and Evaluation (2007)

17. Lapalme, J.: Three schools of thought on enterprise architecture. IT Prof. 14(6), 37–43 (2012)

18. Ross, J.W., Weill, P., Robertson, D.: Enterprise Architecture as Strategy: Creating a Foundation for Business Execution. Harvard Business Press, Boston (2006)

19. Bernus, P., Nemes, L., Schmidt, G.J.: Handbook on Enterprise Architecture. Springer Science & Business Media, Heidelberg (2012). doi:10.1007/978-3-540-24744-9

20. Graves, T.: Real Enterprise Architecture. Tetdradian, Colchester (2008)

21. Christiansen, P., Gøtze, J.: Trends in governmental enterprise architecture: reviewing national EA programs – Part 1. J. Enterp. Architect. 3(1), 9 (2007)

22. Graves, T.: Enterprise Architecture: A Pocket Guide. ITGP, Ely (2009)

23. Lankhorst, M. (ed.): Enterprise Architecture at Work: Modeling, Communication and Analysis, 2nd edn. Springer, Heidelberg (2009)

24. OMG: Model Driven Architecture (MDA); MDA Guide rev. 2.0. OMG document ormsc/2014-06-01

25. Sein, M., Henfridsson, O., Purao, S., Rossi, M., Lindgren, R.: Action design research. MIS Q. 35(1), 37–56 (2011)

26. Valtonen, K., et al.: Government enterprise architecture grid adaptation in Finland. In: 42nd Hawaii 2009 International Conference on System Sciences, HICSS 2009 (2009)

27. Bente, S., Bombosch, U., Langade, S.: Collaborative Enterprise Architecture: Enriching EA with Lean, Agile, and Enterprise 2.0 Practices. Newnes, Boston (2012)

28. Whitehouse, O.: Federal enterprise architecture framework, Version 2, January 2013

29. Dictionary.com. (2016). http://www.dictionary.com/browse/framework?s=t. Accessed 31th Aug 2016

30. Kotusev, S., Mohini, S., Storey, I.: Consolidating enterprise architecture management research. In: IEEE International Conference on HICSS (2015)

31. Pulkkinen, M.: Systemic management of architectural decisions in enterprise architecture planning. four dimensions and three abstraction levels. In: Proceedings of the 39th Annual Hawaii International Conference on System Sciences (HICSS 2006). IEEE (2006)

32. IFIP-IFAC Task Force.: GERAM: Generalised enterprise reference architecture and methodology. IFIP-IFAC Task Force on Architectures for Enterprise Integration, March Version, 1(3) (1999)

33. Winter, R., Fischer, R.: Essential layers, artifacts, and dependencies of enterprise architecture. J. Enterp. Architect. 3(2), 7–18 (2007)

34. Simon, D., Fischbach, K., Schoder, D.: An exploration of enterprise architecture research. Commun. Assoc. Inf. Syst. 32(1), 1–72 (2013)

35. Pulkkinen, M.: Enterprise architecture as a collaboration tool: discursive process for enterprise architecture management, planning and development. University of Jyväskylä, Jyväskylä (2008)

36. Simon, D., Fischbach, K., Schoder, D.: Enterprise architecture management and its role in corporate strategic management. Inf. Syst. and e-Bus. Manag. **12**(1), 5–42 (2014)
37. Spewak, S.H., Hill, S.C.: Enterprise Architecture Planning: Developing a Blueprint for Data, Applications and Technology. Wiley, Chichester (1992)
38. Public Administration: Recommendation for National EA planning and design method (2012). http://www.jhs-suositukset.fi/suomi/jhs179. Accessed 19th Aug 2016
39. Mayo, D., Tiemann, M.: EA: IT's not just for IT anymore. J. Enterp. Archit. **1**(1), 36–44 (2005)
40. Perks, C., Beveridge, T.: Guide to enterprise IT architecture. Springer Science & Business Media, New York (2007). doi:10.1007/b98880
41. Hoogervorst, J.A., Dietz, J.L.: Enterprise architecture in enterprise engineering. Enterp. Model. and Inf. Syst. Architect. **3**(1), 3–13 (2015)
42. Buckl, S., Ernst, A.M., Lankes, J., Matthes, F.: Enterprise architecture management pattern catalog. Technical Report TB 0801, V. 1.0. Technical University of Munchen, Ernst Denert-Stiftungslehrstuhl (2008)
43. Population Register Centre.: Suomi.fi – at your service (2017). https://www.suomi.fi/frontpage. Accessed 15th July 2017
44. Valtonen, K., Leppänen, M.: Business architecture development at public administration – insights from government EA method engineering project in Finland. In: Papadopoulos, G., Wojtkowski, W., Wojtkowski, G., Wrycza, S., Zupancic, J. (eds.) Information Systems Development. Springer, Boston (2009)
45. Levin-Rozalis, M.: Using abductive research logic to construct a rigorous explanation of amorphous evaluation Findings. J. Multidisciplinary Evaluation **6**(13), 1–14 (2009)
46. Valtonen, K., et al.: EA as a tool in change and coherency management - a case of a local government. In: IEEE 43rd International Conference on HICSS (2010)
47. Valtonen, K., et al.: Enterprise architecture descriptions for enhancing local government transformation and coherency management: case study. In: Enterprise Distributed Object Computing Conference Workshops (EDOCW), 2011 15th IEEE International. IEEE, 2011. pp. 360–369 (2011)
48. Mintzberg, H.: The fall and rise of strategic planning. Harv. Bus. Rev. **72**(1), 107–114 (1994)
49. Ratsu information system for strategic planning, Kouvola (2014). https://www.avoindata.fi/. Accessed 15th July 2017

NEXT: Generating Tailored ERP Applications from Ontological Enterprise Models

Henk van der Schuur[1]([⊠]), Erik van de Ven[1], Rolf de Jong[1],
Dennis Schunselaar[2], Hajo A. Reijers[2], Michiel Overeem[1], Machiel de Graaf[1],
Slinger Jansen[3], and Sjaak Brinkkemper[3]

[1] Department of Architecture and Innovation, AFAS Software,
Leusden, The Netherlands
hwschuur@gmail.com, {e.vdven,r.dejong,m.overeem,m.degraaf}@afas.nl
[2] Department of Computer Science, Vrije Universiteit, Amsterdam, The Netherlands
{d.m.m.schunselaar,h.a.reijers}@vu.nl
[3] Department of Information and Computing Sciences, Utrecht University,
Utrecht, The Netherlands
{s.jansen,s.brinkkemper}@uu.nl

Abstract. Tailoring Enterprise Resource Planning (ERP) software to the needs of the enterprise still is a technical endeavor, often requiring the (de)activation of modules, modification of configuration files or even execution of database queries. Considering the large body of work on Enterprise Modeling and Model-Driven Software Engineering, this is remarkable: Ideally, one models one's own enterprise and, at the press of a button, ERP software tailored to the needs of the modeled enterprise is generated. In this paper, we introduce NEXT, a novel model-driven software generation approach being developed with precisely this goal in mind. It uses the expressive power of ontological enterprise models (OEMs) to generate ERP cloud applications. An OEM only describes the real-world phenomena essential to the enterprise, using terms and customizations specific to the enterprise. We present our considerations during development of the OEM modeling language, which is designed to capture the specifics of enterprise phenomena in a way that technical details can be derived from it. We expect NEXT to drastically shorten the time-to-market of ERP software, from months–years to hours–days.

Keywords: Ontological Enterprise Modeling · Model-driven software development · Software generation · Enterprise Resource Planning

1 Introduction

ERP software has become fundamental in the day-to-day operation of enterprises. Although most ERP applications provide functionality to tailor the software to the specific needs of the enterprise, generally, customization possibilities

This work is a result of the AMUSE project. See www.amuse-project.org.

G. Poels et al. (Eds.): PoEM 2017, LNBIP 305, pp. 283–298, 2017.
https://doi.org/10.1007/978-3-319-70241-4_19

are limited and require technical knowledge from the end-user. As an example, a fixed number of free input fields, input records or modules can be activated or deactivated, for instance through advanced management tools, specific configuration files or by executing particular database queries. As a result, enterprises have to tailor their processes to the software, instead of the software being tailored to the enterprise. This is surprising given the comprehensive bodies of work on Enterprise Modeling and Model-Driven Software Engineering. Ideally, one models one's own enterprise and, at the press of a button, ERP software tailored to the needs of the modeled enterprise is generated.

In this paper, we show preliminary results obtained during the ongoing development of NEXT. NEXT is a novel software generation approach using ontological enterprise models (OEMs) to generate ERP cloud applications. With NEXT, functional application requirements are separated from the application logic and the technical foundations of the application: all enterprise-specific requirements are expressed in the OEM through one modeling language, allowing for generation of a functionally tailored ERP application. This work is a first effort to describe the many aspects and ideas encompassing our approach (see Fig. 1). First, we introduce NEXT's declarative OEM Language and present our considerations during its development. The OEM Language allows the modeler to reason and model in terms of real-world enterprise concepts, without having to consider technical implementation details (arrow 1 in Fig. 1). The language is designed such that an OEM forms the basis for generating an integrated ERP cloud application (arrow 2). As a result, the generated application is tailored to the needs of the modeled enterprise by definition (arrow 3).

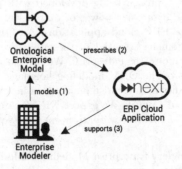

Fig. 1. The NEXT software generation approach

This paper is structured as follows: in Sect. 2, NEXT's OEM Language is outlined. In Sect. 3, we illustrate the model transformation and software generation processes through three concrete models, and show the generated ERP cloud application for each of these models. Finally, we compare our approach with similar enterprise modeling and model-driven software generation initiatives in Sect. 4, and present conclusions and future work in Sect. 5.

2   The Ontological Enterprise Modeling Language

In this section, we describe the OEM Language as well as our considerations during the development of the language.

During the past decade, being ignorant of existing Enterprise Modeling (EM) languages, the OEM Language has been developed within AFAS. Recently, we have started evaluating existing EM approaches for their applicability to automatically generate ERP software and none sufficed [1]; also see Sect. 4. Next to this, from a pragmatic side, by developing our own language we have full flexibility to (re)define the language to best fit our needs (see Fig. 1 and Sect. 2.2). At the same time, we acknowledge that a more thorough analysis is required to further justify the existence of another EM language; this analysis is subject of future work.

In the remainder of this section, we start with an exemplifying model to familiarize the reader with the language and its main constructs. Next, we present our considerations during development of the language.

2.1   EnYoi: An Example Enterprise

Within this example, we suppose there is an enterprise named EnYoi. EnYoi's core business is selling shaving products. Its main customers are hotels. Products are sold both ad hoc and through subscriptions. From time to time, EnYoi sends free trial products to its customers to find out if there is substantial interest in the products to bring them to market. Already from the description of EnYoi, we can identify concepts that are relevant within EnYoi, e.g., selling, products, subscriptions, customers. For particular concepts, one would expect specific application functionality, e.g., when an enterprise sells physical products, the enterprise needs an application to register orders, maintain stock levels, and obtain actual insights in the (historical) economical performance of the enterprise. The identified enterprise concepts of EnYoi map onto the four main stereotypes in the OEM Language: Entity, Role, Event, and Agreement. Using our example enterprise EnYoi, we elaborate on each of them.

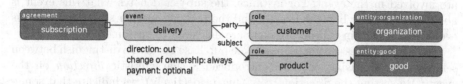

Fig. 2. A simple OEM used by EnYoi

In Fig. 2, we have the OEM of EnYoi. The hotels EnYoi is delivering to are denoted with the block *organization*. Similarly, what EnYoi is delivering are goods (denoted by the block *good*). The organization block and good block are both of the type **entity**. Entities are things in the real world around us, e.g., time, locations, people, organizations. Furthermore, entities have a set of universal, constant properties, i.e., all physical things (goods, persons, etc.) take up space, are tangible and have weight. To capture the semantics of an entity, each entity is of a particular type. Currently, the three most mature types of entities for which we have implemented specific functionality in the application are: organization, person, and good. Using the type of an entity, we deduce common-sense[1] functionality. For instance, for the organization type, we generate functionality to administer, i.a., contact persons, date of establishment, date of closing down, email address (all common-sense in our ERP domain). Analogously, the entity type person entails functionality related to, i.a., date of birth, sick leave, scheduling. Finally, for the entity type good, functionality is generated related to, i.a., physicality (size, location, weight), value, ownership. All common-sense functionality comes for free, i.e., *without the need to model this explicitly*[2]. At the time of writing, we already have additional types in scope such as location, time, room and country, which will be detailed in future work.

Next to entities, we have **roles**. Roles allow the modeler to denote in what way entities are considered from within the enterprise. For instance, for EnYoi, hotels perform the role *customer*. Analogously, some goods perform the role of *product*. Note that not all goods within EnYoi need to be products, e.g., forklift trucks used to move pallets with shaving products will typically not be a product but it is a good. Entities can perform multiple roles from the perspective of an enterprise, e.g., some organizations might be both customer and supplier.

As mentioned, EnYoi delivers products to its customers. The *delivery* of products is modeled using an **event**. Events are used to abstract real-world business activities that are relevant for the enterprise to administer. Although at design-time an event is a static, timeless component, during run-time, an event is executed at a particular moment in time. The potential run-time effects of an event (e.g., stock level decrease) are encoded using *characteristics*. By combining characteristics, we know what an event means, i.e., the meaning of an event is determined by the combination of the meanings of the individual characteristics. Based on the characteristics of an event, we add common-sense to the model. Using the characteristics *subject* and *party* of an event, depicted on the edges between events and roles, we know how these roles and their entities are involved in the event. For instance, the subject denotes what this event is about, e.g., *what* is being delivered, and the party is another stakeholder in this event. Again, within EnYoi, products are delivered to customers.

Some enterprises sell goods, and some purchase goods. To distinguish between selling and purchasing, we have introduced a characteristic *direction* on the events. By setting the direction to *in* (*out* respectively), we indicate that something of value enters (leaves respectively) the enterprise. Next to selling and purchasing goods, enterprises can also rent (or rent out) goods. In the former

---

[1] We use the term 'common-sense' in line with the work of Fox [2], i.e., information that is deduced from the semantics of the model.

[2] Every stereotype can also have modeled (non-semantic) attributes, e.g., description, number of employees, wedding date, margin, or attachment.

case, there is a change of ownership, and in the latter there is not. This resulted in a *change of ownership* characteristic. Next to administering that an enterprise obtained the ownership of a good, the enterprise also differentiates in what capacity they own something, which is supported in the *ownership type* characteristic; currently trade item and asset are supported. The direction, change of ownership, and ownership type characteristics specify the (financial) effects on stock and the general ledger accounts, e.g., if the enterprise obtains the ownership of an asset (direction in), then periodic deprecations of the asset is journalized in the general ledgers. Furthermore, if the enterprise loses the ownership of a trade item (direction out), then the stock levels will be decreased. In the EnYoi example, for some deliveries a payment was expected and some were free of charge. This can be indicated using the *payment* characteristic on an event, i.e., is there a monetary claim created to the party after executing this event. By setting the payment characteristic to *optional*, the generated application will give the user the run-time choice to create a monetary claim for every event instance. Based on the payment characteristic, we deduce common-sense that includes, i.a., accounting functionality to give insights into the ledger accounts and trial balance (see Sect. 3).

The last model element in Fig. 2 is the *subscription* which has type **agreement**. This indicates that deliveries can be performed within the context of an agreement. An agreement in itself only represents the fact that there is an agreement with a second party. The contents of the agreement are represented by events that are connected to the agreement (e.g., delivery for EnYoi).

2.2   Language Considerations

As shown in Fig. 1, an enterprise modeler models the OEM using the OEM Language (1). This OEM prescribes an ERP cloud application (2). In its turn, this application supports the enterprise (3). For each of these arrows, we present our challenges in the form of questions we posed ourselves and our considerations in development of the OEM Language in the remainder of this section.

(1) An Enterprise Modeler models an OEM
What is our target audience? Current ERP software requires people with substantial technical knowledge to configure and tailor the software towards the enterprise needs. Often these people are less familiar with the enterprise itself. As a result, considerable communication is required between people familiar with the enterprise and the more technical application managers. Within NEXT, we have targeted the enterprise modeler familiar with the enterprise as primary audience for the OEM Language. Enterprise modelers are not necessary familiar with technical concepts like foreign keys, database tables, and validations, but are familiar with the people, products, processes, and other concepts within the enterprise. To better connect to the target audiences, we have stereotypes and characteristics in the OEM Language that are named after the real world phenomena they are representing, e.g., agreement, or payment. Please note that the models we are showing are *a* possible visualization. The usability of

language by end users is still subject of future investigation. For the first release of NEXT, all the OEMs for enterprises will be created by modelers from AFAS.

What should be expressible within our language and how? As mentioned in the introduction, we want to separate the functional application requirements from the technical foundation of the application. As a result, our OEM Language should only contain enterprise concepts; it should not contain IT artifacts. To determine which enterprise concepts should be part of the OEM Language, we continuously analyze AFAS' current ERP application named Profit, which is currently used by more than 1.3 million end-users of 10.000 customers. By analyzing the (usage of) functionality provided by Profit, we verify that all enterprise aspects of the current set of customers can actually be expressed in the OEM Language. This analysis is conducted by processing all fields, screens, database tables, etc. of Profit. For each field, screen, database tables, etc., we determine with which functional reason it was introduced. Furthermore, we determine if there is variability of the particular functionality between enterprises, i.e., which functionality is used differently by the customers, e.g., the moment an order is considered finalized differs per enterprise. If functionality is used differently between customers, we investigate what the reason behind this is. Depending on the reason, the level of variation, and the number of customers using a particular variation, we decide whether to encode this variability in the OEM Language by means of characteristics. Finally, based on this analysis, we determine if, and how, the functionality the screen, database table, etc. represents should be part of the OEM Language. We determine this as follows: If there is no variability in a particular part of the functionality among enterprises, then this is not explicitly represented in the OEM Language (this part of the functionality will be generated without modeling it). If there is variability, then we try to map this onto real world phenomena. If such a mapping exists, then the real world phenomenon will be part of the languages, e.g., change of ownership, agreement. So far, we did not encounter any variability in functionality where this mapping to the real world phenomena did not exist. Using this mapping onto real world phenomena, we have created our characteristics and stereotypes.

If all functionality provided by Profit can be modeled using the OEM Language, then the first version of the OEM Language is considered complete. As a result, the OEM Language will, initially, be scoped to the current functionality of Profit. In later phases, this scope is widened for every new release of Profit. Also, when required, the OEM Language will be extended with additional concepts to support functionality (currently) not supported within Profit.

(2) An OEM prescribes an Application

How to ensure every OEM is complete and valid input for generating exactly one application? The goal of an OEM is to prescribe an application tailored towards the needs of an enterprise. As a result, given an OEM, it should always be complete and valid input for generating an application. Furthermore, there cannot be two functionally different applications adhering to one and the same OEM. This would mean that the enterprise modeler cannot anticipate what functionality is provided in the generated application, which is highly undesirable for obvious reasons. To ensure that there cannot exist two functionally different applications based on one and the same OEM, we are formalizing the language. This way, there cannot be any ambiguity with respect to which functionality should be generated based on a particular OEM. To ensure that every OEM is complete and valid input for generating an integrated, fully-functioning application, every stereotype is allowed to exist independently within a model, i.e., an OEM that consists of one stereotype in isolation is already complete and valid input for generating the application. Furthermore, stereotypes can only be composed if the composition maintains the completeness and validity of the OEM. As a result, every OEM is complete and valid by construction.

How to keep the language maintainable when concepts change over time? The environment around an enterprise is always evolving, e.g., rules and regulations change, distribution channels change, more innovative competitors appear. As a result, the OEM Language also needs to evolve, e.g., maternity leave, sick leave, holiday, etc. are concepts that did not always exist. When concepts change, or are introduced, one ideally only changes the stereotypes representing these concepts in the language, i.e., ideally the changes are local. We attempt to achieve these local changes by requiring that the composition of stereotypes only adds behavior and does not change existing behavior. As a result, if a concept changes, we only need to change the stereotypes and compositions representing the concept. Would we not have local changes, then a change of a concept would require a change to the stereotypes and compositions representing the concepts, as well as, stereotypes and compositions affecting the stereotypes and compositions representing the concepts.

(3) An Application supports the Enterprise

How to support variability within enterprises? Not a single enterprise is exactly identical to another enterprise. To capture the variability between enterprises, we have introduced the characteristics on events (Sect. 2.1). Also variability exists *within* an enterprise, e.g., in the case of EnYoi, some deliveries require a payment and some are for free. This internal variability is encoded within the OEM Language by offering the enterprise modeler the possibility to postpone setting characteristics till run-time. This means that for every new run-time instance, the characteristics can be set differently.

How to provide the same run-time support as Profit? Profit provides run-time support related to: workflow, rules, Key Performance Indicators (KPIs), authorization, customer portals, etc. All this run-time functionality should be provided using the OEM. After all, the OEM prescribes the applications. In current approaches, these KPIs are defined by hand. Often they also need to be tailored towards a particular enterprise. In order to automate this manual endeavor, we have created deduction rules, which, given an OEM, automatically can deduce the KPIs and present them and their values during run-time. The other functionality, e.g., workflow, is still under investigation. Particularly, if and how the functionality can be deduced from an OEM and which information is still missing in the OEM Language to automatically deduce this functionality with its possible variability.

3   From Design-Time to Run-Time

How NEXT cloud applications are to be generated and deployed is depicted in Fig. 3 (arrows labeled with numbers correspond to the arrows in Fig. 1). Starting on the ontological layer, the real-world enterprise is abstracted by an OEM. OEMs are expressed in the OEM Language using our modeling tool called Studio. Studio understands the OEM Language as well as the common-sense (see Sect. 2) that is part of it. The resulting OEM serves as input for the cloud application generation process, which is orchestrated by the NEXT Cloud Manager. The Cloud Manager's responsibilities are fourfold:

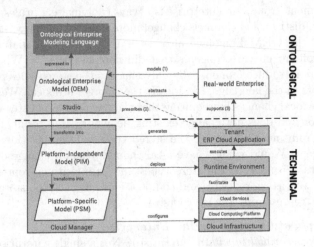

Fig. 3. Model-Driven Software Generation with NEXT

First, the Cloud Manager reads the OEM and transforms it to a Platform-Independent Model (PIM), which contains high-level application constructs that establish the required run-time functionality. Next, it uses the PIM to create a Platform-Specific Model (PSM) that forms the basis for the actual software generation process. Secondly, the Cloud Manager configures the cloud infrastructure. The cloud infrastructure consists of (1) a cloud computing platform such as Microsoft Azure, Amazon Web Services or Google Cloud Platform and (2) cloud services on top of the cloud computing platform such as application hosting services, event buses or database services. The Cloud Manager determines the type and amount of services required. Thirdly, the Cloud Manager deploys the runtime environment in which the tenant ERP cloud application is executed. For example, generic frontend and backend framework code used by the cloud application is deployed. Also, generic runtime services such as an authentication service and logging service are deployed. Finally, the tenant ERP cloud application itself is generated. The application is generated based on the PSM, which was created earlier from the PIM (and indirectly, the OEM). After the Cloud Manager has completed its task, a fresh NEXT ERP cloud application tailored to the modeled enterprise is generated and ready for use by that enterprise. Many technical details involving our software generation approach are omitted to conserve space, and are detailed elsewhere[3].

The remainder of this section describes how an OEM transforms to a corresponding PIM and onwards to a PSM. In three steps, we build the OEM of the EnYoi example enterprise from Sect. 2. See Fig. 4. Each of the columns depicts one particular OEM (top 'OEM' layer), as well as the transformation to the corresponding PIM and PSM ('PIM' and 'PSM' layers). We will start with a simple OEM on the left and expand the model as we go from left to right. This is done in such a way that a model in a particular cell c is a fragment of the model in the cell to the right of c. Every OEM is self-contained: an OEM in itself is sufficient to generate an application from. The cells in the PIM and PSM rows are complementary, i.e. PIM/PSM elements in cell c should also be considered to be part of every cell to the right of c. The colors of the blocks with black text in the OEM and PIM layers denote a causal relationship: colored rectangular blocks in a particular column's cell c are the result of the rectangular blocks with the same color(s) in the cell above c. For example, the green elements Organizations and Goods in columns ❶ and ❸ in the PIM layer result from the green organization and good entities in the OEM layer, respectively. Below, the transformations in each of the columns ❶–❸ are described in more detail.

❶ An Organization Performs a Customer Role...

The first OEM is composed of a customer *role* which is performed by an organization *entity*. The design-time entity organization results in functionality to create, read, update, and delete (CRUD) organization instantiations in the PIM. As mentioned, the fact that organizations can have contact persons is considered common-sense in our ERP domain. CRUD is therefore *also* generated for contact persons. In addition, functionality is generated to assign contact persons to organizations. Similarly, because of the customer role in the OEM, the role customer can be assigned to an organization. Furthermore, generic application functionality is generated irrespective of the source OEM. This is represented by the PIM level Runtime Framework block. The runtime framework establishes basic navigation (including pages, lists, forms, etc.), search, and reporting functionality for each application.

Next, all PIM blocks (CRUD, Runtime Framework) and their elements are transformed into technical counterparts in the PSM. The PSM consists of code generator templates for both the front end and back end of the NEXT runtime[4]. For example, the CRUD block is translated into code generator templates to accommodate the run-time creation, presentation, revision and deletion of

---

[3] For example, NEXT uses Event Sourcing [3] to ensure that all changes to the application state are stored as an event sequence. Using this sequence of events, application-wide features such as auditing, logging of in-the-field software operation and usage [4] as well as application rollbacks are implemented [5,6].

[4] At the time of writing, we have front end code generator templates for HTML, Javascript, and CSS. The back end generator templates currently generate C# code.

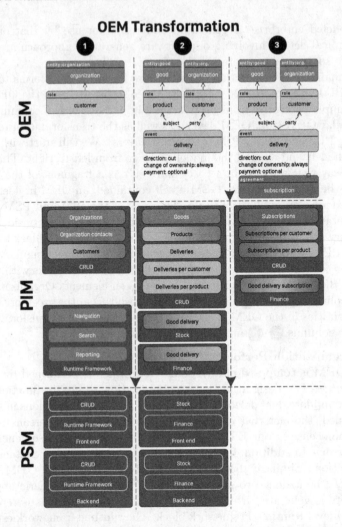

Fig. 4. Three OEMs and their transformations to corresponding PIMs and PSMs. Each OEM cell is independent, whereas the PIM and PSM cells also implicitly include the cells to the left. All OEMs result in a functioning cloud application (see Fig. 5).

organizations. Using the same techniques, the Navigation, Search and Reporting functionality of the Runtime Framework are transformed to the PSM level.

② ...in a Delivery Event...

In column ②, the OEM is further extended with three elements. First, the delivery *event* is added. Secondly, by assigning a role to the event's subject characteristic, one models what is going to be delivered by the modeled enterprise. In the OEM of column ②, goods that perform the product role can be subject of the delivery event.

The extension of the OEM with the delivery event, the product role, and the good entity results in additional PIM elements. First, CRUD functionality specific to the good entity is added, including functionality to assign the product role to existing goods. Furthermore, CRUD functionality is added specific to the delivery event so that new deliveries of products to customers can be created.

As mentioned in Sect. 2.1, run-time event instantiations are temporal by definition, i.e. an event is always executed at a particular moment in time. Also, events have various characteristics which can be set to configure the precise ontological meaning and resulting run-time behavior of the event. If there is at least one event in the OEM with {subject: good; change of ownership: yes; direction: out} characteristics, Stock logic is generated on the PIM level: if there are enterprise events that move goods (i.e., a physical, tangible, valuable object) outwards, it is plausible that the enterprise would like to have insight in the (remaining) stock levels of the particular good. Analogously, the Finance element is generated on the PIM level if there is at least one event in the OEM with characteristics {subject: good; payment: yes}: if one expects to receive or perform payments, one would also like to obtain insights in financial journal entries, revenue, profit and loss account, the enterprise's trial balance, etc. Note that if there is variability in the stock logic, e.g., deliveries without a change of stock, then this variability should be reflected in the OEM Language, e.g., by means of characteristics.

On the PSM level, for both the front end and back end, additional code generator templates are instantiated to generate the code required for the additional Stock and Finance functionality from the PIM level.

❸ ...According to a Subscription Agreement

Finally, in column ❸, a subscription *agreement* is added to the OEM. The delivery event can now be part of an agreement: as opposed to delivering in an ad hoc and impromptu fashion (column ❷), the delivery event can now be the consequence of, and governed by, a subscription agreement. The subscription forms an agreement in which delivery concerns such as the delivery frequency, the amount to be delivered, subscription duration, etc. are established. A single agreement can govern multiple events, e.g. delivery, invoicing, and payment.

Again, the addition of a new OEM element results in an extension of the PIM. First, CRUD functionality specific to the subscription agreement is added, including functionality to assign subscriptions to existing customers. Also, the Finance block that was added to the PIM in column ❷, is extended in the PIM of column ❸ because of the addition of the subscription element in the OEM. Since the delivery can now be governed by the subscription, both the outgoing value and the expected revenue can be calculated within the subscription context and period. Additional financial overviews, such as an operations overview and operations forecast, are generated in the PIM.

On the PSM level, no additional elements are introduced: all PIM elements from column ❸ are expressed with the PSM elements in columns ❶ and ❷.

Current State of the Runtime

To show the current state of the NEXT runtime, Fig. 5 shows run-time screenshots of generated NEXT cloud applications for each of the OEMs in Fig. 4. The application of ❶ is rather basic and straightforward: organizations can be created and listed, and they can be assigned a customer role (note that already with application ❶, basic functionality such as navigation and search is available). With the application generated from ❷, good deliveries can be created. Based on run-time deliveries, stock mutations, a stock overview as well as ledger balances are automatically derived. Finally, with the application based on OEM ❸, delivery subscriptions can also be created. Note that the start and end date, as well as the subscription duration are automatically derived.

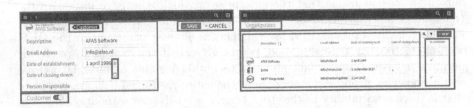

❶ *Organizations can be created and can be assigned the customer role*

❷ *Good deliveries can be created; a stock overview and a ledger balance are derived*

❸ *A subscription and subscription (delivery) lines can be created*

Fig. 5. Screenshots of NEXT applications based on the three OEMs in Fig. 4. UI elements are annotated with the color of the particular stereotype(s) causing generation of the elements, i.e., green: entity (organization, person), blue: role (customer, product), yellow: event (delivery), red: agreement (subscription). Purple indicates generic application functionality that is generated irrespective of the underlying OEM. Full-size versions can be downloaded from www.amuse-project.org/portal-amuse/nextruntime. (Color figure online)

At the time of writing, NEXT itself consists of more than 580 KLOC and the most substantial OEMs currently generate 1.2 MLOC.

4   Related Work

With NEXT, we connect the worlds of enterprise modeling (EM) and model-driven software engineering. Next to this, work has been done on creating models of ERP functionality. We provide related work from all three domains.

4.1   Enterprise Modeling

In our previous work [1], we compared EM approaches on their applicability for automatically generating ERP Software. These approaches included, among others: ArchiMate [7], ARIS [8], CIMOSA [9], DEMO [10], MEMO [11], MERODE [12], and UEML [13]. We show some of the highlights of [1] in the context of this paper. We do so, by going through the steps listed in Fig. 1 and show the requirements on the EM approach. We omit step (3) since none of the approaches are applicable to automatically generate ERP software [1].

(1) An Enterprise Modeler Models an OEM
One aspect on which NEXT sets itself apart from existing EM approaches is the ontological aspect [1]. With this, we do not mean that existing approaches do not have ontologies, but that the NEXT ontology is on a different level; it has more detail. For example, within DEMO [10], there are so-called transactions. The ontological characteristics of a transaction is that it represent a set of steps, i.a., request, promise, and accept. Within DEMO, the transaction itself only has a label associated to it. In NEXT, we aim to add more information, e.g., within *events* (Sect. 2.1), we have characteristics to detail the semantics of a particular event and not only the steps every event goes through. If we would translate the ideas from NEXT to DEMO, this would mean that more information is known about transactions, e.g., whether it entails the sale of an item, or borrowing a book. Similarly, in the MEMO approach [11], there are processes. These processes do have an ontological distinction between automatic, semi-automatic, and manual. But apart from this, processes have a label with no further semantics for the application. Another differentiating aspect between NEXT and some EM approaches is the targeted audience. Within some approaches, information needs to be provided in a programming-like style. In NEXT, we take the business user as a target audience. This target audience is usually not familiar with programming. If we take the DEMO approach again [10], then within DEMO there is a so-called *action model*. The action model specifies the action rules that serve as guidelines for the actors. The specification of an action model is syntax-wise very close to the syntax of a programming languages. Other approaches where some aspects of the approach require a user with programming skills include [1]: ARIS [8], CIMOSA [9], and MERODE [12].

(2) An OEM Prescribes an Application

One of the most essential parts for describing the application from an enterprise model is formal (execution) semantics. After all, without clear semantics, either functionally different applications would adhere to the same enterprise model, or it is not possible at all to generate an application. Most of the EM approaches have formal (execution) semantics [1]. Some, like ArchiMate [7], CIMOSA [9], DEMO [10], and UEML [13], are not completely formally defined with respect to (execution) semantics [1].

4.2   Model-Driven Software Engineering

Kulkarni [14] reflects on decades of experience in delivering large business applications using a model-driven development approach, and concludes that models with a higher level of abstraction and expressive power lead to many advantages such as (a) more significant operational involvement of functional experts, (b) early determination and elimination of errors, (c) application-wide implementation of design decisions and policies, and (d) separation of the functional application specification from technology concerns. The NEXT ontological enterprise models encompass a high level of abstraction and we pursue these advantages. Since the OEM Language abstracts from technical elements such as window types, forms, and batch functionality (see Sect. 2), we believe it provides a higher level of abstraction than the high-level language Q++ developed by Kulkarni [14]. Existing model-driven enterprise engineering solutions such as Mendix, Servoy, or Betty Blocks[5] are not based on ontological models; these require technical knowledge from the modeler to enable and influence architectural aspects such as storage, business logic, and frontend behavior [15]. While the aforementioned solutions allow for the creation of generic business applications which support communication, collaboration, and content creation between business functions, NEXT is specifically designed to model, understand and generate integrated ERP applications. The model-driven enterprise engineering solutions from IBM[6] and OpenText[7] specifically allow for the creation of business process management (BPM) applications and are often used on top of legacy software. Contrarily, NEXT is not designed to be used on top of legacy software; with the NEXT approach, integrated, fully-functioning ERP applications are generated.

4.3   ERP Modeling

Work has been done on creating models of ERP systems with the goal to configure an ERP system to the requirements an enterprise, e.g., [16]. Within these approaches, an abstraction is made of an existing ERP system by means of a model, a model is created of the customer requirements, and manually a mapping is made between both models to see how to configure the ERP system.

---

[5] www.mendix.com, www.servoy.com, www.bettyblocks.com.

[6] www.ibm.com/software/products/en/business-process-manager-family.

[7] www.opentext.com/what-we-do/products/business-process-management.

Our approach sets itself apart from these approaches in a number of ways: (1) similar to existing EM approaches, the ontological aspect is limited, (2) we are aiming for an automated approach; no manual mapping, and (3) NEXT is not intended to be used on existing software systems.

5   Conclusions and Future Work

The paper is a first effort to describe the many aspects and ideas that encompass our NEXT software generation approach. We show that ontological enterprise models can form the basis for generating integrated, fully-functioning Enterprise Resource Planning (ERP) cloud applications.

We have presented the NEXT Ontological Enterprise Modeling Language, a language specific to the ERP domain. The language is being designed to provide sufficiently powerful semantics for modeling real-world enterprises, i.e., express concepts such as an enterprise's people, products, and business processes. Every model created with the language forms the basis for an integrated, fully-functioning ERP cloud application, tailored to the needs and requirements of the modeled enterprise. The OEM Language is being designed for the modeler to easily comprehend and maintain the enterprise model, while requiring minimal technical knowledge. Apart from the language itself, we have presented our considerations during development of the language.

Through three exemplifying OEMs, we have illustrated the OEM transformation process, and how we are able to generate sophisticated run-time ERP application functionality and behavior from (the composition of) basic modeling language stereotypes. More complex OEMs will be subject of future work.

As NEXT is under development, its OEM Language and software generation approach are further enriched, refined and evaluated continuously. Also, many technical aspects that encompass NEXT, such as (partial) code generation techniques, blue green deployment, and real-time monitoring, are considered out of the scope of this paper and are or will be detailed elsewhere [6].

NEXT is designed to allow for creation of tailor-made software using one toolset and modeling language. We expect NEXT to drastically shorten the average time-to-market of ERP software, from months–years to hours–days. Despite the developmental stage of NEXT, we hope that this paper sheds new light on the potential of (ontological) enterprise modeling.

Acknowledgements. This paper was supported by the NWO AMUSE project (628. 006.001): a collaboration between Vrije Universiteit Amsterdam, Utrecht University, and AFAS Software in the Netherlands.

References

1. Schunselaar, D.M.M., Gulden, J., van der Schuur, H., Reijers, H.A.: A Systematic evaluation of enterprise modelling approaches on their applicability to automatically generate ERP software. In: CBI 2016. IEEE Computer Society (2016)
2. Fox, M.S.: The TOVE project towards a common-sense model of the enterprise. In: Belli, F., Radermacher, F.J. (eds.) IEA/AIE 1992. LNCS, vol. 604, pp. 25–34. Springer, Heidelberg (1992). doi:10.1007/BFb0024952
3. Fowler, M.: Event Sourcing (2005). https://martinfowler.com/eaaDev/EventSourcing.html. Accessed 9 Nov 2017
4. van der Schuur, H., Jansen, S., Brinkkemper, S.: Reducing maintenance effort through software operation knowledge: an eclectic empirical evaluation. In: CSMR, pp. 201–210. IEEE Computer Society (2011)
5. Overeem, M., Spoor, M., Jansen, S.: The dark side of event sourcing: managing data conversion. In: SANER, pp. 193–204 (2017)
6. Overeem, M., Jansen, S.: An exploration of the it in it depends: generative versus interpretive model-driven development. In: MODELSWARD (2017)
7. Open Group: Archimate 2.1 Specification. Van Haren Publishing, December 2013
8. Scheer, A.W.: Aris-Business Process Modeling, 2nd edn. Springer, Heidelberg (1999)
9. Vernadat, F.: The CIMOSA languages. In: Bernus, P., Mertins, K., Schmidt, G. (eds.) Handbook on Architectures of Information Systems. International Handbooks on Information Systems, pp. 251–272. Springer, Heidelberg (1998). doi:10.1007/3-540-26661-5_11
10. Dietz, J.L.G.: Enterprise Ontology - Theory and Methodology. Springer, Heidelberg (2006)
11. Frank, U.: Multi-perspective enterprise modeling: foundational concepts, prospects and future research challenges. SoSyM 13(3), 941–962 (2014)
12. Snoeck, M.: Enterprise Information Systems Engineering - The MERODE Approach. The Enterprise Engineering Series. Springer, Switzerland (2014)
13. Vernadat, F.: UEML: Towards a unified enterprise modelling language. Int. J. Prod. Res. 40(17), 4309–4321 (2002)
14. Kulkarni, V.: Model driven development of business applications: a practitioner's perspective. In: ICSE Companion, pp. 260–269 (2016)
15. Fortuin, S.: Model Driven Engineering: Incipient Environments with Imperative Views. Master's thesis, Utrecht University (2016)
16. Rolland, C., Prakash, N.: Matching ERP system functionality to customer requirements. In: 5th IEEE International Symposium on Requirements Engineering, pp. 66–75 (2001)

An Integrated Enterprise Modeling Framework Using the RUP/UML Business Use-Case Model and BPMN

Yves Wautelet[✉] and Stephan Poelmans

KU Leuven, Leuven, Belgium
{yves.wautelet,stephan.poelmans}@kuleuven.be

Abstract. Various frameworks are available for modeling an organizational setting. Their constituting models nevertheless mostly choose a particular decision level to represent perceived reality meaning that some introduce coarse-grained (i.e. abstract) elements and some others fine-grained (i.e. detailed) ones. Sometimes, in a same model, elements of various levels of granularity can be mixed like for example in the i* strategic rationale model. The main drawback is that this leads to hard to read and complex models, not ideal for easy and quick understanding of the software problem. Also, within the industry, poor unification in the use of models does exist. The various Unified Modeling Language (UML) models and the Business Process Model and Notation (BPMN) are nevertheless rather popular. In this paper, we study the use of the Business Use Case Model – an extension of the classical UML use-case model defined in the Rational Unified Process (RUP) – and the BPMN Business Process Model (BPM) as a unified framework for knowledge representation at strategic, tactical and operational levels. By default, the RUP advises to use UML activity diagrams for operational-level knowledge representation. Their main drawback is that they have been engineered to model software behavior with respect to the user and not business process modeling at large. The BPMN BPM thus offers more perspectives for pure business process modeling; that is why it mostly used in the industry for this purpose. The use of these models in a unified way is ensured by traceability at the various levels of modeling.

Keywords: Business use-case model · Business modeling · BPMN · Business goal

1 Introduction

1.1 Research Context

Business (often refereed to as enterprise) modeling provides guidance for the analyst on how to understand and represent the organizational setting through all

G. Poels et al. (Eds.): PoEM 2017, LNBIP 305, pp. 299–315, 2017.
https://doi.org/10.1007/978-3-319-70241-4_20

of its processes. *As-is* process understanding is required for further process re-engineering or determining possible software systems support. In order to furnish adequate models to support such an activity, we need to model different levels of abstraction. Traditionally, a company structures around three (complementary) abstraction (or decision) levels – the *strategic*, *tactical* and *operational* level – each one requiring representation models. Furthermore, guidance for a follow-up between all hierarchy levels is required; i.e. knowledge must – at least partially – be refined and traceable.

Within the the *Rational Unified Process* (*RUP*) [10,12,25], the RUP/UML *Business Use-Case Model*[1] (*BUCM*) offers a syntax and semantic to represent the situation *as-is* at tactical and (at least partially[2]) strategic level. The BUCM is, indeed, an extension of the *Unified Modeling Language* (*UML*) [17] Use-Case Model supported by the RUP and many *Computer Aided Software Engineering* (*CASE*) tools. Then, at the operational level, the representation is ensured by the UML activity model as defined in the OMG specification (see [17]). These are, nevertheless, primarily designed to document the *to-be* system behavior through the interaction with users. RUP defines no alignment (anchoring of elements) between the tactical and operational levels.

1.2   Towards the Combined Use of the RUP/UML Business Use Case Model and the BPMN Business Process Model

The RUP/UML BUCM and the *Business Process Modeling Notation* (*BPMN*) [1,16,26] *Business Process Model* (*BPM*)[3] have in common that they are targeted to pure business process modeling so that they dispose of a richer set of elements associated with precise semantics for this purpose. Even if they come from different semantic domains, some elements are semantically close enough and they can be used for anchoring (and traceability) among representation levels. That is why, previous research (see [29]) studies the possible anchoring between the RUP/UML BUCM and the BPMN BPM.

The conjunct use of these two frameworks is supported by CASE-tools like *Rational Software Architect* [23] or *Visual Paradigm* [18].

---

[1] We do not refer here to the use case model as defined by the OMG in [17] but to the refinement proposed in the business modeling discipline from the RUP (see [8,10,12,15,25]). That is why, in this paper, we refer to it as the RUP/UML *Business Use-Case Model*.

[2] The strategic elements within the BUCM are the business goal and objective (see Sect. 5).

[3] Note that we do not include the BPMN *Process Maps* in our study but only the Business Process Model (i.e. the classical workflow), see Sect. 3. Also, when we refer to the BPMN BPM, we refer to the entire theoretical set of elements defined by the OMG while when we refer to a BPMN process diagram we refer to an instance of the model (applied to a case).

1.3 Research Context and Objective

As evoked, [29] evaluates the possible anchoring between the RUP/UML BUCM and BPMN BPM, but focuses exclusively on tactical and operational levels representation. It does not detail the strategic level and is thus an incomplete solution for full business modeling knowledge levels coverage.

The research developed in this paper further justifies the choice of the integration of the two frameworks and furnishes a meta-model for the full integration of the 2 frameworks and their use for knowledge representation and traceability among the three knowledge level representations. This unified-model has been used within the context of the *Design of a Business Information System* (*DBIS*) course within the Master in Business Information Systems (faculty of economics and business) at KU Leuven (campus Brussels). Further justification of the choices for framework selection can be found in Sect. 2. We specifically wanted to adopt BPMN BPM within the *as-is* business process modeling of a case study given to students. Within the context of the course, we (the teachers) have initially decided to integrate the use of the BPMN BPM for process operational level representation instead of the UML activity model because:

- The BPMN BPM offers a set of (relevant) stereotypes with associated semantics to represent business processes in an operational manner because these were primarily engineered for enterprise modeling. The activity model does not offer these; this misalignment comes from the fact that they have been engineered to model user behavior with respect to a *to-be* software system;
- The BPMN BPM is an increasingly important industry standard for enterprise modeling (see [14]);
- The BPMN BPM offers the possibility to easily execute modeled workflows with a language as the *Business Process Execution Language* (*BPEL*, see [5,19–21]);
- Further extensions of the BPMN BPM include the definition of Key Performance Indicators (e.g. [7]) that could be applied to the BPMN BPM in our approach to evaluate their support to tactical and strategic aspect(s). This is left for future work.

Finally, poor (we could even say no) documentation and support is offered for the use of strategic modeling within the RUP/UML BUCM. That is why we distinguish here the strategic modeling level as a separate diagram to be built in parallel with the classical (business) use case model and allowing to trace the impact of processes (i.e. business use-cases) on the long term strategic goals and objectives. This is discussed in Sect. 5.

1.4 Added Value of Defining Anchoring Points Between the RUP/UML Business Use Case Model and the BPMN Business Process Model

The set of elements defined by the BPMN BPM allows better anchoring between the operational and tactical levels than the classical UML activity model. A preliminary question is, however, the utility of defining such anchoring points to ensure traceability between the different abstraction levels. We highlight the following benefits:

- *Ensure consistency during the refinement process.* Providing anchoring points of elements from the models at the different abstraction levels helps to ensure that the vision of the reality built and shown in the different models (thus at different knowledge levels) is aligned rather than divergent. In other words, it allows building complementary models envisioning reality with the same perspective rather than building concurrent models envisioning reality with various perspectives;
- *Giving guidelines to modelers.* By defining a set of anchoring points, modelers dispose of a clear set of guidelines for building and structuring their models; this is very useful for novice modelers (see Sect. 1.5);
- *Simplify the structuring in the refinement process.* A set of elements present at the tactical level need to be present at the operational level, these can immediately be included in the operational view simplifying the structuring of diagrams;
- *Help communicating with stakeholders.* The correct use of the anchoring guidelines allows to explain and justify modeling choices when communicating the produced models to stakeholders.

As said, the definition of these anchoring points has been done in [29] and are summarized in Sect. 4.

1.5 Added Value of the Integrated Framework and Contributions

As said, the integrated framework presented in this paper has been developed and applied in the context of an applied software engineering course at master level. When the course was initially defined and given, the BPMN BPM was integrated in the *Business Modeling* discipline of the RUP for operational workflow representation but without specific anchoring points with the RUP/UML BUCM. During the two first academic years, the teachers only gave the indication to use the BPMN BPM instead of the UML activity model in order to practice skills with the former framework (it was judged relevant for the reasons evoked previously). The course format stipulates that students receive real-life process descriptions (submitted to a major consultancy company, partner in the students' solutions evaluation) and have to produce an initial *as-is* representation of the business processes. In practice, when modeling the case, students made a lot of round-trip between the abstraction levels (thus the RUP/UML BUC diagram and the BPMN process diagrams) while understanding and modeling the processes. This resulted often in a poor linkage between the tactical and operational diagrams. When questioned about it, students could hardly relate the different modeling levels and justify their choices. In the next (and last) two academic years, students received theoretical information about the anchoring points and could use these as modeling guidelines leading to more consistent models and the ability to justify some modeling choices. A formal evaluation of this is left for future work.

The primary contribution of this paper is the meta-model furnishing an integrated view for the conjunct use of the RUP/UML BUCM and the BPMN BPM; this one is intended to be used as guideline for the building diagrams documenting the organization and its processes on three layers (see Sect. 5).

The goal is not (necessarily) to push the adoption of "our integrated framework" into the industry but to teach business process modeling as a prerequisite in software development using industry adopted practices. This paper highlights possible anchoring between the frameworks to force the modeler to consider traceability when depicting the three knowledge (or decision) levels of an organization increasing the level of consistency between levels.

1.6 Paper Structure

The paper is structured as follows. Section 2 justifies the choice of the software engineering methodology guiding developments and its constituting artifacts. Section 3 overviews related work. Section 4 explains the theoretical background through the presentation of the mapping of elements from the RUP/UML BUCM and the BPMN BPM. The Section summarizes the work realized in [29] used as a basis for the present research. Section 5 studies the use of an integrated model on the basis of the alignment study performed and shows its applicability on an illustrative example. Finally, Sect. 7 concludes the paper.

2 Selecting a Methodology and Artifacts

The main issue when starting up the course in 2012 was to find a methodology being an adequate compromise between the best suiting method for a structured learning of software engineering and industry adopted practices. Indeed, one of the characteristics of the institution is the so called *business-orientation* and, since the students are in their Master year, they are very likely to be on the job market soon so that using industry adopted practices is of course favored. The first possible option to use methodologies and artifacts mainly used in the academic world like for example the i* modeling framework [30] or KAOS [27] was thus abandoned. Despite the real interest of these for their broad representation capabilities and their formal approach, they are far from being industry-adopted which partially conflicts with the objectives expressed earlier.

In order to conciliate with the objectives, we did a small informal survey of the frameworks used by the main consulting companies that are also teaching partners of the institution. This lead to the conclusion that each of them used their custom development method mostly documented internally within the company or group. A few common patterns could nevertheless be distinguished. They all:

- devote significant effort to representing the as-is situation before depicting the situation to-be;
- represent operational workflows using the BPMN BPM or very similar formalisms.

Pure agile methods are too informal and operational in their requirements definition so that we did not want to push them neither. The *Rational Unified Process* (*RUP*) nevertheless made a perfect candidate to be adopted as a guidance development methodology for the purpose of our course. Indeed, the *business modeling* discipline devotes significant effort to the representation *as-is*. This allows a structured approach of the development of software systems for heavy processes organizations and has already been identified in [2] as a strength of the framework for educational purpose. Indeed, from a strong identification of the *as-is* situation, the added value of the *to-be* situation can be showed/demonstrated.

We thus decided to select the RUP as a methodology but to study the possible integration of the BPMN BPM instead of the UML activity model within the business modeling discipline.

3   Related Work and Positioning

[24] claims that using of the UML use-case model associated with workflows in the context of business process analysis is useful and needs to be further studied. It thus advocates for the interest of our research.

[6] proposes yPBL, a learning methodology applied to Software Engineering (SE). The methodology is based on the well-known PBL method and adapted to SE unified processes. It specifies the relationship between the roles and phases considered in PBL methods and the roles, iterations and phases considered in the Two Tracks Unified Process (2TUP). The yPBL method concentrates on the realization of three tracks (i.e. functional, technical and development). The functional track considers a tactical level, the used models are the UML Use Cases and Activity ones.

As already evoked, [2] points to the use of the RUP for educational purpose notably because of the presence of the *Business Modeling* discipline. Within this discipline the RUP/UML business use-case model is defined and by including the BPMN BPM instead of the UML activity model in the RUP process, more formality and traceability is required which could have a positive impact on their approach of complex software problems. This approach is followed by this paper's authors in the evoked course.

Artifacts for a tactical representation are present in the global BPMN framework and artifacts for an operational one are present in the UML, indeed:

- Process Maps (PM) are included in BPMN; PM are made of coarse-grained elements with limited expressiveness. PM are only constituted by a set of elements representing sets of business processes and the triggering actors represented as lanes. PM are comparable to a classical use-case model but the RUP/UML BUCM offers richer representation possibilities;
- The UML Activity Model define a set of elements for workflow modeling, but, as discussed earlier, the set of available elements is much poorer for pure business (enterprise) modeling than the ones of BPMN's BPM because they are mostly oriented on representing software system behavior with user interaction.

Traceability studies and referrals between use-cases and business processes have been studied in both top-down and bottom-up perspectives.

[3] proposes an approach to obtain a use-case model from a business process model. It builds a complete use case model – including the identification of actors, uses cases and the corresponding descriptions – which are created from a set of predefined natural language sentences mapped from the BPMN BPM elements. The approach is divided in two parts. The first one presents a set of rules to obtain a use-case diagram from a BPMN process diagram. Then, the rules are used to derive the description of the uses cases previously identified. When sub-processes are involved, the approach demands that they are fully expanded which induces losing some structure information. [22] details how to make use of the Visual Paradigm Model Transitor function to build a use case model from a BPMN process diagram. It nevertheless remains a tool-based approach with no formal rules.

In opposition to the previous approaches, [9] suggests to use the BPMN BPM instead of the UML activity model in the RUP process. Their study showed that the perceived complexity of a BPMN process diagram is lower than the one of an activity diagram. The only guideline given in the paper is the use of one BPMN process diagram to depict one particular use-case; no further traceability rules are given. Similarly, [13] studies traceability between use-case elements and the BPMN BPM. They distinguish the same integration approach as we do plus distinguish an upper level to depict the sequence of the use-cases themselves. Such an encapsulation is notably supported by Visual Paradigm (see for example [28]) and was already supported in the same way in Rational Rose but with UML activity diagrams only and we inherently encompass the same encapsulation in our approach (see Sect. 4). We suggest to have a **finer level of traceability** meaning to trace elements constituting the RUP/UML BUCM with elements from the BPMN BPM.

Finally, [4] proposes a mapping from the BPMN BPM to a formal language, namely Petri nets, for which efficient analysis techniques are available. This work is complementary and could be integrated into the RUP for the forward engineering of business process models. As evoked in the introduction, the BPMN BPM has also mapping approaches to other execution languages like for example BPEL.

4   Theoretical Background

[29] has studied the alignment between the elements from the RUP/UML BUCM and BPMN's BPM. To such an extend, the RUP/UML BUCM's elements defined in the business modeling discipline of the *RUP knowledge base* (see [11,12,15]) were taken as input elements to be mapped. More precisely, three categories of elements were distinguished: *Inheriting from Use Case* (*IUC*), *Inheriting from the Actor* (*IA*) and *Links* (*UMLLink*). The icons of the RUP/UML BUCM are represented in Fig. 1. Similarly, on the basis of the documentation found in [16], Wautelet et al. [29] has built four categories of elements within the BPMN BPM

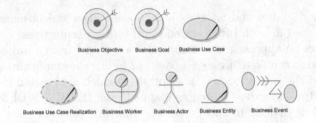

Business Objective   Business Goal   Business Use Case

Business Use Case Realization   Business Worker   Business Actor   Business Entity   Business Event

Fig. 1. Icons of the RUP/UML business use-case model.

ones: *Events* (*Evt*), *Activity* (*Act*), *Gateway* (*Gwy*) and *Connections* (*Cnt*). In this section, we relate the transformations in a top-down manner meaning that we start from tactical elements (from the RUP/UML BUC Model) and see how they are mapped to the operational elements (from the BPMN BPM).

We are, of course, aware of the fact that we are facing two different semantic domains and that a perfect alignment is illusive. Nevertheless, since the two frameworks are devoted to business modeling their semantic coverage is rather close and (as will be seen in the next section) the mappings that have been made are (rather) consistent.

4.1   Traceability of Inheriting from Use Case Elements

The elements from the IUC category (which could be seen as stereotypes of the classical UML use-case element) are coarse grained (so very abstract) ones. It means that each elements of this category encapsulate an entire (business) process so are not suited for traceability at individual level with elements grouped in the categories of the BPMN BPM. [29] indicates to map a *Business Use Case Realization* (BUC Realization) element with one *BPMN Process Model*. Following the RUP knowledge base, *a Business Use Case (instance) is a sequence of actions that a business performs that* **yields an observable result of value** *to a particular business actor.* The BUC Realization represents an entire business

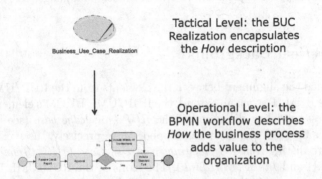

Business_Use_Case_Realization

Tactical Level: the BUC Realization encapsulates the *How* description

Operational Level: the BPMN workflow describes *How* the business process adds value to the organization

Fig. 2. Tracing business use cases and BPMN process diagrams (from [29]).

process and [29] thus suggests to encapsulate the details of its realization within a BPMN process diagram; this is represented in Fig. 2. This two-level abstraction view is fully supported by Visual Paradigm (see for example [28]).

4.2   Traceability of Inheriting from Actor Elements

Contrarily to the elements of the IUC category, the ones of the IA (which could be seen as stereotypes of the classical UML Actor element) can be traced (with BPMN BPM elements) at an individual level. Table 1 summarizes the mapping of elements between the RUP/UML BUCM IA category elements and the BPMN BPM ones performed by [29]. The interested reader can refer to the former sources for full justifications.

Table 1. Mapping of inheriting from actor (*IA*) elements

RUP/UML BUC element	Business actor	Business worker	Business entity	Business event
Mapped BPMN element	Pool	Lane	Data object	Event

4.3   Traceability of Link Elements

The impact of the elements of the Link category present in the RUP/UML BUCM can be traced as a set of constraints within the BPMN BPM elements. The rules established by [29] are the following:

- *Association directed from IA to IUC element*: the IA category element triggers the action so that the Start Event from the BPMN process diagram depicting the IUC category element should be placed in the swimlane corresponding to the IA category element;
- *Association directed from IUC to IA element*: the IA category element is involved in the realization of the process but not triggering the action so that this IA category elements must be found as a swimlane or pool in the BPMN process diagram, but does not host the start event (it can possibly host an intermediate or an end event);
- *Include*: A IUC category element is included in another IUC category one so that the IUC element representing the "main" process includes as a sub-process in its BPMN process diagram the second one; the latter **must be** executed in any path of achievement of the main process;
- *Extend*: A IUC category element is thus extended by another IUC category one so that the IUC element representing the "main" process includes as a sub-process in its BPMN process diagram the second one; the latter **may be** executed in the path of achievement of the main process but not necessarily.
- *Generalization*: A generalization can take place both between elements of IA category or the IUC one in the RUP/UML BUCM.

- When there is a generalization between 2 elements of the IA category, it cannot be traced at the level of the BPMN process diagram;
- When there is a generalization between two elements of the IUC category and the parent is abstract, only a BPMN process diagram is build for the realization of the child IUC category element. If it is not abstract, a BPMN process diagram is also associated with the parent IUC category element.

5   Three Layered Approach for Business Modeling

This section integrates the findings of [29] and suggests a way to integrate the strategic, tactical and operational levels in a unified framework based on the RUP/UML BUCM and the BPMN BPM. The findings of the mapping/alignment study are finally presented and summarized through a meta-model in the form of a class diagram in Fig. 3 and illustrated on a case study. The case study takes place in the chocolate industry.

My Chocolate Factory[4] (*MCF*) is a company producing and selling chocolates that has commercial presence in 3 continents and manufacturing activity in 2 of them. The focus of growth of MCF is the Asian region, and its main competitive advantage is the vertical integration with providers and customers, developing quality through all the production stages. In order to support this, MCF requires a system able to integrate the most important activities, in a non-redundant, stable and user-friendly way. The company of Thailand is the scope and the first phase of the new system implementation because it covers both manufacturing and sales process, and is the center of operations in the actual market of Asia. Part of this case is presented in this in Fig. 4; The goal of the Section is to give a perspective on the use of the integrated framework and not to illustrate each cases of tactical/operational traceability. It depicts a reinterpretation of the strategic aspects of the RUP/UML BUCM – because that perspective is not formally defined and illustrated in literature[5] – as well as the integration of the strategic, tactical and operational levels on one case.

5.1   Strategic Modeling: The Business Goal Model

The Strategic Level is concerned with decisions including the general direction i.e. long term goals, philosophies and values. In a SE perspective, we would be willing to represent the goals of the organization as well as the processes it is

---

[4] For confidentiality reasons the name of the company has been changed.

[5] The effective use in real-life of the strategic elements of the RUP/UML BUCM is hard to evaluate. Often, this level is neglected or modeled with documents in natural language. We recognize that strategic modeling using only business goals and objectives does not lead to an exhaustive strategy description. However, this (limited) graphical representation has many benefits in terms of communication; textual documents can be used in parallel.

involved in but in a coarse-grained, non-sequential and non-prioritized manner in order to trace support.

The RUP knowledge base defines a business goal as *a requirement that the business must satisfy*. It argues that *business goals describe the desired value of a particular measure at some future point in time and can therefore be used to plan and manage the activities of the business*. It also distinguishes *business objectives* as *high-level business goals* and emphasizes that *because business objectives are usually abstract, they are difficult to measure and are therefore translated into more measurable lower-level business goals*. Both elements are represented with the same icon.

Business Goals in the large sense (including business objectives) are very interesting in the context of modeling a software system since they allow to include a representation of the business strategy. Indeed, [11] highlights that *the purpose of business goals is to translate the business strategy into measurable steps with which the business operations can be steered in the right direction, and, if necessary, improved*. In that context, both concepts of business goals and objectives are interesting, they are mainly distinguishable by the fact that the first one can be directly associated with a metric while the second needs to be refined in more business goals for measurement. Business goals can then be supported by BUC themselves realized through BUC Realizations allowing to draw a full and clear hierarchy. This will be further discussed into Sect. 5.1.

The RUP knowledge base defines a business goal as *a requirement that the business must satisfy*. It argues that *business goals describe the desired value of a particular measure at some future point in time and can therefore be used to plan and manage the activities of the business*. It also distinguishes *business objectives* as *high-level business goals* and emphasizes that *because business objectives are usually abstract, they are difficult to measure and are therefore translated into more measurable lower-level business goals*. Both elements are represented with the same icon.

Business goals and objectives are very interesting for enterprise modeling since they allow representing the business strategy. Indeed, [11] highlights that *the purpose of business goals is to translate the business strategy into measurable steps with which the business operations can be steered in the right direction, and, if necessary, improved*. These two elements are mainly distinguishable by the fact that the first one can be directly associated with a metric while the second needs to be refined in more business goals for measurement. Business goals can then be supported by BUC themselves realized through BUC Realizations allowing to draw a full and clear hierarchy.

Few sources and examples are available to depict how they can/should be used in a project. In [11], the business objectives and goals are decomposed in a tree structure and, within the RUP/UML BUCM, business use cases trace their support of lowest level goals only. To clearly highlight the strategic level, we point to the use of an independent model (that we simply call the *business goal model*) at strategic level only relating the business objectives, goals and their refinement as well as the business use-cases supporting these goals[6]; no actor should be present in it (actors will be later documented at tactical level). RUP/UML business goals are related using a *Dependency* relationship (arrow) originating on the highest level goal and pointing to the lower level one. Similarly, when a RUP/UML business use-cases supports a business goal it is linked using a *Dependency* relationship stereotyped *supports* from the the former to the later.

The upper left part of Fig. 3 (the transparent classes) concerns the *RUP/UML Business Goal Model*. The latter is composed of the *Business_Objective*, the *Business_Goal* and the *Business_Use_Case* classes. Instances of the *Business_Goal* class (so Business Goal elements) can be linked through a *Refine_Dependency_Link*. Similarly, different instances of the *Business_Goal* class (thus different Business Goal elements) can be linked through a *Refine_Dependency_Link*. Instances of the *Business_Use_Case* class (so Business Use Case elements) support the *Business_Goal* class by offering support so through a *Supports_Dependency_Link*.

The strategic layer in Fig. 4 illustrates the Goal Model. The business objective *Sustainable Growth* is refined in another business objective (*Increase Customer Loyalty*) and more business goals. Also, business use-cases support the realization of certain goals, we can notably cite the goal *Manage Procurement* that, within its realization, can favor the performance of the goal *Acquire Raw Material Locally*.

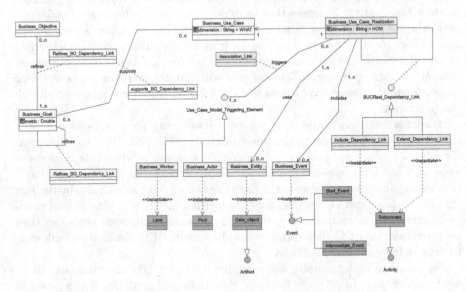

Fig. 3. Unified business modeling framework: Meta model.

---

[6] We emphasize that BUC are thus represented to trace the support of the strategic level while – as will be seen later – BUC realizations are represented at tactical level.

5.2   Tactical Modeling: The Business Use-Case Model

The upper middle and left part of Fig. 3 (the mid-dark classes) concerns the *Business_Use_Case_Model*. The latter is composed of the *Business_Use_Case_Realization*, the *Business_Actor*, *Business_Worker*, *Business_Entity*, *Business_Event*, the *Include_Dependency_Link* and the *Extend_Dependency_Link* classes. *Business_Use_Case_Realization* elements are instantiated and correspond to the *Business_Use_Case* elements depicted in the goal model in a 1 to 1 fashion. These *Business_Use_Case_Realization* elements are triggered by *Business_Worker* or *Business_Actor* elements.

The tactical layer of Fig. 4 is illustrated by a business use-case diagram. Each BUC Realization in the diagram (i) corresponds to a BUC distinguished at strategic level that prescribes what should be done to obtain value (and thus linked with the Business Goals and Objectives) and (ii) encapsulates a description in the form of a BPMN process diagram of the process realization scenarios. Traceability between the strategic and the tactical layers is thus ensured through the mapping of BUC and BUC realizations.

5.3   Operational Modeling: The BPMN Business Process Model

The lower part of Fig. 3 (the darkest classes) concerns the *BPMN_Business_Process_Model*. The latter is composed of the *Lane*, *Pool*, *Data_Object*, *Start_Event*, *Intermediate_Event* and *Subprocess* classes (only elements that are traceable from the (tactical level) business use-case model are represented). As evoked previously, a *Business_Use_Case_Realization* element should lead to one BPMN process diagram. The latter inherently instantiates a main *Pool* element corresponding to the main organization modeled. Within this *Pool*, a *Business_Worker* element instantiates a *Lane* element. Similarly, a *Business_Actor* element instantiates another (thus separate) *Pool* element.

The operational layer in Fig. 4 illustrates a BPMN process diagram. The Make-to-Stock BUC Realization is here depicted as a set of activities. We can highlight that the *Salesman* which is a *Business_Worker* can be traced in the form of *Lane* in the *My_Chocolate_Factory Pool*. Also, the *Customer* which is a *Business_Actor* can be traced in the form of a separate *Pool*. The *Sales_Order* which is a *Business_Entity* can be traced in the form of a *Data_Object*. Traceability between the tactical and the operational layers is thus ensured by (i) the BPMN process diagram describing realization scenarios for BUC realizations and (ii) elements constituting the BUC Model described in the BPMN process diagram.

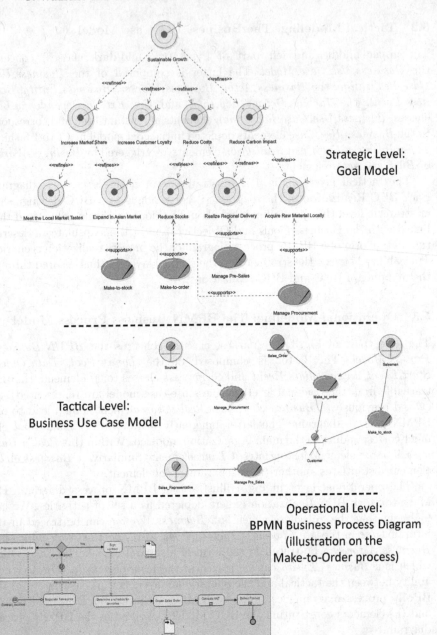

Fig. 4. Unified business modeling framework applied on the case study.

5.4   Integration in the RUP Process

The integration of the framework into the Business Modeling discipline must be done at *artifact* level. Indeed, following [10], *An artifact is a piece of information that is produced, modified, or used by a process. Artifacts are the tangible products of the project, the things the project produces or uses while working towards the final product. Artifacts are used as input by workers to perform an activity, and are the result or output of such activities.* The BUCM is already part of the process' artifacts; the Goal Model can be integrated into strategic activities as a new artifact allowing Goal reasoning. Similarly, BPMN process diagrams could just substitute UML activity diagrams since they have the same representation possibilities but offer richer semantics.

6   Framework Acceptance and Results

The framework is currently being further validated through the use of students' produced models. The validation is made longitudinally and cross-sectionally. We are comparing the work produced by cohorts of students from different generations. Concretely a same case has been modeled by students that have only been taught the basic artifacts from the RUP and BPMN and by students that have received a specific training on the structure and traceability rules. All of the students reports are given a score in function of the (i) the quality of the application of the structure and traceability (including the cohort not familiar with the framework of this paper), and (ii) on the general quality and completeness of the models produced. We then compare the results of the 2 cohorts (without and with knowledge of the framework). Across the cohorts, traceability scores are also correlated to the general scores. The full validation of the framework will be part of a future communication in the form of a scientific article.

7   Conclusion

The conjunct use of the RUP/UML BUC Model and the BPMN BPM leads to an integrated framework that allows to model both the strategic, tactical and operational layers of a business modeling problem. The framework has been used in the context of structured learning of software engineering in a master course on information management. With respect to the traditional RUP approach, the pedagogical approach is enhanced because of the strength of the framework to enforce traceability at all levels thanks to the richer semantics proposed by BPMN's BPM compared to the classical UML activity model. Also, it allows to use the BPMN BPM that is widely adopted in the industry.

The coupling of elements could be made stronger if backed by an empirical evaluation of the choices that would be made by practitioners. This particular point will also be the subject of a study in the coming months. Future work includes the evaluation of the benefits of framework use in various contexts.

Indeed, as evoked, the primary willingness of its use is pure business modeling so not necessary leading to software development. It can indeed be used to audit business processes in order to point out weaknesses and optimization flows, for modeling the as-is situation in off-the shelf software development (like for integrated ERP systems), etc.

References

1. Chinosi, M., Trombetta, A.: BPMN: an introduction to the standard. Comput. Stand. Interfaces **34**(1), 124–134 (2012)
2. Ciancarini, P.: On the education of future software engineers. In: Roman, G.C., Griswold, W.G., Nuseibeh, B. (eds.) ICSE, pp. 649–650. ACM (2005)
3. Cruz, E.F., Machado, R.J., Santos, M.Y.: From business process models to use case models: a systematic approach. In: Aveiro, D., Tribolet, J., Gouveia, D. (eds.) EEWC 2014. LNBIP, vol. 174, pp. 167–181. Springer, Cham (2014). 10.1007/978-3-319-06505-2_12
4. Dijkman, R.M., Dumas, M., Ouyang, C.: Semantics and analysis of business process models in BPMN. Inf. Softw. Technol. **50**(12), 1281–1294 (2008)
5. Dumas, M.: Case study : BPMN to BPEL model transformation. In: 5th International Workshop on GraphBased Tools (GraBaTs) (2009)
6. Exposito, E.: yPBL methodology: a problem-based learning method applied to software engineering. In: 2010 IEEE Education Engineering (EDUCON), pp. 1817–1823, April 2010
7. Friedenstab, J., Janiesch, C., Matzner, M., Müller, O.: Extending BPMN for business activity monitoring. In: Proceedings of the 45th Hawaii International International Conference on Systems Science (HICSS-45 2012), Grand Wailea, Maui, HI, USA, 4–7 January 2012, pp. 4158–4167. IEEE Computer Society (2012)
8. Gibbs, R.D.: Project Management with the IBM®Rational Unified Process®: Lessons From The Trenches. IBM Press (2006)
9. Herden, A., Farias, P.P.M., Albuquerque, A.B.: An approach based on BPMN to detail use cases. In: Elleithy, K., Sobh, T. (eds.) New Trends in Networking, Computing, E-learning, Systems Sciences, and Engineering. LNEE, vol. 312, pp. 537–544. Springer, Cham (2015). 10.1007/978-3-319-06764-3_69
10. IBM: The Rational Unified Process, Version 7.0.1 (2007)
11. Johnston, S.: Rational®uml profile for business modeling. Technical report (2004)
12. Kruchten, P.: The Rational Unified Process : An Introduction. Longman (Wokingham), Addison-Wesley, Boston (2003)
13. Lubke, D., Schneider, K., Weidlich, M.: Visualizing use case sets as BPMN processes. In: Requirements Engineering Visualization, REV 2008, pp. 21–25, September 2008
14. Zur Muehlen, M., Recker, J.: How much language is enough? theoretical and practical use of the business process modeling notation. In: Bubenko, J., Krogstie, J., Pastor, O., Pernici, B., Rolland, C., Sølvberg, A. (eds.) Seminal Contributions to Information Systems Engineering, 25 Years of CAiSE, pp. 429–433. Springer, Heidelberg (2013). 10.1007/978-3-642-36926-1_35
15. Nailburg, E.J., Maksimchuk, R.A.: UML for Database Design, 1st edn. Addison-Wesley Longman Publishing Co., Inc., Boston (2001)
16. OMG: Business process model and notation (BPMN). version 2.0.1. Technical report (2013)

17. OMG: Omg unified modeling language (omg uml). version 2.5. Technical report (2015)
18. Oscar, S.: Visual Paradigm for Uml. International Book Market Service Limited, Beau Bassin-Rose Hill (2013)
19. Ouyang, C., Dumas, M., ter Hofstede, A.H.M., van der Aalst, W.M.P.: From BPMN process models to BPEL web services. In: 2006 IEEE ICWS, Chicago, Illinois, USA, pp. 285–292. IEEE Computer Society (2006)
20. Ouyang, C., Dumas, M., Hofstede, A.H.M., et al.: From business process models to process-oriented software systems: The bpmn to bpel way (2006)
21. Ouyang, C., Dumas, M., ter Hofstede, A.H.M., van der Aalst, W.M.P.: Pattern-based translation of BPMN process models to BPEL web services. Int. J. Web Serv. Res. (JWSR) 5(1), 42–62 (2007)
22. Paradigm, V.: From business process to use case. https://www.visual-paradigm.com/tutorials/from-business-process-to-use-cases.jsp
23. Quatrani, T., Palistrant, J.: Visual Modeling with IBM Rational Software Architect and UML. The developerWorks Series. IBM Press, Boston (2006)
24. Shishkov, B., Xie, Z., Liu, K., Dietz, J.: Deriving use case from business process models developed using norm analysis. In: Gazendam, H., Jorna, R., Cijsouw, R. (eds.) Dynamics and Change in Organizations, pp. 117–131. Springer, Netherlands (2003). 10.1007/978-94-010-0161-8_7
25. Shuja, A., Krebs, J.: Ibm®; Rational Unified Process®; Reference and Certification Guide: Solution Designer, 1st edn. IBM Press, Boston (2007)
26. White, S.A., Miers, D.: BPMN Modeling and Reference Guide. Future Strategies Inc., Lighthouse Pt (2008)
27. Van Lamsweerde, A.: Requirements engineering: From System Goals to UML Models to Software Specifications. Wiley, Chichester (2009)
28. VisualParadigm: From use case to business process (2012). https://www.youtube.com/watch?v=jkIZuBZ876c
29. Wautelet, Y., Poelmans, S.: Aligning the elements of the RUP/UML business use-case model and the BPMN business process diagram. In: Grünbacher, P., Perini, A. (eds.) REFSQ 2017. LNCS, vol. 10153, pp. 22–30. Springer, Cham (2017). 10.1007/978-3-319-54045-0_2
30. Yu, E., Giorgini, P., Maiden, N., Mylopoulos, J.: Social Modeling for Requirements Engineering. MIT Press, Cambridge (2011)

Short Papers

A Method for Effective Use of Enterprise Modelling Techniques in Complex Dynamic Decision Making

Souvik Barat[1]([⊠]), Vinay Kulkarni[1], Tony Clark[2], and Balbir Barn[3]

[1] Tata Consultancy Services Research, Pune, India
{souvik.barat,vinay.vkulkarni}@tcs.com
[2] Sheffield Hallam University, Sheffield, UK
t.clark@shu.ac.uk
[3] Middlesex University, London, UK
b.barn@mdx.ac.uk

Abstract. Effective organisational decision-making requires information pertaining to various organisational aspects, precise analysis capabilities, and a systematic method to capture and interpret the required information. The existing Enterprise Modelling (EM) and actor technologies together seem suitable for the specification and analysis needs of decision making. However, in absence of a method to capture required information and perform analyses, the decision-making remains a complex endeavour. This paper presents a method that captures required information in the form of models and performs what-if calculations in a systematic manner.

Keywords: Enterprise decision making · Method · Bottom-up simulation

1 Introduction

Modern organisations try to meet their goals by adopting appropriate courses of action. Evaluation of alternative courses of action and deciding best amongst them call for precise understanding of organisational aspects such as goals, organisational structure, operational processes and the past data [6]. The dynamic organisational structure, socio-technical aspects and emergent behaviour contribute to making it a complex dynamic decision making (CDDM) endeavour [12].

An effective CDDM hinges on the availability of: (i) the information required for decision-making in a structured and machine-interpretable form, (ii) suitable machineries to interpret the information, and (iii) a method to help identify the relevant information, capture it in model form, and perform *what-if* analyses. The current practice of organisational decision-making that relies heavily on human experts making use of the primitive tools such as spreadsheets, word

G. Poels et al. (Eds.): PoEM 2017, LNBIP 305, pp. 319–330, 2017.
https://doi.org/10.1007/978-3-319-70241-4_21

processors, and diagram editors *etc.* fares poorly on all the three criteria mentioned above [12].

The existing Enterprise Modelling (EM) techniques and technologies, such as Zachman Framework [19], ArchiMate [9], i* [18], BPMN [17], System Dynamics (SD) [13], and Multi-Perspective Enterprise Modeling (MEMO) [7], help to capture information of interest and perform rigorous analyses. Similarly, the actor technologies, such as Scala Actors [8] and Akka [2], help specify and analyse the system with autonomous, adaptive and emergent behaviours.

Essentially, the EM technologies and actor technologies together support two of the three requirements of CDDM: (i) the ability to capture relevant information in a structured and machine interpretable form and (ii) the ability to perform required analyses. However, to the best of our knowledge, there is no work reported on how to address the third requirement of a method for CDDM.

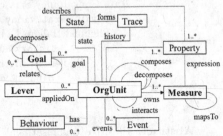

Fig. 1. Schema of an organisation

This paper presents a method that helps systematically represent the necessary aspects of an organisation in terms of suitable models, and perform simulation-based analyses leading to effective CDDM. The proposed method refines the management view of decision-making advocated by Richard Daft [6] (described in Sect. 2), and the model construction and validation method advocated by Robert Sargent [15] (described in Sect. 3). An illustration of the proposed method on a representative sample from real life is presented in Sect. 4. Section 5 provides a summary and outlines further research plans.

2   Background and Requirements of CDDM

The management view of organisational decision-making [6] (henceforth referred as *Management Decision Cycle*) recommends an iterative process flow involving six process steps namely, *Recognition of Decision Requirement* [D1], *Diagnosis and Analysis of Causes* [D2], *Development of Alternatives* [D3], *Selection of Desired Alternative* [D4], *Implementation of Chosen Alternative* [D5], and *Evaluation and Feedback* [D6]. The process steps D1-D4 among them are arguably critical for CDDM as the cost and effort of implementing an alternative in D5 are often prohibitively high for most of the modern organisations. Moreover, an inappropriate selection of alternative in D4 may reduce the options in subsequent iterations of Management Decision Cycles.

The selection of best possible alternative in process step D4 requires precise understanding of Organisational *Goal*, *Structure*, *Behaviour*, *State* and *Trace* (or historical information) [3]. We represent these aspects using a unified abstraction of *OrgUnit* as shown in Fig. 1. Essentially, an OrgUnit contains the structural aspect through *composes*, *decomposes* and *interacts* relationships. It contains a set of *Goals* that represent the objectives of the OrgUnit, *Behaviour* that helps in achieving Goals, a set of *Measures* that describe key performance indicators, and a set of *Levers* that describe possible courses of action.

In this formulation, the *Organisation* is a specialised OrgUnit that composes multiple [de]composable OrgUnits along multiple levels; the Organisational Goals flow from bottom-to-top along Organisational structure; the Organisational behaviour exhibits compositional and emergent characteristics; and the Measures are typically localised and they flow from bottom-to-top along goal decomposition structure.

Therefore, organizing the relevant information for CDDM faces several fundamental dichotomies such as top-down/bottom-up [16], composional/decompositional, and localized/globalized. In addition, the analysis techniques need to be cognizant of reductionist/emergentism principles [4].

The existing enterprise modeling and actor technologies are cognizant of these dichotomies at a varying degree. For example, the goal specification languages such as i* [18] advocate a top-down method for goal modelling. The EM languages, such as ArchiMate [9], MEMO [7] and 4EM [14], advocate a top-down method, decomposition abstraction, and globalized view of the system to represent the Goal, Structure and Behaviour of organisation in an integrated manner. The BPMN [17] and SD model [13] predominantly support top-down specification and analysis approach. On the other hand, actor languages and frameworks [2,8] advocate localised view, bottom-up approach, composition and emergentism. While the technologies have provision for the required primitives for CDDM, a means for a seamless integrated use of the technologies is missing. This lacuna is further aggravated by conflicts in promoting a top-down reductionist approaches such as in DESIRE (DEsign Specification of Interacting REasoning components) [11] and bottom-up approaches such as that advocated by Kinny et al. using Belief-Desire-Intention (BDI) paradigm [10].

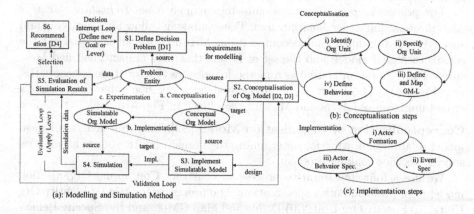

Fig. 2. Overview of modelling and simulation method

Principally, none is capable of combining top-down/bottom-up design principle, reductionist/emergentism analysis techniques, compositional/decompositional
abstractions, and localized/globalized perspectives as desired. They are also found
wanting in terms of ensuring model validity and correlating with the management
view of decision-making. The next section describes our proposed method.

3   Approach

We conceptualise an iterative method to construct a reliable and simulatable
models of organisation and conduct required *what-if* analyses in a systematic
manner. The proposed method contains six method steps namely *Define Decision
Problem* [S1], *Conceptualisation of Organisation Model* [S2], *Implement Simulatable Model* [S3], *Simulation* [S4], *Evaluation of Simulation Results* [S5], and
Recommendation [S6] as shown in Fig. 2(a). Principally, these steps implement
the modelling and validation method proposed by Robert Sargent in [15] (henceforth referred as M&V Method) to realise the decision steps D1-D4 of Management Decision Cycle. The proposed method uses three representations namely
problem entity, *conceptual model*, *computerized model* to transform a problem
entity (*i.e.*, description of real organisation) into an analysable model as advocated in M&V Method. Proposed method also adopts the operational validity
technique described in M&V Method to establish veracity of constructed models
for what-if analyses.

3.1   Method Definition

The detailed activities of six method steps of Fig. 2(a) are illustrated below:

Define Decision Problem [S1]: The method step *Define Decision Problem*
formalises decision problem and defines the scope for *what-if* scenario playing
by identifying the *Goals*, *Measures* and *Levers* from problem entity.

The process step S1 uses three sub-steps namely *Goal Definition*, *Measure
Identification* and *Lever Identification*. These sub-steps allow for identifying and
specifying: a top-down goal decomposition; Measures for all leaf goals of the
constructed goal model; and the set of Levers that may impact identified Measures. The i* notation is used as a methodological device for these concepts [18]
(*see* Fig. 3(a)). The Lever set is augmented by a decision table comprising a
cross-tabulation of Levers and Measures as shown in Fig. 3(b).

Conceptualisation of Organisation Model [S2]: This step defines a logical
model of an organisation for determining the domain information relevant to a
specific decision making problem.

We use a four-step iterative process to construct Conceptual Organisation
model from problem entity specification. The process steps are: (i) Identify Org
Units, (ii) Specify Org Unit, (iii) Define and Map GM-L, and (iv) Specify Behaviour as shown in Fig. 2(b). Process step *Identify Org Units* identifies prospective OrgUnits such as organisation, organisational units, sub-units, stakeholders,
resources from problem entity.

Together, these two process steps provide representational capability for describing states and trace information; interacting Events; compositional relationships; interactions between OrgUnits. The process steps also allow for refining of Goals, Measures and Levers as well as defining micro-behaviour of OrgUnits.

The ordering of the process steps allow for both a top-down decompositional approach starting from specification of an OrgUnit and a middle-out approach that uses behaviours to specify details of other OrgUnits. As well as using i* model to specify Goals and Measures, an extended form of class diagram to represent OrgUnits and the their structure, and a form of state machine to depict behaviours are used.

Implement Simulation Model [S3]: This method step converts a Conceptual Organisation model into machine interpretable specification, which we term as Simultable Organisation Model as shown in Fig. 2(a). We use the notion of *actor* [1] and an extended actor language ESL [5] to represent a machine interpretable organisation specification. A three step process (as shown in Fig. 2(c)), for example, maps OrgUnits into an actor specification and interactions between OrgUnits into event specifications. The full mapping is shown in the example in Sect. 4.

Simulation [S4]: We use an actor-based simulation (in particular ESL simulator [5]) to analyse what-if scenario formulated in method step S1. This step simulates the simulatable organisation model (with or without lever) and captures Measures from simulation results. Each simulation run captures a row of the decision table (as depicted in Fig. 3(b)) formulated in method step S1.

Evaluation of Simulation Results [S5]: In this step, during the evaluation, a human expert interprets the simulation results and may continue exploration of the problem where operational validity is not satisfied. This may be done by

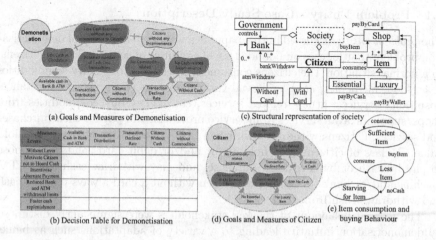

(a) Goals and Measures of Demonetisation

(c) Structural representation of society

(b) Decision Table for Demonetisation

(d) Goals and Measures of Citizen

(e) Item consumption and buying Behaviour

Fig. 3. Produced model artefacts

adjustment of levers, selection of different levers or identification of new levers through iterative actions. (See Fig. 2(a)).

Recommendation [S6]: This step recommends one or more Levers that can be implemented in real organisation.

3.2 Validation

Our method uses a validation loop that iterates over the method steps S2-S3-S4-S5 and compares simulation results with real or predicted data to establish operational validity [15] of constructed Conceptual Organisation model and Simulatable Organisation model. We consider operational graphics [15] of Trace and Measures as a basis for evaluation, and rely on human experts to certify the validity.

4   Illustration

On November 8, 2016, the Indian government pulled out 86.4% of the cash in circulation by derecognising two of the highest denominations currency notes - 500 rupee note and 1000 rupee note. The primary objective of demonetisation[1] was to reduce cash-based transactions that led to a shadow economy. This sudden and disruptive initiative resulted into prolonged cash shortages, financial crisis and inconvenience to the Indian population. The initiative was criticised for inadequate a-priori decision-making. This is a real life example of CDDM involving a socio-technical system with significant dynamism, uncertainty and emergentism. This section introduces the problem entity and illustrates how proposed method can be applied for a CDDM.

4.1   Problem Entity - Case Study Description

The *problem entity* discussed in this paper is a well-formed subset of demonetisation problem that focuses on bounded set of activities of common Indian citizens. In a normal situation, the citizens consume essential and/or luxury commodities (*e.g.*, food, medicines, *etc.*), and avail various services (*e.g.*, medical assistance, hospitality services, fitness related services, *etc.*). They buy commodities from shops/suppliers, avail services from service providers, and pay for their purchases and services. Citizens withdraw cash when cash-in-hand dips below a threshold value. A class of citizens may hold credit and/or debit cards and may choose to pay by cash or by card for a purchase, and may withdraw cash from ATM machine and/or bank. In contrast, a citizen without a card always pays by cash and withdraws cash from bank.

The normal behaviour of the key stakeholders were significantly disrupted by demonetisation initiative leading to a variety of adaptations such as banks enforcing set of restrictions on cash withdrawals to manage a fairer distribution

---

[1] https://en.wikipedia.org/wiki/2016_Indian_banknote_demonetisation.

of the introduction of new currency notes being introduced at a fixed rate - a mint-centric constraint. Shops adapted by accepting alternate payment options such as mobile wallet and card payment whenever they observed drops in sales. Individual citizens adapted by changing their payment patterns using mobile wallets and debit/credit cards to avoid using ATMs. Some citizens also resorted to temporary cash hoarding *i.e.*, withdrawing cash way in excess of their needs.

Given the above scope or problem entity description, the key objective of decision-making is to identify the set of appropriate *Levers* that can restore normalcy after demonetisation, *i.e.*, no notable denial of service from banks and ATM machines, no cash related inconvenience and no commodity related inconvenience to the citizens. The next subsections describes the execution of proposed method steps and their outcomes.

4.2   Define Decision Problem [S1]

The method starts with the Define Decision Problem [S1] step that produces goal models and decision tables. The problem entity described in Subsect. 4.1 aims for a high level Goal namely "Less-Cash Economy without any inconvenience to Citizens" as shown in Fig. 3(a). Method step S1 decomposes the high-level Goal with three sub-Goals namely "Less Cash in Circulation", "Increased number of Cash-Less Transactions", and "Citizens without any Inconvenience". The latter sub-Goal is further decomposed to two sub-sub-Goals namely "No Commodity-related Inconvenience" and "No Cash-related Inconvenience".

The method step S1 identifies five Measures: "Available Cash in Bank and ATM"; "Transaction Distribution" (*i.e.*, distribution of cash, alternate payment or wallet, and Card payments); "Citizens without Commodities"; "Transaction Declined Rate"; and "Citizen without Cash" for leaf-level goals as shown in Fig. 3(a). The method step S1 also identifies the possible Levers that may influence the Measures and therefore the Goals. The identified Levers are - "Motivate Citizen not to hoard Cash", "Incentivise Alternate Payment", "Reduce Bank and ATM Withdrawal Limit", and "Faster Cash Replenishment".

The decision formed using table using identified Levers and Measures is illustrated in Fig. 3(b). The resultant structural, goal and measure, and state behaviour models from S2 form the basis for implementing a simulatable specification for decision-making related analysis.

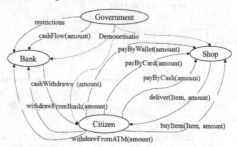

Fig. 4. Schema of simulatable model

4.3   Conceptualisation of Organisation Model [S2]

S2 and its sub-steps are used to construct the Conceptual Organisation Model from the problem entity description. Here, five key OrgUnits namely "Bank", "Shop", "Item", "Government", and "Citizen" are identified together with their structural relationships through an iterative process. The resultant artefact is depicted using a class diagram in Fig. 3(c). Sub-steps are used to define the Goal and Measures of identified OrgUnits. Figure 3(d) depicts the Goal and Measures of Citizen OrgUnit. Finally the behaviour of Government, Shop, Bank, Citizen, and their specilised OrgUnits is defined. A depiction is shown using firmed line box in Fig. 3(c). A part of citizen behaviour that describes the item consumption and buying behaviours of a citizen is illustrated using a state machines notation in Fig. 3(e).

4.4   Implement Simulatable Model [S3]

In this step, the models generated from earlier steps are (manually) translated into a schema of an actor specification depicted in Fig. 4. Here, OrgUnits are translated into actors namely Government, Shop, Bank and Citizen; the interactions are translated as events; the behaviours (*i.e.*, state machines) are translated into actor behaviour; and the demonetisation is specified as an event of the Government actor.

We also configure ESL simulator to display Measures using appropriate graphics. We have chosen 8 graphics panels to represent and help understand Measures as shown in Fig. 5. The "Trace on Payment Transaction Distribution" chart represents the Trace of "Transaction Distribution" Measure where the card transactions are displayed in green, wallet transactions in blue, and cash transactions in red. (*i.e.*, Transaction Declined Rate Measure). The "Payment Distribution" pie chart shows distribution of Card (green), Wallet (blue) and Cash (red) payments (*i.e.*, Transaction Distribution Measure at a specific time).

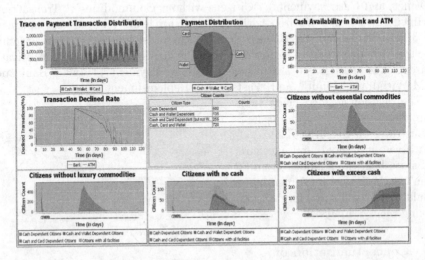

Fig. 5. Simulation dashboard - operational graphics for measures (Color figure online)

The "Citizen with no Cash" and "Citizen with excess Cash" charts describe the financial condition of those citizens with cash concerns (No cash Measure) and those hoarding cash (Excessive Cash Measure). Similar charts depict measures related to essential Items.

4.5   Simulation and Evaluation of Simulation Results [S4, S5]

A demonetisation scenario is simulated by considering a Society having one Government, one Bank, 15 Shops and 1710 Citizen actors for 150 'Days' where the Demonetisation event is triggered at Day 45. A snapshot of simulation dashboard with graphs at the Day of 115 (*i.e.*, after 70 days of Demonetisation) is depicted in Fig. 5.

Overall, we observe the Measure values in pre-demonetisation phase (*i.e.*, before Demonetisation event) are stable and normal: (i) Banks and ATMs have enough cash to service Citizens without noticeable denial of service, and (ii) Citizens are not experiencing any deficiency for essential or luxury items.

The Demonetisation event is triggered at 'Day' 45 causing a sudden reduction of 86.4% cash from the Banks and Citizens. Subsequently, the withdrawals from bank and ATM decline whilst wallet payment and card payment increase significantly: the citizens have started facing a financial crisis and the citizens who are solely dependent on cash have started starving for essential and/or luxury items (as shown in Fig. 5). The adverse effects continue for 52 days and then the situation returns back to normal.

We capture simulation results in an extended form of the decision table formulated in method step S1 and shown in Fig. 3(b). The extended table with simulation results is depicted in Table 1. Each row of Table 1 is the Measures captured by interpreting graphs of the simulation dashboard (refer Fig. 5) produced from a simulation run.

The observations of demonetisation specification without any Lever are captured in Row 1 of Table 1. The values of Row 1 of Table 1 signify that the Cash availability is low in post-demonetisation phase, the transactions distribution of Cash, Wallet and Card payments after 100 Days of Demonetisation are <50%, 42%, 8%> respectively, the bank and ATM transactions declined rate returns to normalcy after 52 Days, 8.1% citizens faced inconvenience due to cash, 7% citizens faced inconvenience due to essential items, and 26.3% citizens faced inconvenience due to luxury items.

Table 1. Consolidated simulation results

	Scenario	Cash Available in Bank and ATM	Transaction Distribution (After 100 Days)	Transaction Declined Rate	Cash Related Inconvenience		Commodity Related Inconvenience	
					Citizens without Cash	Citizens with excessive Cash	Citizen without essential commodities	Citizens without Luxury Commodities
1	Without Lever	Low	<50,42,8>	52 days	8.1%, 45	9.4%	7%, 41	26.3%, 42
2	Motivate Citizen not to Hoard Cash	Low	<50,43,7>	40 days	7%, 39	0	6.1%, 38	25.7%, 40
3	Insentivise Alternate Payment	Low	<35,57, 8>	45 days	7%, 31	9.4%	5.8%,34	25.7%, 35
4	Reduced Bank and ATM withdrawal limits	Low	<50,45,5>	48 days	5.8%, 46	9.4%	4.7%, 40	23.4%, 39
5	Faster cash replenishment	Low	<70,15,15>	18 days	5.4%, 17	0	3.2%,16	22%, 15

4.6   Validation Loop

We observed simulation results of demonetisation specification without any Lever (*i.e.*, Row 1 of Table 1) and correlated with the information found in authentic press-releases and newspapers. The trends on cash conditions of different citizens, the inconvenience due to deficiency of essential items, and luxury items, and service of denial at Bank and ATM withdrawal are consistent with ground truths. In reality, the cash conditions in ATMs and Banks at the end of January 2017 (after 3 and half months of demonetisation) were just sufficient to serve their customers - this observation relate with the graph shown in "Cash Availability in Bank and ATM" graph of Fig. 5. The alternative payment volume trend "Trace on Payment Transaction Distribution" chart (the value recorded in column "Transaction distribution" of Table 1) also matches with the Bloomberg report[2]. These observations and close correlations with reality ensure the operation validity of the constructed models.

4.7   Decision-Making and Recommendation

After ensuring the operation validity of demonetisation models, we explored four Levers as described in decision table of Fig. 3(b). Due to the space limitation, the simulation results of relevant simulation runs[3] are summarized using decision table in Table 1. A comparative analysis of rows 1–4 of Table 1 shows that the hoarding behaviour is one of the contributing factors for prolonged cash shortage - note row 2 is addressing the cash shortage issue in 40 Days, which is better than Row 1, 3 and 4. However, ATM and Bank withdrawal limits, as shown in row 4, are found as most critical to mitigate cash-less condition and deficiency of essential and luxury items (*i.e.*, citizen inconvenience).

A simulation run with faster cash-replenishment (five times more than standard cash replenishment rate) resulted into less cash shortage and less inconvenience to the citizens as compared to other alternatives as shown in Row 5 of Table 1. However, we found this option is not helping in moving toward a less-cash society as payment distribution of Cash, Wallet and Card payments is <70%, 15%, 15%> respectively.

5   Conclusion

This paper has contributed a method uses a top-down approach for defining goals, a middle-out approach for defining structural aspect of an organisation, and a bottom-up approach for behavioural specification, addresses methodical needs. The method incorporates best practice from both the simulation and management sciences disciplines. Critically, it addresses a significant gap in the

---

[2] https://www.thequint.com/business/2017/02/17/demonetisation-100-days-indian-economy.

[3] https://www.dropbox.com/s/q6xtz9el3sa6qzs/Demonetisation%20Experiment.pdf?dl=0.

methodology space for appropriate methods for supporting effective CDDM. While we have used specific techniques (such as i*, and ESL), our ongoing research suggests that several other alternative specifications can seamlessly be used in this method (such as Archimate and Akka). Our future research aims to improve the agility of the proposed method by exploring human guided, semi-automated language transformations between the stages of problem entity specification through to simulatable models.

References

1. Agha, G.A.: Actors: A model of concurrent computation in distributed systems. Technical report, DTIC Document (1985)
2. Allen, J.: Effective Akka. O'Reilly Media, Inc., USA (2013)
3. Barat, S., Kulkarni, V., Clark, T., Barn, B.: A model based realisation of actor model to conceptualise an aid for complex dynamic decision-making. In: 5th International Conference on Model-Driven Engineering and Software Development (2017)
4. Beckermann, A., Flohr, H., Kim, J.: Emergence or Reduction?: Essays on the Prospects of Nonreductive Physicalism. Walter de Gruyter, New York (1992)
5. Clark, T., Kulkarni, V., Barat, S., Barn, B.: ESL: an actor-based platform for developing emergent behaviour organisation simulations. In: Demazeau, Y., Davidsson, P., Bajo, J., Vale, Z. (eds.) PAAMS 2017. LNCS, vol. 10349, pp. 311–315. Springer, Cham (2017). doi:10.1007/978-3-319-59930-4_27
6. Daft, R.: Organization Theory and Design. Nelson Education, Toronto (2012)
7. Frank, U.: Multi-perspective enterprise modeling (memo) conceptual framework and modeling languages. In: 35th Annual Hawaii International Conference on System Sciences, pp. 1258–1267 (2002)
8. Haller, P., Odersky, M.: Scala actors: unifying thread-based and event-based programming. Theoret. Comput. Sci. **410**(2), 202–220 (2009)
9. Iacob, M., Jonkers, D.H., Lankhorst, M., Proper, E., Quartel, D.D.: Archimate 2.0 Specification: The Open Group. Van Haren Publishing, Zaltbommel (2012)
10. Kinny, D., Georgeff, M., Rao, A.: A methodology and modelling technique for systems of BDI agents. In: Van de Velde, W., Perram, J.W. (eds.) MAAMAW 1996. LNCS, vol. 1038, pp. 56–71. Springer, Heidelberg (1996). doi:10.1007/BFb0031846
11. van Langevelde, I., Philipsen, A., Treur, J.: Formal specification of compositional architectures. In: 10th European Conference on Artificial Intelligence, pp. 272–276 (1992)
12. Locke, E.: Handbook of Principles of Organizational Behavior: Indispensable Knowledge for Evidence-based Management. Wiley, Chichester (2011)
13. Meadows, D.H., Wright, D.: Thinking in Systems: A Primer. Chelsea Green Publishing, White River Junction (2008)
14. Sandkuhl, K., Stirna, J., Persson, A., Wißotzki, M.: Enterprise Modeling: Tackling Business Challenges with the 4EM Method. Springer, Heidelberg (2014)
15. Sargent, R.G.: Verification and validation of simulation models. In: Proceedings of the 37th Conference on Winter Simulation, Winter Simulation Conference, pp. 130–143 (2005)
16. Thomas, M., McGarry, F.: Top-down vs. bottom-up process improvement. IEEE Softw. **11**(4), 12–13 (1994)

17. White, S.A.: BPMN Modeling and Reference Guide: Understanding and Using BPMN (2008)
18. Yu, E., Strohmaier, M., Deng, X.: Exploring intentional modeling and analysis for enterprise architecture. In: Enterprise Distributed Object Computing Conference Workshops (2006)
19. Zachman, J., et al.: A framework for information systems architecture. IBM Syst. J. **26**(3), 276–292 (1987)

Streamlining Structured Data Markup and Agile Modelling Methods

Ana-Maria Ghiran[1], Robert Andrei Buchmann[1(⊠)], Cristina-Claudia Osman[1], and Dimitris Karagiannis[2]

[1] Business Informatics Research Center, Babeş-Bolyai University, Cluj-Napoca, Romania
{anamaria.ghiran,robert.buchmann,cristina.osman}@econ.ubbcluj.ro
[2] Knowledge Engineering Research Group, University of Vienna, Vienna, Austria
dk@dke.univie.ac.at

Abstract. Structured Data Markup allows Web developers to embed semantics in HTML pages, thus enabling clients (search engines, client apps etc.) to distil machine-readable resource descriptions from HTML code. This approach emerged from the Semantic Web paradigm as a powerful alternative to traditional Web scraping. Its enablers are dedicated HTML extensions (e.g., RDFa) and controlled vocabularies (e.g., Schema.org). Originating in a different context, Enterprise Modelling methods rely on diagrammatic means for describing and analysing an enterprise system in terms of key properties and conceptual abstractions. Hence, both the Semantic Web and Enterprise Modelling paradigms share a common interest in machine-processable semantics towards the goal of elevating semantics-awareness in information systems and decision support. Inspired by this overlapping, the paper proposes a mechanism for streamlining semantics between Structured Data Markup and enterprise modelling methods. Towards this goal, it employs the Resource Description Framework and the Agile Modelling Method Engineering Framework.

Keywords: Structured Data Markup · Resource Description Framework · Agile Modelling Method Engineering · Schema.org · ADOxx

1 Introduction

Structured Data Markup is being advocated as a search engine optimisation (SEO) technique enabled by semantic technology grafted on traditional Web development practices [1]. The origins of this approach may be traced back to data gleaning from XML documents [2] and to microformat profiles [3]. More recently, the lessons learned from microformats have led to the centralisation of prominent description vocabularies under the Schema.org "umbrella terminology" [4] founded and maintained by the big search engine providers (e.g., Google, Yahoo, Microsoft). From a conceptual perspective, Schema.org can be considered an ontology – i.e., it provides a consensus on terms (categories and properties) that should be used to describe often searched types of resources: organisations, persons, events, actions etc. The Schema.org terminology is

G. Poels et al. (Eds.): PoEM 2017, LNBIP 305, pp. 331–340, 2017.
https://doi.org/10.1007/978-3-319-70241-4_22

complemented by syntaxes that can extend HTML content with machine-readable descriptions of arbitrary resources – e.g., RDFa [5] introduced by the Resource Description Framework (RDF) [6].

In parallel developments, technologies and practices dealing with semantics have also emerged from the Enterprise Modelling paradigm – originating in data modelling, then evolving in complexity towards system modelling, business process modelling and multi-view enterprise modelling [7]. Although conceptual modelling is commonly perceived as being based on standards, the literature on modelling pragmatics [8] raised awareness on the need for domain-specificity or situational customisation of modelling methods, languages and tools. This is especially relevant in Enterprise Modelling where enterprise context or multi-perspective consistency concerns [9, 10] may raise requirements on semantic customisation. Methodologies and fast prototyping enablers have emerged to allow knowledge engineers to tailor and deploy modelling methods and languages for narrow domains or situational cases [11, 12]. They rely on metamodels that integrate concepts in *graphical language terminologies* which are comparable, to some extent, to ontological terminologies such as Schema.org.

This intuitive observation inspired the work at hand, as it proposes a streamlining between conceptual descriptions made available through semantic HTML markup and modelling languages that are synchronised to this markup with the help of the Agile Modelling Method Engineering (AMME) methodology [11]. The Resource Description Framework (RDF) [6] is employed as a bridging medium.

Therefore, the problem statement of this paper can be outlined as follows: *assuming that an organisation publishes machine-readable conceptual descriptions in their Web pages* (either for SEO purposes or for arbitrary client agents), *how can these be made available to a diagrammatic Enterprise Modelling environment?* The proposed solution extends the previously published method of Agile Modelling Method Engineering (AMME) with a mechanism for importing model contents in a modelling environment, from the RDF knowledge graph that can be distilled from Structured Data Markup; the necessity of AMME comes from the need to customize the targeted modelling language in order to align its semantics with those provided by the Structured Data Markup - especially if the markup uses the Schema.org terminology and not one that is under the control of the organisation using the modelling environment.

The remainder of the paper is organised as follows: Sect. 2 will introduce the technological and methodological enablers for the work at hand - Structured Data Markup and the Agile Modelling Method Engineering. Section 3 will present the mechanism through a running example. Section 4 will comment on related works. The paper ends with conclusions and outlook.

2   Technological and Methodological Enablers

2.1   The Structured Data Markup Processing Workflow

Structured Data Markup emerged from the convergence between traditional SEO practices and semantic technology. SEO aims to make the contents of HTML documents "understandable" for search engines. Structured Data Markup allows Web developers to embed machine-readable semantics (i.e., resource descriptions governed by some ontology) directly in the HTML source, with the help of dedicated syntactic formats – e.g., RDFa. This brings drastic changes to SEO practices, as the traditional techniques are replaced with precise ways of describing content meaning. The Structured Data Markup may be "distilled" into RDF graphs – a data model that is amenable to knowledge representation and reasoning. Arbitrary client agents (not limited to search engines) can thus shift from traditional string-based scraping towards powerful semantic queries and reasoning over the distilled knowledge graphs.

Complementary to the mentioned syntactic formats, a centralised, extensible terminology was set up at Schema.org [4], incorporating concepts and properties that were previously available in scattered and narrow-scoped microformat profiles or RDF vocabularies (e.g., hCard [13], FOAF [14], GoodRelations [15]).

Figure 1 shows an example of Structured Data Markup and the typical knowledge flow from a public HTML document to a client agent (not limited to search engine crawlers).

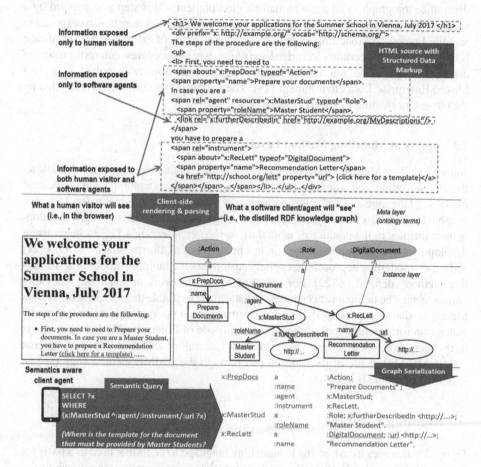

Fig. 1. From Structured Data Markup to machine-readable knowledge graphs

On the client side, the document content is formatted by a browser for a human visitor (mid-left side of the figure); the same document can also be distilled into a knowledge graph (bottom side). The example in the figure employs RDFa as a Structured Data Markup syntax [5], Turtle as a graph serialisation syntax [16] and SPARQL as a graph query language [17]. The meta layer of the graph uses concepts (Action, Role, Digital-Document) and properties (name, agent, instrument) from the Schema.org ontology. The example also indicates three categories of information that can be embedded in the HTML source: (i) statements that are *human-readable but not machine-readable* (i.e., the first statement, written in natural language); (ii) statements that are *machine-readable but not human-readable* in the browser (i.e., that the Master Student role has additional properties at the given URL); (iii) statements that are *both machine-readable and human-readable* (that the application requires a Master Student to provide a Recommendation Letter and a template is available at the given URL).

The conversion to the "pure" knowledge graph is performed by openly available "distillers" (see [18]). The additional step proposed by the work at hand is to further deserialise the graph in an agile modelling environment – this step is supported by a metamodelling plug-in (details in Sect. 3). The graph semantics may thus be exposed to an agile Enterprise Modelling method for further analysis or extension. The ideal case is to have models of certain enterprise facets (e.g., work procedures, enterprise resource descriptions) generated out of Web pages where they are already described – e.g., in a Linked Enterprise Data environment [19]. The possibility is currently investigated by the project motivating this work, EnterKnow [20].

2.2   Agility at Modelling Method Level

Agile Modelling Method Engineering [11] is a framework and methodology that allows the customisation and alignment of modelling methods (including their associated modelling language and software) with respect to targeted requirements (on language or model-driven functionality). As the name suggests, AMME transfers agile development principles to the practice of *modelling method engineering* – i.e., an incremental development cycle is applied, based on fast prototyping platforms such as ADOxx [21] and a metamodelling approach that agilely customises the building blocks of a "modelling method" defined in [22]. For the purposes of the work at hand, the modelling language must be tailored to accept the contents made available through Structured Data Markup so that the typical modelling procedure may be supported with automated model generation for specific types of models. A multitude of Enterprise Modelling methods have been developed in the Open Models Laboratory collaborative environment (OMiLAB) [23], some of them developed through the AMME methodology (see an inventory of methods in [24]).

3   Running Example

Figure 2 showcases a custom-made modelling language to be further used as a basis for the running example. The language is tailored to describe "application procedures" –

i.e., bureaucratic processes of applying for certain programs or benefits, extended with descriptions of required documents and dependencies on responsible persons.

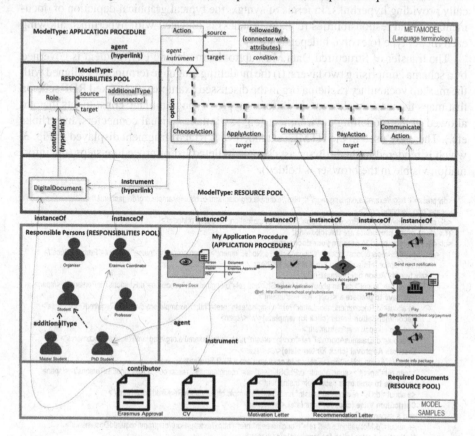

Fig. 2. The application procedure modelling language

Several customisations may be noticed, compared to the established business process modelling languages: the language concepts (including "action types") are hereby aligned with the Schema.org terminology, with some extensions added whenever properties that are necessary in the modelling environment are not available in Schema.org (e.g., the "condition" attribute, the "followedBy" connector). Certain concepts are enriched with user-editable attributes – e.g., the "ChooseAction" provides a table of alternatives – i.e., what kind of documents must be prepared depending on the applicant type. The language is partitioned into three "views" (types of models): (i) the actual procedure, (ii) the required documents and (iii) the responsibilities. Relations are established across these views (e.g., "agent" to indicate responsibility for an action, "contributor" to indicate required input to a document, "instrument" to indicate documents involved in an action, "target" to indicate the URL where a certain action can be performed on-line). The labels of these concepts and relations are abstracted here to be fully aligned with Schema.org, to keep the example easy to follow. In pragmatic cases, one may encounter cases where they must differ to make models easier to read, hence involving an additional mapping effort. Semantics are reflected in notation by dynamically providing hyperlinks. In terms of syntax, the typical graphical depiction of documentation and responsibilities (e.g., swimlanes) is replaced with hyperlinks, allowing each model type to evolve independently.

The transfer of Structured Data Markup to the modelling environment is governed by a schema comprising two layers: (i) the modelling language terminology aligned with the markup vocabulary (Schema.org in the discussed example); (ii) a fixed RDF schema that maps the markup elements to different types of diagrammatic constituents that are allowed in the modelling environment (e.g., swimlanes, visual connectors, hyperlinks etc.). These are used in the HTML (extended with RDFa) fragment displayed in Fig. 3, which is rendered in the browser as a simple bulleted list of procedure steps (the information visible in the browser is bolded).

```
<div prefix="l: http://example.org/language/ d: http://example.org/diagram/ o: http://example.org/diagschema/"
vocab="http://schema.org/">
<div about="d:MyApplicationProcedureGraph" typeof="l:ApplicationProcedure o:Model">
The steps of the procedure are the following:
<ul><li> First, you need to prepare your documents
    <div about="d:PrepareDocs" typeof="ChooseAction o:NodeElement"><span property="name" content="Prepare Docs"/>
        <div rel="option">In case you are a Master Student
        <div typeof="Action o:NonVisualEntity">
            <span rel="agent"><span about="d:MasterStudent" rel="o:originatesIn" resource="d:ResponsiblePersons"/></span>
            you have to prepare a <span rel="instrument">
            <a about="d:RecommendationLetter" rel="o:originatesIn" href="http://example.org/diagram/RequiredDocuments">
            Recommendation Letter (click for template)</a></span>
            and the  <span rel="instrument">
            <a about="d:ErasmusApproval" rel="o:originatesIn" href="http://example.org/diagram/RequiredDocuments">
            Erasmus Approval (click for template)</a></span>
        <div typeof="Action o:NonVisualEntity"> In case you are a PhD Student
            <span rel="agent"><span about="d:PhDStudent" rel="o:originatesIn" resource="d:ResponsiblePersons"/></span>
            you have to prepare a <span rel="instrument">
            <a about="d:CV" rel="o:originatesIn" href="http://example.org/diagram/RequiredDocuments">
            Curriculum Vitae (click for template) </a></span>
            and a <span rel="instrument">
            <a about="d:MotivationLetter" rel="o:originatesIn" href="http://example.org/diagram/RequiredDocuments">
            Motivation Letter (click for template)</a></span>
    </div>
    <span typeof="l:followedBy o:ComplexConnector">
        <span rel="o:from" resource="d:PrepareDocs"/><span rel="o:to" resource="d:RegisterApplication"/>
    </span></li>
    <li> Next, you need to register your application
    <span about="d:RegisterApplication" typeof="ApplyAction o:NodeElement">
        <span property="name" content="Register Application"/>
        <span rel="agent" resource="d:Student"/> at the following link:
        <a rel="target" href="http://summerschool.org/submission"> Registration </a>
    </span>
    <span typeof="l:followedBy o:ComplexConnector">
        <span rel="o:from" resource="d:RegisterApplication"/><span rel="o:to" resource="d:DocsAccepted"/>
    </span></li>
    <li> Then, we will check your documents
    <span about="d:DocsAccepted" typeof="CheckAction o:NodeElement" rel="agent" resource="d:Organiser">
        <span property="name" content="Docs accepted?"/>
    </span>
    <span typeof="l:followedBy o:ComplexConnector">
        <span rel="o:from" resource="d:DocsAccepted"/><span rel="o:to" resource="d:Pay"/>
        <span property="l:condition" content="yes"/>
    </span></li>....</ul></div></div>
```

Fig. 3. Structured markup aligned with the application procedure modelling language

From the same HTML fragment, RDFa distillers will extract the process description as a machine-readable knowledge graph (Fig. 4). This further becomes the input for the import plug-in prepared for the modelling environment (current implementation is based on ADOxx) to generate model elements. The terms employed in the machine-readable descriptions may be distinguished by their prefices: prefix **s:** (or no prefix in the HTML fragment) corresponds to Schema.org terms; prefix **l:** corresponds to terms that are not found in Schema.org but are necessary in the modelling language (e.g., the connectors between actions); prefix **d:** corresponds to model elements, i.e. those terms that will become diagrammatic constituents (nodes, connectors etc.); prefix **o:** corresponds to the schema of diagrammatic constituents allowed in ADOxx.

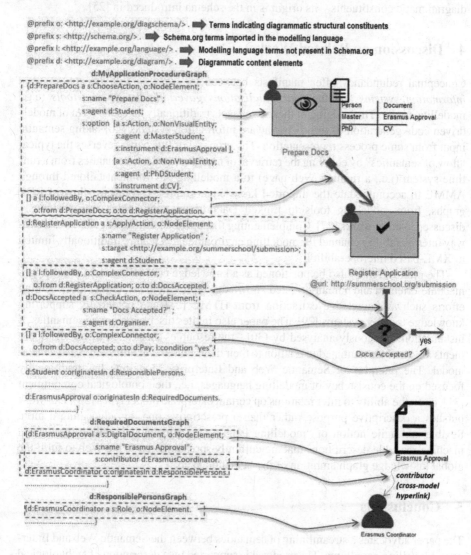

Fig. 4. Distilled application procedure model

The schema of diagrammatic constituents makes an explicit mapping indicating what kind of constructs are to be generated in the modelling tool (rather than relying on labels which may be ambiguous): "Node Element" is the class of all diagrammatic nodes; a "ComplexConnector" corresponds to any connector that has attributes attached to it; Hyperlink properties allow navigation between elements in different models; "NonVisualEntity" is any resource that is not present on the modelling canvas (has no graphical symbol attached), but is editable as table structure annotation attached to model elements. A taxonomy of such constituents is the outcome of analysing the extensive corpus of modelling languages presented in a first volume authored by the OMiLAB global community [24] and is currently being developed towards an ontology of diagrammatic constituents – its origin is in the schema introduced in [25].

4   Discussion on Related Works

Conceptual redundancy often manifests between the *data models driving run-time information systems* and the *conceptualisations governing design-time tools* (e.g., modelling tools). The bridging of these two facets traditionally takes the form of model-driven code generation or of process-aware information systems [26] taking semantic input from some process representation. The proposal of this paper reverses the typical "flow of semantics" by enabling the retrieval of machine-readable semantics from a run-time system (i.e., a running Web page) to a modelling environment tailored through AMME to accommodate the imported knowledge graphs. The reverse flow of RDF graphs, from modelling tools to Linked Data-driven applications was previously discussed in other works [27]. Complementing those works, this paper completes a two-way interoperability channel for modelling environments, a feature traditionally limited to XML-based interoperability.

The proposal may also be positioned as a knowledge conversion step, as it bridges machine-oriented and human-oriented knowledge representations, thus complementing efforts such as knowledge extraction from HTML [28] and potentially supporting knowledge transfer systems [29]. The paper also invites discussion on the semantics of instantiation, previously analysed by [30] - the resources mentioned in HTML documents are dually instantiated in relation to their diagrammatic manifestation and a meta-model. The interplay of Semantic Web and Enterprise Modelling has traditionally focused on the consistency of modelling languages, i.e., their ontological commitment [31], or on the ability to infer relations on certain enterprise model types [32]. Our work pursues a descriptive purpose rather than a prescriptive one, by advocating a more flexible and agile notion of "modelling languages", with models taking input from machine-readable descriptions that are currently spreading across the Web to fulfil the global knowledge graph ambition of the Semantic Web.

5   Conclusions

The paper advocates a streamlining of semantics between the Semantic Web and Enterprise Modelling paradigms. The proposal is supported by a description of technological and methodological enablers - RDF for interoperability and AMME for tailoring a modelling language to targeted semantic requirements. The streamlining proposal presented in the paper is being investigated in the EnterKnow [20] project on more realistic use cases than the showcase modelling language presented here.

Schema.org is frequently enriched and it may take valuable input from the use cases served by the work at hand (e.g., currently the Action concepts in Schema.org are lacking properties required to express action flows). Enterprise Modelling use cases may inspire the addition of concepts for describing enterprise assets.

In terms of limitations, the current implementation is not fully optimised, as it requires manual manipulation to prepare the import – i.e., to add position coordinates for the graphical layout of models (such information cannot be expected to be available in the general case for Structured Data Markup); since named graphs are not supported by the current specification of RDFa, conventions are necessary (e.g., one graph per HTML page). Finally, technical evaluations are still necessary to assess the usability and speed of model generation compared to manual creation of comparable models.

Acknowledgment. This work is supported by the Romanian National Research Authority through UEFISCDI, under grant agreement PN-III-P2-2.1-PED-2016-1140.

References

1. Google Structured Data (2017). https://developers.google.com/search/docs/guides/intro-structured-data
2. W3C: Gleaning Resource Descriptions from Dialects of Languages (GRDDL) (2007). https://www.w3.org/TR/grddl/
3. Microformats.org (2017). http://microformats.org/wiki/about
4. Schema.org – official website (2011). http://schema.org/
5. W3C: Rich Structured Data Markup for Web Documents (2015). https://www.w3.org/TR/rdfa-primer/
6. W3C. RDF 1.1 – official website (2014). https://www.w3.org/TR/rdf11-concepts/
7. Frank, U.: Multi-perspective enterprise modeling (MEMO) – conceptual framework and modeling languages, In: Sprague Jr., R.H. (ed.) Proceedings of the 35th Hawaii International Conference on System Sciences, pp 1258–1267. IEEE (2002)
8. Bjeković, M., Proper, H.A., Sottet, J.-S.: Embracing pragmatics. In: Yu, E., Dobbie, G., Jarke, M., Purao, S. (eds.) ER 2014. LNCS, vol. 8824, pp. 431–444. Springer, Cham (2014). doi: 10.1007/978-3-319-12206-9_37
9. Jeusfeld, M.A.: SemCheck: checking constraints for multi-perspective modeling languages. In: Karagiannis, D., Mayr, H., Mylopoulos, J. (eds.) Domain-Specific Conceptual Modeling, pp. 31–53. Springer, Cham (2016). doi:10.1007/978-3-319-39417-6_2
10. Karagiannis, D., Buchmann, R.A., Bork, D.: Managing consistency in multi-view enterprise models: an approach based on semantic queries. In: Proceedings of ECIS 2016, Association for Information Systems, p. 53 (2016)
11. Karagiannis, D.: Agile modelling method engineering. In: Karanikolas, N., Akoumianakis, D., Mara, N., Vergados, D., Michalis, X. (eds.) Proceedings of the 19th Panhellenic Conference on Informatics, pp. 5–10. ACM (2015)

12. Frank, U.: Domain-specific modelling languages: requirements analysis and design guidelines. In: Reinhartz-Berger, I., Sturm, A., Clark, T., Cohen, S., Betin, J. (eds.) Domain Engineering, pp. 133–157. Springer, Heidelberg (2013). doi:10.1007/978-3-642-36654-3_6

13. Microformats.org: H-Card (2017). http://microformats.org/wiki/h-card

14. Brickley, D., Miller, L.: FOAF Vocabulary Specification 0.99 (2014). http://xmlns.com/foaf/spec/

15. Hepp, M.: GoodRelations: an ontology for describing products and services offers on the web. In: Gangemi, A., Euzenat, J. (eds.) EKAW 2008. LNCS, vol. 5268, pp. 329–346. Springer, Heidelberg (2008). doi:10.1007/978-3-540-87696-0_29. http://www.heppnetz.de/projects/goodrelations/

16. W3C: Terse RDF Triple Language (2014). https://www.w3.org/TR/turtle/

17. W3C: SPARQL 1.1 Query Language (2013). https://www.w3.org/TR/sparql11-query/

18. W3C: RDFa 1.1 Distiller (2013). https://www.w3.org/2012/pyRdfa/Overview.html

19. Wood, D. (ed.): Linking Enterprise Data. Springer Science & Business Media, Heidelberg (2010)

20. EnterKnow project (2017). http://enterknow.granturi.ubbcluj.ro/

21. BOC-Group: ADOxx tool (2017). https://www.adoxx.org/live/home

22. Karagiannis, D., Kühn, H.: Metamodelling platforms. In: Bauknecht, K., Tjoa, A.M., Quirchmayr, G. (eds.) EC-Web 2002. LNCS, vol. 2455, p. 182. Springer, Heidelberg (2002). doi:10.1007/3-540-45705-4_19

23. The Open Models Initiative Laboratory (2017). http://www.omilab.org/psm/home

24. Karagiannis, D., Mayr, H.C., Mylopoulos, J. (eds.): Domain-Specific Conceptual Modelling. Springer, Heidelberg (2016)

25. Karagiannis, D., Buchmann, R.A.: Linked open models: extending linked open data with conceptual model information. Inf. Syst. 56, 174–197 (2016)

26. Dumas, M., van der Aalst, W.M.P., ter Hofstede, A.H.M. (eds.): Process-Aware Information Systems: Bridging People and Software through Process Technology. Wiley-Interscience, New York (2005)

27. Buchmann, R.A., Karagiannis, D.: Domain-specific diagrammatic modelling: a source of machine-readable semantics for the Internet of Things. Cluster Comput. 20(1), 895–908 (2017)

28. Wu, X., Cao, C., Wang, Ya., Fu, J., Wang, S.: Extracting knowledge from web tables based on DOM tree similarity. In: Lehner, F., Fteimi, N. (eds.) KSEM 2016. LNCS, vol. 9983, pp. 302–313. Springer, Cham (2016). doi:10.1007/978-3-319-47650-6_24

29. Marumo, N., Beppu, T., Yamaguchi, T.: A knowledge-transfer system integrating workflow, a rule base, domain ontologies and a goal tree. In: Buchmann, R., Kifor, C.V., Yu, J. (eds.) KSEM 2014. LNCS, vol. 8793, pp. 357–367. Springer, Cham (2014). doi:10.1007/978-3-319-12096-6_32

30. Laarman, A., Kurtev, I.: Ontological metamodeling with explicit instantiation. In: van den Brand, M., Gašević, D., Gray, J. (eds.) SLE 2009. LNCS, vol. 5969, pp. 174–183. Springer, Heidelberg (2010). doi:10.1007/978-3-642-12107-4_14

31. Guizzardi, G.: Ontological foundations for structural conceptual models. CTIT, Centre for Telematics and Information Technology, Ph.D. thesis Series, No. 05-74 (2005)

32. Lantow, B., Sandkuhl, K., Fellmann, M.: Visual language and ontology based analysis: using OWL for relation discovery and query in 4EM. In: Abramowicz, W., Alt, R., Franczyk, B. (eds.) BIS 2016. LNBIP, vol. 263, pp. 23–35. Springer, Cham (2017). doi:10.1007/978-3-319-52464-1_3

Integrating Local and Global Optimization in Capability Delivery

Kurt Sandkuhl[✉]

University of Rostock, Albert-Einstein-Str. 22, 18059 Rostock, Germany
kurt.sandkuhl@uni-rostock.de

Abstract. Efficient value creation and service delivery processes are considered as key factor to competitiveness in a globalized market. The systematic management of the capabilities of an enterprise is emerging into a key activity for achieving efficiency. In capability management, the capability design and delivery approach (CDD) has been proposed and its utility was demonstrated in previous work. An essential activity in CDD is the analysis of the context of capability delivery in order to understand the cause of variations in delivery of capabilities. This paper builds on CDD and elaborates on the feature of CDD to combine local context information from individual clients with global context information from the capability provider when optimizing capability delivery. An additional method component for the CDD methodology is proposed and demonstrated using a case from business process outsourcing.

Keywords: Capability · BPO · Local context · Global context

1 Introduction

In many industrial sectors efficient value creation and service delivery processes are considered as the key factor to competitiveness in a globalized market environment with information technology as enabler and strategic instrument for service management. The systematic management of the capabilities of an enterprise, which often are reflected in the business services offered to customers and the technical services associated to them, is emerging into a key activity for achieving efficiency. The term capability is used in various industrial and academic contexts with often different meanings (see Sect. 4.1). Most conceptualizations agree that capability includes the ability to do something (know-how, organizational preparedness, competences) and the capacity for actual delivery in an application context.

In order to facilitate capability management, we propose to not only consider business services but also to explicitly analyze their delivery contexts and to model both, the service and the context. This approach, which is called capability-driven design and development (CDD), aims at capturing the factors that are decisive for flexibility, dynamics and variability. CDD is grounded in industrial requirements and includes method components, a common meta-model and a tool environment (see Sect. 2). The method provides mechanisms for adjustment of capability delivery.

© IFIP International Federation for Information Processing 2017
Published by Springer International Publishing AG 2017. All Rights Reserved
G. Poels et al. (Eds.): PoEM 2017, LNBIP 305, pp. 341–351, 2017.
https://doi.org/10.1007/978-3-319-70241-4_23

For business process outsourcing (BPO), which is in focus of the industrial case selected for this paper (see Sect. 2.1), the adjustments during capability delivery are based on the service level agreements between client and business process service provider (BSP) as well as on BSP-internal policies, such as the responsible units for a capability and their schedule. Currently, the CDD approach includes primarily adaptation mechanisms, which focus on this "local view" for separate capabilities and/or clients. However, in industrial practice the BSP also would like to have an additional "global" view encompassing several capabilities or clients. Examples are the business transactions of a certain client in all capabilities, all business transactions of a certain category, the cases currently processed in a department, etc. In order to provide the global view and to offer integrated local and global optimization, an aggregation and filtering of local view data on a higher level is required. CDD has to be prepared for this purpose, e.g. by reflecting the indicators required for optimization in context elements and different optimization strategies in context sets (see Sect. 2.2). The focus of this paper is on methodical aspects of this CDD extension.

The main contributions of this paper are (a) the analysis of requirements for integrating local and global views, (b) the concept of local-as-global and global-as-local and (c) an example for using the method extension. Section 2 presents an industrial case form BPO motivating the work and summarizes previous work in capability management. Section 3 presents an approach for integrating local and global optimization manifested in a method component for CDD. Section 4 discusses related work and Sect. 5 summarizes initial experiences and gives an outlook.

2   Context-Aware Business Services: The CaaS Approach

Work in this paper was performed as a part of the EU-FP7 project "Capability-as-a-Service in Digital Enterprises (CaaS)". This section introduces an industrial case in BPO (2.1) motivating the work, and the CDD approach developed in CaaS (2.2).

2.1   Business Process Outsourcing of Energy Distribution Companies

Main partner in the industrial case is the company SIV.AG from Rostock (Germany). SIV offers BPO services to a variety of medium-sized utility providers and other market roles of the energy sector in Germany and several European countries. BPO, i.e. the performance of a complete business process for a business function by a BSP outside an organization, has to offer and implement solutions with variations for different cases. One variation is inherent in the business process as such. Even though core processes can be defined and implemented in standard software systems, configurations and adjustments for the organization in question are needed. The second cause of variation is the configuration for the country of use, i.e. the implementation of the actual regulations and bylaws. The third variation is related to the resource use for implementing the actual business process for the customer, i.e. the provision of technical and organizational capabilities.

Basis for these services is SIV's software product kVASy4. Integrated with the business process environment, kVASy4 provides business logic for the energy sector. Different deployment models are used including a provider-centric model (kVASy4 and the business processes are run at SIV), a client-centric model (kVASy4 is installed at the client site and the manual work of the business process is performed at SIV) and mixed models (e.g. kVASy4 in the cloud, process performed partly at the client and partly at SIV). SIV envisioned a more dynamic way of providing BPO services to their customers for ad-hoc up-scaling of services for existing customers.

As a basis for the research work presented in this paper, we performed a case study in SIV's BSP business unit. Qualitative case study is an approach to research that facilitates exploration of a phenomenon within its context using a variety of data sources. This ensures that the subject under consideration is not explored from only one perspective, but rather from a variety of perspectives which allows for multiple facets of the phenomenon to be revealed and understood. Within the case study, we used three different perspectives, which at the same time represent sources of data: We observed the activities during business service provision, we examined the business process models used for execution of the outsourcing and we interviewed different roles involved in BPO services. The case study work resulted in a better understanding of the characteristics of local and global context in the case and in requirements to the method extension presented in Sect. 3. After the case study, SIV also formed the basis for evaluating the new method extension (see Sect. 3.4).

2.2   Capability-Driven Design and Delivery (CDD)

Business services are IT-based services which digital enterprises provide for their customers. Business services usually serve specified business goals, they are specified in a model-based way and include service level definitions. The CDD approach explicitly defines (a) the potential delivery contexts of a business service, (b) the potential variants of the business service for these delivery contexts and (c) what aspect of the delivery context would require what kind of adaptation. The potential delivery context basically consists of a set of parameters (context elements) which characterize the differences in delivery. The combination of all context elements and their possible ranges defines the context set. The potential variants of the business service are represented by process variants. Since in many delivery contexts it will be impractical to capture all possible variants, we propose to define patterns for the most frequent variants and to combine and instantiate these patterns to create actual solutions. The connection between context elements, patterns and business services has to be captured as transformation or mapping rules. These rules are defined during design time and interpreted during runtime. CDD has been further elaborated by defining a meta-model (see, e.g. [9]), a methodology and a tool environment.

The *CDD methodology* consists of method components. To structure the methodology the method components have been divided into upper-level method components, describing a certain application area with method components relevant for that area. The upper-level method components are the following:

- Getting Started with CDD. Supports decision making whether or not CDD is suitable for an organization, and how to get started with CDD.
- Capability Design Process. Contains an overview on how to design, evaluate and develop capabilities using process models, goal models and other models.
- Enterprise Modelling. The component contains method components that guide the creation of enterprise models that are used as input for capability design.
- Context modelling. Describes the method components needed for analysing the capability context, and the variations needed to deal with variations.
- Reuse of Capability Design. This component contains guidelines for the elicitation and documentation of patterns for capability design.
- Run-time Delivery Adjustment. Describes the components needed to adjust a capability at runtime.

The *CDD tool environment* includes the following functional components:

- capability design tool CDT - provides modeling elements defined in the capability meta-model and models the required capability including business service, business goals, context and relations to delivery patterns.
- Pattern composition module and repository - identifies patterns for capability delivery, composes them and offers storage and maintenance of patterns.
- Context platform - captures and provides data from external data sources including sensing hardware and Internet based services such as social networks.
- Capability delivery navigation application (CNA) - provides means for monitoring and adjustment of capability delivery. It includes a module for monitoring context and goal KPI, predictive evaluation of capability delivery performance and delivery adjustment algorithms.
- Capability delivery application (CDA) is developed following the process and technologies used by a particular company. The CDD methodology only determines interfaces required for the CDA to be able to receive capability delivery adjustment commands from the capability delivery navigation.

3   Local and Global Optimization in Capability Delivery

3.1   Purpose of the Method Extension

This section proposes a method extension for the methodology part of CDD which has the focus on monitoring and optimizing a capability in BPO. The method extension was motivated by and developed and applied in the industrial case presented in Sect. 2.1. In BPO monitoring of capability delivery primarily focuses on two different aspects which might cause capability adjustments:

- the business service provider has to make sure that the capability is provided in accordance to the contractual service-level agreement with the client. Typically, such agreements include maximum processing time for a business transaction, maximum waiting time before a business transaction is processed, capacity to provide for the client in terms of knowledge workers, etc.

- internal policies of the business service provider have to be met. Examples are the way to decide what business unit is responsible for a business transaction and in what order the cases have to be processed (dispatching), the quality assurance measures to be performed for each case, the targeted maximum processing time, average processing time or waiting time until processing.

Both aspects usually are reflected in performance indicators which ideally can be captured automatically in the runtime environment. Furthermore, the context model for a capability often reflects both aspects by including context elements mirroring the decision strategies. An advantage of the CDD approach is the possibility to differentiate between different levels of monitoring during capability delivery. From a technical perspective, BPO frequently uses different installations of the capability delivery application (e.g. separate installations for clients with high volume of business transactions) which potentially are deployed on different technical platforms (e.g. in the computing center of the client, at the service provider's premises or on cloud resources). Thus, the "local view" of each CDA installation and the "global view" of all local installations will have to be subject of monitoring and optimization. Furthermore, the BPO also is interested in additional views while monitoring, like all business transactions of a certain client, all business transactions of a certain category, the cases currently processed in a department, all cases delayed independently of the installation and service type, etc.

The local view of each CDA installation usually is equipped with an own monitoring application (e.g. a business process activity monitor), but the global view cannot easily be provided as they require an aggregation and filtering of local view data on a higher level. Furthermore, an optimization strategy on global level might require modifications in the decision logic on local level and vice versa. With many local installations a manual intervention on either local or global level is too time consuming, i.e. dynamic adjustments require a technical integration of local and global level. In the CDD approach, CNA offers the possibility to establish a global monitoring and optimization level on top of local CDA installations with the additional option to not only use indicators captured in the runtime environments but also from other context sources, even outside the enterprise IT. However, if the subject of integrated local and global optimization is addressed, capability model and adjustment algorithms have to be prepared for this purpose, e.g. by reflecting the indicators required for optimization in context elements. The method extension proposed is addressing the subject of capability modelling for integrated local and global monitoring and optimization. One of the aims in this context is to minimize the interventions in local systems.

The issue of optimizing a set of systems with potentially different "local" strategies from a global perspective, i.e., for a "global" strategy, has been subject of study in operations research and production systems before. Often, the optimization problem can be expressed in a formal way, e.g., as optimization model, and established optimization approaches can be applied, e.g. linear optimization, mixed integer programming, network-based optimization or non-linear optimization. In this context, the method component aims at supporting problem analysis and development of the optimization model by identifying the required decision variables and restrictions. However, the actual development of the optimization model is not part of this method component, as this topic is already covered in existing literature.

3.2 Global-as-Local or Local-as-Global

Independently of the actual optimization approach, there are different ways to implement the actual optimization in enterprise IT on local level (i.e. in CDA) and global level (i.e. in CNA). In the context of this method component, we consider two different approaches and support decision making on what approach to use. Global-as-local assumes that the overall optimization requires changes in behavior of the local system which requires information about the global situation. Local-as-global assumes that local systems adapt their behavior using only information about their local situation and the overall optimization is done by coordinating local systems on a global level. Global-as-local typical would be applicable in the following situations:

- Implementation of specific strategies for overall resource usage which depend on actual situation of these resources
- Strategies which require human intervention at central point
- Strategies which require information not available at local systems

  Selected situations when local-as-global is adequate are

- Low update frequency of global parameters, often with high latency
- High performance requirements for transactions, i.e. there is no possibility to suspend a process for receiving information from the central unit
- Local status affects global optimization (e.g. rare kind of exception)

  Implementation of global-as-local typically would either include that the local system asks the global system for instructions how to continue before proceeding with a business case, which technically is similar to a blocking remote procedure call. If non-blocking behavior is required, the global system would have to update decision variables of the local system whenever there is a change in scheduling strategy. However, this is only adequate if the scheduling is not dependent on the individual case but the overall resource availability. In an implementation of local-as-global the local system typically decides independently but notifies the global system. The global system will have to re-assign resources based on the notification information.

3.3 Procedure of the Method Extension

The method extension consists of several steps, which can be summarized as its procedural part. The steps and their purposes are as follows:

- Step 1 - Scoping: to decide for which capability or capabilities local or global optimization shall be prepared
- Step 2 - Identify and gather relevant information. This includes earlier analysis results, in particular from capability modelling, contractual agreements with the client, internal policy documents and ideas about potential optimization strategies
- Step 3 - Extract desired decision logic: To draft an idea how the desired optimization could be reached and to prepare the identification of decision variables needed for implementing the desired decision logic

- Step 4 - Identify decision variables: To identify the decision variables needed for implementing the desired decision logic
- Step 5 - Decide on local-as-global or global-as-local: To decide whether local-as-global or global-as-local should be implemented
- Step 6 - Implement either local-as-global or global-as-local, i.e. to design the way of implementing the capturing of decision variables and the communication between local system and global level.

3.4 Example

For brevity reasons, the example will only include the first 4 steps which are essential to demonstrate the intention of the method component. In step 4, we will only show the details of one of the example capability variations, variation V2 (see below).

Step 1- Scoping: As an example we will use a capability of the business service provider introduced in Sect. 2.1. This capability includes two major variations V1 and V2. The required services for the two variations are performed by two organization units A and B which have a need to achieve better load balancing between them. The use of the method component aims at (a) identifying the decision variables and restrictions for implementing workload balancing between organization units A and B, and (b) at deciding whether local-as-global or global-as-local has to be implemented for V1 and V2.

Step 2- Information gathering: If the BSP is handling exceptions in the first variation (V1) the knowledge workers from organization unit A are responsible. For variation 2 (V2), organization unit B is taking care of the exceptions. As the exceptions from V2 are related to those of V1 but V2 exceptions are far more complex, the knowledge workers from organization unit B would also be qualified to work on exceptions from V1, but not vice versa. Balancing of work load between the two units currently is not optimal as no overall view on global level is available. If the capability owner has the impression that organization unit A has too much work and the organization unit B has free capacity, work is redistributed from A to B until B starts to complain. For V2, the service-level agreements with the clients are structured similar to V1. For V2 it states that up to 10 exceptions per working day will be handled by the client; each exceptions on top until max. 50 has to be managed by the BSP. In case of more than 50, the exceptions will be handled by the client unless the client changes the upper limit. All exceptions to be handled by the BSP are sent to the task management system of organization unit B. For V2, the BSP receives a compensation based on the number of exceptions handled. The service-level agreement with two of the clients includes a penalty for each exception whose handling time exceeds a certain time limit.

Step 3 - Extract desired decision logic: The desired optimization for V1 is as follows: IF the sum of jobs in the task management queue is higher than what is the capacity of organization unit A for a given time period AND organization unit B still has capacity available THAN the dispatcher on duty asks organization unit B to also work on exceptions of V1 OTHERWISE additional resources have to be called in by the dispatcher for the next shift. For V2 the capability owner puts the priority on avoiding penalties with at the same time optimizing resource use in unit B. The wish of the capability owner is to assign priorities to exceptions, i.e. each exception should get a priority number. The priority number is calculated using the average waiting time and contracted maximum processing time agreed on with the client.

Step 4 - Identify decision variables: To identify decision variables includes different activities including a separate view on local and global level and context modeling. The final lists of decision variables for V2 are shown in Table 1 (global level) and Table 2 (local level).

Table 1. Final list of decision variables for V2 on global level

Decision variable	Measurable property	Captured in the local system?
BSP human resources	Schedule (planned capacity per date and org. unit)	NO
SUM of the backlog sizes of all local systems for the exception leading to V1	Backlog size	YES
Exception type	BAM notification	YES
Maximum processing time	SLA information (for each exception type and client: max. hours)	NO
Average processing time	operations average (for each exception type: average processing time)	NO
Current workload in BSP	Task management data (current number of tasks and average processing time per org. unit)	NO

Table 2. Final list of decision variables in the local system for V2

Decision variable	Measurable property	Captured in the local system?
Backlog threshold for the exception leading to V2	Backlog size	YES
Exception type	BAM notification	YES
Processing priority	Calculated based on maximum processing time, average processing time and current workload at BSP	NO

Step 5 - Decide on local-as-global or global-as-local: As shown in Tables 1 and 2, for V2 not all decision variables in the local systems are captured locally. Thus, "global-as-local" has to be implemented. For V1, all decision variables required in the local systems are captured locally. Here, "local-as-global" has to be performed.

4   Related Work

4.1   Capability Management

The term capability is used in different areas of business information systems. In the literature there seems to be an agreement about the characteristics of the capability, still there is no generally acceptance of the term. The definitions mainly put the focus on "combination of resources" [2], "capacity to execute an activity" [1], "perform better than competitors" [4] and "possessed ability [8]". The capabilities must be enablers of competitive advantage; they should help companies to continuously deliver a certain business value in dynamically changing circumstances [5]. They can be perceived from different organizational levels and thus utilized for different purposes. According to [6] the firm performance is the greatest, when the enterprises map their capabilities to IT applications. In this perspective the capabilities are provided as business services, i.e. designed and delivered in a process-oriented fashion. Capabilities are directly related to business processes that are affected from the changes in context, such as, regulations, customer preferences and system performance. As companies in rapidly changing environments need to anticipate variations and respond to them [3], the affected processes need to be adjusted quickly.

In the CaaS project capability is defined as *the ability and capacity that enable an enterprise to achieve a business goal in a certain context* [7, 9]. Ability refers to the level of available competence, where competence is understood as talent intelligence and disposition, of a subject or enterprise to accomplish a goal; capacity means availability of resources, e.g. money, time, personnel, tools. This definition focuses on the components of enterprise modelling such as goal modelling and utilizes the notion of context, thus stresses the variations of the standard processes.

4.2   Adaptive Case Management

During the last years, adaptive case management (ACM) has attracted a lot of attention in the field of business process modelling. Whenever business processes are only weakly structured or include a lot of exceptional situations, they cannot be fully specified and automated. Such business processes typically show many situations where a human agent, the so called knowledge worker, has to be involved in completing a business process or has to fully take over this process. In this context, the term ACM-system was defined as follows: "Systems that are able to support decision making and data capture while providing the freedom for knowledge workers to apply their own understanding and subject matter expertise to respond to unique or changing circumstances within the business environment" [10].

Service providers in BPO are interested to perform as many activities in a business process in an automatable way, i.e. to only base BPO on IT resources only. If case handling has to be done by knowledge workers, BPO service providers are interested to reduce the costs for this step because of economic reasons: case work requires personnel with the right knowledge, coordination of this personnel and definition of service levels and quality attributes in relationship to the client. The main focus of ACM is the "case", which has three main features [11]:

- Organization: conventional business process models always include a control flow, which often is missing in ACM. ACM often is data-centred in contrast to the process-centred approach of a process model,
- Case handling: case handling often is performed not only by one individual knowledge worker, but includes the interaction of several workers. This requires a high level of cooperation form each individual participant.
- Adaption: in comparison to business process management which attempts to treat all instances of a process in an identical way, ACM requires adaption of the case handling to each individual case.

5 Summary

New situations in business environments arise due to changes in regulations, bylaws and customer preferences. Capabilities help companies to continuously deliver a certain business value in these dynamically changing circumstances by adjusting the service delivery to different contexts. This paper focuses on a specific aspect of capability management: integration of local and global optimization. A method extension is proposed which focuses on analyzing the optimization context and identifying the required decision variables. The method extension complements the CDD methodology. An example of using the methodology in an industrial case of BPO illustrates the method extension use. Future work has to include application of the method extension in more real-world application in order to facilitate a systematic evaluation and improvement of the method extension.

Acknowledgments. This work has been performed as part of the EU-FP7 funded project no: 611351 CaaS – Capability as a Service in Digital Enterprises.

References

1. Jiang, Y., Zhao, J.: An empirical research of the forming process of firm inter-organizational e-business capability: based on the supply chain processes. In: 2010 2nd International Conference on Information Science and Engineering (ICISE), pp 2603–2606 (2010)
2. Antunes, G., Barateiro, J., Becker, C., et al.: Modeling contextual concerns in enterprise architecture. In: 2011 15th IEEE International Enterprise Distributed Object Computing Conference Workshops (EDOCW), pp. 3–10 (2011)
3. Eriksson, T.: Processes, antecedents and outcomes of dynamic capabilities. Scand. J. Manage. **30**(1), 65–82 (2014). doi:10.1016/j.scaman.2013.05.001
4. Boonpattarakan, A.: Model of thai small and medium sized enterprises' organizational capabilities. JMR **4**(3), 15 (2012). doi:10.1016/j.scaman.2013.05.001

5. Stirna, J., Grabis, J., Henkel, M., Zdravkovic, J.: Capability driven development – an approach to support evolving organizations. In: Sandkuhl, K., Seigerroth, U., Stirna, J. (eds.) PoEM 2012. LNBIP, vol. 134, pp. 117–131. Springer, Heidelberg (2012). doi: 10.1007/978-3-642-34549-4_9

6. Chen, J., Tsou, H.: Performance effects of 5IT6 capability, service process innovation, and the mediating role of customer service. J. Eng. Technol. Manage. **29**(1), 71–94 (2012). doi: 10.1016/j.jengtecman.2011.09.007

7. Zdravkovic, J., Stirna, J., Henkel, M., Grabis, J.: Modeling business capabilities and context dependent delivery by cloud services. In: Salinesi, C., Norrie, M.C., Pastor, Ó. (eds.) CAiSE 2013. LNCS, vol. 7908, pp. 369–383. Springer, Heidelberg (2013). doi: 10.1007/978-3-642-38709-8_24

8. Ben Mena, T., Bellamine-Ben Saoud, N., Ben Ahmed, M., Pavard, B.: Towards a methodology for context sensitive systems development. In: Kokinov, B., Richardson, D.C., Roth-Berghofer, T.R., Vieu, L. (eds.) CONTEXT 2007. LNCS, vol. 4635, pp. 56–68. Springer, Heidelberg (2007). doi:10.1007/978-3-540-74255-5_5

9. Bērziša, S., Bravos, G., Gonzalez Cardona, T., Czubayko, U., España, S., Grabis, J., Henkel, M., Jokste, L., Kampars, J., Koç, H., Kuhr, J.-C., Llorca, C., Loucopoulos, P., Juanes Pascual, R., Pastor, O., Sandkuhl, K., Simic, H., Stirna, J., Zdravkovic, J.: Capability driven development: an approach to designing digital enterprises. Bus. Inf. Syst. Eng. (BISE) **57**(1), 15–25 (2015)

10. Swenson, K.D.: Mastering the Unpredictable: How Adaptive Case Management will Revolutionize the Way that Knowledge Workers get Things do. Meghan-Kiffer Press, Tampa (2010)

11. Herrmann, C., Kurz, M.: Adaptive case management: supporting knowledge intensive processes with IT systems. In: Schmidt, W. (ed.) S-BPM ONE 2011. CCIS, vol. 213, pp. 80–97. Springer, Heidelberg (2011). doi:10.1007/978-3-642-23471-2_6

The Digital Business Architect – Towards Method Support for Digital Innovation and Transformation

Matthias Wißotzki[✉] and Kurt Sandkuhl

University of Rostock, Chair of Business Information Systems,
Albert-Einstein-Str. 22, 18059 Rostock, Germany
{matthias.wissotzki,kurt.sandkuhl}@uni-rostock.de

Abstract. Digitalization is currently the most important driver of economic growth. Inspired by increasing digital networking and smart automation possibilities, omnipresent access technologies and dynamic customer requirements, modern enterprises work more and more on additional and new digital business models. The aim is to exploit potentials for new and especially digital business models much faster and to cope with the resulting challenges. This requires a technical integration of different disciplines, new qualification profiles and new methodical approaches. The paper proposes the aggregation of selected approaches from the areas of digital business model development, capability management and enterprise architecture management as a methodical basis for the training profile of a "Digital Business Architect" and "Digital Innovation and Transformation Process (DITP)".

Keywords: Digital business modeling · Capability management · Enterprise modeling · Enterprise architecture management · Digital Business Architect · Small and medium business

1   Introduction

The successful development and integration of digital business models requires a high degree of agility in enterprises. From an economic perspective, agility is only recommendable if the effects of changes in an enterprise can be determined at any point in time [1, 2]. Furthermore, digital business models usually depend on technological innovations and the exploitation of their potential in a way, which creates entirely new products and services and leads to new operational procedures in enterprises or completely redefines the existing ones. This calls for a methodical and technical integration of approaches from different areas facilitating the required changes, such as digital business model management (BMM), capability management (CM) and enterprise architecture management (EAM) [2].

The integration of these issues shape a modern qualification profile [2, 3] which we name "Digital Business Architect" (DBA). The DBA has to have multi-disciplinary expertise and a corresponding method support, the Digital Innovations and Transformation Process (DITP). The latter, in particular, enables the DBA to moderate as part

G. Poels et al. (Eds.): PoEM 2017, LNBIP 305, pp. 352–362, 2017.
https://doi.org/10.1007/978-3-319-70241-4_24

of the business executive team in an enterprise between business management and technology experts in order to support implementing their requirements under consideration of an integrative Business-IT-Alignment (iBITA) concepts [2]. The industrial demand for this qualification profile and organizational role showed in different digitalization projects and the experiences collected in these projects [2, 4]. The new qualification profile should not only enable personnel and students to develop digital business models but also to carry out the planning and implementation of changes and to provide suitable methods to do so. This paper presents first results of work in progress on the DBA qualification profile and the DITP process. The first process version is currently being evaluated in the context of a master thesis at the University of Rostock [5].

An introduction, the research methodology used for the data collection and its analysis as well as the foundations for the (DITP are outlined in Sect. 1. Section 2 discusses the required methods and Sect. 3 presents the core activities of DITP. Finally, the results of this work in progress are summarized and an outlook on further research activities is given in the last section.

1.1 Research Approach

A literature analysis was conducted to elaborate the theoretical foundations. In general, two methods are used: The "systematic method" [6] and the snowballing method [7, 8], whereas for the initialization of the literature review, we opted the second approach. This procedure should ensure the inclusion of both scientific and journalistic publications. For a first evaluation, a specific scenario was considered in the context of a case study [9, 10]. The case study was carried out within the frame of a master thesis at the University of Rostock. The aim was to observe version one of the DBA's proposed process model within a start-up environment and then derive new insights for the improvement of its practicability by means of an argumentative-deductive analysis [10–12].

The process was realized according to [11] and consists in the process steps of planning, data collection, analysis and report (Fig. 1).

Fig. 1. Process of carrying out a case study according to Göthlich [11].

In the *planning phase*, we decided on the design of the study as well as on its objective that we defined as follows:

- *Explorative goal*: Based on the observations and documentations, insights should be obtained und optimization potentials of the DBA's processing should be identified.
- *Evaluation goal:* The case study serves to validate the process in practice, explicitly considering the scenarios presented in Sect. 4.

During *data collection*, information determined in the planning phase is continuously documented. For this purpose, survey forms such as interviews, documentations (protocols) and observations were adopted [13]. During *analysis*, results on the hypotheses elaborated in the planning phase were collected. At the same time, the practicability of the DBA approach was tested and process optimizations were demonstrated. The case study is completed with the publication of the results in a *report*. The report can be published separately, or, like in our case, as part of further studies [11].

1.2 Fundamentals

Profound knowledge of the anatomy of business models, necessary capabilities for adaptation or reorganization and the structures affected thereby within or without the enterprise (e.g. processes, IT systems, roles) is a prerequisite for a DBA. As part of new management approaches, they complement established disciplines. To maintain this prerequisite, various techniques, methods and tools are necessary. It also implies that enterprises have to rethink and upgrade the established management approaches to be able to change quickly within a digital environment.

For a successful digital transformation and an integrative approach, knowledge is required in three disciplines: business model management [14–18], capability management [2, 19] and enterprise architecture management [20–23]. All three of them are connected through their respective outputs in the form of models in order to support enterprises with:

- Analysis and documentation of the current *company situation* comprising business model and the necessary architectural objects such as processes, structures and products,
- *Analysis of digital potentials* for additional and new value chains,
- Development and *concretization of the business strategy* for the implementation of digital objectives as well as derivation of the required business capabilities,
- *Determining the need for change* and planning of the architectures required for the digital transformation,

The approach presented in this work should provide a methodological basis for the role and training profile of the DBA. Its content will focus on the interdisciplinary application of these different management approaches (BMM, CM, EAM) within a procedure model developed for this purpose (Fig. 2).

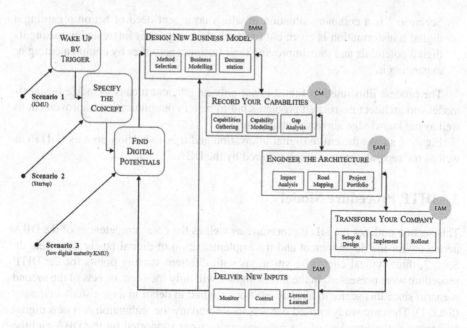

Fig. 2. Digital innovation and transformation process (DITP) including required disciplines.

2   Spectrum of Methods and Scenarios

This section introduces the interaction of the disciplines (BMM, CM, EAM) and presents indications on how to use discipline-specific methods in particular scenarios of digital transformation and thus denote one of the action bases of the DBA.

There already exist scientific books and textbooks for the development of business models and enterprise architecture management providing methods and tools [14, 18, 23–25]. In the area of capability management that is supposed to act as a link between the disciplines, numerous approaches exist. However, there is only on integrative approach addressing this topic [2]. So far, a higher level procedure for the integrative use of the single disciplines in the form of a process model is not yet available [5].

A special feature of the approach presented in this work is the focus on the interaction of available methods of the respective disciplines considering a choice that should be preferably needs-based.

The following scenarios exemplify typical situations in enterprises which require the integrative use of different disciplines and the different possible fields of actions of the DBA:

1. The first scenario is an existing enterprise which is facing new product-related, customer-related and/or competitive challenges due to digitalization and which needs to react on them promptly.
2. In scenario 2, the main concern is implementing a business concept in a start-up company.

3. Scenario 3 is a company situation in which no urgent need of action regarding a digital transformation is given but in which the company is interested in raising its digital potentials and thus improving their business activities by complementing or expanding it.

The process illustrated in Fig. 2 is not only an efficient means to tackle business-model and architecture-related problems but to foster communicative improvement as well as the knowledge about the enterprise.

Figure 2 shows the entire digital innovation and transformation process (DITP) as well as the separate process steps required by the DBA.

3 DITP Procedure Model

This section outlines the DITP procedure as well as the core competences of the DBA necessary for the development and the implementation of digital business models. In Sect. 2, three typical enterprise situations with different starting points for the DITP procedure were presented. In the following, we will only focus on aspects of the second scenario since this scenario already has been studied in detail in a case study company (Sect. 1). The case study carried out was to accompany the realization of a new digital business i.e. the founders of the new enterprise were supported by the DBA and the DITP procedure during the start-up process.

Starting point for the second scenario is the so-called *"Specify the Concept"* phase in which an existing idea is elaborated with the help of creative methods. This idea should have a clear business purpose. This elaboration follows an idea process that helps identifying and formulating, among others, internal/external factors, requirements and implementation approaches. The process is divided in three activities: *DITP1.1 Identification of the idea, DITP1.2 Activation method, DITP1.3 Elaboration of the concept.* To provide a common methodological starting point, the activities for the elaboration of the basic idea are carried out by all founders. The competence required of the DBA consists in being able to derive a concept from ideas in a systematic way according to the requirements of the concept, e.g. by applying one of more than 60 existing creativity techniques. The outcome of this phase is a comprehensively documented business concept.

The process step *"Find Digital Potentials"* focusses on the analysis of digital trends and building blocks and helps finding possible digital approaches that could be relevant for the business concept. This phase is divided into the activities *DITP2.1 Research of digital trends/building blocks, DITP2.2 Evaluation of digital trends/building blocks.* Based on the documented business concept, the first activity allows the research of different data sources in order to find digital trends/building blocks such as *Gartner Hype Cycle* [26], *Technology Radar* [27], *TechTrends* [28] und *Producthunt* [29]. Examples for digital technology building blocks are: *Automatisation* (Robotik, adaptive manu-facture, autonomous vehicles), *Digital accesses* (social networks, mobility, apps, market places, gesture and voice control) *interconnectivity and exchange* (broadband, mobile Internet, IoT, Industrie 4.0, Cloud), *artificial intelligence* (smart cities & homes, agents

& bots, machine learning), *Data* (big data, blockchain, predictive maintenance), *User Experiences* (Wearables, Virtual Reality, context-related individualization).

The founders involved preselect potential digital trends/building blocks for the business model development of the next phase by means of feature or priority evaluations. When a trend/building block is from the list of candidates, we speak of a digital potential, because, from the founding team's perspective, it will support the realization or the improvement of the business idea. This phase has also to be carried out by all founders. It is recommendable but not imperative to involve team members with a high affinity to technology. In this phase, the DBA supports the research of digital trends/building blocks and gives advice on how to use them in possible application scenarios. The outcome of this phase is a technology map with suitable digital potentials that will be considered in the context of the business model development. The accuracy of this map will be specified more precisely later on.

The third phase includes the modelling of the business model *"Design New Business Model"*. Different approaches can be used for modelling according to personal preferences or the requirements of the project [14, 17, 18, 25]. For this purpose, the following activities have to be accomplished: *DITP3.1 Choice of business modelling approach, DITP3.2 Modelling of the business model, DITP3.3 Visualization of the business model & documentation.* For scenario 2, we selected the business model innovation method according to [14] which is one of the most comprehensive and most detailed approach for the detailed development of business models.

The founding team was convinced by this approach because of its comprehensive methodological support (metamodel, questionnaires, examples) during the different phases of the business model development. The graphical representation of the business model using visualization software is a possibility of documenting the results. Another possibility of documentation is based on the proposed meta model by [14] that can be represented by means of modelling tools. This process step is accounted for by the executive manager who is actively taking part in the specific activities. The DBA plays the implementing role in this process step and supports the choice of the business model approach, the business model development and the choice of suitable documentation software. The outcome of this process is a comprehensive digital business model that serves as basis for the following operationalization activities.

In the process step *"Record Your Capabilities"*, we will resolve the following question: *"What capabilities are needed by our company or our future company in order to implement the developed business model?"* As a starting point, the discipline of capability management gaining growing attention in theory and practice will help to answer this question [1, 30]. At present, capabilities are considered as missing link between business units and IT and therefore support the business IT alignment [2, 31, 32]. For the present phase, we suggest an efficient method (Capability Management Guide) that supports the identification, the structuring and the management of capabilities [2]. In scenario 2, the following activities were carried out in the context within the framework of the Capability Management Guide (CMG): *DITP4.1 Collection of required and existing capabilities, DITP4.2 Capability modeling, DITP4.3 Gap analysis and adaptations.* The CMG is based on an integrated capability approach that was developed from different scientific studies. The approach is integrated in a process comprising four building blocks. They propose suitable procedures, concepts and supporting tools derived from specific theoretical and practical applications in order to detect and structure capabilities within the company [2]. The process is accounted by the management team of the start-up. The DBA takes over the executing role during this process step and conducts the four building blocks. In doing so, the DBA integrates the founder and the disciplines in the elaboration of the capabilities catalogue. The outcome of this process is a catalogue describing the required capabilities for the implementation of the business model.

In the phase **"Engineer the Architecture"**, the future enterprise architecture model is derived and defined by means of the detected capabilities and possibly considering the present architecture. The aim of this phase is to draft an enterprise architecture model (EA) including the required architecture objects and their dependencies in order to obtain a transparent picture about the aspects necessary for the implementation of the business model [33]. The defined capabilities catalogue serves as a basis for the retrieval of required enterprise architecture objects [2]. In this context, we propose the following activities: *DITP5.1 Choice of an approach for the impact analysis, DITP5.2 Development of the enterprise architecture including roadmap for integration, DITP5.3 Project portfolio for the implementation*. For DITP5.1, it is necessary to select a suitable modelling approach and tool. This can be done primarily on the basis of the detected requirements and/or on the basis of existing experiences [33–35]. Since scenario 2 is about an initial EA and with the resources of the founders being limited, they will need an uncomplicated and easy-to-learn method for the modelling. This method, however, has to be able to represent the entire architecture (e.g., processes, IT, roles, resources, objectives). A method that meets these requirements is the 4EM-Method [36]. It describes an approach for a systematic and controlled procedure for the analysis, development and documentation of a company or an organizational unit. The aim is to represent structures and processes incrementally in the form of an EA, whereas the single elements can be already derived from the capabilities of the catalogue.

To complete the elaboration of the enterprise architecture, the specific models have to be documented appropriately. For this purpose, we recommend software tools ranging from simple text programs, spreadsheet applications or graphic programs to comprehensive enterprise architecture modelling and management tools that need to be selected in accordance with the profile of requirements and maturity [33, 37]. Since scenario 2 described a start-up with an uncomplicated approach of enterprise architecture modelling, a single graphical modelling tool was used initially in order to visualize the required dependencies. The DBA plays an implementing role in this process step and supports the choice of the modelling approach according to the requirements as well as the establishment and documentation of the architecture by means of suitable software tools. The outcome of this phase is the enterprise architecture required for the operationalization of the business model.

The way in which the elaborated EA is implemented and the change measures evolving from it are crucial for the success of the enterprise. The phase *"Transform Your Company"* focusses the activities *DITP6.1 Project set up, DITP6.2 Implementation and DITP6.3 Roll out* of the EA in the enterprise. The planning of strategic initiatives and/or single projects provides the framework for the following change measures and the implementation of the planned EA. Furthermore, this phase comprises the definition of typical project management activities such as, for instance, the definitions of milestones, supply of information, personnel, escalation handling, implementation and roll out reporting [20]. Here, the recurrence of single parts of the DITP is possible. On the one hand, the successful implementation of an EA depends on the planning already mentioned, but also on the degree of maturity of the EA models – any insufficient degree will become evident during the planning phase of the project and must be increased in an iterative process [35]. On the other hand, the users (e.g. executive board, business developers, line managers) must be convinced of the emerging structures [20, 36]. In order to obtain a successful roll out as well as an extensive use, we recommend the following procedure: The roll out process should start with a specific change measure within the frame of a pilot project in a selected organizational unit. The project has to prove whether the expected advantages actually occur or rather unexpected challenges emerge. After successful completion of the pilot project, the implemented change measures can be rolled out on additional organizational units or on the entire organization. This procedure can be repeated for further changes and organizational units whereas different organizational unit could be in charge of this. On the basis of the EA and by means of graphical models and simulations, different implementation approaches can be tested. The DBA supports the project teams(s) with the implementation. The result of this phase is an operationalized business model based on an EA.

Regarding the fact that enterprises are permanently facing new digital challenges in increasingly shorter time intervals, monitor and control activities must be set up in the enterprise. They control the new digital components of the enterprise architecture and can detect signals for digital changes at an early stage [15]. In this context, one of the most important functions of the phase *"Deliver New Inputs"* is to safeguard the digitalization objectives. In order to monitor the quality of short, medium and long-term digitalization objectives within the entire enterprise and the changes related to it, enterprises determine suitable indicators to be sustained by a corresponding data base [18]. Especially usage-oriented, trend and context-related data of introduced digital changes form the basis for new inputs of the DITP. Measuring tests, risk assessments and compliance tests are activities based on indicators that could support the implementation and the evaluation of goals as well as the derivation of new inputs for the procedure based on the collected data. The DBA supports the information needs analysis [38] of the management regarding the definition of appropriate indicators and compiles the required elements of the enterprise architecture.

4   Conclusion and Outlook

The successful development and integration of digital business models requires a high degree of agility which is only given economically when the effects of the changes in an enterprise or the development of new enterprises can be determined at any point in time. Basic prerequisites are innovative ideas, knowledge about the development of business models, capabilities necessary for the adaptation or restructuring and the architectures affected within and without the enterprise. To maintain these prerequisites, various methods and tools of different disciplines are necessary. These methods and tools were presented as elements of an integrated procedure of the DBA in this work.

In particular, the DBA profile could be taught to students of universities and higher education institutions, especially in business information systems studies, but also in addition to computer science and economic science. For this purpose, the procedure and its methodological contents in the area of electronic business, business model management, enterprise architecture management and business analysis can be used. But it could also serve for practitioners in enterprises for self-study or as manual and thus demonstrate first possibilities and approaches for the digital transformation. The presented DBA profile and the DITP are currently examined in two additional case studies for scenario1 and 3 and will be adapted according to the results.

References

1. Wißotzki, M.: Exploring the nature of capability research. In: El-Sheikh, E., Zimmermann, A., Jain, L.C. (eds.) Emerging Trends in the Evolution of Service-Oriented and Enterprise Architectures. ISRL, vol. 111, pp. 179–200. Springer, Cham (2016). doi: 10.1007/978-3-319-40564-3_10
2. Wißotzki, M.: Capability Management Guide, 1st edn. Springer Vieweg Research, Wiesbaden (2017)
3. Lemke, C., Brenner, W.: Verstehen des digitalen Zeitalters. Springer Gabler, Berlin (2015)
4. Wißotzki, M., Köpp, C., Stelzer, P.: Rollenkonzepte im enterprise architecture management. Lect. Notes Inf. **244**, 127–138 (2015)
5. Plewka, T: Die Entwicklung einer Fallstudie zur Integration von digitalen Geschäftsmodellen und Architekturen (2017)
6. Kitchenham, B.: Procedures for performing systematic reviews. Keele, UK, Keele University **33**(2004), 1–26 (2004)
7. Sandberg, B.: Wissenschaftlich Arbeiten von Abbildung bis Zitat: Lehr- und Übungsbuch für Bachelor, Master und Promotion, 2nd edn. Oldenbourg Wissenschaftsverlag, München (2013)
8. Wohlin, C.: Guidelines for snowballing in systematic literature studies and a replication in software engineering. In: The 18th International Conference on Evaluation and Assessment in Software Engineering, EASE 2014, London, May 12th-14th, 2014, pp. 1–10. Association for Computing Machinery, New York (2014)
9. Wilde, T., Hess, T.: Methodenspektrum der Wirtschaftsinformatik (2006)
10. Yin, R.: Case Study Research. SAGE Publications, Thousand Oaks (2013)
11. Göthlich, S.E.: Fallstudien als Forschungsmethode: Plädoyer für einen Methodenpluralismus in der deutschen betriebswirtschaftlichen Forschung. Manuskripte aus den Instituten für Betriebswirtschaftslehre der Universität Kiel, Christian-Albrechts-Universität zu Kiel, Institut für Betriebswirtschaftslehre 578, Jan. 2003. http://EconPapers.repec.org/RePEc:zbw:cauman:578
12. de Vries, E.:Epistemology and methodology in case research: a comparison between European and Americans is journals. American IS Journals. In: Primavera Working Paper, 2004. Dispon, Jan. 2007 http://is2.lse.ac.uk/asp/aspecis/20050113. Accessed 25 Nov 2007
13. Dubé, L., Paré, G.: Rigor in information systems positivist case research: current practices, trends, and recommendations. MIS Q. **27**(4), 597–636 (2003). http://www.jstor.org/stable/30036550

14. Schallmo, D.: Geschäftsmodelle erfolgreich entwickeln und implementieren: Mit Aufgaben und Kontrollfragen. Springer Gabler, Berlin (2013)
15. Schallmo, D., Rusnjak, A., Anzengruber, J., Werani, T., Jünger, M.: Digitale Transformation von Geschäftsmodellen: Grundlagen, Instrumente und Best Practices. Springer Gabler, Wiesbaden (2016)
16. Schallmo, D.R.: Jetzt digital transformieren: So gelingt die erfolgreiche Digitale Transformation Ihres Geschäftsmodells. Gabler, Wiesbaden (2016)
17. Hoffmeister, C.: Digital Business Modelling: Digitale Geschäftsmodelle entwickeln und strategisch verankern. Hanser, München (2015)
18. Wirtz, B.W.: Electronic Business, 5th edn. Springer Fachmedien Wiesbaden GmbH, Wiesbaden (2016)
19. Anastasios, P.: Capability-based planning with TOGAF and ArchiMate. Master Thesis, Business Information Technology School of Management and Governance, University of Twente, Twente, (2014)
20. Ahlemann, F.: Strategic Enterprise Architecture Management: Challenges, Best Practices, and Future Developments. Springer, Berlin (2012)
21. Simon, D., Fischbach, K., Schoder, D.: Enterprise architecture management and its role in corporate strategic management. Inf. Syst. E-Bus. Manage. 12(1), 5–42 (2014)
22. Simon, D., Schmidt, C. (eds.): Business Architecture Management: Architecting the Business for Consistency and Alignment. Springer, Cham (2015)
23. Stelzer, P., Wißotzki, M.: Enterprise Architecture Management in kleinen und mittleren Unternehmen - Ein Vorgehensmodell: Wie Business-IT-Alignment im Zeitalter der Digitalisierung auch in KMU gelingen kann, 1st edn. Kovac, Dr. Verlag, Hamburg (2017)
24. Lemke, C., Brenner, W.: Einführung in die Wirtschaftsinformatik: Band 1: Verstehen des digitalen Zeitalters. Springer Gabler, Berlin (2015)
25. Osterwalder, A., Pigneur, Y.: Business Model Generation: A Handbook for Visionaries, Game Changers, and Challengers. Wiley, Hoboken (2013)
26. Gartner, Gartner Hype Cycle 2016. http://www.gartner.com. Accessed 19 Jun 2017
27. Thoughtworks, Technology Radar. https://www.thoughtworks.com/de/radar. Accessed 19 Jun 2017
28. Deloitte, Deloitte Tech Trends (2017). https://www2.deloitte.com/global/en/pages/technology/articles/tech-trends.html. Accessed 19 Jun 2017
29. Producthunt, Producthunt Protfolio. https://www.producthunt.com/. Accessed 19 Jun 2017
30. Offerman, T., Stettina, C.J., Plaat, A.: Business Capabilities: A Systematic Literature Review and a Research Agenda (2017)
31. Greski, L.: Business capability modeling: Theory & practice. Architecture & Governance Magazine (2009)
32. Loucopoulos, P. et al.: Enterprise Capability Modeling: Concepts, Method, and Application. In: Proceedings of the 2015 Third International Conference on Enterprise Systems - ES 2015, Basel, Switzerland, 14–15 October 2015, pp. 66–77. IEEE, Piscataway (2015)
33. Schekkerman, J.: Enterprise Architecture Good Practices Guide: How to manage the enterprise architecture practice. Trafford Publ, Victoria (2008)
34. Matthes, D.: Enterprise Architecture Frameworks Kompendium: Über 50 Rahmenwerke für das IT-Management. Springer-Verlag, Heidelberg (2011)
35. Hanschke, I.: Enterprise Architecture Management - einfach und effektiv: Ein praktischer Leitfaden für die Einführung von EAM, 2nd edn. Hanser, Carl, München (2016)
36. Sandkuhl, K., Stirna, J., Persson, A., Wißotzki, M.: Enterprise Modeling: Tackling Business Challenges with the 4EM Method. Springer, Heidelberg (2014)

37. Schekkerman, J.: How To Survive in the Jungle of Enterprise Architecture Frameworks: Creating or Choosing an Enterprise Architecture Framework, 3rd edn. Trafford, Victoria (2006)
38. Lundqvist, M., Sandkuhl, K., Levashova, T., Smirnov, A.: Context-driven information demand analysis in information logistics and decision support practices. In: Workshop on Contexts and Ontologies: Theory, Practice and Applications, Riva del Garda, Italy (2005)

Author Index

Printed in the United States
By Bookmasters